Teaching English Abroad

Susan Griffith

Distributed in the U.S.A. by Peterson's Guides, Inc.,
202 Carnegie Center, Princeton, N.J. 08543

Published by Vacation Work, 9 Park End Street, Oxford

TEACHING ENGLISH ABROAD
by Susan Griffith

Copyright © Vacation-Work 1991

ISBN 1 85458 048 5 (softback)
ISBN 1 85458 049 3 (hardback)

Cover Design by
Miller Craig & Cocking Design Partnership

Illustrations by John Taylor

Printed by **Gibbons Barford Print**, Wolverhampton, England

Teaching
English Abroad

Contents

PART I INTRODUCTION

PART II COUNTRY BY COUNTRY GUIDE

PART III APPENDICES

Acknowledgments

Many teachers of English have helped in the writing of this book. In particular the assistance of Michael Frost, who researched and wrote the chapter on Eastern Europe, and of Dick Bird who wrote at humorous length about Turkey, have been invaluable.

Substantial contributions were made by the following people to whom we are grateful for their information and insights:

France	Andrew Boyle, Kathryn Kleypas, Julian Peachey, Richard Pitwood
Greece	Andrew Boyle, Loraine Christensen, Sarah Clifford
Italy	Ian Abbott, Laurence Koe, Bruce Nairne, Sue Ratcliffe
Spain & Portugal	Dennis Bricault, Stuart Britton, Marta Eleniak, Michael Frost, Glen Williams
Eastern Europe	Dennis Bricault (Hungary), Graham Johnston (Czechoslovakia), Colin Boothroyd (USSR)
Rest of Europe	Paul Greening (Sweden), Susanna Macmillan (Switzerland)
China	Adam Hartley, Richard McBrien
Hong Kong	Brett Muir, Martyn Owens, Leslie Platt
Taiwan	Lee Coleman, Adam Hartley, David Hughes, Greeba Hughes, Helen Welch
Japan	Steven Hendry, Bryn Thomas, Claire Wilkinson
Indonesia	Colin Boothroyd, Paul Greening
Thailand	Steven Hendry, Laurence Koe
Africa	Judy Kendall (Zimbabwe), Ian MacArthur and Bryn Thomas (Egypt)
Latin America	Rupert Baker and Stuart Britton (Mexico), David Hewitt (Brazil), Edwin Hunt (Chile)

In addition, Kevin Boyd, Carl Hart, Judy Kendall and Sue Nuttall supplied background information on preparing for a stint of teaching abroad. Rachael Robinson provided admirable assistance in the later stages

Also, we gratefully acknowledge the kind assistance of British Rail International, who donated a trans-Europe railway ticket, and of Eurotrain, who supplied a complimentary Polish rail pass, which facilitated the writing of the chapter on teaching in Eastern Europe.

Finally I would like to thank Carol Lawson who (unwittingly) made the production of this book possible.

NOTE: While every effort has been made to ensure that the information contained in this book was correct at the time of going to press, details are bound to change, especially those pertaining to visa requirements for teachers, exchange rates and the conditions offered by the schools listed in the country directories. Readers are invited to write to Susan Griffith, Vacation Work, 9 Park End Street, Oxford OX1 1HJ, with any comments or corrections.

Preface

English teaching is surely one of the most civilized ways to finance a sojourn abroad. There are other jobs which allow people to travel not just as tourists, but these tend to be more short-term and menial, such as hotel and agricultural work. English teaching appeals to a wide range of people and the beauty of it is that it is accessible to so many. It is possible to find employment (and do a good job) without any training whatsoever. Of course it is even better to obtain some training, which will open many more doors abroad. The standard introductory courses in Teaching English as a Foreign Language last no more than a month, are widely available and are open to almost everyone.

This book tries to maintain a fine balance. On the one hand, it is not aimed primarily at the serious professional EFL teacher who is likely to have already at his or her disposal a wide range of information on working abroad at the more prestigious teaching establishments. Neither is it intended to encourage layabouts and illiterates to masquerade as teachers, nor to bluster their way into jobs abroad on the dubious grounds that they are native speakers of the language. But between these two extremes, there is a huge pool of people both young and old who have the appropriate background and personality to become successful teachers of their mother tongue.

While compiling this book, the response to our request for help with the research has been staggering. Language schools from the south of Chile to Iceland and from Korea to Cordoba have contacted us with their teacher requirements. Countless organizations involved in the dissemination of the English language have provided background information, which we have interwoven with the actual experiences (both enjoyable and disappointing) of people who have taught abroad. Like every enterprise, teaching English in foreign cultures has its specific rewards and risks which we have attempted to identify in the hope of easing the path for those who are tempted but remain hesitant. This book may be the stepping stone to a brilliant year abroad.

Susan Griffith
Oxford
December 1990

PART I

Introduction

Training
Finding a Job
Preparation
Problems

Introduction

It is said that one thousand million people speak or are learning to speak English in the world today. Mind-boggling statistics aside, the demand for instruction at all levels by people who happen to speak English as their mother tongue is enormous and set to continue increasingly for the forseeable future. English speakers who want to see the world simply have to display the most basic of talents, i.e. talking, and someone somewhere will be willing to employ them.

For whatever historical and economic reasons, English has come to dominate the world, the late twentieth century sequel of colonialism. When the newly liberated nations of Eastern Europe sloughed off Russian, they turned in very large measure to English rather than to the other main European languages. Countries as far-flung as Mongolia and Namibia are busy making English one of the keystones of their educational systems. English is the international language of science, of air traffic control and to a very large extent of trade and export. This is bad news for all those Germans, Swedes and French Canadians who would like to market their language skills in order to fund a short or long stay abroad. But it is English speakers, mainly from Britain, Ireland, North America and Australia/New Zealand who accidentally find themselves in possession of such a sought-after commodity.

Some Definitions

The commonly used acronyms TEFL, TESL and TESOL can be confusing, especially since they are often used interchangeably. TEFL (pronounced "teffle") is Teaching English as a Foreign Language. TESL stands for Teaching English as a Second Language, and TESOL means Teaching English to Speakers of Other Languages. English is learned as a *foreign* language by people who may need the language for certain purposes such as business or tourism but who live in countries where English has no official status. English is learned as a *second* language when it will have to be used for day to day life, for example by emigrants to the UK and the USA or by inhabitants of ex-colonies where English retains official status and may well be the medium of instruction in schools. (English is the official or joint-official language in 70 countries.)

Because this book is for people who want to travel abroad to teach, the term TEFL is preferred. Teachers of ESL are normally involved with multicultural education. In the US, the vast majority of English language teaching is of ESL because of the huge demand for English among foreigners who have emigrated to the US. Therefore the term ESL dominates in American contexts, even when (technically) EFL is meant.

The acronym TESOL covers both situations, yet it is not widely used apart from in institutions which favour the Trinity College qualifications known as the Certificate and Licentiate Diploma in TESOL (see page 22) and also in the context of the American organization TESOL, which is the largest English teachers' organization in the world claiming 11,000 members (see page 63).

There is no shortage of other acronyms in the world of TEFL. One of the main ones is ESP which means English for Specific Purposes. Specialist English courses have been designed for business, banking, medicine, science and technology, secretaries, etc. Business English is probably the most important in this category (and "English for Shopping" as sometimes offered in Japan is the least important). EAP stands for English for Academic Purposes, i.e. English at an advanced level taught to students who are normally planning to study at foreign universities. EAP is largely in the hands of government-funded programmes, such as those run by the British Council.

SCOPE OF OPPORTUNITIES

The range of locations and situations in which English is in demand covers an enormous spectrum. If TEFL is booming in Mongolia, there can be few corners of the world to which English has not penetrated. English has been called a "barometer of Western influence" and there is only a handful of countries in the world which have rejected Western influence outright; post-revolutionary Iran, Burma, Albania and a few others do not have any call for EFL teachers. More important nations like India and the USSR are also not promising destinations for the aspiring teacher (though the situation in the Soviet Union may well change in the next few years).

With the approach of the single European market in 1992, Europe will become an even greater consumer of English than it already is. There has been an enormous increase in demand especially from companies and professionals prompted by the media bombardment: "Are you ready for 1992?". The field of teaching English to young chidren is also flourishing especially in Mediterranean countries. The attraction of European Community countries for Britons is even greater since they don't need to worry about work permits.

The kinds of people who want to learn English are as numerous as the places in which they live. Possibly there has been some decline in the number of "leisure students", i.e. people attending English classes simply for pleasure. But people

around the world can think of a dozen reasons why they need English. A Korean student dreams of studying at UCLA, the wife of the Peruvian ambassador in Islamabad wants to be able to speak English at official functions. A Greek secondary school student has to pass her English exams in order to proceed to the next year and, like most of her classmates, attends a private tutorial college for conversational English. A Czech worker associates English with the language of freedom and liberalism and wants to be able to read one of the newly available foreign newspapers. A Turkish youth wants to be able to flirt with tourists from northern Europe. A Mexican waiter wants to get a job in the Acapulco Hilton. A Saudi engineer has to be able to read reports and manuals in English for his job. The list is open-ended, and prospects for hopeful teachers are therefore excellent.

TEFL is booming even in Mongolia

But the situation is not all rosy for the prospective teacher. As the profile of the English language has risen, so has the profile of the profession which teaches it, and the number of qualified and experienced English teachers has increased along with the rise in demand, even if it hasn't kept pace with it. Some people who have cruised into a country expecting to be hired as an EFL teacher straightaway have come a cropper, surprised to be asked for evidence of the ability to teach their language or at least a university degree as proof of a sound educationl background. Certainly without a degree, a TEFL qualification or any relevant experience, the scope of opportunities shrinks drastically without dwindling away completely.

Who is eligible to teach?

Anyone who can speak English fluently and has a lively positive personality has a fighting chance of finding an opening as a teacher somewhere. Geordies,

Tasmanians and Alabamans have all been known to be hired as English teachers, though of course most employers would rather avoid hiring teachers with heavy regional accents. Depending on the economic and cultural orientation of a country, schools will prefer British English (what the Director-General of the British Council likes to call "standard English") or North American English. For obvious geopolitical reasons Europe and Africa incline towards Britain while Latin America and the Far East incline towards the US. Many countries have no decided preference, for example Indonesia and Turkey. Clear diction is usually more important than accent.

English language teaching is an industry which is seldom regulated, giving rise to a host of cowboy schools, which are mentioned (usually disparagingly) throughout this book. The other side of the coin is the proliferation of cowboy *teachers*, who have no feel for language, no interest in their pupils and no qualms about ripping them off. The issue of qualifications must be considered carefully. It is obviously unwise to assume that fluency in English is a sufficient qualification to turn someone into an EFL teacher. Many experienced teachers of English come to feel very strongly that untrained teachers do a disservice both to their pupils and to their language. Certainly anyone who is serious about going abroad to teach English should turn to page 18 to consider the training options.

Among the army of teachers-cum-travellers, there are undoubtedly some lazy, spiritless and ungrammatical people who have bluffed their way into a teaching job. Most books and journals about language teaching are unanimous in their condemnation of such amateurs. Yet there are some excellent teachers who have learned how to teach by practising rather than by studying. For certain kinds of teaching jobs, a background in business and commerce might be far more useful than any paper qualifications in teaching. Therefore we have not excluded the unqualified teacher-traveller from our account. As long as they take their responsibilities seriously and bear in mind that their pupils have entrusted them with significant quantities of time and money to help them learn, they are unlikely to bring the EFL profession into disrepute. Some untrained teachers we talked to during the research for this book found the responsibility so unnerving that they promptly enrolled in a TEFL course before unleashing themselves on an unsuspecting language-learning public.

At an extreme opposite from the casual teacher-traveller is the teacher who makes EFL a career. Only a minority of people teaching English abroad are professional teachers. Career prospects in TEFL are in fact not very bright. After teachers have achieved a certain level of training and experience, they can aspire to work for International House and then for the British Council. From there, they might become a director of studies at a private language institute, though are unlikely to become a director unless their primary interest is business and administration or unless they have some capital to invest in order to buy and run their own school.

What employers are looking for

Between the dodgy operators and the British Council is a vast middle ground of respectable English teaching establishments. Many would prefer to hire only qualified staff, yet there are not enough to go around. On the whole these schools are looking for teachers with a good educational background, clear correct speech, familiarity with the main issues and approaches to TEFL and an outgoing personality. A BA and/or TEFL certificate is no guarantee of ability as Marta

Eleniak observed in Spain where she taught during her "gap" year (after doing a one-week introductory TEFL course with Pilgrims):

I've seen graduate teachers make such a mockery of the enterprise that it's almost criminal. TEFL is creative teaching. Forget about your educational experiences. In TEFL you have got to be able to do an impression of a chicken, you've got to be a performer. And you have to be flexible. If the pupils are falling asleep, conduct a short aerobics class and change tack to something more interesting. A good teacher builds a rapport with the class, and is enthusiastic, patient, imaginative and genuinely interested in the welfare of the pupils.

A sophisticated knowledge of English grammar is not needed, since in most cases, native speakers are hired to encourage conversation and practise pronunciation, leaving the grammar lessons to local teachers. On the other hand, a basic grasp is necessary if only to keep up with your pupils.

MOTIVES FOR TEACHING ENGLISH

There are perhaps four main types of individual to be found teaching English from Tarragona to Taipei: the serious career teacher, the student of the prevailing language and culture who teaches in order to fund a longer stay, the long-term traveller who wants to prolong and fund his or her travels and finally the misfit or oddball perhaps fleeing unhappiness at home or using TEFL as an excuse for spreading the gospel.

In many countries, English teaching is the most easily attainable employment, in fact the *only* available employment for foreigners. Anyone who wants to transcend the status of mere tourist in a country like Thailand, Peru or Japan will probably be attracted to the idea of teaching English. The assumption behind some thinking at the snobbish end of the EFL spectrum is that people who do it for only a year or two as a means to an end (e.g. learning Chinese, studying Italian art, eating French food) are necessarily inadequate teachers.

There are small pockets of people (mainly in the Far East) whose sole ambition is to earn as much money as possible in order to fund further world travels. These "bread-heads" are probably not ideal teachers if only because they take on so many hours of teaching that they can't possibly prepare properly for their lessons. But for most teachers, making a lot of money is not a priority or, if it was at the outset, they are soon disillusioned.

Salaries in popular tourist destinations (like Paris, Barcelona, Chiang Mai) may actually be lower than in less appealing neighbouring towns, even though the cost of living is higher. Pay scales are relatively meaningless out of context. For example the high salaries paid in Japan are usually eaten up (at least in the first year) by extortionate rents and other expenses. When converted into sterling a salary in Brazil or Turkey might sound reasonable, but chronic inflation and currency devaluations could soon alter the picture. Converting salaries into pounds is often misleading unless you are well acquainted with the cost of living. At the time of writing, the pound was stronger than it had been for years, and as a result foreign salaries sound low when translated. For example the standard TEFL salary of 90,000 escudos in Portugal was "worth" £385 in June 1990 and £333 in August. The vast majorty of people who spend time abroad teaching English are able to afford to live comfortably and have an enjoyable time without feeling pinched, but end up saving little.

RED TAPE

The European Community consists of the UK, Ireland, Netherlands, Belgium, Luxembourg, Denmark, France, Germany, Italy and Greece, the latter four of which have enormous EFL markets. Spain and Portugal, though members, will not participate in the free exchange of labour until January 1993. From 1992, all EEC nationals will carry a lilac-coloured Community passport. Within the EEC the red tape is minimal for all nationals of member states who wish to work in any capacity. Anyone who intends to stay for more than three months requires a residence permit, which may be a bureaucratic hassle to obtain but should not be cause for anxiety, once you have a teaching job. All of this means that Britons have a significant advantage over Americans, Canadians, Australians and New Zealanders. Although not impossible for other nationalities, it is very difficult for them to find an employer willing to undertake the task of proving to the authorities that no EEC national is available or able to do the job. The handful of Americans who apply to do the RSA Certificate course in the UK are often discouraged by the training centre and warned that jobs are very difficult to get in the European Community. However many do find ways of bending the rules.

Outside the EEC, legislation varies from country to country, but many countries accord English teachers a special status recognizing that their own nationals cannot compete as they can for other jobs. For example, Sweden has one of the most restrictive immigration policies in the world and yet every year allows in a contingent of English teachers (on an approved scheme). However this is not always the case: most English language schools in Switzerland find it impossible to hire teachers from outside Switzerland. Other countries may lack the mechanism for granting work visas to English teachers (as in Thailand) but will usually turn a blind eye to those who teach on tourist visas, since everyone knows that Thais are not being deprived of jobs, rather they're being given an advantage by having the chance to learn English.

Teachers who fix up a job before leaving home can usually sort out their visas or at least set the wheels in motion before arrival, which greatly simplifies matters. The majority of countries will process visas only when they are applied for from outside the country. Otherwise it may be necessary to go to your chosen country on a tourist visa, find a job, then leave the country to apply for the work visa. The restrictions and procedures for obtaining the appropriate documentation to teach legally are set out in *Part II* of this book country by country. Prospective teachers should contact the relevant Consulate for the official line (addresses in *Appendix 2*). If there is any doubt, ring the embassy a second time to confirm the original information. It is amazing how inconsistent such sources of information can be. Always enlist the help of your employer who should be familiar with procedures (assuming he or she has hired native speakers before) and who should be willing to pay the often considerable costs (e.g. £50 for a teaching visa for Spain and Turkey).

If you do get tangled up in red tape, always remain patient with consular officials. If things seem to be grinding to a halt, it may be helpful to pester them, provided this is done with unfailing politeness.

REWARDS AND RISKS

The rewards of teaching abroad are mostly self-evident: the chance to become integrated in a foreign culture, the pleasure of making communication possible for your students, the interesting characters and lifestyles you will encounter, a feeling of increased self-reliance, a better perspective on your own culture and your own habits, a base for foreign travel, a good suntan . . . and so on. Good teachers (e.g. those who enjoy doing impressions of chickens?) often find their classes positively fun. One-to-one teaching can also be enjoyable since you have a better chance to get to know your pupils. Off-site teaching provides glimpses into a variety of workplaces and private homes, perhaps even resulting in hospitality and friendship with your pupils.

Working conditions can be luxurious at the elite end of the profession. For example, the British Institute in Madrid offers its established teachers 14 salary payments a year, 4 months of paid holiday and job security virtually for life. But this description of a TEFL paradise applies to only a handful of teachers. The norm is nine salary payments a year, two weeks of holiday and no job security.

Uninitiated teachers run the risk of finding themselves working for a cowboy operation which does not care a fig about the quality of teaching or the satisfaction of the teachers, as long as pupils keep signing up and paying their fees. The job of teaching English is demanding; it demands energy, enthusiasm and imagination, which are not always easy to produce when confronted with a room full of stonily silent faces. Instead of the thrill of communication, the drudgery of language drills begins to dominate. Instead of the pleasure of exchanging views with people of a different culture, teachers become weighed down by sheafs of photocopies and visual aids. Like most jobs when done right, teaching English is no piece of cake and is at times discouraging, but invariably it has its golden moments.

Coming home

Teaching abroad can be addictive. The prospect of returning home to scour the local job adverts may be distinctly unappealing as you eat *tapas* in a Spanish bar or spend the weekend at a Brazilian beach resort. Once you have completed one teaching contract, it will be very much easier to land the next one, and it can be an exhilarating feeling to think that you can choose to work in almost any corner of the globe.

But after a year or two or three, homesickness catches up with most EFL teachers and they begin to pine for a pint of bitter, a test match or baseball game, the *Guardian* or *New York Times*, and mum's home cooking. The bad news is that there are few jobs in EFL in Britain except at summer schools. Even professional teachers frequently fail to find a job in the UK. Americans will probably fare better due to the growth industry of ESL in the US. The good news is that a stint of teaching English abroad is an asset on anyone's c.v. Employers of all kinds look favourably on people who have had the get-up-and-go to work at a respectable job in a foreign land. Such experience can always be presented as valuable for increasing self-assurance, maturity, a knowledge of the world, communication skills and any other positive feature which comes to mind. Very few teachers have regretted their decision to travel the world, even if the specific job they did was not without its drawbacks and difficulties.

Training

THE VALUE OF TEFL QUALIFICATIONS

Training in teaching English as a foreign language is not absolutely essential for successful job-hunting; but it makes the task easier by an order of magnitude. For example, anyone with the RSA Certificate (discussed in detail below) is virtually guaranteed a job in any country where English is widely taught, from Austria to Zimbabwe. This magical passport to jobs abroad can be gained in just one month (admittedly at great expense), and so anyone interested in spending some time teaching abroad should seriously consider enrolling in a "Cert" course.

There are numerous other kinds of qualifications available, some obtainable after a weekend course and others after years of university study. All are described in this chapter, with an assessment of their usefulness.

Increasing your marketability is not the only reason to get some training. The assumption that just because you can speak a language you can teach it is simply false. There may be plenty of people who have a natural flair for teaching and who can do an excellent job without the benefit of an RSA or any other TEFL qualification. There are, however, many others who, when faced with a class full of eager adolescents, would not have a clue where to begin. Doing a TEFL course cannot fail to increase your confidence and provide you with a range of ideas on how to teach and (just as important) how not to teach. Even a short introductory course can usually illustrate methods of making lessons interesting and of introducing the range of teaching materials and approaches available to the novice teacher. A perpetual problem which a TEFL course solves is the general level of ignorance of grammar among native speakers. Native-speaker teachers often find that their pupils, who are much better informed on English grammar than they are, can easily catch them out with questions about verb tenses and subjunctives, causing embarrassment all round.

Some training courses can also introduce you to the cultural barriers you can expect to encounter and the specific language-learning difficulties experienced by various nationalities (many of which will be touched on in the country chapters).

Some teachers who have invested the money and effort in doing a TEFL course go so far as to see this as a moral obligation. Completely untrained teachers may end up being responsible for teaching people who have paid a great deal of money for expert instruction. If you happen not to be a natural in the classroom, you may well fail to teach anything sensible to your pupils, whether they be young children in Hong Kong or businessmen in northern Portugal.

Not satisfied that the one week inlingua course was enough to qualify him as a teacher, Ian Abbott went on to do the RSA Certificate at International House in Rome and summarizes his view of TEFL training.

I wouldn't recommend teaching English as a foreign language without investing in a course first. You've got to remember that the people coming along to your lessons are desperate to learn your language and it is costing them a small fortune. It is only fair that you know what you are doing and can in the end take that money without guilt, knowing you haven't ripped them off to increase your travel funds.

One of the practical advantages of joining a TEFL course is that many training centres have contacts with recruitment agencies or language schools abroad and can advise on, if not fix up, a job abroad for you at the end of the course. Even in countries where it may be commonplace to work without a formal TEFL qualification (for example Thailand and Japan), people without a TEFL qualification will often be at a disadvantage, since the jobs they are likely to get will be with schools at the cowboy end of the market who may in turn be more likely to offer exploitative conditions. In some countries (such as Turkey) a TEFL certificate is a prerequisite for a work visa, which is yet another justification for doing some formal training before setting off.

RANGE OF COURSES

There is a bewildering array of courses available, at vastly different levels and costs, so it is wise to carry out some careful research before choosing. A comprehensive guide to all the courses on offer both in Britain and abroad is contained in the *EFL Careers Guide,* which includes tables comparing duration, cost and starting dates. This book is revised annually by the publishers of the monthly *EFL Gazette* and is available from EFL Ltd., 64 Ormly Road, Ramsey, Isle of Man; the 1990/1 edition cost £6.75.

For a free list of courses with their addresses only, contact the English Language Information Unit of the British Council (10 Spring Gardens, London SW1A 2BN). They distribute separate lists headed: Academic Courses in TEFL for the RSA/UCLES Certificate, for the RSA/UCLES Diploma, for the Trinity College Certificate and Licentiate Diploma, and for the PGCE, all of which are described below. The British Council does not advise on any non-academic introductory courses. For information about these, see the short entries below under the heading *Introductory Courses.*

RSA Courses

The Royal Society of Arts has been the main regulatory body and examination board of TEFL courses for many years. Its Preparatory Certificate or Prep. Cert. (acquired after an intensive 100 hour course) and more advanced Diploma or Dip. are the most widely recognized qualifications in the international EFL field. In 1988 the RSA handed over responsibility for the administration of the courses to the University of Cambridge Local Examinations Syndicate or UCLES (Syndicate Buildings, 1 Hills Road, Cambridge CB1 2EU; tel: 0223 61111) so that the qualifications are now known respectively as the RSA/UCLES Certificate in TEFLA (Teaching English as a Foreign Language to Adults) shortened to CTEFLA, and the RSA/UCLES Diploma in TEFLA or DTEFLA. In fact the old term of RSA Prep. Cert. is so engrained that many schools still refer to the qualification that way, and so this book occasionally follows their example. Full information about the content of the course and its assessment (which is continuous rather than by examination) is available from UCLES, together with a list of centres where the course is offered, for £1.50.

The **RSA Certificate** has always been the most popular choice of qualification for beginners and the number of people doing it has increased by over 75% in the past five years. In order to be accepted on a course you need have no prior experience of teaching English, but you must be at least 20 years of age and have a good standard of education, which may mean at least two A levels, if not a university degree. Most schools will send you a "task sheet" or grammar quiz as part of the application. Two questions taken from the International House literature illustrate the language awareness they are looking for: "How would you explain the difference in meaning between 'he's gone to Paris' and 'he's been to Paris'? and "Explain the difference between 'he robbed the bank' and 'he stole the money'." Some schools interview prospective candidates and ask questions such as "how would you convey the idea of 'regret' to a language learner?" Places are often difficult to get because of high demand, especially in summer and it is not unusual to have to wait four to six months for an opening in the most popular venues such as International House in London.

The price of the RSA Certificate courses is a major stumbling block. In 1990/91 the range was from £400 to £800 plus the RSA registration fee of £52. These fees do not include food and accommodation, nor in some cases the cost of books and teaching materials. International House, which is the largest and most famous TEFL training institute, training nearly half of all Certs. worldwide, was charging £570 at its London headquarters and slightly more or less in its various other locations like Newcastle, Hastings, Barcelona and Cairo. Many people have grumbled that the RSA course is grossly overpriced but there is little option unless you happen to live near a state-run course at a college of further education or polytechnic where prices are a fraction of the private schools (e.g. £65) but waiting lists are long. These inexpensive courses are almost always offered on a part-time basis only, usually one or two evenings a week for the academic year plus one day a week for full teaching observation and practice (which rules out most people in full-time employment). Many universities and colleges have language institutes which run intensive TEFL courses at various levels on a commercial basis, and so fees at public institutions are often equivalent to private training courses.

Once accepted on the course, you will be subjected to about 110 hours of rigorous training (full-time for four weeks or part-time over several months).

The standard of teaching is high and the emphasis is on the practice of any theory taught. By the end of the course, students are expected to teach a full hour's lesson, unaided, to "guinea pig" foreign language students. Pass grades are A, B and Pass, though employers (apart from International House) are not normally concerned to know your grade.

A summary of the course content includes the principles and techniques of language learning, linguistic form, function and meaning, teaching materials both commercially available and home-made, how to motivate your pupils, teaching aids including language labs, videos and computers, lesson planning, teaching the four skills of reading, listening, speaking and writing, plus testing and evaluation. Most RSA Cert. courses are organized so that morning classes and lectures are devoted to methodology and developing language awareness, whereas afternoons involve putting the theory into practice in the classroom.

All Prep. Cert. graduates complain of the crushing workload, as Kevin Boyd describes here:

Anyone attempting to do the RSA Certificate is in for the hardest four weeks of their lives. It is like a year of university crammed into one month. At the course I did (with inlingua in Hove), the day would start at 9am with an hour's preparation for the afternoon teaching practice (dummy teaching sessions with real students). We would have lessons all day until 3.30pm. During teaching practice we all had to teach a lesson finishing at 5.30pm, followed by an hour's post-mortem on everyone's lessons. Then home to work until at least midnight preparing for the next day's teaching practice. Your social life disappears, and if you do meet friends at the weekend, all you can talk about is gerunds and infinitives.

The RSA/UCLES **Diploma** in TEFLA is a high-level qualification open to graduates who have at least two years of recent EFL classroom experience. Normally applicants have either Prep. Cert. or a teaching qualification. Although the Diploma covers such topics as theoretical linguistics, it is a practical course which covers syllabus design, evaluation of EFL courses on the market and so on. The Diploma course standardly lasts 8 to 10 weeks, costs anything up to £1,000 (plus an RSA examination fee of £123.50) and is only for those intending to make TEFL a career. Technical colleges and other public educational institutions offer part-time courses usually costing about £200.

According to most people in the profession, there is a world shortage of Diploma-qualified teachers, who are in great demand especially at language schools in Britain. Unfortunately salaries for Dip. holders are not sufficiently higher than for Cert. holders to entice many people to do the Diploma course.

There are 40 authorized RSA centres in the UK, many of which are listed in the Directory section below.

RSA Certificate Courses Abroad

RSA courses are offered in a surprising number of locations from Majorca to Australia. In fact there are 30 overseas centres. The British Council run a number of Diploma and a few Certificate courses, mostly outside Europe, for example in Thessaloniki, Cairo, Oman, Penang, Hong Kong, Tokyo and Caracas, while International House offer RSA courses in five Spanish cities (Barcelona, Madrid, Palma de Mallorca, San Sebastian and Valencia), plus Paris, Rome, Lisbon, Cairo, Rio de Janeiro and Porto Alegre in Brazil. Other foreign venues are listed in the information from UCLES.

Possible advantages of doing an RSA Prep. Cert. abroad are that you may already be teaching or living in that country and want to upgrade your qualifications locally; the course and cost of living may be cheaper than in England; and course participants would almost certainly be put in touch with local employers, making it much easier to land a job than if they were to apply from home.

Details of some RSA courses offered abroad are listed in the *Directory of TEFL Training Courses* below.

Other Recognized Qualifications

The main rival to the RSA/UCLES Certificate and Diploma is Trinity College London (11-13 Mandeville Place, London W1Y 6AQ). When job adverts say "RSA or equivalent", they are probably thinking primarily of Trinity College qualifications which are newer on the scene and therefore less well known, but gaining ground at a faster rate than the RSA. The content of the Trinity Certificate for Teachers of English to Speakers of Other Languages (TESOL) and of the Licentiate Diploma (TESOL) is similar to the RSA Cert. and Dip. respectively though with an emphasis on oral communication and the ability to speak conversational English. If the RSA qualifications are as internationally well known as, say, American Express travellers cheques, the Trinity College qualifications are more like National Westminster travellers cheques. They serve the same function and cost about the same but are less instantly recognized. The Director of Examinations prefers to compare Trinity to Avis with their famous slogan "We try harder," and and says that in a few years time, the order may be reversed. Details of Trinity College courses are given below.

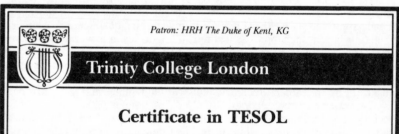

Patron: HRH The Duke of Kent, KG

Trinity College London

Certificate in TESOL

If you have always wanted to teach English but have never known how to begin, this is the course for you. There are over twenty centres now offering courses leading to the Certificate TESOL.

Licentiate Diploma in TESOL

For those who already have at least 2 years' English teaching experience, this provides a widely respected professional qualification.

For syllabus booklets and details of courses contact:
Group Administrator (Language), External Examinations Dept, Trinity College,16 Park Crescent, London W1N 4AH
Tel: 071-323 2328 Fax: 071-323 5201

The two choices of post-university academic qualification available to TEFL specialists are the MA and the PGCE (Post Graduate Certificate in Education). The latter confers teacher accreditation and allows you to teach in the UK state educational system. Some other countries also recognize the PGCE. A further advantage is that British citizens are eligible for a grant. For a list of the universities and colleges which offer a PGCE in teaching English as a foreign (or second) language, get the relevant list from the British Council as mentioned above, or write to the Graduate Teacher Training Registry (GTTR) at 3 Crawford Place, London W1H 2BN for an application form and details any time after September 1st before the year of entry. A PGCE with TEFL as a main component is offered at five institutions (Bangor, Birmingham, Leicester, London and Manchester) and as a secondary subject at 14 others. Some complain that when EFL is a subsidiary subject, the content is superficial. Applications start being processed in September but it is often possible to get a place on a course at the last minute.

MA courses in ELT and Applied Linguistics are offered at dozens of universities and colleges. It should be noted that in contrast to the demand for RSA Diploma holders, there is a world oversupply of MAs. There is a relatively small number of high level posts which require an MA; for example the British Council has only ten or so positions a year specifically for MA-qualified English language teachers.

Some academic institutions such as Brighton Polytechnic offer diplomas in TEFL which are not affiliated to RSA/UCLES or to Trinity College. These are listed after the Trinity College courses in the *Directory*.

Introductory Courses

Although the RSA and Trinity College Certificates are often called "introductory courses", there are many cheaper, shorter and less rigorous introductions to the subject.

The more upmarket introductory courses often present themselves as an opportunity to sample the field to see whether you want to go on to do an RSA Cert. at a later stage. Others make their course sound as if it alone will be sufficient to open doors worldwide. It would be unreasonable to expect a 5-day course to equip anyone to teach, but most participants find them helpful.

A number of private language centres offer their own short courses in TEFL which may focus on their own method, developed specifically with the chain of schools in mind (for example Linguarama and inlingua), or may offer a more general introduction. Almost all will issue some kind of certificate which, without having the clout of an RSA Cert., can sometimes be used to impress prospective employers.

Because there are so many commercial enterprises and "cowboy" operators cashing in on the present EFL boom, standards vary and course literature should be studied carefully before choosing. In particular you should be a little skeptical of "distance learning" courses, i.e. self-study by correspondence since most people who have done a TEFL training course claim that the most worthwhile part is the actual teaching practice, whether in teaching mock lessons to your fellow participants or to living breathing foreigners. In fact, many short introductory courses do not allow for much chance to do teaching practice.

The majority of courses last one week (i.e. five days) and cost between £100 and £150, not counting accommodation. Anyone who wants a job after doing a short course should aim to do it in the spring when the majority of jobs are advertised for the following academic year. Many people who complete an introductory or "taster" course go on to do the RSA Certificate, which may even be available at the same centre.

Details of introductory courses both in Britain and abroad are provided at the end of the *Directory* which follows.

Training in the US

There is no equivalent of the Royal Society of Arts in the US and therefore there are no short intensive courses which provide an internationally recognized qualification. Americans who wish to pursue a career in TEFL or TESL normally study for a BA or MA in TESL/Applied Linguistics at their state university. There are also one-semester courses in TESL offered at some American colleges and universities. For a guide to the various courses on offer, consult the *Directory of Professional Preparation Programs in TESOL in the US* available from TESOL, 1600 Cameron Street, Suite 300, Alexandria, Virginia 22314, USA; the 1989-91 edition costs $22.50.

It is easier to get practical experience of teaching English (without a qualification) by joining one of the many voluntary ESL programmes found in almost every American city. Literacy Volunteers of America operate in 35 states and offer volunteer tutors a training programme. Public high schools often have after-hours classes in ESL taught by local volunteers, coordinated by the National School Volunteers organization.

A TEFL course which is affiliated with the UK-based St. Giles Educational Trust is offered in San Francisco (see entry on page 38). Occasionally American institutions advertise in the UK. For example the TESL Institute at Ohio University runs high-level summer courses for ELT professionals. Details are available from Summer TESL/TEFL Institutes, Gordy Hall 201 TG, Ohio University, Athens, Ohio 45701.

DIRECTORY OF TRAINING COURSES

RSA Certificates in the UK

All courses last four weeks full-time unless otherwise stated. The RSA Certificate assessment fee in 1991 is £52 and the Diploma fee is £123.50.

ANGLO-CONTINENTAL TEACHER TRAINING CENTRE
29-35 Wimborne Road, Bournemouth BH2 6NA. Tel: (0202) 27414.
Duration: 4 weeks (125 hours of instruction, observation and teaching practice).
Frequency: 3-4 courses per year.
Cost: £550 (plus RSA fee).
Accommodation: can be arranged on bed and breakfast basis for about £50 per week.

ANGLOSCHOOL
146 Church Road, Upper Norwood, London SE19 2NT. Tel: 081-653 7285. Fax: 081-653 9667.
Duration: 4 weeks (140 hours).
Frequency: 6 times a year.
Cost: £636.50 (including RSA fee).
Accommodation: can be arranged with local families.
Comments: also run part-time evening RSA Dip. course.

BASIL PATERSON SCHOOL OF ENGLISH
22 Abercromby Place, Edinburgh EH3 6QE. Tel: 031-556 7696.
Frequency: 7 times a year.
Cost: £600.

Accommodation: accommodation officer can place trainees with host families.
Comments: courses usually booked up well in advance. Have a Teacher Recruitment Agency which can assist with placement abroad.

BELL SCHOOL OF LANGUAGES
1 Red Cross Lane, Cambridge CB2 2QX. Tel: (0223) 247242.
Duration: 4 weeks (130 hours) or 5 weeks (140 hours). Also part-time course (Tuesday and Thursday evenings) October to June.
Frequency: full-time course 6 times per year between January and September.
Cost: £686 (plus RSA fee); £626 for part-time course.
Accommodation: can sometimes advise on possible host families.
Comments: also offer the RSA Diploma course part-time (fee is £702 plus RSA fee). Opportunities for employment may arise from the Overseas Division of the Bell Educational Trust.

BELL SCHOOL OF LANGUAGES
Bowthorpe Hall, Norwich NR5 9AA. Tel: (0603) 745 615.
Frequency: 6 times per year.
Cost: £690 (plus RSA fee).
Accommodation: assistance can be provided on request.
Comments: also offer the 10-week RSA Diploma course (fee is £1,040 plus RSA fee).

🔔 The *Bell* School
Bowthorpe Hall · Norwich

* *Do you want to travel when you've finished your degree?*
* *Do you enjoy communicating with others?*
* *Do you want to learn a foreign language while living abroad?*
* *Do you want to make sure you're not left behind in 1992?*
* *Have you considered teaching English as a Foreign Language?*

Since 1973 we have successfully trained more than 1,000 people on our intensive teacher training courses leading to the Cambridge/RSA Certificate & Diploma in the Teaching English as a Foreign Language. These are internationally recognised qualifications which can lead to jobs almost anywhere in the world and ultimately to a rewarding career in TEFL. Teachers trained by us are now working in more than 55 countries throughout the world. Why not think about it?

Each year we run six four-week courses leading to the Certificate in TEFL and a full-time course leading to the Diploma in TEFL. For further details and an application form please write to:

**The Registrar (Teacher Training), The Bell School
Bowthorpe hall, Norwich NR5 9AA
or telephone Norwich 745615 or fax Norwich 747669**

The Bell School, Bowthorpe Hall is recognised as efficient by the British Council for the teaching of English as a Foreign Language.

BELL COLLEGE
South Road, Saffron Walden, Essex CB11 3DP. Tel: (0799) 22918/22119.
Duration: 5 weeks (125 hours).
Frequency: 3 times per year.
Cost: £775 (plus RSA fee).
Accommodation: board and lodging available at Bell College for £100 per week or can be arranged with local families on bed & breakfast basis.
Comments: also run 10-week RSA Diploma course once a year and a 3-stage job-linked Certificate course.

BELL LANGUAGE INSTITUTE LONDON
Regents College, Inner Circle, Regents Park, London NW1 4NS. Tel: 071-487 7411.
Frequency: occasional.   30 sept – 25 October
Cost: £635 (plus RSA fee).

BRUNEL COLLEGE OF TECHNOLOGY
Ashley Down, Bristol BS7 9BU. Tel: (0272) 241241.
Duration: 5 weeks.
Frequency: October and February.
Cost: £350.
Accommodation: college accommodation officer can assist.

CILC (Cheltenham International Language Centre)
Cheltenham & Gloucester College of Higher Education, Francis Close Hall Campus, Swindon Road, Cheltenham, Glos. GL50 4AZ. Tel: (0242) 222077.
Duration: 5 weeks (full-time) and September to June (part-time).
Frequency: full-time course begins September, November, January, February, April and May.
Cost: £550 (plus RSA fee).
Comments: also offers introductory course and RSA Diploma course for £950 (plus RSA fee).

CONCORDE INTERNATIONAL
Hawks Lane, Canterbury, Kent CT1 2NU. Tel: (0227) 765537/451035.
Frequency: occasional.
Cost: £590 (plus RSA fee).
Comments: also run one-week introductory courses. All successful participants are offered Easter and summer jobs in the UK with Concorde.

EF INTERNATIONAL LANGUAGE SCHOOLS
EF House, 1 Farman Street, Hove, Sussex BN3 1AL. Tel: (0273) 723651.
Location: courses held at EF School in Hastings: 76 Warrior Square, St. Leonards on Sea, Hastings, Sussex TN37 6BP; tel: (0424) 423998. Course may also be held in Brighton and Cambridge.
Frequency: every 2 or 3 weeks.
Cost: £615 (including RSA fee).
Accommodation: bed and breakfast in local homes available for £42 per week plus £15 booking fee.
Comments: guarantee a summer job in the UK and can assist with placements in 24 countries where EF have schools.

FILTON TECHNICAL COLLEGE
Filton Avenue, Bristol BS12 7AT. Tel: (0272) 694217.
Duration: part-time September to May.
Cost: £200.
Comments: open to County of Avon residents only.

GODMER HOUSE
Oxford School of English, 90 Banbury Road, Oxford OX2 6JT. Tel: (0865) 512538.
Frequency: 10 times a year.
Cost: £795 (plus RSA fee). One of the most expensive in the country.
Accommodation: can be arranged witih local families.
Comments: trainer to trainee ratio 1 to 3. Advance booking essential. Help given with job-finding, based on files of reports from ex-trainees.

GREENHILL COLLEGE
Lowlands Road, Harrow, Middlesex HA1 3AQ. Tel: 081-422 2388.
Duration: November to June (Wednesday evenings) and January to June (Tuesdays 9.30am-4.30pm).
Cost: £200 inclusive.
Comments: also offer RSA Diploma course September to June for £200 (plus RSA fee).

HILDERSTONE COLLEGE
Broadstairs, Kent CT10 2AQ. Tel: (0843) 69171.
Location: part-time course held in Canterbury.
Duration: 4 weeks (full-time) or October to June (part-time) 2 evenings a week.
Frequency: full-time course offered September, October, January, April and June.
Cost: £595 full-time (including RSA fee); £575 part-time.
Accommodation: can be arranged with a local family on self-catering or half-board basis, or in small hotel.
Comments: maximum group size of 10. Also offer introductory and RSA Diploma courses.

INTERNATIONAL LANGUAGE CENTRE
International House, White Rock, Hastings, East Sussex TN34 1JY. Tel: (0424) 720104.
Member of the ILC Group which is affiliated to International House.
Frequency: monthly.
Cost: £586.50 (plus RSA fee).
Accommodation: approximately £40 a week self-catering.
Comments: also offers RSA Diploma, 2-week course on teaching young learners and a wide range of 5-day specialist courses. Helps with recruitment in one of their 20 summer schools in the UK and in an overseas school via ILC Recruitment (see page 57).

INTERNATIONAL HOUSE —NORTHUMBERLAND
14-18 Stowell Street, Newcastle upon Tyne NE1 4XQ. Tel: 091-232 9551.
Frequency: spring and autumn only.
Cost: £644 (plus RSA fee).
Accommodation: can be arranged on request.
Comments: 12 participants per course, so oversubscribed.

INTERNATIONAL TEACHER TRAINING INSTITUTE (INTERNATIONAL HOUSE)
106 Piccadilly, London W1V 9FL. Tel: 071-491 2598.
Duration: 4 weeks full-time or 12 weeks part-time (Tuesday and Thursday evenings plus 5 Saturdays).
Frequency: once a month (full-time); 3 times a year (part-time).
Accommodation: can be arranged by accommodation department at International House.
Comments: pioneering organization in the TEFL field and now one of the largest and best known organizers of RSA courses. Several IH schools abroad offer RSA courses (see following list of overseas RSA centres). Has 70 affiliated language schools in 20 countries which often employ International House graduates: employment is virtually guaranteed to candidates who achieve A or B grade. (Failure rate is 2-3%.) Also offer RSA Diploma course (£925 plus RSA fee) and range of specialist courses. For a complete list of International House training courses request the ITTI Training booklet from the above address.

INTERNATIONAL TEACHING & TRAINING CENTRE (ITTC)
674 Wimborne Road, Bournemouth BH9 2EG. Tel: (0202) 531355.
Frequency: once a month.

Cost: £550 (plus RSA fee).
Accommodation: can be arranged with local host families, in guest houses, etc.
Comments: also offer the RSA Diploma course.

MARBLE ARCH TEACHER TRAINING
21 Star Street, London W2 1QB. Tel: 071-724 2217.
Duration: 4 weeks (full-time) or 4 months (part-time: Tuesday and Thursday evenings).
Frequency: 10 times per year (full-time); twice a year (part-time: September-December and January-May).
Cost: £550 plus RSA fee.
Accommodation: can advise.
Comments: also teach a one-week introductory course.

MILLBROOK HOUSE
Bankfield Site, Bankfield Road, Liverpool L13 0BQ. Tel: 051-259 1124.
Duration: 9 weeks (part-time).
Frequency: twice a year.
Cost: £550.
Comments: also offer RSA Diploma course on demand.

NEWCASTLE UPON TYNE POLYTECHNIC
Lipman Building, Sandyford Road, Newcastle upon Tyne NE1 8ST. Tel: 091-232 6002 ext. 3107.
Duration: academic year (one evening a week).
Cost: £44 (plus RSA fee).
Comments: also offer RSA Diploma course.

PILGRIMS LANGUAGE COURSES
8 Vernon Place, Canterbury, Kent CT1 3HG. Tel: (0227) 762111.
Location: University of Kent campus.
Frequency: 2 courses per year (summer only).
Cost: £800.
Accommodation: £280 for self-catering accommodation in 5-bedroom on-campus house or £500 for private room in college residence and full board.
Comments: Pilgrims invite groups of students from abroad specifically for RSA teaching practice (which they attend for free). Offer more teaching practice time than prescribed minimum. Steady stream of job offers from Europe, Asia, etc. are received. Pilgrims also offer one-week introductory courses.

ST GILES COLLEGE
51 Shepherd's Hill, Highgate, London N6 5QP. Tel: 081-340 0828/9207.
Frequency: once a month.
Cost: £540 (plus RSA fee).
Accommodation: advice can be given.

ST GILES COLLEGE
3 Marlboroug Place, Brighton, Sussex BN1 1UB. Tel: (0273) 682747.
Frequency: 5 times a year (between September and June).
Cost: as above.
Accommodation: can be arranged with local families for £56 per week.

Comments: the St Giles Educational Trust also offers TEFL training in San Francisco (see page 38).

SOAS (School of Oriental and African Studies)
University of London, Thornhaugh Street, Russell Square, London WC1H 0XG. Tel: 071-637 2388 ext. 2589.
Frequency: September only.
Cost: £575 (including RSA fee).
Accommodation: university accommodation service can advise.

SOUTH DEVON COLLEGE OF ARTS & TECHNOLOGY
Newton Road, Torquay, Devon TQ2 5BY. Tel: (0803) 217524/217553.
Duration: 26 weeks from September (Tuesday evenings).
Cost: £260 (including RSA fee).
Comments: also offer RSA Diploma course for £110 (plus RSA fee).

STANTON SCHOOL OF ENGLISH
167 Queensway, London W2 4SB. Tel: 071-221 7249.
Frequency: occasional.
Cost: £516 (including RSA fee).
Accommodation: assistance can be given.
Comments: compulsory interviews held in London and Madrid.

STEVENSON COLLEGE OF FURTHER EDUCATION
Bankhead Avenue, Sighthill, Edinburgh EH11 0NX. Tel: 031-453 6161 ext. 301.
Duration: 19 weeks from October to March (Tuesday and Thursday evenings) plus teaching observation and practice on Wednesday mornings.
Cost: £150 (plus RSA fee).

UNIVERSITY OF STIRLING
Centre for English Language Teaching, Stirling FK9 4LA. Tel: (0786) 73171.
Duration: 4 weeks.
Frequency: June only.
Cost: £500.
Comments: also run B.Ed., M.Ed. and postgraduate degree courses in TEFL.

WESTMINSTER COLLEGE
Peter Street, London W1V 4HS. Tel: 071-437 8536.
Frequency: September, April and June.
Cost: £620.
Comments: very large state sector EFL school with 1,500 adult students learning English in any one term. Also offers range of other teacher training courses.

Several colleges of further education offer only the RSA Diploma course, such as Mid-Cheshire College (Hartford Campus, Northwich, Cheshire CW8 1LJ) and Oxford College of Further Education (Oxpens Road, Oxford OX1 1SA) which charge about £120 and £61 respectively plus the RSA Diploma examination fee of £123.50.

RSA Certificate Courses Abroad

Spain

INTERNATIONAL HOUSE — BARCELONA
Trafalgar, 14 entlo, 08010 Barcelona. Tel: (3) 318 84 29.
Frequency: 9 times per year.
Cost: 77,000 pesetas (plus RSA fee)
Accommodation: help can be given.
Comments: full-time and part-time RSA Diploma courses also offered (for 160,000 pesetas plus RSA fee).

INTERNATIONAL HOUSE — MADRID
Zurbano 8, 28010 Madrid. Tel: (1) 410 13 14.
Frequency: July and September.
Cost: 92,000 pesetas.
Comments: part-time Diploma course may be offered in the autumn.

Other International House schools in Spain which occasionally offer RSA courses
are: International House — Mallorca,
      Paseo de Mallorca 36,
      07012 Palma de Mallorca
      Tel: (71) 72 64 08

International House — San Sebastian,
Urbieta 14-1,
San Sebastian
Tel. (43) 42 77 07

International House — Valencia,
Pascual y Genis 16,
46002 Valencia
Tel: (6) 352 29 71

YORK HOUSE
English Language Centre, Muntaner 479, 08021 Barcelona. Tel: (3) 211 32 00.
Duration: 5 weeks.
Frequency: starting mid-February, mid-May, early July and early November.
Cost: 98,000 pesetas (plus RSA fee).
Accommodation: can be arranged. Single rooms available for between 11,000 and 15,000 pesetas per week.
Comments: RSA Diploma course also offered.

Portugal

INTERNATIONAL HOUSE — LISBON
Rua Marquês Sá da Bandeira 16, 1000 Lisbon. Tel: (1) 57 14 96.
Frequency: starting dates in July, August and September.
Cost: £449 (including RSA fee).
Accommodation: hotel/pension accommodation can be arranged.
Comments: introductory and specialist courses also held.
RSA Diploma offered part-time October to May for 130,000 escudos.

Italy

INTERNATIONAL HOUSE — ROME
Viale Manzoni 57, 00185 Rome. Tel: (6) 757 68 94.
Frequency: June, July and August/September (full-time) and October to May (part-time).
Cost: 1,600,000 lire (plus 110,000 lire RSA fee).
Accommodation: can be arranged in hotels or with families. Prices from 40,000 lire per night for a single room or 500,000 lire for 4 weeks of bed and breakfast.
Comments: RSA Diploma course also offered. Useful notice board with job vacancies.

REGENT SCHOOL (INTERNATIONAL HOUSE)
Via Uguccione da Pisa 6, 20145 Milan. Tel: (2) 469 24 19.
Frequency: 4 per year.
Comments: RSA Diploma offered once a year.

France

INTERNATIONAL LANGUAGE CENTRE
20 Passage Dauphine, 75006 Paris. Tel: (1) 43 25 40 55.
Affiliated to International House.
Frequency: 8 times a year (between March and November).
Cost: 6,250 French francs (including RSA fee).
Accommodation: advice can be given, but is the responsibility of course participants.

Ireland

LANGUAGE CENTRE OF IRELAND
9-11 Grafton Street, Dublin 2, Ireland. Tel: (1) 716266.
Duration: 9 or 12 weeks (3 or 4 evenings per week).
Frequency: April and September.
Cost: IR£600.
Accommodation: help provided on request.
Comments: only RSA centre in Ireland. Diploma courses also offered (part-time October to June) for IR£900 plus introductory courses.

Turkey

ITBA (Istanbul Turco-British Association)
Süleyman Nazif Sokak 68, Nişantaşi, 80220 Istanbul. Tel: (1) 132 8200.
Postal address: P. K. 520, Şişli, 80224 Istanbul.
Affiliated to the British Council.
Duration: 16 weeks (part-time); 4 weeks (intensive).
Frequency: end of October to late February (part-time) and May/June (intensive).
Cost: £550 (plus RSA fee).
Comments: British Council in Istanbul also offers RSA Diploma course.

Egypt

INTERNATIONAL LANGUAGE INSTITUTE — CAIRO
3 Mahmoud Azmy Street, Off Ahmed Oraby Street, Medinet El Sahafeyeen. Tel: (2) 346 3087/346 8597.
Postal address: Teacher Training Department, ILI, P.O. Box 13, Embaba, Cairo.
Affiliated to International House.
Frequency: 5 times a year.
Cost: £350 (plus RSA fee).
Accommodation: can be arranged in shared flats or hotels.
Comments: RSA Diploma course offered in the spring.

Brazil

BRITANNIA
Av. Borges de Madeiros 67, Ipanema/Leblon CEP 22430, Rio de Janeiro (RJ). Tel: (21) 511 0143.
Affiliated to International House.

Frequency: December only.
Cost: US$400.
Accommodation: help can be given if 2 months notice is given.
Comments: RSA Diploma course held in January/February.

BRITANNIA
Rua Dr. Timóteo 752, Moinhos de Vento CEP 90460, Porto Alegre (RS).
Tel: (512) 229 663.
Affiliated to International House.
Frequency: January only.
Cost and accommodation: as above.

Trinity College Certificate (TESOL) Courses

ABERDEEN COLLEGE OF COMMERCE
Holburn Street, Aberdeen AB9 2YT. Tel: (0224) 572811.
Duration: September to May/June (5-6 hours a week).
Cost: £110.
Comments: also offer the Licentiate Diploma Course.

CICERO LANGUAGES INTERNATIONAL
42 Upper Grosvenor Road, Tunbridge Wells, Kent TN1 2ET. Tel: (0892) 547077.
Duration: 4 weeks.
Frequency: monthly except July/August and December/January.
Cost: £575.
Accommodation: available in hotels or on half-board basis with local families for £335.
Comments: acceptance is either conditional on an interview or unconditional, depending on applicant's background.

/**COLCHESTER INSTITUTE**
Sheepen Road, Colchester, Essex CO3 3LL. Tel: (0206) 761660.
Duration: 4 weeks (intensive) or 10 weeks (part-time Tuesday and Thursday evenings).
Frequency: intensive course in autumn only; part-time course starting October, January and April.
Cost: £128 (plus exam fee).
Accommodation: can be arranged for about £55 a week.
Comments: also offer RSA Diploma course (£280 plus exam fee).

COVENTRY TESOL CENTRE
Coventry Technical College, Butts, Coventry CV1 3GD. Tel: (0203) 256793.
Duration: 4 weeks (full-time) or academic year (part-time one evening a week).
Frequency: full-time course offered every month.
Cost: £550 inclusive.
Accommodation: can be arranged in guest houses or YM/WCA.
Comments: also offers one-week introductory and Licentiate Diploma courses. Setting up its own recruitment service.

CROYDON ADULT EDUCATION SERVICE
Coombe Cliff, Coombe Road, Croydon, Surrey CR0 5SP. Tel: 081-686 9191.
Duration: 3 months home study plus 4 weeks intensive plus further 3 weeks of distance learning.
Frequency: 2 starting dates in January plus part-time option September to May.
Cost: £480.

EATON HALL INTERNATIONAL
Retford, Nottinghamshire DN22 0PR. Tel: (0777) 706441.
Owned by Nottinghamshire County Council.
Duration: 6 weeks home study plus 4 weeks residential course.
Frequency: residential part of course offered 5 times a year.
Cost: £595.
Accommodation: available on-site at Eaton Hall for £243 bed and breakfast.
Comments: also offers Licentiate Diploma.

its ENGLISH SCHOOL, HASTINGS
43-45 Cambridge Gardens, Hastings, Sussex TN34 1EN. Tel: (0424) 438025.
Duration: 4 weeks (135 hours).
Frequency: February and August.
Cost: £595 inclusive.
Comments: also offers one-week introduction to TEFL and Licentiate Diploma course (distance learning plus 3 weeks) from £565 to £1,090.

LANGUAGE CENTRE OF GUILDFORD
53 Woodbridge Road, Guildford, Surrey GU1 4RF. Tel: (0483) 35118. Fax: 34777.
Duration: 4 weeks.
Frequency: starting dates in January, March, April, June, August, September and November.
Cost: £690 plus Trinity College fee.
Accommodation: full board accommodation with host families available at £300 for 4 weeks plus booking fee of £15.
Comments: launched in 1991.

THE REGENCY SCHOOL OF ENGLISH
Royal Crescent, Ramsgate, Kent CT11 9PE. Tel: (0843) 591212.
Duration: 4 weeks.
Frequency: April and November.
Accommodation: can be arranged in neighbouring hotel (at £15 a night bed and breakfast) or with a local family (£65 a week half board).
Comments: also offers one-week introductory course and part-time Licentiate Diploma.

SHEFFIELD CITY POLYTECHNIC TESOL CENTRE
Totley Hall Lane, Sheffield S17 4AB. Tel: (0742) 369941.
Duration: 12 weeks home study plus 4 weeks residential course plus further 3 weeks study for completion of extended essay.
Frequency: 7-8 times a year.

Cost: £550.
Accommodation: can be arranged in private houses or student residences.
Comments: open only to degree holders or certified teachers. Also offers
Licentiate Diploma course (£800). The TESOL Centre pioneered the distance
learning element of the course and oversees the same arrangement in other centres.

THURROCK TECHNICAL COLLEGE
Woodview, Grays, Essex RM16 4YR. Tel: (0375) 391199.
Duration: 12 weeks home study plus 4 weeks intensive course and further 3
weeks distance learning.
Frequency: twice a year, starting January and August with intensive course held
in April/May and November/December.
Cost: about £325 (plus £40 Trinity College moderation fee).
Accommodation: advice can be given. From £35 a week for self-catering
accommodation with a local family.

WOKING & CHERTSEY ADULT EDUCATION INSTITUTE
**"Danesfield", Grange Road, Woking, Surrey GU21 3DA. Tel: (0483)
21425.**
Offers Licentiate Diploma course only, part-time for one year from November
or intensively on a residential basis.

Other Recognized Courses

ASTON UNIVERSITY
**Language Studies Unit, Department of Modern Languages, Aston
Triangle, Birmingham B4 7ET. Tel: 021-359 3611 ext. 4236.**
Duration: 4 weeks.
Frequency: July and August only.
Cost: £400.
Accommodation: available in halls of residence for £30 per week.
Comments: open to graduates only. Offer detailed career guidance and a
certificate which it is claimed is equivalent to RSA Prep. Cert.

BRIGHTON POLYTECHNIC
The Language Centre, Falmer, Brighton, Sussex BN1 9PH. Tel: (0273) 606622.
Duration: September to June (full-time) or 2 years (part-time).
Cost: £607.
Comments: open to graduates or qualified teachers. Qualification gained is the Brighton Polytechnic Diploma in TEFL.

UNIVERSITY OF WALES

Centre for Applied English Language Studies
offer each October a thorough, full-time,
three month postgraduate university

CERTIFICATE IN TEFL

*Friendly, active Centre, keen to help
inexperienced trainees to develop teaching
skills and confidence.*

Teaching Workshops
Pre- and in-sessional Teaching Practice
Principles and Methods of Language Teaching
Introductions to Grammar and Phonetics
Introduction to Computing (optional)

Tuition Fee: £662 (UK & EC applicants)
Further information from the Secretary, Centre for Applied English Language Studies,
UWCC, PO Box 94, Cardiff, CF1 3XE. Tel: (0222) 874243 Fax: (0222) 371921

ANGLO ENGLISH SCHOOL
Grosse Bäckerstrasse 7, Im Geno Haus, 2000 Hamburg, Germany. Tel: (040) 362151.
Duration: 4 weeks.
Frequency: irregular intervals; dates on application.
Cost: £360 (equivalent in German marks).
Accommodation: can be arranged with local families.
Comments: intensive TEFL courses designed for native English speakers.

ST. GILES COLLEGE
Language Teaching Center, 2280 Powell Street, San Francisco, California 94133, USA. Tel: (415) 788-3552.
Affiliated to St. Giles Colleges in London and Brighton.
Duration: 4 weeks (full-time) or 12 weeks (part-time).
Frequency: 5 times a year (full-time) and summer only (part-time).
Cost: $1,075 plus $65 extra fees.
Accommodation: can be arranged in private homes, hotels and apartments.
Comments: course concentrates on practice rather than theory. Interview for acceptance on course can be conducted by telephone. School is recognized by the California State Department of Education. Back-up services offered such as files of case histories of former course participants who have gone abroad to work.

WEST SUSSEX INSTITUTE OF HIGHER EDUCATION

10 WEEK CERTIFICATE IN TEACHING ENGLISH AS A FOREIGN LANGUAGE IN SECONDARY SCHOOLS OVERSEAS

Apart from a 3-day induction in Britain, this course is run by West Sussex tutors at Faro Polytechnic in Portugal.

The course aims to provide an introduction to the teaching of English in secondary schools overseas where large classes are the norm.

The course consists of 5 components:

> **Principles of Classroom Practice**
>
> **Language Description**
>
> **Syllabus Materials**
>
> **Practical Teaching**
>
> **Learning Portuguese**

Travel grants may be available for EEC nationals.

For details and application for this and other teacher training courses contact:
Ian Forth, Senior Lecturer — TESOL Section,
West Sussex Institute of Higher Education,
The Dome, Upper Bognor Road, Bognor Regis, West Sussex. PO21 1HR.
Telephone: 0243-8650503.

Introductory Courses

ABON LANGUAGE SCHOOL
25 St. John's Road, Clifton, Bristol BS8 2HD. Tel: (0272) 730354.
Duration: 25-hour course offered as an intensive 5-day course or part-time 10-week course.
Frequency: intensive course offered in February, June and September; part-time course offered mid-January to March, late March to May and late September to November.
Cost: £110.

BERLITZ SCHOOLS OF LANGUAGES
Wells House, 79 Wells Street, London W1A 3BZ. Tel: 071-580 6482.
Comments: do not run open TEFL training courses. Compulsory method training course for all employees, lasting 1-2 weeks. This can be taken in the country in which the employee has been successfully interviewed rather than in the country where they'll be working. In the UK the course is unpaid, whereas in some countries (e.g. Spain) you are paid a modest sum to help defray living expenses.

BUTLER SCHOOL OF LANGUAGES
170 Victoria Street, London SW1E 5LB. Tel: 071-834 0606.
Duration: one week (30-40 hours).
Frequency: sporadically throughout the year.

BUTLER

SCHOOL OF LANGUAGES

LONDON & SHANNON

Intermittently during the year this school offers short EFL training courses outlining the principles of Direct Method Teaching with special emphasis on 'The Butler Question Method'.

These courses serve as an introduction to EFL teaching and some immediate vacancies are available at associate schools in Europe. They are also helpful to potential teachers who cannot afford the time and expense of longer courses and to foreign language teachers in this country who would like to improve their teaching techniques.

The courses are too short to deal with grammar points or the anomalies of English usage. In this context, 'Students English Grammar' by Allsopp and 'Practical English Usage' by Swan are highly recommended.

The courses usually last a week and the current cost is £100+VAT. They are advertised in the Tuesday *Guardian* EFL section.

170 Victoria Street	**Monument Cross**
London	**Newmarket-on-Fergus**
SW1E 5LB	**Shannon, Co. Clare**
Tel: 071-834 0606	**Tel: 061 71659**
Fax: 071-828 1184	**Fax: 061 71660**

Cost: £115.
Comments: use their own method, the "Butler Question Method". Have associate schools abroad, especially in Germany, Spain and Italy for whom they recruit teachers. Also based in Ireland (Monument Cross, Shannon, Co. Clare; tel: 061-71659).

CILC (Cheltenham International Language Centre)
Cheltenham & Gloucester College of Higher Education, Francis Close Hall Campus, Swindon Road, Cheltenham, Glos. GL50 4AZ. Tel: (0242) 222077.
Duration: one week (25 hours).
Frequency: 9 times per year.
Cost: £100.
Accommodation: can be arranged with local familes for about £75.
Comments: Course ends with tutor's assessment of participant's aptitude for teaching EFL. Also offers RSA Certificate and Diploma courses.

CONCORDE INTERNATIONAL
Hawks Lane, Canterbury, Kent CT1 2NU. Tel: (0227) 765537.
Duration: one week.
Frequency: December, January, April and June.
Cost: £120.
Accommodation: can be arranged.
Comments: also run RSA Certificate courses.

COVENTRY TESOL CENTRE
Coventry Technical College, Butts, Coventry CV1 3GD. Tel: (0203) 256793.
Duration: one week.
Frequency: once a month.
Cost: £99.
Accommodation: can be arranged in the YMCA.
Comments: introductory course is integrated with Trinity College Certificate course and so successful candidates can choose to enter the Certificate course in week 2 at a later date.

DIANA INTERNATIONAL SCHOOL OF LANGUAGES
Head Office, 69A Burgess Avenue, Kingsbury, London NW9 8TX. Tel: 081-200 6810.
Duration: 5 days intensive or 6 weeks part-time (Monday and Wednesday evening classes or Tuesday and Thursday afternoon classes).
Location: mostly in central London but also centres in Hastings and Sydney, Australia.
Frequency: intensive courses offered every month.
Cost: £330 for both full-time and part-time courses.
Accommodation: must be arranged independently.
Comments: all courses held at YWCA, Great Russell Street, London WC1. Also offers distance learning courses for £360.

EDINBURGH LANGUAGE FOUNDATION
11 Great Stuart Street, Edinburgh EH3 7TS. Tel: 031-225 8785.
Duration: one week.
Frequency: several per year; dates on application.
Cost: £100.
Accommodation: £60 (half board); £45 (bed and breakfast); £38 (self catering).
Comments: specializes in English for specific purposes.

EXPRESS LANGUAGE INSTITUTE
Express House, 6 Baches Street, London N1 6UB.
Duration: 10 weeks of distance learning for standard home-study course. Can also be done in five weeks ("express course") or part-time over a period of up to 18 weeks.
Frequency: throughout the year.
Cost: £195 (standard), £225 (express).
Comments: assessment based on three 1,000 word assignments. No contact with learners and no practice teaching possible.

THE GLOBE ENGLISH CENTRE
71 Holloway Street, Exeter, Devon EX2 4JD. Tel: (0392) 438102.
Duration: 10 weeks (Thursday evenings 6.45-9am).
Frequency: occasional.
Cost: £40.

HILDERSTONE COLLEGE
Broadstairs, Kent CT10 2AQ. Tel: (0843) 69171.
Duration: 6 days.

Frequency: October, January and April.
Cost: £135.
Accommodation: can be arranged on self-catering or half-board basis, or in small hotel.
Comments: also offer RSA courses.

inlingua Method Courses
Essex House, Temple Street, Birmingham B2 5DB. Tel: 021-643 3472.
Duration: 10 days (residential summer courses).
Location: Lancaster, Oxford and London.
Frequency: 4 courses in Lancaster, 2 in Oxford and 1 in London in July and August; one-week Birmingham courses held at intervals throughout the year.
Cost: £220 for 10-day course plus £230 full board accommodation or £180 half-board accommodation. A proportion of the fee (possibly about £80) will be refunded after fulfilling a one year contract in an inlingua school abroad.
Accommodation: college accommodation provided on residential course in St. Mary's College, Lancaster and Magdalen College, Oxford.
Comments: candidates cannot be accepted without a university degree; preferred age 22-35. Residential courses are held in conjunction with summer schools for foreign learners so teaching practice can take place on actual Italian or Spanish students. inlingua method course designed to equip people to teach in the chain of 200 inlingua schools, and successful participants are virtually guaranteed a job, usually in Spain, Germany or Italy. See page 58 for details of inlingua's teacher placement service.

INSTITUTE OF COMMUNICATION STUDIES
28 Nottingham Place, London W1M 3FD. Tel: 071-487 5665.
Duration: variable because participants work at their own pace.
Frequency: throughout the year.
Cost: £195.
Comments: distance learning only.

INTERNATIONAL LANGUAGE INSTITUTE
County House, Vicar Lane, Leeds LS1 7JH. Tel: (0532) 428893.
Duration: one week.
Frequency: once a month.
Cost: £98.
Accommodation: can be arranged.

its ENGLISH SCHOOL HASTINGS
43-45 Cambridge Gardens, Hastings, Sussex TN34 1EN. Tel: (0424) 438025.
Duration: one week (28 hours).
Frequency: 4 per year.
Cost: £120.
Accommodation: £48 bed & breakfast.
Comments: also offer Trinity College Certificate and Licentiate Diploma courses.

LANGUAGE CENTRE OF GUILDFORD
53 Woodbridge Road, Guildford, Surrey GU1 4RF. Tel: (0483) 35118. Fax: 34777.

Duration: one week (5 days).
Frequency: 8 times a year throughout the year.
Cost: £170.
Accommodation: can be arranged with host families at £75 (full board) or in hotels and bed and breakfasts, plus a booking fee of £15.
Comments: also launching Trinity College Certificate courses in 1991.

LANGUAGE 2 ASSOCIATES
16 Normanby Road, London NW10 1BX. Tel: 081-452 5495.
Duration: variable because participants work at their own pace.
Frequency: throughout the year.
Cost: £100 for the Certificate; £145 for the Diploma.
Comments: distance learning courses which follow the RSA syllabus without being entitled to issue RSA qualifications.

LINGUARAMA
New Oxford House, 16 Waterloo Street, Birmingham B2 5UG. Tel: 021-632 5925.
Duration: $5\frac{1}{2}$ days.
Location: Birmingham, Manchester, Nottingham and Winchester (non-residential); Canterbury (residential).
Frequency: non-residential courses held throughout the year; residential courses in Christmas, Easter and summer holidays only.
Cost: £160 non-residential; £235 residential.
Comments: often place their graduates in jobs abroad in the Linguarama chain, mainly Germany, Finland, France, Spain and Italy.

MARBLE ARCH TEACHER TRAINING
21 Star Street, London W2 1QB. Tel: 071-724 2217.
Duration: one week (25 hours).
Frequency: monthly between March and November.
Cost: £120.
Accommodation: can advise.
Comments: also run RSA Cert. courses.

NORD ANGLIA INTERNATIONAL
10 Eden Place, Cheadle, Cheshire SK8 1AT. Tel: 061-491 4191. Fax: 061-491 4410.
Duration: one week (30 hours).
Location: Manchester.
Cost: £125.
Accommodation: can be arranged.
Comments: operate many summer schools in UK and recruitment agency for schools abroad.

PILGRIMS LANGUAGE COURSES
8 Vernon Place, Canterbury, Kent CT1 3HG. Tel: (0227) 762111.
Duration: one week.
Location: mainly at University of Kent at Canterbury; other courses in Bristol, London, Edinburgh, Manchester and Canterbury city.
Frequency: throughout the year.

Cost: £170.
Accommodation: self-catering accommodation can be arranged for £60, full-board accommodation for £100.
Comments: also offer RSA Certificate courses.

PRIMARY HOUSE
300 Gloucester Road, Horfield, Bristol BS7 8PD. Tel: (0272) 444503.
Duration: 40 hours self-study plus 20 hour weekend course.
Location: weekend courses in various locations including Bangor, Southampton, York, Nottingham, Manchester and Edinburgh as well as Bristol.
Frequency: 3 weekend courses held per month in various locations.
Cost: £55 for self-study part plus £120 for weekend course. Students and unemployed people can join both parts for £100.
Accommodation: can be arranged in most venues in campus accommodation, bed and breakfasts or guest houses. Maximum cost is £17.50 per night (in London).
Comments: has links with the organization Teachers in Greece (see page 114 and guarantees a job in Greece to successful candidates. Course emphasizes teaching young children.

THE REGENCY SCHOOL OF ENGLISH
Royal Crescent, Ramsgate, Kent CT11 9PE. Tel: (0843) 591212.
Duration: 5 days.

Frequency: occasional (usually held in April).
Cost: £120.
Accommodation: can be arranged in next door hotel (£15 a night bed and breakfast) or with a local family (£65 a week).
Comments: also offer Trinity College Certificate and Licentiate Diploma.

SCOTTISH INTERNATIONAL LEARNING CENTRE (SILC)
24 Polwarth Gardens, Edinburgh EH11 1LW. Tel: 031-229 2611.
Duration: completely variable because courses are distance learning (i.e. self study by correspondence).
Frequency: throughout the year.
Cost: £160.

SOUTHAMPTON INSTITUTE OF HIGHER EDUCATION
East Park Terrace, Southampton SO9 4WW. Tel: (0703) 229381.
Duration: 10 weeks (2 hours each Monday afternoon or Tuesday evening).
Frequency: once a term.
Cost: £60.
Accommodation: must be arranged independently.
Comments: no entry requirements other than early enrolment.

SURREY LANGUAGE CENTRES
Sandford House, 39 West Street, Farnham, Surrey GU9 7DR. Tel: (0252) 723494.
Duration: one week.
Frequency: once a month.
Cost: £125.
Accommodation: £45 (bed & breakfast up to 5 nights); £60 (half board for up to 7 nights).
Comments: teacher placement service which may be able to assist graduates to secure jobs, especially in Spain, Greece and Italy.

TEACHER TRAINING INTERNATIONAL
Harrington Hall, 11 Harrington Gardens, South Kensington, London SW7 4JJ. Tel: 071-835 1945.
Duration: 6 weeks part-time (evening courses offered Mondays and Wednesdays

or Tuesdays and Thursdays; afternoon courses on Mondays and Wednesdays.
Frequency: new course begins each month.
Cost: £299.
Comments: has links with schools in Spain and France for whom they recruit teachers.

WESTERN LANGUAGE CENTRE
Forge House, Limes Road, Kemble, Nr. Cirencester, Glos. GL7 6AD. Tel: (0285) 770447.
Duration: 3 days (Wednesday to Friday).
Frequency: every 2 months.
Cost: £161.
Accommodation: will advise.
Comments: courses are specifically about teaching English for business.

Ireland

ACADEMY OF EDUCATIONAL DEVELOPMENT
44 Lower Leeson Street, Dublin 2, Ireland. Tel: (1) 610007.
Duration: weekend course held between Friday 6pm and Sunday 5pm (15 hours).
Frequency: occasional.
Cost: IR£75.
Comments: graded certificate granted after final assignment has been submitted.

Participants are given a list of language schools in Ireland, Britain, Europe and Japan which might have vacancies.

BLUEFEATHER SCHOOL OF LANGUAGES
35 Montpelier Parade, Monkstown, Dublin, Ireland. Tel: 806288.
Duration: 5 weeks (minimum), comprised of 4 weeks part-time home study (3 hours per day) plus 1 week (30-40 hours) at Bluefeather School.
Frequency: starting dates for home-study units entirely flexible; intensive course offered in Dublin throughout the year, September to June.
Cost: IR£180.
Accommodation: can be arranged with families, in bed and breakfasts or hotels. Host family charges are approximately IR£70 per week.
Comments: emphasis on practice rather than theory so course is billed as a "survival kit for the tutor". Participants accompany language learners on outings to gain experience teaching outside the classroom. Course also includes unit on how to prepare students for the Cambridge exams.

GRAFTON TUITION CENTRE
34 Grafton Street, Dublin 2, Ireland. Tel: (1) 772507/719288.
Location: as well as Dublin, summer courses offered at Stranmills College, Belfast (at £150).
Duration: 2 weeks (daytime) or 3 weeks (evenings Monday to Thursday).
Frequency: evening courses offered every month; daytime courses offered June to September.
Cost: IR£120.
Comments: free placement service for successful participants, plus file of language schools abroad which might be recruiting. Also offer Trinity College Licentiate Diploma course full-time or part-time for a fee of IR£275.

LANGUAGE CENTRE OF IRELAND
9-11 Grafton Street, Dublin 2, Ireland. Tel: (1) 716266.
Duration: 3 weeks (2-7pm, Monday to Friday).
Frequency: 4 times per year (starting April, June, September and November).
Cost: IR£180.
Comments: also offers RSA courses.

Abroad

ENGLISH FAST
Altiyol, Yoğurtçu Şükrü Sokak 29, Kadiköy, Istanbul, Turkey. Tel: 338 91 00.
Duration: 4 weeks.
Frequency: once a month.
Cost: £700 includes tuition, free accommodation and return flight from UK.
Comments: job guaranteed with English Fast or other Turkish language schools on completion of course. Candidates must have a university degree or equivalent.

INTERNATIONAL HOUSE — LISBON
Rua Marquês Sá da Bandeira 16, 1000 Lisbon, Portugal. Tel: (1) 57 14 96.
Duration: 2 weeks (10 days).

Frequency: late August/early September only.
Cost: £153.
Comments: also offer an introductory course specifically for teaching children and several RSA Certificate courses in the summer.

Other introductory courses which occasionally advertise but of which we have no recent confirmation are:

Inner Track Learning, 10/9 Forge House, Kemble, Glos. GL7 6AD. Tel: (0285) 770635. 5-day courses based on Suggestopaedia, the method of teaching which concentrates on relaxing the students' minds to make them more receptive. The cost is £200.

Living Language Centre, Clifton Gardens, Folkestone, Kent CT20 2EF. Tel: (0303) 58536. One-week course in June aimed at teachers on summer courses, leading to a "TEVAC" Certificate (Teaching English for Vacation and Activity Courses). The cost is £200 (of which up to £130 is refundable during employment). Accommodation is available for £50. Employment of 3-8 weeks in UK summer schools is guaranteed to successful participants.

OISE (Oxford Intensive School of English), OISE House, Binsey Lane, Oxford. Tel: (0865) 792799. 2-week evening courses for their own teachers. The cost is £70. Concentrates on theory and grammar with no teaching practice.

Oxford Tutorial Services, 44 Ashurst Close, Off Jasmine Grove, Anerley, London SE20. One-week course during the day or evenings/weekend.

Polyglot, Bennet Court, 1 Bellevue Road, London SW17 7EG. Tel: 081-767 9113. One-week intensive courses held throughout the year.

Video English Schools, 860 Sokak No. 1/4, Konak, İzmir, Turkey. Tel: (51) 137273. 4 week intro courses held occasionally. The cost is £600 which includes air fare from the UK, free accommodation and the guarantee of a one-year teaching contract in Izmir. This is affiliated to Cinar Language School (see page 204).

Finding a job

Teaching jobs are either fixed up from home or sought out on location. Having a job arranged before departure obviously removes much of the uncertainty and anxiety of leaving home for an extended period. It also allows the possibility of preparing in appropriate ways, e.g. sorting out the right visa, researching the texts which are used in your school, etc. Others prefer to meet their employer and inspect the school before signing a contract. It is always an advantage to meet other teachers and learn about the TEFL scene in that particular place firsthand before committing yourself, rather than accepting a job in complete ignorance of the prevailing conditions. But of course this is not always feasible.

Employers normally choose their staff several months before they are needed, so most schools advertise between April and July for jobs starting in September. If you want to fix up a job in person, you will either have to go on a reconnaisance mission well in advance of your proposed starting date or take your chances of finding a last-minute vacancy.

There are three ways of fixing up a teaching job in advance: by answering an advertisement, using a recruitment agency (which includes the large international English teaching organizations like International House) or conducting a speculative job search, i.e. writing letters to all the schools whose addresses you can find.

ADVERTISEMENTS

Luckily for the job-seeking teacher in the UK, two publications have a virtual monopoly on TEFL adverts: the Education section of the *Guardian* every Tuesday and the *Times Educational Supplement* published on Fridays but available in newsagents throughout the week. Although the monthly *EFL Gazette* is an excellent source of news and developments in TEFL, the recruitment adverts are surprisingly few. (A subscription to the *EFL Gazette* costs £14 a year and is available from 10 Wrights Lane, London W8 6TA; tel: 071-938 1819.) Relevant adverts occasionally appear in other places such as the *Guardian Weekly, The Times* (on Wednesdays), the *Graduate Post,* etc. but these are insignificant compared to the main two.

The best source of job ads for Americans is the TESOL Placement Bulletin. This listing of English teaching jobs appears every two months and is sent to TESOL members who register for the Placement Service, and pay an extra fee of $12 in North America, $18 abroad (see page 63). Another American publication in the field of overseas education is called *The International Educator.* In fact it concentrates on jobs in international English-medium schools abroad (normally with an American curriculum) which almost exclusively employ state-certified teachers, so it is of limited interest to straight EFL/ESL teachers.

Interpreting Adverts

Between Easter and mid-summer, the TEFL columns of the Tuesday *Guardian* and the *TES* are bursting with jobs for the next autumn. Jobs are listed year round, though schools which advertise in February or October are often advertising a very urgent vacancy — "to start immediately . . . good salary, air fares, accommodation . . ." — but these are in relatively short supply.

Almost all adverts specify TEFL training/experience as a minimum requirement. But this is often mere rhetoric. Those who lack such a background should not feel defeated before they begin, since quite often a TEFL background turns out not to be essential. A carefully crafted c.v. and enthusiastic personality could well persuade a school that they don't really have to insist on an RSA Certificate after all, especially if there is a shortage of qualified applicants.

The *Times Educational Supplement* (or *TES*): includes two relevant headings. "Overseas Appointments" primarily (but not exclusively) lists jobs in English-medium schools, while "English as a Foreign Language" is often disappointingly skimpy on TEFL jobs outside Britain. When checking the *Guardian* bear in mind that display adverts placed by VSO and the British Council do not appear under the "TEFL" heading but on an adjacent page. Although there is no guarantee that schools which use the hallowed pages of the British educational press for their siren songs of employment will be reasonable employers, most are established schools which go to the trouble and expense of recruiting abroad.

Apart from newspapers, there are a few other places where vacancies abroad might be mentioned. TEFL training centres often have numerous links with foreign schools and may have a notice board with posted vacancies. Unless you are a trainee it will probably be tricky consulting such a notice board, but a cooperative secretary might not mind a *potential* trainee consulting the board. University careers offices may also have contacts with schools abroad to which their graduates have gone in the past, so if you have a university connection, it is worth making enquiries.

THE BRITISH COUNCIL

Among the heaviest advertisers of all is the largest ELT (English language teaching) employer in the world. The British Council represents the elite end of the English language teaching industry. The Council runs its own language teaching centres in 33 countries, which claim to offer the highest quality language teaching available in those countries. Each centre employs between 3 and 80 teachers virtually all of whom are qualified to at least the RSA Certificate level and many to the Diploma level. The Council hires about 150 teachers a year from Britain (compared with over 200 by International House) as well as others on a local basis. Many of the locally recruited teachers are part-time and often the spouses of working expatriates.

The Royal Charter of the British Council defines its aims as "promoting a wider knowledge of the United Kingdom and the English language abroad and developing closer cultural relations with other countries." Financed by public funds, it is non-profit-making and works non-politically in over 80 countries. It employs about 4,500 staff in all, divided between Britain and abroad, a good percentage of whom are involved with the teaching of the English language in some capacity. Other work which the Council carries out includes the running of libraries, the organization of cultural tours and exchanges, etc. But language teaching and teacher recruitment remain one of its central concerns.

A useful starting place for understanding the various roles which the Council plays in the world of TEFL is to request the small format brochure "Teaching Overseas" which is available free of charge from the Overseas Education Department, 65 Davies Street, London W1Y 2AA (tel: 071-389 7660).

Structure of the British Council

The British Council in London is not an easy institution to fathom and it sometimes seems as though the receptionists on the switchboard (tel: 071-930 8466) have yet to master its complexities. In the first place the Council is divided between two buildings, both of which contain departments of interest to potential teachers. (The building at 65 Davies Street is in Mayfair, off Oxford Street and 10 Spring Gardens is near Trafalgar Square.) Unless you know exactly which department you need (and preferably its direct telephone number) you may be in for a frustrating time.

Here is a layman's guide to the sections and departments of possible interest to prospective teachers, complete with their acronyms:

CMDT, 10 Spring Gardens, London SW1A 2BN. Tel: 071-389 4931.
The acronym stands for Central Management of Direct Teaching. The Council refers to its own teaching centres abroad as Direct Teaching Operations (DTOs) or sometimes DTE operations for Direct Teaching of English.

CMDT is the department which oversees these 52 centres and the recruitment section is responsible for the bulk of the hiring of teachers. Anyone interested in applying for a Council teaching post should write to CMDT requesting the brochure "Teaching English World-wide," a glossy but moderately informative document which includes some personal accounts from people working in the Council's network of English language centres. The last page is headed "How to Apply".

CMDT Recruitment regularly advertises in the educational press. A sample advert (taken from the May 1990 issue of *EFL Gazette*) stated that the British Council's English Language Centres had over 150 teaching post vacancies for August/September in Europe, the Middle East, North Africa, the Far East and Latin America, and went on to list the 23 countries with vacancies. "Applicants should have a degree plus an RSA Diploma, PGCE or equivalent and a minimum of 2 years experience. Candidates with experience plus an RSA Preparatory Certificate will be considered." Interviews for these one or two year contracts are held between May and July. By early June, CMDT still had over 50 vacancies in six countries (including the relatively unpopular destinations of Algeria and Bangladesh). By July, the advertised vacancies were for supervisors and middle managers in eight countries. But it is worth contacting CMDT at any time of the year, as they maintain a file of teachers available for work.

OEAD, 65 Davies Street, London W1Y 2AA. Tel: 071-389 7660.
The Overseas Educational Appointments Department recruits senior educational personnel for posts abroad in universities, teacher training colleges, ministries of education, etc. The majority of vacancies are related to ELT but by no means all, since the Council is often asked to provide technical experts for educational establishments abroad.

A substantial part of OEAD's work is on behalf of the Overseas Development Administration (*ODA*) and large display adverts bearing both logos can regularly be seen in the *Times Educational Supplement* and the *Guardian*. One such advert (chosen at random from an April *TES*) listed the following vacancies, which will give an idea of the level of position available from OEAD: ELT Media Adviser for the College of the Air in Mauritius, an ESP Adviser for Rwanda, an ELT Consultant for Colombia, an English Teaching Adviser for the Ministry of Education in the Cameroons, an Examinations Officer in Aden and a teacher trainer for Angola. The basic qualifications for these 2-year contract posts are: UK citizenship, a British educational background, MA in Applied Linguistics or TEFL and 3-5 years relevant overseas experience. The rewards are commensurate with the seniority of these posts and include free family passages, superannuation, etc.

Unlike CMDT, OEAD does not keep a register of applications, so people must apply for vacancies as they crop up and are advertised.

ELIU, 10 Spring Gardens, London SW1A 2BU. Tel: 071-389 4036.
The English Language Information Unit (formerly ETIC, the English Teaching Information Centre) provides information to members of the public on all aspects of English language teaching. They produce various free publications of special interest to people who want to pursue a TEFL qualification, principally lists of centres which offer the RSA/UCLES Certificate and Diploma, the Trinity College Certificate and Licentiate Diploma and the PGCE.

They also publish and distribute free of charge a large number of English Teaching Profiles, a series of country-specific papers which describe the state of English language teaching in that country. Although these cover most countries of the world, many are sadly outdated; the worst example is the profile of Jordan which was published in 1974. The bulk of the information is about English language teaching in the state sector, usually with a rather sniffy paragraph about private language schools. But if you are keenly interested in one country, it can't hurt to request a copy of the relevant profile. ELIU can send you a list of the country profiles with the date of the most recent edition.

ELIU also holds other relevant publications such as the *Keltic Guide* (which is a complete guide to ELT materials) and other sources of reference for EFL teachers.

ELPU, 10 Spring Gardens, London SW1A 2BU. Tel: 071-389 4375.
The English Language Promotion Unit is of interest to prospective teachers merely

as the publisher of various "Surveys of English Language Teaching and Learning". The country surveys available at the time of writing were: Austria, Colombia, Cyprus, Denmark, Japan, Korea, Switzerland, Taiwan and Turkey, all at a cost of £25. These are subtitled "Guides to the Market" and are intended for companies and organizations which are in the TEFL business. But they do contain lists of private and public English language schools to which it is possible to send speculative applications. There are no facilities for consulting reference copies of these Surveys at the Council, which is both disappointing and shocking for an institution famed for its library facilities around the world.

Teaching for the Council

Since the Council's requirements are more stringent than most other employers, it normally attracts teachers who are serious about their profession. It is very common for newly qualified teachers who work abroad in a private school or for a private chain such as International House or inlingua to aspire after a job in a British Council DTO.

In the first instance DTOs normally try to fill a vacancy from the pool of expatriates living locally. Teachers on local contracts are paid in local currency and not provided with accommodation. Failing this, they turn to CMDT in London. The advantages of a British Council contract are numerous, though terms and conditions vary substantially from centre to centre. Teachers recruited through London always have their air fares paid and an allowance for shipping their belongings. Salaries probably average £10,000. Considering that living expenses are often considerably less in foreign parts than in the UK, and that the salary is tax-free, this is reasonably favourable. Many teachers value all the intangible benefits such as the security of working for an established institution, and encouragement of professional development with such perks as a subsidy to study for the RSA Diploma, etc. Some Council offices abroad offer the RSA Cert. and/or RSA Dip. course, which are open to anyone. Once you have secured one job with the Council, it is easy to move to other jobs in other places, since the Council regularly notifies its network of all vacancies.

On the minus side is a tendency to snobbishness. British Council staff are sometimes unnecessarily condescending about local language schools who may be satisfactorily meeting a local need and for a fraction of the cost which the British Council charges its language learners. Also, the Council is a very large and ponderous bureaucracy with all the problems which that entails, such as inflexibility and cumbersome procedures for doing anything at all original or out-of-the-way.

RECRUITMENT ORGANIZATIONS

As mentioned above, the British Council often recruits teachers on behalf of the Overseas Development Administration, though the ODA increasingly carries out its own recruitment on behalf of foreign ministries of education. ODA projects are funded under the British Government's Aid Programme.

ODA, Abercrombie House, Eaglesham Road, East Kilbride, Glasgow G75 8EA. Tel: (03552) 41199, ext. 3486. Fax: (03552) 38432. Publishes a free booklet "Opportunities in Education Overseas" (revised July 1989) which sets out the broad categories of teaching posts for which the ODA recruit and gives a rough idea of the terms and conditions under which candidates are asked to serve.

Requirements fluctuate very much from year to year. The ODA is occasionally asked to assist when a country is setting up a new English teaching operation and there will be a one-off demand for staff, usually with specialist qualifications. Normally they are looking for candidates who are more than just EFL teachers, for example teachers who have experience of curriculum development. Their literature states categorically that there are no opportunities for untrained teachers.

In addition to these official government-sponsored agencies, there is a large range of teacher placement organizations in Britain (and in the US — see below). Some are international educational foundations like the Bell Educational Trust; some are charities or voluntary organizations like VSO; some are the head office of language school chains like Berlitz; and others are small agencies run by one or two individuals who act as intermediaries between independent language schools abroad and prospective teachers.

It is fair to say that most agencies and recruitment consultants deal with the elite end of the EFL market. It is hardly worthwhile for a family-run language school in northern Greece or southern Brazil to pay the high costs which most agencies charge schools just to obtain one or two native speaker teachers. Advertisements placed by commercial agencies tend to be for specialized or high level positions. Often the clients for whom they are trying to recruit staff are corporations with in-house EFL programmes or foreign governments. Agencies make their money by charging client schools; the service to teachers is normally free of charge. Some of the best recruitment organizations to deal with are ones which specialize in a single country, such as English & Spanish Studies or English Teachers for Greece (see the relevant chapters). They tend to have more first-hand knowledge of their client schools, though there is never any guarantee of this. The most established agencies such as Gabbitas, Truman & Thring deal only secondarily or peripherally with EFL vacancies. Their main task is to find qualified and experienced teachers for English-medium international schools following the British curriculum. Of the main agencies in this field, the first three do carry out some EFL recruitment.

Gabbitas, Truman & Thring, Broughton House, 6-8 Sackville Street, London W1X 2BR. Tel: 071-734 0161. Maintain a register of qualified and experienced teachers available for teaching posts in South America, the Middle East and Africa, including some English language teaching jobs.

Centre for British Teachers, Quality House, Gyosei Campus, London Road, Reading RG1 5AQ. Tel: (0734) 756200. Fax: (0734) 756365. Recruits EFL teachers for its own projects in Brunei (primary and secondary), Oman, Malaysia, Turkey and Germany. Candidates must have recognized teacher status in the UK and considerable experience for most posts. There are exceptions, for example their new project at Bilkent University in Ankara requires only that candidates have a BA and one year's teaching experience.

Worldwide Education Service, 10 Barley Mow Passage, Chiswick, London W4 4PH. Tel: 081-994 3689. Educational charity which recruits qualified teachers including a few EFL teachers for some 80 schools all over the world.

ECIS (European Council of International Schools), 21B Lavant Street, Petersfield, Hants. GU32 3EL. Tel: (0730) 68244. Has links with independent international schools in Europe and worldwide. Placement service for fully qualified teachers normally with 2 years' experience; professional dossiers of members are circulated among appropriate schools. They only have about 15 EFL vacancies annually.

Major EFL Agencies

One way in which these agencies work is to create a database of teacher's c.v.'s and to try to match these with suitable vacancies as they occur. In order to be registered with such an agency it is normally essential to have at least the RSA Prep. Cert. Alternatively agencies place advertisements (often expensive display adverts) in the educational press for specific vacancies.

Bell Educational Trust, Overseas Department, The Lodge, Redcross Lane, Cambridge CB2 2QX. Tel: (0223) 246644. Fax: (0223) 410282. Frequently advertise EFL posts for its own affiliated schools abroad or on behalf of independent client schools. Countries in which Bell has recently advertised jobs include Brazil, Saudi Arabia, Indonesia, Italy and Hungary.

ILC Recruitment (International Language Centres), 1 Riding House, London W1A 3AS. Tel: 071-580 4351. Fax: 071-631 0741. Offer a computerized recruitment service for English language teachers and employers throughout the world. The TEFL Register is free and open to all qualified (degree plus TEFL) native-speaker teachers whether British, American, Irish, etc. Recent advertised vacancies have been in Greece, Japan, Korea, Oman, Abu Dhabi, Portugal, Spain, Turkey and Czechoslovakia.

International House, 106 Piccadilly, London W1 9FL. Tel: 071-491 2598. Fax: 071-495 5848. IH is a non-profit educational charity which was founded in 1953 and is now the largest British-based organization for teaching English.

The vast majority of vacancies in the 85 International House affiliated schools worldwide are filled through the Teacher Selection Department in London. The large format "Recruitment Programme" brochure is very useful for prospective teachers, since it provides a description of individual schools and their environs, as well as the terms of contract (salary, hours, housing, etc.). The new edition comes out in March in time for the busy recruitment season.

In order to be considered for an IH teaching post, you must have passed the RSA Certificate course with either an 'A' or 'B' (not easy) and even then employment is not automatic. RSA-qualified teachers with experience will always be given preference. However, once you're in, you're in and it is not difficult to move within the organization; in fact about half the appointments are transfers. There is a lot of competition for choice positions in France, Italy and the UK.

Language School Chains

The hiring of teachers for chain schools abroad is done either at a local level (so direct applications are always worthwhile) or centrally, especially if the affiliated school has trouble filling vacancies on its own.

Berlitz is one of the biggest language training organizations in the world with about 250 schools, though most vacancies occur in Spain, Italy, Germany and France. All their teachers are native speakers trained in the direct "Berlitz Method". Berlitz schools are known for supervising their teachers' techniques very closely, so deviation from the method is not encouraged in any way.

The headquarters of Berlitz International Inc. are in the US (where there are 60 Berlitz schools) at Research Park, 239 Wall Street, Princeton, NJ 08540. In Britain, Berlitz has its main offices at Wells House, 79 Wells Street, London W1A 3BZ (tel: 071-580 6482) and at 101 The Piazza, Piccadilly Plaza, Manchester M1 4AN (tel: 061-228 3607). When Berlitz has urgent vacancies to fill, usually in Spain and Italy, it places an advert in the Tuesday *Guardian* inviting any interested university graduates to attend interviews in London, Manchester, Edinburgh or Dublin. Normally, however, Berlitz schools abroad employ their teachers directly.

inlingua Teacher Service, Essex House, Temple Street, Birmingham B2 5DB. Tel: 021-643 3472. Fax: 021-643 3482. Has 280 schools worldwide for which it recruits about 150 teachers annually. The majority are for schools in Germany, Spain and Singapore. Candidates must have a degree and should have teaching experience. Many people do the inlingua Method Course (see page 43), to enhance their chances of placement within the organization. The inlingua headquarters are in Switzerland at Weisenhausplatz 28, 3011 Berne.

Linguarama, Oceanic House, 89 High Street, Alton, Hants. GU34 1LG. Tel: (0962) 66836. Linguarama's motto is "Language Training for Business" though their short teacher training course does not specialize in business English. They have several offices in London (for teacher interviews, visa services, etc.) as well as the above address which deals with vacancies in France, Spain, Italy and Germany. Vacancies in Finland are administered by Linguarama, King's Court, The Broadway, Winchester, Hants. SO23 9JX.

Benedict Schools, PO Box 300, 1000 Lausanne 9, Switzerland. Have over 50 schools in Europe especially Italy. They look for qualified teachers (RSA Dip./MA in Linguistics preferred) though they also run in-house training courses. They advertise in Britain and interview prospective teachers at a London hotel during the summer.

Other Commercial Agencies

Smaller agencies may have fewer vacancies on their books but they can often offer a more personal service.

Anchor Language Services, 30 Brick Row, Babraham, Cambridge CB2 4AJ. Tel: (0223) 836017. Most jobs are in Turkey (e.g. 20 in language schools and 10 in secondary schools in 1990) but also some in Italian language schools. The RSA Cert. is required for TEFL posts.

Basil Paterson, Teacher Recruitment Agency, 22-23 Abercromby Place, Edinburgh EH3 6QE. Tel: 081-556 7698. An RSA Cert. training centre which has extended its services to include placement abroad of RSA Cert. holders.

ELT Banbury, 49 Oxford Rd., Banbury, Oxon. OX6 9AH. Tel: (0295) 263480. Fax: (0295) 271658. Invite EFL teachers to fax their c.v.'s for possible posts in Italy, France, Greece, Turkey, Yugoslavia, etc.

English Worldwide, 17 New Concordia Wharf, Mill St., London SE1 2BB. Tel: 071-252 1402. Established and serious agency which recruits mostly for Europe and the Middle East.

International Language Services, 36 Fowlers Road, Salisbury, Wilts. SP1 2QU. Tel: (0722) 331011. Majority of its work is for the Folkuniversity of Sweden (see Sweden chapter) but also has occasional vacancies elsewhere, e.g. Japan.

Language Exchange, 7 Panmure Place, Edinburgh EH3 9HP. Tel: 031-228 2755. Fax: 031-229 7666. Currently recruit about 50 teachers (primarily EFL) to schools in Italy, Spain, Portugal, France, Germany, Greece, Turkey,

Czechoslovakia and Hungary. Teachers are advised to apply 5 or 6 months prior to employment date if possible.

Language Matters, 4 Blenheim Road, Moseley, Birmingham B13 9TY. Tel: 021-442 4550. Fax: 021-441 1361. Small new agency run by two experienced EFL teachers, one of whom is based in Spain (c/ Galileo 70, 1º, Ct. Dch, 28015 Madrid; tel: 593 15 83). In 1990 they recruited teachers for several schools in Spain and one in Rhodes, with plans to expand.

Language School Appointments, 27 Delancey Street, Regent's Park, London NW1 7RX. Tel: 071-388 6644. Fax: 071-387 7575. Specialists in Spain and Italy, expanding to cover all EEC countries. Occasional positions for language graduates with no teaching experience but majority require at least an RSA Cert.

Language Specialists International (LSI), 25 Whitwell Road, Southsea, Portsmouth PO4 0QP. Tel. (0705) 291811. Recruit for associate schools in Spain (Madrid and Cordoba), Italy (e.g. Bologna) and the United Arab Emirates.

Nord-Anglia International Ltd. 10 Eden Place, Cheadle, Stockport, Cheshire SK8 1AT. Tel: 061-491 4191. Fax: 061-491 4409. Specializes in EFL vacation courses throughout the UK, but has recently registered as a recruitment agency which is open not only to their own summer school teachers. Most of their contacts are in Spain, Turkey, Greece and Italy. The minimum qualifications are a relevant degree, some EFL experience and preferably an initial TEFL qualification.

Surrey Language Centre, Teacher Recruitment Service, 39 West Street, Farnham, Surrey GU9 7DR. Tel: (0252) 723494. Fax: (0252) 733519. Primarily a training centre, but also advertise occasional vacancies abroad, e.g. in Greece.

Advertisements will very often include a contact name or company in the UK to which enquiries should be addressed for posts abroad. This may be a TEFL training centre (such as the Butler School and Teacher Training International both in London; see Training chapter) or a language school in the UK which is in contact with language schools abroad.

Voluntary and Religious Organizations

A booklet *Jobs Abroad* containing a number of specific vacancies for Christians includes a section called "English Language Teaching Vacancies" and is usually issued twice a year in the spring and autumn. It is available from the Christian Service Centre, Unit 2, Holloway Street West, Dudley, West Midlands DY3 2DZ (tel: 0902 882836). In the most recent issue, 14 separate organizations were looking for EFL volunteers to fill positions in circumstances as varied as an Afghan refugee camp and Christian language schools in Portugal.

There are very few English teaching opportunities for pre-university candidates with the notable exception of two organizations for school-leavers.

GAP Activity Projects, 44 Queen's Road, Reading, Berks. RG1 4BB. Tel: (0374) 594914. Fax: (0734) 576634. Offers work opportunities for school-leavers aged 18 or 19. Includes positions as English teachers in China, India, Indonesia, Mexico, Poland and the Soviet Union. Posts are for at least 6 months and cost the volunteer on average £250 plus air fares and insurance, while board, lodging and pocket money are provided.

The Project Trust, Breacachadh Castle, Isle of Coll, Argyll PA78 6TB. Tel: (087 93) 444. An educational trust which sends British school-leavers overseas for a year. Some examples of projects include teaching English to unemployed lobster fishermen on one of the Honduran Bay Islands, and also teaching in Zimbabwe, China and Indonesia. Participants must raise a proportion of the cost of the placement: £2,350 in 1991.

The two major voluntary agencies in the UK recruit EFL teachers as well as many other kinds of volunteer.

VSO (Voluntary Service Overseas), 317 Putney Bridge Road, London SW15

2PN. Tel: 081-780 1330. Regular advertisements headed "Wanted urgently . . . " appear in the educational press. All postings are for a minimum of two years. Requirements vary, but the EFL teachers are normally expected to have at least the RSA Cert. and 6 months experience. Demand has been strongest lately in China and Southeast Asia (Indonesia, Thailand and Laos) and also Poland. Pay is always based on local rates, though VSO provides flights, accommodation and insurance, plus other perks such as national insurance contributions, equipment grants and a gratuity on return to Britain.

Christians Abroad, 1 Stockwell Green, London SW9 9HP. Tel: 071-737 7811. Ecumenical charity which provides information to prospective volunteers and recruits a limited number of teachers for schools in Japan, Malawi and Zimabwe. Publishes a leaflet on Education in its "A Place for You Overseas?" series, and also a list of vacancies, *Opportunities Abroad* issued every 6 months, in which over 30 mission, volunteer and aid agencies list their voluntary requirements. These are open to both Christian and secular teachers.

Other charities and mission societies which occasionally require EFL teachers include:

CIIR (Catholic Institute for International Relations), Overseas Programme, 22 Coleman Fields, London N1 7AF. Very occasional professional positions only, especially in Latin America.

Methodist Church Overseas Division, 25 Marylebone Road, London NW1 5JR. Tel: 071-486 5502. Long-term appointments only.

OMS International, 1 Sandileigh Avenue, Manchester M20 9LN. Tel: 061-445 3513. Publish a "Missing Persons Bulletin" which lists the mission's annual vacancies. TEFL vacancies occur occasionally and are filled by applicants with a good standard of education but not necessarily a TEFL qualification.

Wycliffe Bible Translators, Horsleys Green, High Wycombe, Bucks. HP14 3XL. Tel: (0494) 482521. Most teaching positions are for teachers with a PGCE.

For US Teachers

Recruitment agencies in the United States have stronger links with Latin America and the Far East than with Europe. As in Britain, some organizations are involved primarily with English-medium international schools following an American curriculum and are looking to recruit state certified teachers. Organizations such as International Schools Service (PO Box 5910, Princeton, NJ 08543) are in this category, as is the quarterly journal *The International Educator* (which has a "Jobs Only" supplement in July) and various job placement fairs held at universities such as Ohio State University. The Institute of International Education (809 United Nations Plaza, New York, NY 10017) publish *Teaching Abroad: Opportunities for US Educators Worldwide;* the 1988 edition costs $21.95 plus postage.

USIA (United States Information Agency), English Language Teaching Division, 301 4th Street West, Washington, DC 20547. Roughly the American equivalent of the British Council with many English teaching programmes especially in developing countries. Most teachers for these Bi-National Centers are hired directly by the centre in question — hence the inclusion of many USIS (US Information Services) addresses in the country directories — however the above address may be able to advise on possibilities and can send a complete list of centres. Some attend the TESOL Convention in the US in order to recruit teachers.

TESOL Inc. (Teachers of English to Speakers of Other Languages), 1600 Cameron Street, Suite 300, Alexandria, Virginia 22314. Tel: (703) 836-0774. A key organization for American English language teachers, TESOL is a non-profit organization which offers various services to members including a placement service and a quarterly journal. Membership is $42 ($22 for students). Of immediate interest to the job-seeker is TESOL's Placement Bulletin, a listing of job vacancies worldwide published six times a year. Members do not receive the Bulletin automatically, but must pay an extra $12 in North America and $18 overseas. Another central function is to organize TESOL Conventions (mentioned frequently in language school entries later in the book). The Conventions are attended by many language schools looking to recruit teachers through the Employment Clearinghouse.

TESL Recruiting Service Inc., Route 6, Box 174, New Orleans, LA 70129. Tel: (504) 662-5569. Non-profit employment service for ESL teachers (both American and non-American) which uses a computer to match teacher's c.v.'s with one of their more than 150 client schools. Operate in 21 countries but specialize in Turkey where they have an office at Akarsu Yokusu 4, Istanbul/Cihangir, Turkey 80060 (tel: 152-1334). They are hoping to open a branch office in Japan in the near future. The service is free of charge to teachers.

ELS International Inc., 5761 Buckingham Parkway, Culver City, CA 90230. Tel: (213) 642-0982. Fax: (213) 410-4688. The Californian headquarters recruits specifically for the two ELS schools in Seoul and one in Madrid. Other schools

in the network are responsible for their own recruitment, though a list of addresses is available from the above address. (At present there are ELS schools in Rio de Janeiro, Sao Paulo, Lima, Jakarta, Bangkok, Kuala Lumpur, Taipei, Kaohsiung, Tokyo, Osaka and Pusan, as well as Seoul and Madrid.)

ELS are normally looking for candidates (American and British) with a BA and one year's full-time experience (or a degree in TESL) as a minimum. If hired to teach in Seoul or Madrid, return air fares are paid, as well as a package of other benefits. The UK office of ELS is Meridian House, Royal Hill, Greenwich, London SE10 8RT.

Aspect International Language Schools, 26 Third Street, San Francisco, CA 94103. Tel: (415) 777-9555. A smaller chain with language schools in Japan and Czechoslovakia and plans to open others. They recruit up to 30 teachers, preferably with an MA in TESL and two years experience.

St. Giles Educational Trust, 2280 Powell Street, San Francisco, CA 94133. Like most TEFL training centres, help is given to graduates who are looking for jobs. This independent centre (with sister schools in the UK) has links with language schools worldwide and tries to advise its newly qualified EFL teachers accordingly.

The Council for International Exchange of Scholars, 3400 International Drive NW, Suite M-500, Washington, DC 20008-3097. Tel: (202) 686-7866. Adminster about 80 Fulbright grants in TEFL/Applied Linguistics for academic TEFL specialists who wish to lecture in universities or carry out TEFL research in any of 40 countries.

A number of voluntary agencies in the US are active in the TEFL field, such as the following:

Peace Corps, 1990 K Street NW, Washington DC 20526. Toll-free tel: 1-800-424-8580, ext. 93. Volunteers are sent on 2-year assignments. TEFL has historically been one of the major programme areas and is expanding with invitations from Poland and Hungary to supply EFL teachers.

AFS International/Intercultural Programs, AFS International Teachers Programs, 313 E. 43rd Street, New York, NY10017. Tel: 1-800-AFS-INFO. Recruits ESL (and other) teachers for Argentina, Chile, China, Costa Rica, Peru, Thailand and the USSR.

WorldTeach, Institute for Int. Devt., 1 Eliot St., Harvard, Cambridge MA 02138. Tel: (617) 495-5527. Fax: (617) 495-9120. Non-profit organization which recruits volunteers to teach English (and other subjects occasionally) for one year in China, Costa Rica, Kenya, Namibia, Poland and Thailand. Volunteers pay about $3,200 for air fares, orientation and insurance, and are provided with housing and a stipend based on local rates. Participants do not have to be US citizens, but must have a BA and must complete a one-semester course in TEFL or do at least 25 hours of EFL/ESL tutoring in their local setting.

ICMC, 1319 F Street NW, Suite 820, Washington, DC 20004. The American office of the Intergovernmental Committee for Migration which also has an office in Geneva. Responsible for refugee processing which often involves English teaching programmes in refugee camps, as in the Philippines.

International Rescue Committee. 386 Park Avenue South, New York, NY 10016. Works with refugees (including English teaching projects) in Thailand, Pakistan, Costa Rica, etc. The minimum commitment is 6 months. IRC pay $1,000 per month and provide housing, insurance and transport.

SPECULATIVE JOB HUNT

Only a small percentage of language schools advertise in the foreign press or use an agency. The vast majority depend on local adverts, personal contacts and direct approaches. Therefore a speculative job search probably has a better chance with TEFL jobs than in many other fields of employment. For a successful campaign, only two things are needed: a reasonable c.v. and a list of addresses of potential customers.

Applying in Advance

Entire books and consultancy companies are devoted to showing people how to draw up an impressive curriculum vitae (or resumé as it is known in the US). But it is really just a matter of common sense. Obviously employers will be more inclined to take seriously a well presented document than something scribbled on the back of a dog-eared envelope. Obviously any relevant training or experience should be highlighted rather than submerged in the trivia about your schooling and hobbies. If you lack any TEFL experience, try to bring out anything in your past which demonstrates your "people skills", such as voluntary work, group counselling, one-to-one remedial tutoring, etc. and your interest in (and ability to adapt to) foreign countries.

Attitudes are probably even more important than educational achievements in TEFL, so anything which proves an aptitude for teaching and an extrovert personality will be relevant. Because this is difficult to do on paper, some eager job-hunters have gone so far as to send off a video of themselves, preferably a snippet of teaching. This is not worth doing unless (a) a school has expressed some interest and (b) you can make a good impression on an amateur video. A cheaper alternative might be to send a photo and a cassette of your speaking voice, again assuming this will be a help rather than a hindrance.

The other essential ingredient is a list of addresses. Each of the country chapters in this book recommends ways of obtaining such a list, for example by contacting a federation of language schools (if there is one) or looking at one of the British Council's *Surveys of English Teaching* all of which contain lists of schools. The book in your hand provides a good starting place, by including over 500 schools which regularly hire native speaker teachers. The most comprehensive source of addresses in most cases is the Yellow Pages which you may be able to consult in advance at the Embassy or Consulate, at large reference libraries (in particular the City Business Library, Basinghall Street, London EC2), at the Chamber of Commerce if there is one, etc. If you have a contact in your proposed destination city you could impose on them to photocopy the relevant destination city you could impose on them to photocopy the relevant section. With luck, the British Council might be prepared to do you this favour. It is always worth writing to the British Council in any case, since very often they maintain a list of selected language schools in their region (for the benefit of enquiries from local language learners) and might be prepared to send it to you. This will be at the discretion of the English Language Adviser or her/his secretary.

Americans can try requesting a similar list from the relevant USIS offices who may also be able to offer general advice about language teaching in that country. You can exploit connections (e.g. nationality) in other respects: Canadians might have a strong chance of being hired by the Manitoba Centre in Portugal; Cambridge graduates might be welcomed by the chain of Cambridge Language

Centres and Americans could concentrate on the Abraham Lincoln Center or Thomas Jefferson Center in South America.

Of course you have to recognize that it is difficult to set up a firm job offer simply by correspondence. It is a good idea to follow up any hint of interest with a phone call. Perhaps the school has a contact in your country who would be willing to conduct an informal interview on their behalf. If your credentials are not the kind to wow school directors, it might still be worth sending off a batch of warm-up letters, stating your intention to present yourself in person a couple of weeks or months hence. Even if you don't receive a reply, such a strategy may stick in the mind of employers, as an illustration of how organized and determined you are.

Interviews

Schools which advertise in foreign journals often arrange for candidates to be interviewed either by their own representative or by a proxy, such as a previous teacher or an appointed agent. Interviews can take place in a variety of locations from a South London pub to a ritzy hotel where large organizations like Berlitz sometimes hold open days and invite anyone who wants to be interviewed to come along. Chances are that British job-seekers will have to travel to London for an interview. Whether you are interviewed at home or abroad, slightly different rules apply. For example smart casual dress, neither flashy nor scruffy, is appropriate in Britain, while something a little more formal might be called for in certain cultures (e.g. Japan). Even if all your friends laugh when you pack a suit before going abroad, you may find it a genuine asset when trying to outdo the competition. As Steven Hendry, who has taught English both in Japan and Thailand with none of the usual advantages apart from traveller's canniness, says: you may not need a tailor-made suit but you definitely need to be able to present a conservative and respectable image.

As with the c.v. so at interview. Highlight anything that is remotely connected with teaching even if it has nothing to do with the English language, and do it energetically and enthusiastically. Yet keenness will seldom be sufficient in itself. You do not have to be an intellectual to teach English; in fact the quiet bookish type is probably at a disadvantage. But you can't be clueless either. It is not unknown for an interviewer to ask a few basic grammar questions; to help you deal with this eventuality you might turn to the list of recommended reading on page 81. Without a TEFL background you should do a certain amount of research, e.g. acquainting yourself with some of the jargon such as "notional", "communicative-based", "total immersion", etc. By visiting the ELT section of a bookshop, you can begin to familiarize yourself with the range of materials on offer. Always have some questions ready to ask the interviewer, such as "Do you use Cambridge or Streamline?", "What audio materials do you have?" "Do you encourage the use of songs?", "Do you teach formal grammar structures?" or (in some settings) "Do you have a photocopier?"

You will certainly be asked how long you intend to stay and (depending on the time of year) nothing less than nine months will be considered. They will also want to know whether you have had any experience. With luck you will be able to say truthfully that you have (at least) taught at a summer school in Britain (see chapter on Preparation). Some applicants who are convinced that they can do a good job make a similar claim, untruthfully, knowing that at the lower end of the TEFL spectrum this will never be checked. Similarly some candidates claim to have done a TEFL course and pretend to have left the certificate at home. A certain amount of bluffing goes on in all interviews, so you'll just have to decide how far you are prepared to go. Bear in mind that the true depths of your ignorance could easily be plumbed ("Ah, so you've used Cambridge. Why do you prefer it to Streamline?").

Another of your skills you may be tempted to exaggerate is your knowledge of the local language. Philip Dodd was hired by a language teaching agency in Madrid on the understanding that he could speak fluent Spanish and was sent out on his first assignment, to give English lessons to a young boy living in a wealthy suburb. He was greeted at the door by the boy's mother who wished to make sure of a few things before she entrusted her precious son to this stranger.

Pretending to speak the language can get you into hot water

Not able to follow her voluble stream, Philip nodded affably and said "si" whenever he guessed it was appropriate. After one of his affable "si's", the woman's face turned grey and she ordered him out of her house. He still doesn't know what he said that was so shocking. On the other hand, a certain inflation of your abilities may be expected, and will be met with distortions of the truth from the employer as you both decide whether you are going to hit it off.

Of course many applicants will be able to avoid potential embarrassment at interview by having prepared themselves for a stint as a teacher. If you have done a TEFL course of any description, be sure to take along the certificate, however humble the qualification. Schools in farflung places may not make any significant distinction between the RSA Diploma and a correspondence course. If you have a university degree, do take the diploma along. Even if the interviewer is prepared to take your word for it, the school administration may need the document at a later stage either to give you a salary increment or to obtain a work permit. Adam Hartley, who taught English in China, hadn't realized that his MA would have earned him a higher salary; although he arranged for two separate copies to be sent from Britain, neither arrived and he had to be content with the basic salary. (Anyone planning to do the RSA Certificate who doesn't have a degree wil be interested to learn that the Cambridge Examination Syndicate, which now administers the exam, helpfully emblazons the University of Cambridge crest on the Certificate, which can be of use.) Americans should take along their university transcripts; any school accustomed to hiring Americans will be familiar with these.

ON THE SPOT

It is almost impossible to fix up a job in advance in some countries, due to the way the TEFL business operates. For example, written applications to the vast majority of language schools in Taiwan (assuming you could compile a list of addresses) are a waste of time since the pool of teacher-travellers on the spot is appropriate to the unpredictable needs of Taiwanese schools. Even in countries like Spain and Turkey for which a large number of adverts appear in the UK, the bulk of hiring goes on on-the-spot.

When you arrive in a likely place, your initial steps might include some of the following: transcribing a list of schools from the Yellow Pages consulted in the telephone office, reading the classified column of the local newspapers including the English language papers, checking notice boards in likely locations such as the British Council, USIS, universities, TEFL training centres, English language bookshops (where you should also notice which EFL materials are stocked), or hostels which teacher-travellers frequent.

Before contacting any potential employer obtain a detailed map and guide to the public transport network so you can locate the schools. Phone the schools and try to arrange a meeting with the director or director of studies (DOS). Even if an initial chat does not result in a job offer, you may learn something about the local TEFL scene which will benefit you at the next interview, especially if you ask lots of questions. You might also be able to strike up a conversation

Cowboy schools abound

with one of the foreign teachers who could turn out to be a valuable source of information about that school in particular and the situation generally. It is very common to have to begin with just a few hours a week. Make it clear that you are prepared to stand in at short notice for an absent teacher. The longer you stay in one place, the more hours will come your way and the better your chances of securing a stable contract.

This gradual approach also gives you a chance to discover which are the cowboy schools, something which is difficult to do before you are on the scene. The British Council has called for an EEC-wide recognition scheme for language schools, to force cowboys out of business. But this is a long way off, and in the meantime disreptutable schools flourish in Europe just as they do in other parts of the world. It is not always easy to distinguish them, though if a school sports a sign "Purrfect Anglish" you are probably not going to need an MA in Applied Linguistics to get a job there. Working for a cowboy outfit may not be the end of the world, though it often spells trouble, as the chapter on Problems will reveal. But without qualifications you may not have much choice.

FREELANCE TEACHING

One way to avoid having to take up bow and arrow to defend your rights in the face of a cowboy employer is to go into business for yourself. Private English lessons are always more lucrative than contract teaching simply because the middle man has been cut out. Pupils may prefer it as well, not only because of the more personal attention they receive in a private lesson but because it costs them less. As a private tutor working from your own home or visiting pupils in theirs, you can undercut the big schools with their overheads (and desire for profit). The best deal of all for the independent EFL teacher is to organize private classes.

Given the relative attractions for teachers of private lessons, they are understandably in great demand and a newly arrived native speaker cannot expect to set up as a freelance teacher immediately, no matter how great the local demand for EFL. Most teachers who are based at schools also have a few private pupils, and it is very difficult to maintain yourself solely on private lessons until you became a fixture in a place.

In order to round up private pupils, you will have to sell yourself as energetically as any salesman. Turn to page 156 for some ideas which have worked in Spain but it could work anywhere. It might be possible to persuade companies to pay you to run English classes for employees during the lunch hour, though you would have to be a confident teacher and dynamic salesman to succeed. You are far more likely to find one or two pupils by word of mouth and build from there.

Self-promotion is essential. Steven Hendry recommends plastering neatly printed bilingual notices all over town, as he did to good effect in Chiang Mai in northern Thailand. Meanwhile Ian McArthur in Cairo made a large number of posters (in Arabic and English) and painstakingly coloured in the Union Jack by hand in order to attract attention. (Unfortunately these were such a novelty that many posters were pinched.) Putting a notice up on appropriate notice boards (in schools and universities for example) and running an advertisement in the local paper are good ideas for those who have the use of a phone (since few people would reply by post to such an advert). Some have gone so far as to hire a paging device so that they can be contacted anytime. These methods should put you in touch with a few hopeful language learners. If you are any good, word will spread and more paying pupils will come your way, though it can be a slow process.

To counterbalance the advantages of higher pay and a more flexible schedule, freelance teaching has its disadvantages too. Everyone, from lazy Taiwanese teenagers to busy Parisian businessmen, cancels or postpones one-to-one lessons with irritating frequency. It is essential to agree on a procedure for cancellations which won't leave you out of pocket. If possible, arrange to be paid a month in advance so that missed lessons will be paid for.

Other considerations when teaching privately are that you may have to spend considerable periods of time travelling between clients' homes and workplaces for which you will not be paid. There will be no one to pay for social security or to provide teaching materials, professional support (or social support either). The life of the freelance teacher can be quite a lonely one.

If you are less interested in making money than integrating with a culture, exchanging conversation for board and lodging may be an appealing possibility. This too can only be set up after building up a network of contacts.

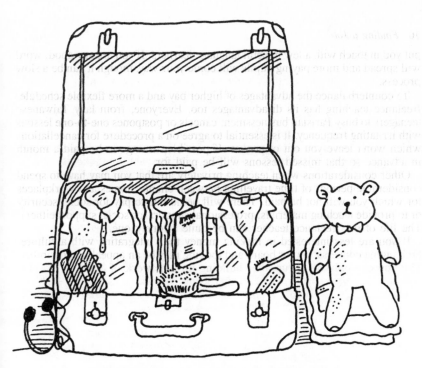

Preparation

The preceding chapters on how to find a job and on training set out ways in which you can make yourself more attractive to potential employers. One of the best ways in which to prepare for a stint of teaching abroad is to teach English locally. Relevant experience can usually be gained by volunteering to tutor immigrants in your home town; this is particularly feasible in the US where English language teaching takes place on a massive scale. It might also be a good idea to contact the director of a local commercial language school and ask to sit in on some lessons to see what it's all about and to talk to teachers. A polite note expressing your interest in TEFL would probably meet with a positive response. EFL teachers are like everyone else; they are experts at what they do and don't mind sharing that knowledge with interested outsiders.

More prolonged exposure to TEFL can best be gained by working at a language summer school. This not only provides a chance to find out whether you will enjoy English teaching for a longer period, but may put you in touch with people who are well-informed on overseas possibilities.

UK SUMMER SCHOOLS

Language summer courses take place throughout the British Isles, especially in tourist areas. The short-term nature of the teacher requirements means that schools cannot possibly find enough qualified staff. Wages are higher than for most student summer jobs and so you must expect a certain amount of competition for teaching jobs. Dressing smartly may be enough to land you a job in a language "lounge" in Taipei but it won't be sufficient in Torquay. You may have to use the same wiles as described above in the section on Interviews in order to be hired.

It is estimated that there are about 1,000 English language schools in operation in Britain during July and August, mainly catering for foreign students especially from France, Spain and Italy. Many of these schools advertise heavily in the spring, "Teach English on the English Riviera". Quality varies dramatically of course. About a quarter of language schools have been "recognized as efficient" after inspection by the British Council. These more established schools are then entitled to join ARELS-FELCO, the association which tries to raise standards (and whose 210 members are less likely to hire novice teachers). The organization is located at 2 Pontypool Place, Valentine Place, London SE1 8QF and will send a list of members to enquirers. Another list of respectable British language schools is contained in the booklet *Learning English in Britain* published by Gabbitas, Truman and Thring (6-8 Sackville Street, London W1X 2BR) every March; the 1990 edition cost £7.95.

At the other end of the spectrum are the entrepreneurs who rent space (possibly ill-suited to teaching) and will take on almost anyone to teach. Teachers are thrown in at the deep end with little preparation and few materials. Marta Eleniak was not very happy with her employer:

> *I have got nothing good to say about my employer. We were expected to do nearly everything including perform miracles, with no support and pathetic facilities. I can only liken it to being asked to entertain 200 people for 4 hours with a plastic bowl. The pupils got a raw deal too because of false promises made to them.*

She does admit that it was on the basis of this 3-week job that she got a job in a Madrid language school.

Schools at both extremes are listed in the Yellow Pages and advertise in the educational press. They are located throughout the UK, but are concentrated in London and the South-East, Oxford, Cambridge and resorts from Bournemouth to Blackpool. Without any TEFL background it is easier to get taken on as a non-teaching sports and activities supervisor which at least would introduce you to the world of TEFL. Even EFL teachers must expect a certain number of extracurricular duties such as chaperoning a group of over-excited adolescents to a West End theatre or on an art gallery visit. The average wage for teachers in 1990 was £150 per week with accommodation (since many schools are residential); £175 without. Since most schools are located in popular tourist destinations, private accommodation can be prohibitively expensive and the residential option attractive. The best rates of pay are at schools which teach foreign business people, where it is possible to earn up to £15 an hour.

Here is a short list of major language course organizations which normally offer a large number of summer vacancies:

Anglo-European Study Tours, 8 Celbridge Mews, London W2 6EU.

Bell Educational Trust, 1 Red Cross Lane, Cambridge CB2 2QX. Summer courses at Bath, Bloxham, Cambridge, Ely, Norwich, etc. Considered among the most prestigious.

Concorde International, Hawks Lane, Canterbury CT1 2NU.

EF Language Travel, 1-3 Farman Street, Hove, Sussex BN3 1AL.

Elizabeth Johnson Organisation, West House, 19/21 West Street, Haslemere, Surrey GU27 2AE.

English Home Holidays, 4 Albert Terrace, High Street, Bognor Regis, Sussex PO21 1SS.

Eurocentre, 26 Dean Park Road, Bournemouth BH1 1HZ. Also with prestigious centres in Cambridge, London and Brighton which recruit individually.

Eurolanguage Ltd., Greyhound House, 23/24 George Street, Richmond, Surrey TW9 1HY. Centres throughout England.

Euro-Students Organisation, 12 George IV Bridge, Edinburgh EH1 1EE.

International Study Programmes, The Manor, Hazleton, Nr. Cheltenham, Glos.

JAC Educational Services, 14 Gloucester Road, London W7 4RB.

Living Language Centre, Highcliffe House, Clifton Gardens, Folkestone, Kent.

M M Oxford Study Services Ltd., 44 Blenheim Drive, Oxford OX2 8OQ.

Milestone International, c/o Box 261, 19 South End, Kensington Square, London W8 5RU.

Nord-Anglia, 10 Eden Place, Cheadle, Stockport, Cheshire SK8 1AT. Has over 80 centres around Britain, especially the North.

OISE, 1 Kings Meadow, Ferry Hinksey Road, Oxford OX2 0DP. 500 summer and Easter vacancies in dozens of their Youth Language Centres.

Passport Language Schools, 37 Park Road, Bromley, Kent BR1 3HJ.

TASIS England American School, Coldharbour Lane, Thorpe, Surrey KY20 8TE. Of special interest to American EFL teachers who want to teach in Britain for eight weeks; only suitably qualified Americans are eligible for work permits.

Tjaereborg Schools of English, Castle Chambers, Union Street, Torquay, Devon TQ14 4BU.

Vacational Studies, Pepys' Oak, Tydehams, Newbury, Berks. RG14 6JT.

WHILE YOU'RE WAITING

After you have secured a job, there may be a considerable gap which will give you a chance to organize the practicalities of moving abroad and to prepare yourself in other ways. If you are going to a country which requires immigration procedures (i.e. any country outside the EEC) you can start — and perhaps even complete — the visa procedures. In addition to deciding what to take and how to get to your destination, you should think about your tax position and health insurance, plus find out as much as you can about the situation in which you will find yourself. Many teachers take out a subscription to the *Guardian Weekly* to guarantee access to world news, though you might prefer to wait until you arrive to see what newspapers are available.

It is also worth contacting the BBC World Service Broadcast Coverage Department (PO Box 76, Bush House, Strand, London WC2B 4PH) for one of their "Learn English" posters which list programmes of interest to language learners (e.g. "Pop Talk Words" which explains song lyrics), together with times and wavelengths for all parts of the world. It might be worth subscribing to *London Calling,* the monthly listing of World Service programmes which can be sent anywhere in the world for £12 a year.

EFL professionals should consider joining the International Association of Teachers of English as a Foreign Language (IATEFL, 3 Kingsdown Park, Tankerton, Whitstable, Kent CT5 2DJ). Membership entitles you to various services including a quarterly newsletter.

To guard against culture shock, you should learn as much as you can about the country which will become your temporary home. If your local library does not stock up-to-date travel and live-abroad books, you might want to visit the

Centre for International Briefing (Farnham Castle, Farnham, Surrey GU9 0AG; tel: 0252 721194) which runs fairly expensive residential courses for expats-to-be and also allows them to use their extensive library for a fee. Here you can consult various expatriate briefing papers and current magazines such as *Resident Abroad* in which you can learn about the climate, politics, customs, medical facilities, housing, household requirements, food, leisure activities, etc. of each country. The Women's Corona Society (Commonwealth House, 18 Northumberland Avenue, London WC2) publishes *Notes for Newcomers* on over 100 countries (for £3 each) and also runs one-day seminars "Living Overseas" for £80.

Contracts

This is the point at which a formal contract or at least an informal agreement should be drawn up. Any employer who is reluctant to provide something in writing is definitely suspect. Horror stories abound of the young unsuspecting teacher who goes out to teach overseas and discovers no pay, no accommodation or even no school. For this reason it is not only very important to sign a contract, but also to have a good idea as to what it is letting you in for.

The following items might be covered in a contract or at least should be given some consideration:
1. Name and address of employer.
2. Details of the duties and hours of the job. (A standard load might be 24 contact

teaching hours a week, plus 3 hours on standby to fill in for an absent teacher, fill all the board markers in the staff room, etc.)
3. The amount and currency of your pay. Is it adequate to live on? How often are you paid? Is any money held back? Can it be easily transferred into sterling or dollars? What arrangements are there if the exchange rate drops suddenly or the local currency is devalued?
4. The length of the contract and whether it is renewable.
5. Help with finding and paying for accommodation. If accommodation is not provided free, is your salary adequate to cover this? If it is, are utilities included? Does the organization pay for a stay in a hotel while you look for somewhere to live? How easy is it to find accommodation in the area? If it is unfurnished what help do you get in providing furniture? Can you get a salary advance to pay for this and for any rent deposits?
6. Your tax liability both locally and in the UK.
7. Provisions for health care and sick pay, maternity allowance, etc.
8. Payment of pension or national insurance contributions.
9. Bonuses, gratuities or perks.
10. Paid flights home if the contract is outside Europe, and mid-term flights if you are teaching for 2 years.
11. Luggage and surplus luggage allowance at the beginning and end of the contract.
12. Any probationary period and the length of notice which you and the employer must give.
13. Penalties for breaking the contract and circumstances under which the penalties would be waived (e.g. extreme family illness, etc.)

Obviously any contract should be carefully studied before signing and returning. Even though you may not be looking for a whole range of expatriate perks — if you can't live without your microwave or CD player, perhaps you shouldn't be going abroad — it is important to be aware of the potential costs of going to work abroad, so that these do not come as a nasty shock when you are down to your last traveller's cheque.

In normal circumstances, it is to the teacher's advantage to have a signed contract. However in a few countries, such as Greece and possibly France, teachers' unions urge their members not to sign any contract because legalislated wages and working conditions are in fact better than most contracts stipulate. Although contracts which fall short of compulsory legislation are not legally valid, they are in circulation and signing one may make it difficult for a teacher to claim the rights which have been won through union negotiation.

Health and Insurance

Reputable schools will make the necessary contributions into the national health insurance and social security scheme. Even if you are covered by the national scheme, however, you may find that there are exclusion clauses such as dental treatment, non-emergency treatment, prescription drugs, etc. Or you may find that you are only covered while at work. Private travel insurance is very expensive (not less than £300 for 12 months) so it is important to clarify the position before departure.

If you are British and intending to work in Germany, France, Italy, Spain, Portugal, Greece, Denmark, Netherlands or Belgium, you should acquire form E-111, which is a certificate of entitlement to medical treatment within the EEC.

The application form is contained inside leaflet SA 40, available from doctors' surgeries, the DSS, etc. Even if your employer will be paying into a health scheme, cover may not take effect immediately and it is as well to have the ordinary tourist cover for the first three months.

If your destination is tropical, consult an up-to-date book on health such as *Travellers' Health: How to Stay Healthy Abroad* by Richard Dawood (OUP, 1989; £6.99). British Airways has set up a network of travel clinics which will give advice on specific destinations, administer jabs and prescribe the correct anti-malarials, etc. These clinics are run in conjunction with MASTA, a profit-making consultancy based at the London School of Hygiene and Tropical Medicine, Keppel Street, London WC1. MASTA (Medical Advisory Services for Travellers Abroad) issues personal health briefs which cost £7, £12.50 or £25 according to the depth of detail required.

If you are heading off to central Africa or any other place where the incidence of AIDS is high, you will be understandably worried about the standards of health care in general and the quality of blood and syringes in particular. AIDS packs are now available which contain hypodermic needles, intravenous drip needles, etc. for about £12 or £15. Again MASTA can advise.

Americans should obtain the booklet "Health Information for International Travel" which is distributed free and includes information on vaccination requirements, malaria prophylactics, etc. The US Public Health Service updates it annually; to request a copy of this document (number 017-023-00183-3), write to the Superintendent of Documents, US Government Printing Office, Washington, DC 20402.

National Contributions and Social Security

If you are a national of an EEC country working in another member state, you will be covered by Social Security regulations. Advice and the leaflet "Your Social Security Health Care and Pension Rights in the European Community" may be obtained from the Department of Social Security, Overseas Branch, Newcastle-upon-Tyne NE98 1YZ. Payments made in any EEC country count towards entitlement when you return home. The UK also has Social Security agreements with other countries. If you are planning to teach in Austria, Cyprus, Finland, Iceland, Israel, Malta, Mauritius, Norway, Sweden, Switzerland, Turkey or Yugoslavia, write to the Overseas Branch for the appropriate leaflet.

In countries where no Social Security agreement exists, the leaflet NI38 "Social Security Abroad" gives an outline of the arrangements and options open to you. If you fail to make National Insurance contributions while you are out of the UK, you will forfeit entitlement to benefits on your return. You can decide to make contributions either class 2 ("self-employed") or class 3 ("voluntary contributions") in order to retain your rights to certain benefits. Unfortunately this entitles you only to a retirement/widow's pension, not to sickness benefit or unemployment benefit. Since teachers abroad are seldom in a pension scheme, it is usually worth maintaining your right to a UK state pension; class 3 contributions can be made up to six years in arrears.

Tax

Calculating your liability to tax when working outside your home country is notoriously complicated so, if possible, check your position with an accountant. Also consult the Inland Revenue information leaflet IR20. Everything depends on whether you fall into the category of "resident", "ordinarily resident" or "domiciled". Most EFL teachers count as domiciled in the UK since it is assumed that they will ultimately return. If you are working abroad and are absent from the UK for a complete 365 days, you are classified as non-resident and get 100% exemption on overseas earnings. This can be critical for teachers on, say, the one-year JET programme in Japan; if they return to Britain a few weeks short of 365 days, they will technically be liable for about 25% of their (otherwise tax-free) salary of £14,500. With the normal 9-month contract, you are more likely to return to Britain and lose your UK tax exemption. If the country in which you have been teaching has a double taxation agreement with Britain then there should be no problem. See Inland Revenue leaflet IR6 "Double Taxation Relief". But not all countries have such an agreement (Sweden for example) and it is not inconceivable that you will be taxed twice. Keep all receipts and financial documents in case you need to plead your case at a later date.

Possible sources of further information on tax are the annually revised book *Working Abroad* published by Kogan Page in conjunction with the *Daily Telegraph*. Also the organization Expats International (62 Tritton Road, London SE21 8DE) offers legal and financial advice to members. A useful booklet is available from Ocean International Marketing Services (rue du Nord 66, 1000 Brussels, Belgium) called "Tax Notes for UK Expatriates". As an incentive to consult one of their participating financial advisers, they send this booklet free of charge.

Travel

London is the cheap fare capital of the world and the number of agencies offering discount flights to all corners of the world is seemingly endless. To narrow the choice you should find a travel agency which specializes in your destination. The Air Travel Advisory Bureau (tel: 071-636 5000) wil give you the phone numbers of a few discount travel agents appropriate to your needs. But because not all travel agencies are registered with them, this does not guarantee the best fare. Consult the quality press, especially the Saturday editions of *The Times, Independent* and *Guardian* or magazines such as *Time Out, Law* and *TNT* (London weeklies). By ringing a few of the agencies with advertisements you will soon discover which airlines offer the cheapest service. Student travel offices such as STA and Campus Travel are always worth consulting, though their popularity often means that there are queues both in their offices and on their telephones. Trailfinders Ltd. (42-50 Earls Court Road, London W8 6EJ; tel: 071-938 3366) are well-established and efficient.

In North America, the best newspapers to scour for cheap flights are the *New York Times* (the Sunday edition has a section devoted to travel with cut-price flights advertised), the *LA Times, San Francisco Chronicle-Examiner, Miami Herald, Dallas Morning News, Chicago Sun Times,* the *Boston Globe* and the *Toronto Globe.* Recommended agencies include Community Travel Service (5237 College Avenue, Oakland, CA 94618; tel: 415-653 0990), the Student Travel Network (with branches in New York, Los Angeles and San Francisco) and Council Travel Services with branches in most major university towns since it is associated with the Council on International Educational Exchange. Travel CUTS, the Canadian student travel bureau, sell discount fares and have offices overseas.

Good maps and guide books always enhance one's anticipation and enjoyment of going abroad. If you are in London, visit the famous map shop Edward Stanford Ltd., (12-14 Long Acre, Covent Garden, WC2E 9LP) which also sends maps by post. The Map Shop (15 High Street, Upton-on-Severn, Worcestershire WR8 0HJ) does an extensive mail order business and will send you the relevant list of their holdings.

In the US one of the best travel book stores in the country is Travel Books (113 Corporation Road, Hyannis, MA 02601-2204; tel: 771-3535). They produce a detailed catalogue on most countries, and do most of their business by mail order. Other good travel outlets include Nomadic Books (201 NE 45th Street, Seattle, WA 98015) and the Travellers Bookstore (Rockefeller Center, New York).

Browsing in the travel section of any bookshop will introduce you to the range of travel guides. The Rough Guides series is generally excellent, and the very detailed books published by Lonely Planet are very popular. Anyone going to teach in a country between Turkey and Indonesia might like to look at the *Travellers Survival Kit to the East* (Vacation-Work, 1990; £6.95). If you want a detailed historical and architectural guide, obtain a *Blue Guide* or a *Michelin Green Guide*.

Learning the Language

Even if you will not need any knowledge of the local language in the classroom, the ability to communicate will increase your enjoyment many times over. After a long hard week of trying to din some English into your pupils' heads, you probably won't relish the prospect of struggling to convey your requests to uncomprehending shopkeepers, neighbours, etc. If there is time, you might consider enrolling in a part-time or short intensive course of conversation classes at a local college of further education or using a self-study programme with books and tapes. This will have the salutary effect of reminding you of what difficulties arise when trying to learn a language. There are a great many teach-yourself courses on the market, for example Berlitz Cassettepaks (£7.95) and BBC courses for beginners (£6.95 for the handbook, £4.95 for each of the two tapes). If you are heading for a remote place, you should take a language course with you, since tapes and books may not be available locally and your enthusiasm to learn may be rekindled once you are on-location.

WHAT TO TAKE

The research you do on your destination will no doubt include its climate, which will help you choose an appropriate range of clothing to take. But there is probably no need to equip yourself for every eventuality. EFL teachers normally earn enough to afford to buy a warm coat or boots if required. Be sure to pack at least one smart outfit; even if jeans are acceptable at work, there will be other occasions which will require more formal wear.

Even though you are expecting to earn a decent salary, you should not arrive short of money. It is usual to be paid only at the end of the first month. Plus you may need sizeable sums for rent deposits and other setting-up expenses.

If possible find out from recently returned travellers what items are in short supply or very expensive. For example instant coffee is extremely expensive in Turkey, film is expensive in Zimbabwe and tea strainers are unobtainable in China. A supply of passport photos and copies of your education certificates are often worth packing. Recreational reading in English will be limited, so you should take a good supply of novels, etc. It could take time to establish a busy social life, leaving more time for reading than usual. In such circumstances, having access to the World Service can be a godsend. You will need a good short-wave radio with several bands powerful enough to pick up the BBC. "Dedicated" short-wave receivers which are about the size of a paperback start at £80. If you are travelling via the Middle East or Hong Kong, think about buying one duty free. A further advantage of having access to the BBC is that you can tape programmes for use in the classroom.

Teaching Materials

Try to find out which course your school follows and then become familiar with it. Depending on the circumstances, there may be a shortage of materials, so again enquire in advance about the facilities. You should visit a good ELT department of a bookshop; every year Dillons publish an ELT catalogue which can be obtained by sending an s.a.e. to Dillons, 82 Gower Street, London WC1E 6EQ. Several bookshops in Britain specialize in EFL materials. Among the major stockists is the Bournemouth English Book Centre (9 Albion Close, Parkstone, Poole, Dorset BH12 3LL; tel: 0202 715555) which supplies books by mail order to teachers all over the world. Another good source is Keltic (25 Chepstow Corner, Chepstow Place, London W2 4TT; tel: 071-229 8560).

Here is a list of items to consider packing which most often crop up in the recommendations of experienced teachers: picture dictionary, tapes for listening and role play; blank tapes (and a cassette recorder if necessary with spare batteries); games and activities book; illustrated magazine (or extracts); lyrics of songs; a map of London; flash cards (which are expensive if bought commercially; home-made ones work just as well); grammar exercise book; old Cambridge exam papers (if you are going to be teaching First Certificate or Proficiency classes); general stationery such as carbon paper, Blutack, plastic files, large pieces of paper, coloured markers, etc. If you know that there will be a shortage of materials, it might even be worth shipping some of the bulkier items ahead. (If you are going into a country in order to look for a teaching job, teaching aids in your luggage will alert customs officers that you intend to work.)

Richard McBrien, who taught English in China, recommends taking a collection of photos of anything in your home environment. A few rolls shot of local petrol stations, supermarkets, houses, parks, etc. can be of great interest to pupils in far-off lands. It may of course be difficult to anticipate what will excite your students' curiosity. The anthropoligist Nigel Barley, who writes amusing books on his fieldwork, describes being enlisted to attend an impromptu English conversation club in a remote corner of Indonesia in his book *Not a Hazardous Sport:*

> *I answered questions about the royal family, traffic lights and the etiquette of eating asparagus, and gave a quick analysis of the shipbuilding industry. At the end of the evening, I fled back to the hotel.*

EFL teachers cannot escape so easily, so you should be prepared to be treated like a guru of contemporary British (or American) culture.

Bibliography

There is such a plethora of books and materials that the choice can be daunting to the uninitiated. Here is a selected list of recommended books and teaching

aids which you could consider; obviously you won't want to buy all of them.

Collins Cobuild English Language Dictionary (Collins in association with the University of Birmingham) £8.95. A dictionary designed specifically for the language learner.

The Heinemann English Grammar, by D. Beaumont & C. Granger (Heinemann, 1990) £5.95. A reference-cum-practice book at intermediate level.

Practical English Grammar, by A. J. Thomson & A. V. Martinet (OUP, 1990) £3.95. Has built-in exercises.

Using English Grammar, by Edward Woods & Nicole McLeod (Prentice-Hall) £5.75.

Grammar in Action, by C. Frank & M. Rinvolucri (Pergamon) £5.95.

Practical English Usage, by M. Swan (OUP) £6.95.

The Practice of English Language Teaching, by Jeremy Harmer (Longman) £8.50. Considered by many to be the bible of the EFL teacher.

Grammar Games, by M. Rinvolucri (CUP) £8.50.

Harrap's Communication Games.

Oxford Resource Books for Teachers (OUP) especially the one on *Conversation* by Nolasco & Arthur, and on *Role Play* by Ladousse, both £7.50.

Challenge to Think, M. Berer (OUP). Student book is £3.40 and teacher book is £5.25. Good for unexpected fill-in lessons and as course book supplement.

How to be a Peaceful Teacher (Primary House, see page 45) £5. With 140 practical classroom techniques.

An English Teacher's Scrapbook (Primary House) £5. Collection of teachers' best lessons.

Teaching Tactics for Japan's English Classrooms, by John Wharton (Global Press, distributed in the UK by Vacation Work) £5.95. A slim volume with wider application than just Japan.

Problems

Potential problems fall into two broad categories: personal and professional. You may quickly feel settled and find your new setting fascinating but may discover that the job itself is beset with difficulties. On the other hand the teaching might suit but otherwise you feel alienated and lonely. Those who choose to uproot themselves suddenly should be fairly confident that they have enough resources to rely on themselves, and must expect some adjustment problems. Only you can assess your chances of enjoying the whole experience and of not feeling traumatized. Women may encounter special problems in countries where women have little status. A book which will introduce you to potential difficulties and includes chapters on most of the countries of the world is called *Women Travel* (Harraps, 1990; £6.95).

PROBLEMS AT WORK

Anyone who has done some language teaching will be familiar with at least some of the problems EFL teachers face. Problems encountered in a classroom of Turkish or Peruvian adolescents will be quite different from the ones experienced teaching French or Japanese businessmen. The country chapters attempt to identify some of the specific problems which groups of language learners present.

Although you are unlikely to be expected to entertain 200 people for four hours with a plastic bowl, there may be a fairly complete lack of facilities and resources. The teacher who has packed some of the teaching materials listed above will feel particularly grateful for his or her foresight in such circumstances. Some schools, especially at the cowboy end of the spectrum go to the other extreme of providing very rigid lesson plans from which you are not allowed to deviate and which are likely to be uncongenial and uninspiring. Even when reasonable course texts are provided, supplementary materials like role play tapes and games can considerably liven up classes (and teachers). You can obtain extra teaching aids after arrival from the nearest English language bookshop or make them yourself, for example tape a dialogue between yourself and an English speaking friend or cut up magazies or use postcards to make flashcards. If the missing facilities are more basic (e.g. tables, chairs, heating, paper, pens) you will have to improvise as best you can and (if appropriate) press the administration for some equipment.

Problems with Pupils

A very common problem is to find yourself in front of a class of mixed ability and incompatible aims. How do you plan a lesson that will satisfy a sophisticated businessman whose English is fairly advanced, a delinquent teenager and a housewife crippled by lack of confidence? A good school of course will stream its clients and make life easier for its teachers. But this may be left to you, in which case a set of commercially produced tests to assess level of language acquisition could come in very handy. One way of coping with gross discrepancies is to divide the class into compatible groups or pairs and give tasks which work at different levels. Sub-dividing a class is in fact generally a good idea especially in classes which are too large.

In classes of mixed ages, you may have trouble pleasing everyone

In some places you may even have to contend with racial or cultural friction among pupils, as Bryn Thomas encountered in Egypt:

One of the problems I found in the class was the often quite shocking displays of racism by the Egyptians towards their dark-skinned neighbours from Somalia. Vast amounts of tact and diplomacy were required to ensure that enough attention was given to the Somalis (who tend to be shy, quiet and highly intelligent) without upsetting the sometimes rowdy and over-enthusiastic Egyptians.

Your expectations of what teaching is supposed to achieve may be quite different from the expectations of your students. Foreign educational systems are often far more formal than their British or American counterparts and students may seem distressingly content to memorize and regurgitate, often with the sole motivation of passing an exam. In many countries free discussion is quite alien, whether because of repressive governments or cultural taboos. It is essential to be sensitive to these cultural differences and not to expect too much of your pupils straightaway. The only way of overcoming this reluctance to express an opinion or indeed express anything at all is to involve them patiently and tactfully, again by splitting them into smaller units and asking them to come up with a joint reply.

Discipline is very seldom a problem outside Europe; in fact liberal teachers are often taken aback by what they perceive as an excess of docility, an over-willingness to believe that "teacher is always right".

In some cases, classes of bored and rebellious European teenagers might cause problems, or children who are being sent to English lessons after school simply as an alternative to babysitting for working mothers. Marta Eleniak, who taught in Spain, recommends taking a hard line:

Be a bitch at the start. The kids can be very wicked and take advantage of any good nature shown. Squash anyone who is late, shouts, gossips, etc. the first time or it'll never stop. The good classes make you love teaching. The bad make you feel as if you want to go back to filing.

Each level and age group brings its own difficulties. Anyone who has no experience of dealing with young children may find it impossible to grab and hold their attention, let alone teach them any English. A lack of inhibition is very useful for teaching young children who will enjoy sing-songs, nursery rhymes, simple puzzles and games, etc. Beginners of all ages progress much more rapidly than intermediate learners. Many teachers find adolescent intermediate learners the most difficult to teach. The original fun and novelty are past and they now face a long slog of consolidating vocabulary and structures. (The "intermediate plateau" is a well-known phenomenon in language acquisition.) Adolescents may resent "grammar games" (which are a standard part of EFL) thinking that games are suitable only for children.

The worst problem of all is to be confronted with a bored and unresponsive class. This may happen in a class of beginners who can't understand what is going on, especially a problem if you don't speak a word of their language. It can be extremely frustrating for all concerned when trying to teach some concept or new vocabulary without being able to provide the simple equivalent. If this is the case, you'll have to rely heavily on visual aids. Whole books have been written to show EFL teachers how to draw, for example.

The best way to inject a little life into a lethargic class is to get them moving around, for example have them carry out a little survey of their neighbours and then report their findings back to the class. A reluctance to participate may be because the pupils do not see the point of it. In many countries foreign teachers come to feel like a dancing bear or performing monkey, someone who is expected to be a cultural token and an entertainer. If the students are expecting someone to dance a jig or swing from the chandelier (so to speak) they will be understandably disappointed to be presented with someone asking them to form sentences using the present perfect. At the other extreme, it is similarly disconcerting to be treated just as a model of pronunciation, and you may begin to wonder whether your employer might be better off employing a tape recorder.

Problems with Yourself

Of course lessons which fizzle or never get off the ground are not always the fault of the students. One of the most common traps into which inexperienced teachers fall is to dominate the class too much. Conversational English can only be acquired by endless practice and so you must allow your pupils to do most of the talking. Even if there are long pauses between your questions and their attempts to answer, the temptation to fill the silences should be avoided. Pauses have a positive role to play, allowing pupils a chance to dwell on and absorb the point you have just been illustrating.

A native speaker's function is seldom to teach grammar. You are not there to help the students to analyse the language but to use it and communicate with it. It has been said that grammar is the highway code, the catalogue of rules and traffic signs, quite useless in isolation from driving, which gets you where you want to go. Grammar is only the cookery book while talking is cooking for other people to understand/eat. Persuading some students, whose language education has been founded on grammar rather then communication, that this is the priority may be difficult, but try not to be drawn into detailed explanations of grammatical structures.

This is probably not a very great temptation for many teachers who can barely distinguish prepositions from pronouns. Being utterly ignorant of grammar often results in embarrassing situations. You can only get away with bluffing for so long ("Stefan, I don't think it matters here whether or not it's a subjunctive") and irate pupils have been known to report to school directors that their teachers are grammar-illiterate. Normally it will suffice to have studied a general grammar handbook such as *Practical English Grammar* or *Practical English Usage* (see Bibliography above).

Get the class to act out the title of a popular song

When you are conducting the lesson, stop frequently to check on comprehension, not just by asking whether or not they are following but by asking questions which will allow them to demonstrate that they are. The worst fate which can befall a teacher is to run dry, to run out of ideas and steam completely before the appointed hour has arrived. This usually happens when you fail to arrive with a structured lesson plan. It is usually a recipe for disaster to announce at the beginning of the lesson "tonight let's talk about our travels/hobbies/animals" or whatever. Any course book will help you to avoid grinding to a halt. Supplementary materials such as songs and games can be lifesavers in (and out) of a crisis. If you are absolutely stuck for what to talk about next, try writing the lyrics of a popular song on the board and asking the class to analyse it or even act it out (avoiding titles such as "I Want Your Body"). Apparently songs which have worked well for many teachers include George Michael's "Careless Whispers", the Beatles' "Here Comes the Sun" and "When I'm 64" and "Perfect Day" by Lou Reed. Another way of stepping outside the predictability of a course book might be to teach a short poem which you like, or even a short story (e.g. by Saki) if the class is sufficiently advanced.

A very popular way to structure a lesson is in "notions"; you take a general situation like "praising" or "complaining", teach some relevant vocabulary and structures and then have the class put them into practice in role-play situations. Although repetition is the key to language learning, drilling is very dull and will kill any interest in the language.

Culture shock is experienced by most people who live in a foreign country in whatever circumstances (see below), but can be especially problematic for teachers. Unthinkingly you might choose a topic which seems neutral to you but is controversial to them. A little feature on the English pub for example would not be enjoyed in Saudi Arabia. Asking questions about foreign travels would be tactless in most East European situations since so few people have had a chance to travel abroad, even now that there are fewer restrictions on visas. A discussion about pollution might make a class of Japanese students uncomfortable.

One of the hardest problems to contend with is teacher burn-out. If you invariably arrive just as the class is scheduled to begin, show no enthusiasm, and glance at the clock every 90 seconds, you will not be a popular teacher. Getting hold of some new authentic materials might shore up your flagging enthusiasm for the enterprise. If not, perhaps it is time to consider going home (bearing in mind your contractual commitments).

Problems with Employers

All sorts of schools break their promises about pay, perks and availability of resources. The worst disappointment of all, however, is to turn up and find that you don't have a job at all. Because schools which hire their teachers sight unseen often find themselves let down at the last moment, they may over-hire, just in the way that airlines overbook their flights in the expectation of a certain level of cancellation. Even more probable is that the school has not been able to predict the number of pupils who will enrol and decides to hire enough teachers to cover the projected maximum. Whatever the reason, it can be devastating to have the job carpet whipped from under your feet. Having a signed contract helps. It may also be a good idea to maintain contact with the school between being hired and your first day of work. If the worst does happen, there is probably nothing to be gained by losing your temper. Instead you might play upon the guilt of the director and ask him or her if they know of other schools which might have a last-minute vacancy.

Just because a school does not belong to the EFL establishment does not mean that teachers will be treated badly (and vice versa). However the back street fly-by-night school may well cause its foreign teachers anxiety. The most common complaints revolve around wages — not enough or not often enough or both. Either you will have signed a contract (possibly in ignorance of the prevailing conditions and pay levels) or you have nothing in writing and find that your pay packet does not correspond with what you were originally promised. It is probably not advisable to take up a confrontational stance straightaway since this may be the beginning of a year of hostility and misery. Polite but persistent negotiations might prove successful. Find out if there is a relevant teachers union, join it and ask them for advice. As the year wears on, your bargaining clout increases (especially if you are a half-decent teacher) since you will be more difficult to replace mid-term. If you are being genuinely exploited and you are prepared to leave the job, delivering an ultimatum might work, as Andrew Boyle discovered in Greece:

> *I had an interesting experience last February. I decided that my salary of 53,000 drachmas was a joke and, egged on by friends, marched into the boss's office and got a rise to 65,000 drachmas (23% no less). The boss was not overpleased about this, but the point is she gave me the rise — she had no choice. When you get to this part of the year the seasonal nature of the TEFL market works in your favour, in distant Greece at least.*

Welcome to your conversation class

Most language schools function as profit-making businesses and teachers soon realize that they matter far less to the people in charge than the number and satisfaction of students. You may be asked to conduct a conversation class in a room not much smaller than the Albert Hall. Only prestigious schools offer regular training and opportunities for professional development to teachers.

Whether your employer leaves you entirely to your own devices or interferes to an annoying degree (we've heard of one school director in Spain who bugged the classrooms to make sure the staff were following his idiosyncratic home-produced course outlines), his main interest will probably be "bums on seats" as Martyn Owens puts it. Martyn taught in Hong Kong but recognized early on where his employer's priorities lay:

A lack of students will soon end the career of even the most enthusiastic teacher. Hong Kong students will not tolerate inadequate teachers and will often "vote with their feet". Dissatisfied students will sometimes complain to the school Director, but mostly they simply stop coming to lessons. I've known some inexperienced teachers lose half the class or more within two weeks. The harsh reality (particularly in Hong Kong) is that your position may be terminated, which few teachers realize.

One of the most commonly heard complaints from teachers concerns their schedule. Eager only to satisfy clients, employers tend to mess around teachers' timetables, offering awkward combinations of hours or changing the schedule at the last moment. A certain amount of evening and weekend work is almost inevitable in private language schools where pupils (whether of school or working age) must study English out-of-hours. Having to work early in the morning and then again through the evening ean become exhausting after a while. It can also br annoying to have several long gruelling days a week and other days with scarcely any teaching at all (but still not days off).

One trick to beware of is to find that the 24 *hours* a week you were told you would be working actually means 32 45-minute lessons (which is much harder work than teaching 24 one-hour lessons). Even if the number of hours has not been exaggerated, you may have been deluded into thinking that a 24-hour week is quite cushy. But preparation time can easily add half as many hours again, plus if you are teaching in different locations, travel time (often unpaid) has to be taken into consideration.

In some situations teachers may be expected to participate in extra-curricular activities such as dreary drinks parties for pupils or asked to make a public speech. Make an effort to accept such invitations (especially near the beginning of your contract) or, if you must decline, do so as graciously as possible. There might also be extra duties, translating letters and documents, updating teaching materials, etc. for which you should be paid extra.

PROBLEMS OUTSIDE WORK

Your main initial worry outside your place of employment will probably be accommodation. Once this is sorted out, either with the help of your school or on your own, and you have mastered the essentials of getting around and shopping for food, there is nothing to do but enjoy yourself, exploring your new surroundings and making friends.

Culture Shock

This won't be at all easy if you are suffering from culture shock. Shock implies something which happens suddenly, but cultural disorientation more often creeps up on you. Adrenalin usually sees you through the first few weeks as you find the novelty exhilarating and challenging. You will be amazed and charmed by the odd gestures the people use or the antiquated way that things work. As time goes on, practical irritations intrude and the constant misunderstanding caused by those charming gestures — such as a nod in Greece meaning "no" or in Japan meaning "yes, I understand, but don't agree" — and the inconvenience of those antiquated phone boxes and buses will begin to get on your nerves. Unless you can find someone to listen sympathetically to your complaints, you may begin to think you have made a mistake in coming in the first place.

Experts say that most people who have moved abroad hit the trough after 3 or 4 months, probably just before Christmas in the case of teachers who started work in September. A holiday over Christmas may serve to calm you down or, if you go home for Christmas, may make you feel terminally homesick and not want to go back. Teachers who survive this, often find that things improve in the second term as they cease to perceive many aspects of life as "foreign".

The best way to avoid disappointment is to be well briefed beforehand, as emphasized in the chapter on Preparation. Gathering general information about the country and specific information about the school before arrival will obviate many of the negative feelings some EFL teachers feel. If you are the type to build up high hopes and expectations of new situations, it is wise to try to dismantle these before leaving home. English teaching is seldom glamorous.

Even if you are feeling depressed and disappointed, do not broadcast your feelings randomly. Feeling contempt and hostility towards your host country is actually part of the process of adjusting to being abroad. But not everyone seems to appreciate that it has more to do with their own feelings than with the inadequacies (real or imagined) of the country they are in. So if you feel you have to let off steam about the local bureaucracy or the dishonesty of taxi-drivers or the way one simply cannot walk ten yards down the pavement without people crossing the street for the express purpose of bumping into you, at least have the common courtesy to do it in private, in letters or when there are no local people around.

This is especially important if you have colleagues who are natives of the country. They may find some of the idiosyncracies of their culture irritating too but, unlike you, they have to live with them forever. Some native-speaker teachers have found an unpleasant rift between local and foreign staff, which in some cases can be accounted for by the simple fact that you are being paid a lot more than they are. Sometimes new foreign teachers find their local colleagues cliquey and uncommunicative. No doubt they have seen a lot of foreigners come, and make a lot of noise, and go, and there is no particular reason why they should find the consignment you're in wildly exciting and worth getting to know.

Loneliness

Creating a social life from scratch is difficult enough at any time, but becomes even more difficult in an alien tongue and culture. Unless you are lucky and find youself content to socialize with your fellow teachers and pupils, you will have to take some positive steps to meet people and participate in activities outside the world of English language instruction. This may require uncharacteristically extrovert behaviour, but overcoming initial inhibitions almost always pays worthwhile dividends.

If you are tired of conversations about students' dullness or your director of studies' evident lunacy, you might want to try to meet other expatriates who are not EFL teachers. The local English language bookshop might prove a useful source of information about forthcoming events for English-speakers, as will be any newspapers or magazines published in English such as the *Bulletin* in Belgium or the *Athens Daily News* in Greece. Seek out the overseas student club if there is a university nearby (though when they discover what line of work you are in they may well have designs on you). Even the least devout teachers have found English-speaking churches to be useful for arranging social functions and offering practical advice. If there is a bar in town which models itself on a British pub or American bar, you will no doubt find a few die-hards drinking Watneys Red Barrel or Michelob, who might be more than willing to befriend you.

The most obvious way to meet other foreigners is to enrol in a language course or perhaps classes in art and civilization. Even if you are not particularly serious about pursuing language studies, language classes are the ideal place to form vital social contacts. You can also join other clubs or classes aimed at residents abroad, for example some German cities have English amateur dramatics groups.

Making friends with locals may prove more difficult, though circumstances vary enormously according to whether you live in a small town or a big city, with some gregarious colleagues or by yourself, etc. As long as you don't spend all your free time moping at home, you are bound to strike up conversations with the locals, whether in cafés, on buses or in shops. Admittedly these seldom go past a superficial acquaintance, but they still serve the purpose of making you feel a little more integrated in the community. Local university students will probably be more socially flexible than others and it is worth investigating the bars and cafés frequented by students. If you have a particular hobby, sport or interest, find out if there is a local club where you will meet like-minded people; join local ramblers, jazz buffs, etc. — the more obscure the more welcome you are likely to be. You only have to become friendly with one other person to open up new social horizons if you are invited to meet their friends and family.

Make an effort to organize some breaks from work. Even a couple of days by the seaside or visiting a tourist attraction in the region can revitalize your interest in being abroad and provide a refreshing break from the tyranny of the teacher's routine.

PART II

Country by Country Guide

General Prospects for Teachers
How to Fix up a Job
Pros and Cons
Rules and Regulations
List of Schools

WESTERN EUROPE   **AFRICA**
EASTERN EUROPE   **ASIA**
MIDDLE EAST   **LATIN AMERICA**

Most wages and prices are given in local currencies. For conversion to sterling and US dollars, see *Appendix 1* on page 316.

Embassies and Consulates will normally provide information on working visas to supplement the information provided in this book. A selective list of diplomatic representatives in London and Washington can be found in *Appendix 2* on page 317.

British Council offices abroad are frequently referred to in these chapers. A list of the relevant addresses is provided in *Appendix 3* on page 319.

Schools whose names are italicized in the text are included in the directory of schools which follows each country chapter. Recruitment agencies whose names appear in italics are listed in the appropriate introductory section beginning on page 55.

WESTERN EUROPE

Benelux

NETHERLANDS

Urban Dutch people have a very high degree of competence in English after they finish their schooling. Educated Dutch people are so fluent in English that the Minister of Education was recently able to suggest that English should become the main language used in Dutch universities, a suggestion which caused an understandable outcry, it must be said. This is not a country in which any old BA (Hons) has much chance of stepping into a TEFL job. What private language schools there are tend to provide business English and to be looking for teachers with extensive commercial or government experience as well as a teaching qualification.

So many British people have settled in the Netherlands, attracted by its liberal institutions, etc. that most schools depend on long-term freelancers. The Dutch Embassy in London sends a skimpy list of 7 language schools (6 of them outside Amsterdam) while the British Council in Amsterdam sends a longer list of institutes only in the Amsterdam region (though they are planning to draw up a list which will cover the whole country).

The pay is less than such an EFL profile would suggest. Salaries start at around 1,600 guilders a month which works out at less than £100/$200 for an average working week. Taxes and health insurance will remove nearly a third of that.

BELGIUM

The situation is more hopeful in Belgium with more and better paid opportunities. The list of language schools in the Brussels Yellow Pages runs to several pages, though these are not necessarily for English. As one of the capitals of the European Community, there is a huge demand for all the principal European languages. The British Council in Brussels (which is responsible for Luxembourg as well as Belgium) maintains a register of qualified teachers and will advise on vacancies of which it is notified. They also send out a list of 19 schools.

The casual EFL teacher will probably steer clear of the schools which undertake to teach senior EEC bureaucrats, but there are plenty of other schools. Some, such as Amira (at 251 avenue Louise in Brussels) offer low-cost conversation classes under the guidance of native speakers. Telephone teaching is also catching on in Belgium, especially among French learners of English.

If you intend to stay in Belgium some time, it might be worth contacting your local *commune* (municipal council), most of which offer adult education language courses. Several language teaching organizations are represented in more than one Belgian city, such as Elsevier Languages, Eurospeak, Intercontact and of course *Berlitz* which employs upwards of 150 teachers in Belgium. The pay at most schools is around 550 Belgian francs an hour, though trained EFL teachers earn up to 800 francs.

LUXEMBOURG

There are only two private language schools in the country (the English Language Centre and the International Language Centre), so if anyone has their heart set on working in Luxembourg (for some reason) he or she would not find many opportunities available. There is a British-Luxembourg Society which promotes British culture and the English language in Luxembourg, and they might be able to advise on teaching possibilities.

LIST OF SCHOOLS

Netherlands

BERLITZ
Rokin 87-89 IV, 1012 KL, Amsterdam. Tel: (20) 22 13 75/22 13 76.
*Number of teachers: 8.
Preference of nationality: UK.
Qualifications: teaching experience preferred but not essential. Professional manner needed.
Conditions of employment: no contracts and no guarantee of hours. Hours of work mainly 6-9pm but also morning and afternoon work. Pupils are all adults.
Salary: from 18.50 guilders per 45-minute lesson. Sessions last minimum 90 minutes.
Facilities/Support: no assistance with accommodation. 10 day in-house training is compulsory.
Recruitment: through newspaper adverts. Local interviews essential.

THE HAGUE LANGUAGE CENTRE
Prinsensegracht 31, (PO Box 313), 2501 CH Den Haag. Tel: (70) 365 49 36.
Number of teachers: 10.
Preference of nationality: US, UK.
Qualifications: work experience in business or government outside education.
Conditions of employment: 6-10 month contracts, 10-20 h.p.w. Pupils aged 30-60.
Salary: 36 guilders per lesson and 18 guilders per special task hour (guidance, testing, etc.)
Facilities/Support: no assistance with accommodation. Training given.
Recruitment: through universities and TEFL courses. Local interviews essential.

NIBO
Hettenheuvelweg 16, 1101 BN Amsterdam ZO. Tel: (20) 567 77 77.
Number of teachers: 12.
Preference of nationality: UK.
Qualifications: teaching qualifications plus 3 years experience in business.
Conditions of employment: 6 month contracts. Variable hours. Pupils are all adults.
Salary: competitive.
Facilities/Support: no assistance with accommodation. Training given.
Recruitment: local interviews essential; nearly all recruitment is local.

Belgium

BERLITZ
28, rue Saint-Michel, 1000 Brussels. Tel: (2) 219 02 74.
Number of teachers: approximately 150 throughout Belgium.
Preference of nationality: none.
Conditions of employment: open-ended contracts. Hours of work between 7.30am-9pm. Pupils aged 6-66, mostly between 25-50.
Salary: 45-60,000 francs per month for full-time contract.
Facilities/Support: assistance with accommodation. Compulsory 3-week training course given.
Recruitment: through newspaper adverts, direct applications and contacts with Irish schools.

MAY INTERNATIONAL
40, rue Lesbroussart, 1050 Brussels. Tel: (2) 640 87 03.
Number of teachers: approximately 25.
Preference of nationality: none.
Qualifications: TEFL qualification, minimum 1 year's teaching experience with adults.
Conditions of employment: no contracts. Mostly day-time work, although evening work is available. Pupils are all adults, and mostly in business/professions.
Salary: 565 francs per hour.
Facilities/Support: no assistance with accommodation. Informal training/assistance given.
Recruitment: local newspaper adverts. Local interviews essential.

THE MITCHELL SCHOOL OF ENGLISH
156, rue Louis Hap, 1040 Brussels. Tel: (2) 734 80 73.
Number of teachers: 7.
Preference of nationality: none
Qualifications: BA/post-graduate teaching diploma and TEFL qualification. Require motivated, dynamic and versatile teachers who have preferably learned a foreign language themselves.
Conditions of employment: no contract. Prefer long-term freelancers. Hours of work 9am-8pm weekdays. Pupils aged 18-80.
Facilities/Support: assistance with accommodation unusual, but possible. Training given.
Recruitment: through direct application. Interviews are essential and are rarely held abroad.

PHONE LANGUAGES
65, rue des Echevins, 1050 Brussels. Tel: (2) 647 40 20.
Number of teachers: 8.
Preference of nationality: none.
Qualifications: BA (TEFL).
Conditions of employment: cycles of 15, 25 or 50 hours of private lessons given in half-hour lessons over the phone. Flexible hours of work between 8am-10pm. Pupils are all adults (usually business people). Teachers must have their own telephone and be prepared to stay in Belgium for at least one year.
Salary: 550 francs per hour.

Facilities/Support: no assistance with accommodation. Training given.
Recruitment: local interviews essential.

*The number of teachers in each entry refers to the number of native-speaker teachers.

France

The French used to rival the English for their reluctance to learn other languages. A Frenchman abroad spoke French as stubbornly as Britons spoke English. But things are changing, especially in the business and technical community. French telephone directories contain pages of language institutes, participants in the new era which 1992 is meant to usher in.

Since the 1970s, the law has put pressure on companies to provide on-going training to staff. The *Droit de Formation Continue* stipulates that companies devote 1% of their salary budget to training. English has recently overtaken Computing as the most popular object of investment, and therefore many schools cater purely to the business market. These schools seem to produce very glossy brochures which look more like the annual report of a multinational corporation than an invitation to take an evening course. Many offer one-to-one tuition. A recent innovation designed for the busy Parisian yuppie is learning by telephone, described below. The French government does not neglect the less privileged, either: there is a new scheme whereby the unemployed can take free English lessons at private schools.

Prospects for Teachers

Advanced TEFL qualifications seem to be less in demand in France than "commercial flair". Anyone who has a BA and who can look at home in a business situation has an excellent chance of finding teaching work, particularly if they have a working knowledge of French. In some circles it is fashionable to learn American English which means that, despite the visa difficulties for non-EEC nationals, it is possible for Americans to find work as well.

FIXING UP A JOB

In Advance

Adverts appear regularly in the UK press though rarely in American journals. When applying try to demonstrate your "commercial flair" with a polished presentation. Almost all the major recruitment agencies have client schools in France, so speculative calls to *English Worldwide, ELT Banbury,* the *Language Exchange* in Edinburgh, etc. could be productive. Anyone with an RSA Certificate might consider working for one of the International House schools in Paris, Toulouse, Grenoble, Lyon or Angers.

The British Council in Paris does not have an English teaching centre and is notoriously unhelpful to enquirers. "We would appreciate not being mentioned as a source of information on TEFL opportunities in France" they wrote to us.

Considering what a popular destination France is (and Paris in particular) for all manner of hopefuls, this attitude is perhaps understandable. They keep a list of English language schools for the benefit of local language learners (but not aspiring teachers). For addresses of language schools, the British Council recommends two books: *Dicoguide de la Formation* (published by Formation France, 80 rue de Miromesnil, 75008 Paris; tel: 45 22 12 88) and *International Where and How of Language Schools* (Wie & Wo-Verlag Gmbh, 6 rue Arsene Houssaye, 75008 Paris; tel: 42 89 01 13), though you may have as much trouble extracting a response from these organizations as from the British Council.

Perhaps a better source of language school addresses would be British Consulates in France. For example the Consulate-General in Lyon (24 rue Childebert, 69002 Lyon) keeps a list of 22 schools in the area. It is worth requesting such a list from the other Consulates-General in Bordeaux, Lille and Marseille, and also from the Vice-Consulates in Blagnac, Cherbourg, Pinard, Nantes, Calais, Boulogne, Dunkirk, Nice, Perpignan and Ajaccio.

French Yellow Pages list language schools under the heading *Enseignements Privé de Langues* or *Ecoles de Langues*. As usual it is easier to consult these at the City Business Library in London than at the French Embassy.

Teaching English in exchange for room and board is very widespread and is normally arranged on the spot, but can also be set up in advance. While looking for something to do in her gap year, Hannah Start was put in touch with a French bank executive who had done an English language course in Hannah's home town and who wanted to keep up her English at home in Paris by having someone to provide live-in conversation lessons. So, in exchange for 3 hours of speaking English in the evening (possibly over an excellent dinner), Hannah was given free accommodation in the 17th arrondisement.

On the Spot

The British Council is reputed to have a good notice board, but is rather selective about who it lets in to the building. Before the security was tightened up, Julian Peachey made use of its facilities:

> *I got a job via the British Council notice board looking after a little French boy, but lost that job after a couple of months. I got the British Council's list of English language schools and rang up all 68 of them. One school, desperate for a teacher the next morning, gave me a job over the phone. That was my first break and it paid £10 an hour. I slowly got work at other schools and also found a very cheap studio to sub-rent in Pigalle.*

According to Richard Pitwood who lived in Paris for part of 1990, demand for native speaker teachers was substantial and anyone with a BA and (preferably) some kind of TEFL certificate could usually find work. Watch for adverts in the metro for English language courses, since these are usually the biggest schools and therefore have the greatest number of vacancies for teachers. Certain streets in the 8th arrondisement around the Gare St. Lazare abound in language schools especially the rue de la Pépinière.

Berlitz has a sizeable presence in Paris with 13 schools including a big one near the Opéra and another at La Défense. A teacher's strike in 1990 highlighted Berlitz's poor reputation for staff conditions and pay levels (from 40 francs a lesson); however such discontent leads to a high turnover of staff, so there are always vacancies. Applicants must be prepared to fill out a very detailed — some say impertinent — application form.

Freelance

Language exchanges for room and board are commonplace in Paris and are usually arranged through advertisements or word-of-mouth. You can also offer English lessons privately in people's homes, which often pays 100 francs a session. The magazine *Paris Passion,* for the American community in Paris, is a good source of such adverts, as are the notice boards at various expatriate hang-outs particularly the American Church at 65 quai d'Orsay. This is what Kathryn Kleypas, an American au pair in Paris, did with great success:

> *I contacted the family who had placed an announcement on the job board at the American Church and was invited to come over to their home for an interview and to meet the 3 children to whom I would be teaching English every day. I was not asked if I had any teaching experience, yet was offered the position which involved 18 hours of English teaching/conversation in exchange for room, board and 1,400 francs per month. My family took me with them to the seashore near Bordeaux during July and to their castle near Limoge during August. Even though life was very slow for me that summer, I often look back at that time as one of the most interesting experiences I have ever had.*

You can also make contact with the teaching fraternity at expatriate drinking holes. The Caveau de Montpensier at 11 rue Montpensier near the metro Palais Royale has been recommended for this, though be prepared to pay £3 for a pint of Guinness.

Outside Paris, you could approach local primary schools and ask if they need any English teachers. In September 1990, English became available to primary school children, without any organized attempt to supply trained teachers. Therefore some schools have made use of lay people who happen to live in the vicinity.

REGULATIONS

For Britons, the same situation pertains as throughout the EEC: they are permitted to stay in France for up to 3 months looking for work. Once a job has been found a residence permit (*carte de séjour*) must be applied for from the Aliens Department of the police. The *carte de séjour* is usually valid for a year or (exceptionally) 5 years. Among the documents you will need are an official translation of your birth certificate (which is said to be cheaper if you do it before you leave home), the originals of your diplomas or certificates, plus your contract of employment. A social security number will be assigned to you and employers will probably deduct about 18% for social security contributions. Tax deductions will be a further 12%.

It is much more difficult for Americans, Australians, etc. to get a working visa, although most schools in the list at the end of this chapter do not state that they refuse to consider people from outside the EEC. There are so many Americans teaching in Paris that many people obviously find a way around the difficulty.

CONDITIONS OF WORK

Teaching "beezneezmen" is not everyone's cup of tea, but it can be much less strenuous than teaching children or adolescents. Provided you do not feel intimidated by your pupils' polished manners and impeccable dress, and can keep them entertained, you will probably be a success. As mentioned above, one-to-one teaching is not uncommon, for which TEFL courses (including the RSA Certificate) do not prepare you. However, if you develop a rapport with your client, this can be the most enjoyable teaching of all. Language schools which offer this facility to clients may well expect you to drive (perhaps even own) a car, so that you can give lessons in offices and private homes. Most schools pay between 50 and 85 francs for private lessons, and 10 or 20 francs more for group lessons.

The newest concept in English teaching is teaching by telephone

Recently, teachers' unions in France and EFL management signed the *Convention Collective* which makes stable contracts, sick pay, maternity benefit, etc. compulsory. This will make it much more difficult for small schools to get by with employing part-time teachers. By national agreement, the monthly salary for teachers of English is set at 7,700 francs for $27\frac{1}{2}$ of teaching per week (including paid travel time). Because social security benefits are based on a 39 hour week for all French workers, contracts state that teachers must do a further $11\frac{1}{2}$ of administration, preparation, etc. (which is not usually enforced too strictly). The annual holiday allowance for full-time teachers is 5 weeks plus an extra 5 days.

An interesting innovation in the world of TEFL consists of one-to-one teaching with a difference: telephone teaching is becoming increasingly popular among language learners both for its convenience and for the anonymity. For many people, making mistakes over the phone is less embarrassing than face-to-face. Apparently this method of teaching is great fun for teachers since the anonymity prompts people to spill out all their secrets. It is not necessary and possibly even an advantage, not to speak any French so you won't be tempted to break into French in frustration. Provided you have the use of a telephone, you can earn up to 80 francs for 20 minutes of conversation. Unfortunately this type of teaching rarely exists in isolation and will normally represent only a part of the teaching required by your employer. The Paris firm Languacom (41 rue de la Chaussée d'Antin, 75009 Paris; tel: 42 82 00 44) has pioneered this teaching method and might be worth approaching. International House in Paris has also jumped on this bandwagon, as have a number of firms. Alternatively, anyone fairly settled in a French city could try to fix up this kind of teaching independently.

Split shifts between 8am and 8pm are the norm, with the usual average of 24 contact hours per week. An unusual feature in France is that some schools calculate the salary according to a certain number of teaching hours per 9 or 12 months, and will pay overtime for hours worked in excess of this. Obviously the total can't be calculated until the end of the contract, which is a drawback for anyone considering leaving early.

Partly because of France's proximity to a seemingly inexhaustible supply of willing English teachers, working conditions in France are seldom brilliant. Although Andrew Boyle enjoyed his year teaching English in Lyon and the chance to become integrated into an otherwise impenetrable community, he concluded that even the most respectable schools treated teachers as their most expendable commodity. But for a whole range of Francophiles, the chance to eat and drink and live in France outweights the disadvantages.

LIST OF SCHOOLS

AUDIO-ENGLISH
44 allées de Tourny, 33000 Bordeaux. Tel: 56 44 54 05.
Number of teachers: 4.
Preference of nationality: UK.
Qualifications: BA, and good French. No previous experience necessary, but people who have already lived/worked in France, and who hold a clean driving licence are preferred. Pleasant personality important.
Conditions of employment: minimum 10 month contracts. 34 h.p.w. Hours of work between 8am-8pm. Pupils aged from 6 upwards.
Salary: 5,600 francs per month (gross).
Facilities/Support: no assistance with accommodation. Training provided.
Recruitment: through direct application and adverts in *TES.* Interviews essential; occasionally in UK.

B.E.S.T.
24 Bd. Béranger, 37000 Tours. Tel: 47 05 55 33. Fax: 47 61 29 94.
Number of teachers: 4.

Preference of nationality: none.
Qualifications: BA, RSA Cert. or good teaching experience.
Conditions of employment: 9 month contracts (September-June). 15-27 h.p.w.
Pupils are mostly aged between 23-50.
Salary: 7,500-9,000 francs per month.
Facilities/Support: no assistance with accommodation. A small amount of training given.
Recruitment: through adverts in local papers, and in *TES* and *EFL Gazette*.
Interviews essential, possibly in UK in summer.

BRITISH CONNECTION INTERNATIONAL
279 rue Créqui, 69007 Lyon. Tel: 72 73 02 55. Fax: 72 72 95 94.
Number of teachers: 12
Preference of nationality: none.
Qualifications: BA and adult language teaching experience preferred.
Conditions of employment: no standard length of employment, though teachers should be resident in Lyon. Hours of work are variable between 8am-8pm. Pupils aged between 18-65.
Salary: 70 francs per hour (gross) for individual lessons, 100 francs per hour for group lessons.
Facilities/Support: assistance with accommodation if necessary. Training provided.
Recruitment: through personal contacts. Local interviews essential.

CENTRE D'ETUDES DE LANGUES ETRANGÈRES
Z.I. du Brockus, B.P. 278, 62504 St. Omer. Tel: 21 93 78 45.
Number of teachers: 2.
Preference of nationality: UK.
Qualifications: RSA Cert., TEFL qualification.
Conditions of employment: 9 month contracts (September-June) or for summer holidays. At least 20 h.p.w. Hours of work from 6-8pm weekdays and 8am-12pm and 4-6pm Saturdays. Classes for children 6-10, adolescents 11-19 and adults.
Salary: 100 francs per hour.
Facilities/Support: informal assistance with accommodation. Training provided for teachers staying for a year.
Recruitment: through adverts. Interviews not essential.

CENTRE D'ETUDE DES LANGUES
I.S.F. Montfoulon, 61250 Damigny. Tel: 33 29 06 66.
Number of teachers: 4-5.
Preference of nationality: none.
Qualifications: TEFL qualification plus at least 1-2 years experience.
Conditions of employment: courses run from October to June. Usual hours 9-12am and 5-8pm Monday to Thursday plus Saturday morning. Pupils aged from 25 upwards.
Salary: negotiable.
Facilities/Support: assistance given with accommodation if necessary.
Recruitment: through direct applications and newspaper adverts. Interviews essential, first via telephone, then in France.

CYBELE LANGUES
7 rue d'Artois, 75008 Paris. Tel: (1) 42 89 12 89.
Number of teachers: 35/40.
Preference of nationality: UK, US, Canada and Australia.
Qualifications: BA and at least 2 years teaching experience.
Conditions of employment: 1 year contracts, 4-6 hours work per day between 8.30am-9pm. All pupils are business people.
Salary: 88 francs per hour (gross).
Facilities/Support: no assistance with accommodation. Training provided.
Recruitment: adverts in UK newspapers. Interviews essential and sometimes held in London.

EXECUTIVE LANGUAGE SERVICES
25, Bd. Sebastapol, 75001, Paris. Tel: (1) 42 36 32 32.
Affiliated to International House.
Number of teachers: 35.
Preference of nationality: none.
Qualifications: RSA Cert. (grade 'B') or RSA Cert. plus experience or RSA Dip.
Conditions of employment: minimum 1 year contracts. 27 h.p.w. Pupils range in age from 23-50.
Salary: 8-9,000 francs per month plus 5 weeks paid holiday.
Facilities/Support: assistance with accommodation. Training provided.
Recruitment: through IH Central Department and other IH schools.

F.O.R.M.
58 Av. St. Augustin, 06200 Nice. Tel: 93 71 31 23. Fax: 93 18 07 87.
Number of teachers: 3.
Preference of nationality: none.
Qualifications: good linguistic knowledge of English and a talent for teaching.
Conditions of employment: 40-60 hour contracts. Hours of work between 9am-8pm. Pupils are all adults.
Salary: 80 francs per hour.
Facilities/Support: no assistance with accommodation. Training provided.
Recruitment: through direct application with c.v. Local interviews essential.

FRANCE EUROPE CONSULTANTS
49 rue du Petit Bois, 35235 Thorigné. Tel: 99 83 89 34. Fax: 99 83 46 49.
Number of teachers: 12.
Preference of nationality: none.
Qualifications: BA and teacher training. Must have familiarity with business world.
Conditions of employment: minimum 1 year contracts. Pupils are all business people, and courses emphasize economic English for engineers, bankers, etc.
Salary: varies according to qualifications, etc.
Facilities/Support: no assistance with accommodation. Training provided if necessary.
Recruitment: through newspaper adverts or agencies.

GROUPE E.S.C. LYON
23 Av. Guy de Collongue, B.P. 174, 69132 Ecully Cedex. Tel: 72 20 25 25.
Affiliated to Lyon Graduate School of Business.
Preference of nationality: none.
Qualifications: BA and TEFL experience, preferably in France.
Conditions of employment: part and full time work. Hours of work 8.30am-5.30pm. Pupils aged between 18-65.
Salary: 6,500 francs per month minimum.
Facilities/Support: no assistance with accommodation. Training provided.
Recruitment: through direct application with c.v. Local interviews essential.

IFG LANGUES
37 quai de Grenelle, 75015 Paris. Tel: (1) 40 59 31 34.
Number of teachers: 70.
Preference of nationality: none, but must have permission to work in France.
Qualifications: minimum BA, RSA Cert. or equivalent, and experience.
Conditions of employment: unlimited contracts. 30/39 h.p.w. of which 20/26 are contact hours. 6 weeks paid holidays. Pupils are business people aged between 25-55.
Salary: 121-128,000 francs per year for full-time positions. Hours in excess of 1,166 over 12 months are reimbursed accordingly.
Facilities/Support: some assistance with accommodation. Training provided.
Recruitment: adverts in *Guardian* and French newspapers. Interviews and demonstration class held in Paris.

INFOLANGUES
169 Av. Charles de Gaulle, 69160 Tassin la Demi-Lune. Tel: 78 34 34 00.
Fax: 78 34 78 23.
Number of teachers: 12.
Preference of nationality: UK, Ireland, US.
Qualifications: TEFL background plus in-house training.
Conditions of employment: full-time contracts of unlimited length. Maximum of 1,225 teaching hours per year. Hours of work between 8am-8pm. Pupils range in age from 20-60.
Salary: 94,800-118,000 francs per year.
Facilities/Support: assistance given with finding accommodation only. Training provided.
Recruitment: through direct application and agencies. Interviews essential and can be held in England or Ireland.

ITS LANGUAGES
21 rue des Plantes, 75014 Paris. Tel: (1) 40 44 98 48.
Number of teachers: 7.
Preference of nationality: none.
Qualifications: teaching experience and maturity. TEFL/TESL/PGCE qualifications preferred, plus business/commercial experience.
Conditions of employment: part and full-time work available. 20 h.p.w. Classes of children and adults. Own teaching method in use.
Salary: 6,000 francs per month.

Facilities/Support: no assistance with accommodation. Training provided when necessary.
Recruitment: through direct application with c.v. Local interviews essential.

LINC
B.P. 19, 06220 Golfe-Juan. Tel: 93 63 71 80. Fax: 93 63 71 69.
Number of teachers: 2.
Preference of nationality: UK, US.
Qualifications: trainee teachers.
Conditions of employment: contracts of up to 9 months from September. 32 h.p.w. Pupils aged 3-11. Must be prepared to teach English songs and sports at this bilingual primary school on the French Riviera.
Salary: 2,500-5,000 francs per month.
Facilities/Support: assistance with accommodation. Training given.
Recruitment: through adverts in the *TES*, etc., Interviews not essential.

LA MAISON DES LANGUES
2 av. de la Libération, 45000 Orléans. Tel: 38 72 02 29.
Number of teachers: 5.
Preference of nationality: UK, US, etc.
Qualifications: BA (Modern Languages), TEFL qualification, some experience preferred.
Conditions of employment: minimum 1 year contracts. 39 h.p.w. of which 22-24 are contact hours. Pupils are all professionals.
Salary: 7,500 francs per month.
Facilities/Support: assistance given finding accommodation. Training provided.
Recruitment: through adverts in *TES* and *Guardian*. Interviews compulsory and can sometimes be arranged in UK.

TRANSFER FORMATION CONSEIL
20 rue Godot de Mauroy, 75009 Paris. Tel: (1) 42 66 14 11.
Number of teachers: 30.
Preference of nationality: none.
Qualifications: 2 years EFL experience, RSA Cert. preferred.
Conditions of employment: generally unlimited contracts. 39 h.p.w. of which 25 are contact hours. Pupils aged around 30.
Salary: £12-16,000 p.a.
Facilities/Support: no assistance with accommodation. Training provided.
Recruitment: through direct application with c.v. followed by interview in Paris.

WOOD LANGUAGE SERVICES
33 cours de la Liberté, 69003 Lyon. Tel: 78 60 15 60.
Number of teachers: 18.
Preference of nationality: UK, US.
Qualifications: BA, and 1 year's experience in TEFL or RSA Cert.
Conditions of employment: 1 academic year or January-June. 4 hours per day average between 8am-8pm. Pupils aged between 30-40.
Salary: 6,000 francs per month (for 100 hours) plus 10% paid holidays
Facilities/Support: assistance with accommodation. Training provided.
Recruitment: interviews essential and carried out at Christmas.

Germany

The excellent state education system in Germany ensures that a majority of Germans have a good grounding in English, so very little teaching is done at the beginner level. If German students want exposure to a native speaker they are far more likely to enrol in a language summer course in Britain than sign up for extra tuition at a local institution. Furthermore, some secondary schools in Germany employ native English-speaking *Helferen* (assistants), posts normally reserved for students of German who apply through the Central Bureau for Educational Visits & Exchanges (Seymour Mews, London W1H 9PE).

The reunification of Germany will change this picture to some extent. East Germans who have never studied English (because they have been studying Russian) may suddenly want to learn English at commercial institutes or at *Volkshochschule*, or "folk high schools" where various adult education courses are run free of charge.

But at present the greatest demand for English in Germany comes from the business and professional community. There are government incentives for companies to provide training to their employees and one of the most popular options is English. This means that there are many highly paid in-company positions for EFL and ESP teachers, as well as a number of agencies and consultancies which supply teachers to their clients.

PROSPECTS FOR TEACHERS

Any graduate with a background in economics or business who can speak German should not encounter too many problems finding work in a German city. Part-time work is almost always available to suitably qualified native speakers. In fact experience in business is often a more desirable qualification than a background in teaching. The question is not so much whether you know what a past participle is but whether you know what an "irrevocable letter of credit" or a "bank giro" is. Many schools offer *Oberstufe*, advanced or specialist courses in, for example, Banking English, Business English, or for bilingual secretaries, etc. For none of these is an RSA Certificate or even a Diploma the most appropriate training.

Very few schools are willing to consider candidates who can't speak any German. Although the "direct method" is in use everywhere (i.e. total immersion in English), the pupils will expect you to be able to explain things in German. If the school prepares its students for the Chamber of Commerce exams (known as LCCI), the teacher will be expected not only to understand the syllabus but to interpret and teach it with confidence. Some schools employ the now unfashionable "contrastive" method, again making a knowledge of conversational German essential.

One further requirement of many employers is a driving licence, so that teachers can travel easily from one off-site assignment to another.

FIXING UP A JOB

Professional presentation is even more important for securing work in the German business world than elsewhere. Germans tend to be formal, so dress appropriately and be aware of your manners at an interview. Also good references (*zeugnisse*) are essential.

Many attractive-sounding contracts are advertised in the *Guardian* and *Times Educational Supplement*. University students and graduates can often find out about possible employers from their university careers office. Vacancies occur throughout the year since businessmen and women are just as likely to start a course in April as in September.

Like so many embassies, the German Embassy in London (23 Belgrave Square, London SW1X 8PZ) is not noted for its helpful attitude to aspiring teachers or other job-seekers. It does, however, distribute a list of about 250 *Sprachenschulen* along with an information sheet headed "Teaching in Germany". Apart from directing students to enquire about the exchange programme run by the Central Bureau, it recommends applying to the Zentralstelle für Arbeitsvermittlung Feuerbachstrasse 42, D-6000 Frankfurt am Main 1. This is the Central Placement Office of the Federal Department of Employment, which has a special department for dealing with applications from abroad. A letter addressed to one of the 146 Arbeitsamter (employment offices) around the country will be forwarded to the Zentralstelle for processing. A personal visit to an Arbeitsamt is more likely to produce results, though you are likely to be told that there are far more qualified teachers and translators than there are vacancies.

Of the 4 British Council offices in Germany (Berlin, Cologne, Hamburg and Munich), Munich is the only one which has its own teaching operation. International House has schools in Freiburg, Hamburg, Munich and Pforzheim, relying on a high proportion of part-time teachers.

inlingua has over 50 schools in Germany and is a major employer of teachers. Similarly Linguarama (whose advertisements claim to provide "Language Training for Business") has centres in Cologne, Frankfurt, Hamburg, Munich and Stuttgart. Other chains include Berlitz (with 35 schools), Carl Duisberg, Bénédict and Euro-Sprachschule.

Organizations in Britain which recruit teachers for German language schools and companies include:

ITTC, 674 Wimborne Road, Bournemouth BH9 2EG.

Language Exchange, 7 Panmure Place, Edinburgh EH3 9HP. Tel: 031-228 2755.

Specialist Language Services (International) Ltd., 9 Marsden Business Park, Clifton Moor, York YO3 8XG.

Studio Language Services, 6 Salisbury Villas, Station Road, Cambridge CB1 2JF. Tel: (0223) 324605.

Freelance Teaching

Many commercial institutes refer to their part-time staff as "free-lancers", i.e. resident expatriates who work for between 2 and 20 hours per week. If you want to find private pupils, you could attend a meeting of an Anglo-German club of which there are many. The Deutsch Englische Gesellschaft meets once a month in Bonn and Düsseldorf and fortnightly in Cologne: details from the British Council.

REGULATIONS

EEC nationals are permitted to enter Germany to look for work at any time. Once work has been found, the teacher should obtain an *Aufenthaltserlaubnis* (residence permit) from the local authority (*Ausländeramt* or *Landratsamt*), which is normally valid for 5 years. If it takes more than 3 months to find work, different rules apply, and you should make enquiries at the *Ausländeramt*.

Americans can arrange teaching jobs in Germany more easily than in France or Italy, but they should obtain a work permit before leaving their country of origin. Despite the claim in the Embassy literature that it takes about 6 weeks for a permit to be processed, be prepared for a much longer wait and also for a possible refusal of your application. Much is left to the discretion of individual officials. According to one language school, the precise procedure for non-EEC nationals to obtain a work permit "depends on which civil servant you talk to".

People who want to work in Germany are supposed to obtain a *Lohnsteuerkarte* (tax card). Rates of tax are very high in Germany, as much as 50%; however, anyone who teaches for less than 2 years can collect their salary tax-free, though they may have about 17% deducted for contributions.

CONDITIONS OF WORK

You can almost guarantee that you will be teaching adults, and usually before or after office hours. Contracts for full-time work are normally at least a year long, often with a 3-month probation period.

Wages are undoubtedly among the highest anywhere. DM15 per lesson is standard, DM20 not uncommon and DM35 possible. Many schools, including inlingua, timetable their lessons to last 45 minutes. So a working week of 30 hours could consist of 40 45-minute lessons, which would be a very heavy workload. Off-site teaching hours often incur a premium of DM3-5 to compensate for travel time.

If you are depending solely on one employer for your income try to find an institute which guarantees a monthly minimum number of hours. Monthly salaries are usually between DM2,000 and DM3,000 gross, with the possibility of extra over-time. Considering that a one-bedroom flat in one of the big cities can cost as much as DM1,000 per month, salaries need to be high. Quite a few schools assist with accommodation, including most in the inlingua chain.

LIST OF SCHOOLS

BERLITZ
Freidrich Wilhelm Strasse 30, 4100 Duisburg. Tel: (203) 27168.
Number of teachers: 8-10 in each of the organization's 35 schools throughout Germany.
Preference of nationality: none.
Qualifications: good command of English, no teaching experience necessary.
Conditions of employment: minimum 6 months contracts. Morning and evening work. Pupils range in age from 2-70.
Salary: DM15 per 45-minute lesson.
Facilities/Support: no assistance generally given with accommodation. Training given.
Recruitment: through newspaper adverts. Local interviews essential.

CARL DUISBERG CENTREN
CDC-Sprachendienst, Rathenaustrasse 9, 3000 Hannover 1. Tel: (511) 363904.
Number of teachers: 25.

Preference of nationality: none.
Qualifications: BA or equivalent, TEFL experience required and TEFL qualifications preferred.
Conditions of employment: length of work varies from intensive 5 day contracts to 2 hours/week September-June. Pupils are all professionals aged 35-50.
Salary: unspecified.
Facilities/Support: assistance with accommodation when possible. Training provided.
Recruitment: through personal recommendation. Local interviews essential.

CHRISTOPHER HILLS SCHOOL OF ENGLISH
Sandeldamm 12, 6450 Hanau 1. Tel: (6181) 15015.
Number of teachers: 8+.
Preference of nationality: UK.
Qualifications: minimum RSA Cert, plus 2 years experience or RSA Dip, plus 4 years experience depending upon the position.
Conditions of employment: unlimited contracts. Pupils range in age from students upwards.
Salary: DM30-42,000 p.a.
Facilities/Support: assistance with accommodation. Training provided.
Recruitment: through word of mouth and adverts in *EFL Gazette, Guardian* and *TES*. Interviews essential and held in UK and Germany.
Contact in UK: c/o 11 Victoria Parade, Broadstairs, Kent.

ENGLISH LANGUAGE CENTRE
Bieberer Strasse 205, 6050 Offenbach am Main. Tel: (69) 858787.
Number of teachers: 8.
Preference of nationality: UK.
Qualifications: RSA Cert.
Conditions of employment: 2 year contracts. 30 lessons × 45 minutes per week mainly in the afternoon and evening. Pupils aged 20+.
Salary: DM19 per lesson.
Facilities/Support: assistance with accommodation. No training provided.
Recruitment: adverts in *Guardian*. Interviews possible in UK.

ENGLISH LANGUAGE CLUB
Business English Consulting, Altonaer Chausee 89, 2000 Schenefeld.
Tel: (40) 830 2421/830 1720/21.
Number of teachers: 20+.
Preference of nationality: none.
Qualifications: BA and TEFL experience.
Conditions of employment: hours and contract length are negotiable. Pupils range in age from 12-75. Method used developed by proprietor Joan von Ehren.
Salary: DM50 per 90-minute lesson.
Facilities/Support: no assistance with accommodation. Training provided.
Recruitment: through personal recommendation and universities. Interviews can be held in UK.

ENGLISH LANGUAGE INSTITUTE
Alter Kirchenweg 33a, 2000 Norderstedt. Tel: (40) 525 1600.
Number of teachers: 8-10 (including freelance teachers).

Preference of nationality: UK, US.
Qualifications: BA or TEFL qualification.
Conditions of employment: minimum 1 year contracts. Hours of work between 8am-9pm. Pupils are business people of all ages.
Salary: varies according to qualifications.
Facilities/Support: no assistance with accommodation. No training provided.
Recruitment: through adverts. Local interviews essential.

ENGLISH LANGUAGE SERVICE
Staufenstrasse 1, 6000 Frankfurt am Main.
Number of teachers: 4-7.
Preference of nationality: US.
Qualifications: BA, TEFL experience and conversational German.
Conditions of employment: hours of work and contract lengths vary. Pupils range in age from 20-60.
Salary: competitive rates of pay plus return air fares to US after 2 year contract.
Facilities/Support: assistance with accommodation. Training provided.
Recruitment: via adverts in *TESOL Bulletin*. Interviews may or may not be required.

ENGLISH TRAINING PROGRAMMES
Hirsauerstrasse 138, 7530 Pforzheim. Tel: (7231) 72598. Fax: 73536. Affiliated to International House.
Number of teachers: 4.
Preference of nationality: UK.
Qualifications: RSA Cert/Dip and previous experience required. Business background and knowledge of German are advantages.
Conditions of employment: 9-10 month contracts (September-June). 20 h.p.w. plus admin. work. Pupils are mostly professional people aged between 25-50.
Salary: DM2,000 per month. 17% deducted for social contributions.
Facilities/Support: fully furnished 3-room flat available from school for a low rent. Training provided.
Recruitment: through IH, London. Interviews in UK if necessary.

EURO AKADEMIE
Elsa-Brandström Strasse 8, 5000 Cologne 1. Tel: (221) 736074.
Number of teachers: 7.
Preference of nationality: UK, US, NZ, South Africa.
Qualifications: BA essential, teaching qualification preferred. Knowledge of German a distinct asset.
Conditions of employment: 2 year renewable contracts with 6 month trial period. Hours of work 8.30am-1.30pm weekdays plus 2 afternoons/evenings per week. Pupils range in age from 18-30. Courses are preparatory to the LCCI exams.
Salary: from DM2,200 per month.
Facilities/Support: assistance given finding accommodation. Training provided.
Recruitment: adverts in *TES*. Interviews essential and take place in Cologne or UK.

EUROPEAN LANGUAGE SCHOOL
Hansastrasse 44, 4600 Dortmund 1. Tel: (231) 579496/8.
Number of teachers: 15.

Preference of nationality: UK.
Qualifications: BA minimum, TEFL experience essential for adult classes.
Conditions of employment: 1-2 year contracts. Hours of work between 8am-11.30pm. Pupils aged between 7-70 years.
Salary: DM3,000 per month (gross).
Facilities/Support: no assistance with accommodation. Training provided.
Recruitment: adverts in *Guardian*. Interviews held in UK.

EURO-SCHULE
Gross Bleiche 16, 6500 Mainz. Tel: (6131) 222650.
Number of teachers: 8-10.
Preference of nationality: US, UK.
Qualifications: TEFL experience, BA helpful but not essential.
Conditions of employment: mostly part-time work. Hours of work 4-8pm weekdays and 8.15-11.30am Saturdays. Pupils range in age from 18-70.
Salary: DM20 per 45-minute lesson.
Facilities/Support: no assistance with accommodation. Training provided.
Recruitment: through university recruitment services, the local Arbeitsamt and occasional adverts. Local interviews are essential.

EURO-SPRACHSCHULE
Herzogspital Strasse 3, 8000 Munich 2. Tel: (89) 266076. Fax: 266387.
Number of teachers: 30-35 (seasonal).
Preference of nationality: none.
Qualifications: BA normally required, teaching experience preferred.
Conditions of employment: hours of work between 7.30am-9pm. Pupils are all adults, and mostly business people.
Salary: DM23 per 45-minute lesson, DM28 per lesson for company work.
Facilities/Support: assistance with accommodation provided if possible, Munich has a housing shortage at the moment. Some training given.
Recruitment: through local adverts. Local interviews essential.

HELLIWELL INSTITUTE OF ENGLISH
Markt 15, 5040 Brühl. Tel: (2232) 12893.
Number of teachers: 8 full-time, 40 part-time in 4 centres (in Euskirchen, Siegburg and Düsseldorf).
Preference of nationality: US, UK, etc.
Qualifications: BA, TEFL qualification or equivalent.
Conditions of employment: 10 month renewable contracts. 26 h.p.w. mostly evening work. Overtime available for contract workers.
Salary: negotiable.
Facilities/Support: assistance given with accommodation when possible. Training provided.
Recruitment: through adverts in *TES*. Interviews held in UK.

INLINGUA SPRACHSCHULE
Westenhellweg 66-68, 4600 Dortmund 1. Tel: (231) 149966.
Number of teachers: 15.
Qualifications: minimum BA/MA, TEFL training and experience, must be between 23-28 years old and of well-groomed appearance.

Conditions of employment: hours of work between 8am-9.40pm and Saturday mornings. 34-40 × 45 minute sessions per week. Pupils mostly business people.
Salary: basic minimum DM2,000 per month for full-time staff. DM15-20 per 45-minute class.
Recruitment: local or via inlingua in Birmingham.

INLINGUA SPRACHSCHULE
Königstrasse 61, 4100 Duisburg 1. Tel: (203) 341334.
Number of teachers: 15.
Preference of nationality: UK, US.
Qualifications: BA or equivalent.
Conditions of employment: 2 year contracts. Hours of work between 8am-9pm. Pupils range in age from 18-60.
Salary: DM15-20 per 45-minute lesson.
Facilities/Support: assistance with accommodation. Training provided.
Recruitment: local interviews if possible.

INLINGUA SPRACHSCHULE
Kaiserstrasse 37, 6000 Frankfurt 1. Tel: (69) 231021/23. Fax: 234829.
Number of teachers: 25.
Preference of nationality: none.
Qualifications: BA, TEFL qualification.
Conditions of employment: 13 month contracts. 30-35 h.p.w. Pupils aged between 18-60.
Salary: approximately DM3,000 per month (gross).
Facilities/Support: assistance with accommodation. Training provided.
Recruitment: through inlingua in Birmingham.

INLINGUA SPRACHSCHULE
Knapper Strasse 38, 5880 Lüdenscheid. Tel: (2351) 20275.
Number of teachers: 4.
Preference of nationality: none.
Qualifications: BA.
Conditions of employment: 1-2 year contracts. 25-30 lessons per week. Pupils aged from 16.
Salary: negotiable.
Facilities/Support: assistance with accommodation. Training provided in Frankfurt or UK.
Recruitment: through adverts. Interviews essential and can be arranged in US/UK.

NEUE SPRACHSCHULE
Rosastrasse 1, 7800 Freiburg 1. Tel: (761) 24810/32026. Fax: 39150.
Number of teachers: 9.
Preference of nationality: none.
Qualifications: BA.
Conditions of employment: 2-20 h.p.w. Pupils range in age from 20-60. Use some suggestopaedic techniques.
Salary: DM20 per hour.

Facilities/Support: no assistance with accommodation. Training provided.
Recruitment: through newspaper adverts. Interviews not essential.

PRIVATE FACHAKADEMIE FÜR FREMDSPRACHENBERUFE
Rathausplatz 2, 8960 Kempten.
Number of teachers: 6-7.
Preference of nationality: none.
Qualifications: BA/MA.
Conditions of employment: 1 year contracts or longer. Hours of work 8am-1pm.
Pupils range in age from 19-24.
Salary: DM36 per 45-minute lesson.
Facilties/Support: no assistance with accommodation. No training provided.
Recruitment: local interviews essential.

SPRACHSCHUL-CENTRUM DREIEICH
Frankfurt Strasse 114, 6072 Dreieich. Tel: (6103) 34113.
Number of teachers: 4.
Preference of nationality: Ireland, UK.
Qualifications: TEFL qualification with 2 years experience.
Conditions of employment: 9 month contracts (October-June). 30 h.p.w. Pupils
are all adults, some company courses.
Salary: DM2,00 per month.
Facilities/Support: assistance with accommodation. No training given.
Recruitment: through private contacts. Interviews can be given in UK.

SPRACHSTUDIO LINGUA NOVA
Thierschstrasse 36, 8000 Munich 22. Tel: (89) 221171.
Number of teachers: 10.
Preference of nationality: none.
Qualifications: depends on level of instruction.
Conditions of employment: part-time work only. 10-25 h.p.w. All pupils are
adults.
Salary: DM20-28 per 45-minute lesson.
Facilities/Support: informal assistance given with finding accommodation.
Training provided.
Recruitment: local interviews essential.

VORBECK-SCHULE
7614 Gengenbach. Tel: (049) 7803/3361.
Number of teachers: 6.
Preference of nationality: UK, US, Australia.
Qualifications: BA essential, teaching experience preferred.
Conditions of employment: minimum 1 year contracts with 3 months trial
period. Up to 6 × 45 min. lessons per day between 8.15am-5.10pm. Pupils aged
between 17-24. Vorbeck is a Vocational School of Languages and Foreign
Correspondence which trains bilingual secretaries, etc.
Salary: varies according to experience.

Facilities/Support: assistance with accommodation. Training provided.
Recruitment: through direct applications. Local interviews usually required.

Greece

The huge ELT industry in Greece predates Greece's full membership in the EEC, but can only increase in the present climate. Of all the candidates worldwide who sit the Cambridge First Certificate and Cambridge Proficiency examinations, about one quarter are in Greece. Estimates vary (between 3,500 and 8,500) of the number of private language schools (*frontisteria*) there are in the country, but there are enough to create a huge demand for native speakers. Standards at *frontisteria* vary from indifferent to excellent, but the run-of-the-mill variety is usually a reasonable place to work for 9 months.

Frontisteria come in all shapes and sizes. In a town of 30,000 inhabitants, it would not be unusual to find 10 English *frontisteria*, 3 or 4 of which would be big enough to employ one native English speaker. Any Greek who has passed the Cambridge Proficiency exam can open his or her own private school. These are often in buildings which were not designed to be schools and facilities can be very basic. Secondary school pupils in Greece are obliged to study 15 subjects, all of which they must pass before being allowed to proceed to the next year. In most areas English is taught so poorly that the vast majority of pupils also attend *frontisteria*, and it is not uncommon for a 15 year old to have 2 or 3 hours of lessons a day (in other subjects as well as English) in one or more private establishments to supplement his or her state schooling. Not surprisingly, the students are not always brimming over with enthusiasm; in fact, quite often they are not even awake.

Prospects for Teachers

Prospects for anyone with a university degree are excellent, particularly outside Athens. The government has recently stipulated that in order to obtain a teacher's licence, English teachers must have at least a BA and all but the most dodgy schools will expect to see a university certificate. Although a TEFL certificate will make it easier to get a decent job, it is far from essential. Of the 21 schools listed in the Directory at the end of this chapter, only two mentioned that they are looking for an RSA Certificate.

There are lots of Americans teaching in Greece, though there is an obvious bias in favour of British teachers because of EEC membership.

Another reason why almost any BA can expect to land a job in Greece is that wages are not high enough to attract a great many qualified EFL teachers. Greece tends to be a country where people get their first English teaching job for the experience and then move to more lucrative countries. Also, few schools place any emphasis on staff development or provide in-house training so serious teachers quickly move on. Still, the cost of living is not high in Greece, and the average teaching wage is enough to support a comfortable if not luxurious lifestyle.

With Greece's full entry to the Common Market (as of 1988), the opening of more foreign-owned language schools is anticipated, especially branches of

UK schools. In fact local Greek language school owners, who obviously fear new competition, have been resisting this. If competition does increase, it may be that standards (and teachers' wages) will be forced up and schools will be looking for more qualified teachers. But that remains a distant prospect.

The majority of advertised jobs are in towns and cities in mainland Greece. Athens has such a large expatriate community that most of the large central schools at the elite end of the market, including the British Council and the New Centre (Akarnanias 16, Athens 11526) which specializes in business English are able to hire well qualified staff locally. But this is not the case in Edessa, Larisa, Preveza or any of numerous towns which the tourist to Greece is unlikely to have heard of.

FIXING UP A JOB

In Advance

Getting a list of language schools from outside Greece is not easy. There are two organizations which *frontisteria* may join: the Pan-Hellenic Association of Language School Owners (PALSO, Kallirois 37, 11743 Athens) caters mainly for large schools, while the Pan-Hellenic Federation of Language Schools is for smaller schools. Neither was willing to send a list of their member schools, though anyone in Athens could no doubt obtain a list.

Fortunately plenty of schools and specialist agencies advertise in the UK press and so it is not necessary to send off a lot of speculative applications, except perhaps to the chains of schools mentioned below. Job adverts for Greece abound in the *TES* and *Education Guardian* in June, though some schools can be seen advertising their last minute vacancies into September. Few seem to go in for lavish display adverts, but there is always a sprinkling of 4-line adverts along the lines of "English teachers required. Good salary and housing. Write to Frontisterion X, etc." There are also occasional adverts for live-in tutors. Some adverts will be for chains of schools and these obviously offer the most opportunities, for example the Strategakis Group (6 George Street, Canningos Square, 10677 Athens; also in Thessaloniki — see entry), the *Homer Association* with 110 schools, the *Xeni* Organization and Hambakis Schools (1 Philellinon Street, Syntagma Square, Athens 105 57). Together, these account for hundreds of schools throughout Greece and so it is always worth sending your c.v. to them.

There are several specialist agencies with offices in Greece and/or Britain which undertake to match teachers with *frontisteria:*

English Teachers for Greece (ETFG), Nikaliou Plastira 3, Rethymnon, Crete. Tel: (831) 20750. Fax: 22446. UK address: 160 Littlehampton Road, Worthing, West Sussex BN13 1QT. Tel: (0903) 690729. Fax: 30129/31402. Run by Susan Lancaster who claims to provide candid information about working abroad. Certainly the orientation bumph followed up with a pre-departure seminar for prospective teachers is detailed and helpful, including information on Greek customs, cheap air fares to Greece, etc. She will also try to put new teachers in touch with current or past ones.

Teachers in Greece (TIG), Taxilou 79, Zographou, 15771 Athens. Tel: (1) 779 2587. UK address: 53 Talbot Road, London W2. Tel: 071-243 9260. Run by Carol Skinner who is based in Athens between September and May, but is in London during June, July and August to carry out recruitment.

English Studies Advisory Centre (ESAC), 22 Belestinou Street, 11523 Athens. Tel: (1) 691 0462/692 6272. Has some summer positions as well as 9 month jobs. Greek-run agency with possible UK contact address (which should be confirmed): Mr. G. Pavlopoulos, Ifor Hall, 109 Camden Road, London NW1 9HA.

All three agencies are looking for people with a BA but not necessarily a TEFL qualification (depending on the client school's requirements). Another telephone number regularly advertised in the *Guardian* in this context is 081-671 0904 on which Bill Mackie might be able to advise. Andrew Boyle (who had no TEFL background) answered one of ESAC's adverts in the *Guardian* and secured a job in Tripolis after one telephone call. The service of these agencies is free to teachers. Complaints about a lack of back-up are common (especially with the latter two), so do not expect too much support if you are unhappy with your *frontisterion*.

Other recruitment agencies which have links with Greece are:
ELT Banbury, 20 Horsefair, Banbury, Oxfordshire OX16 0AH. Tel: (0295) 271658.
ESAB, 16 Argyle Street, Bath BA2 4SB. Tel: (0225) 442333.
ETU, 3 Rosewood Avenue, Burnley, Lancs. BB11 2PH. Tel: (0282) 27367.
Language Exchange, 7 Panmure Place, Edinburgh EH3 9HP. Tel: 031-228 2755.
Nord-Anglia International Ltd, 10 Eden Place, Cheadle, Stockport, Cheshire SK8 1AT. Tel: 061-491 4191.
Surrey Language Centre, 39 West Street, Farnham, Surrey GU9 7DR. Tel: (0252) 723494.

On the Spot

Greece is a country in which the idiom "on the spot" must be taken literally, since very little can be reliably accomplished by post or even by telephone. A native English speaker eager to teach Greek young people, who is present in the flesh, has an excellent chance of finding a job. The best times to look are early September, since the academic year begins mid to late September, or possibly again at the beginning of January. Finding work in the summer in Athens is impossible, though a few English language summer courses are run in resorts or on the islands.

Your first step after arrival would be to check the adverts in the English language daily *The Athens News*, where *frontisteria* throughout the country occasionally advertise, though they normally ask for qualifications. If you want to stay in Athens, you can find a list of language schools in the *Blue Guide*, an English version of the Yellow Pages. Once you arrange an interview, be sure to dress well and to amass as many educational diplomas as you can. This will create the right aura of respectability in which to impress the potential employer with your conscientiousness and amiability. Decisions are often taken more according to whether you hit it off with the interviewer than on your qualifications and experience.

Finding work in the provinces is easy if you are around in early September as Sarah Clifford was. She had no trouble lining up part-time work at a *frontisterion* in the Peloponnesian village of Kynoryrias, with "no experience, no teaching qualification, no degree and no knowledge of Greek". The catch was that the hourly wage of 1,000 drachmas was low, but she enjoyed rural Greece more than cosmopolitan Athens.

If you are looking for a more informal arrangement, many Greek families are looking for live-in tutors for their children. Again check the *Athens News* or indeed place your own advert; the newspaper is at 23-25 Lekka Street and charges 800 drachmas for 15 words. There are several English language bookshops in Athens where EFL materials are available and where contacts might be forged, e.g. the one in Nikis Street (off Syntagma Square) and The Bookstall (Harilou Trikoup 6-19).

When you elicit interest from a language school owner or a family, take your time over agreeing terms. Greece is not a country in which it pays to rush, and negotiations can be carried out in a leisurely and civilized fashion. On the other hand, do not come to an agreement with an employer without clarifying wages and schedules precisely.

Freelance

Private lessons, at least in the provinces, are very easy to find. The going rate is 2,000 drachmas an hour, though teachers in Athens can earn 3,000 drachmas. Most teachers do at least 3 or 4 hours a week — more than enough to cover their Retsina bill (according to Loraine Christensen who taught in Kastoria in northern Greece for a number of years). Frontisterion owners don't seem to mind and, curiously enough, even encourage freelance teaching.

Trading English lessons for board and lodging is a common form of freelance teaching in Athens. The rich suburbs of Kifissia and Politia are full of families who can afford to provide private English lessons for their offspring. The suburbs of Pangrati and Filothei are also well-heeled as is the more central suburb of Kolonaki. It is also possible to start up private classes for children. In fact it is easy, provided you have decent accommodation in a prosperous residential area, though this will normally be too expensive if your only source of income is private teaching.

REGULATIONS

EEC nationals do not require a work permit; however English teachers must obtain a teacher's licence and a residence permit, and the bureaucratic procedures involved can be stressful even with a supportive employer. Andrew Boyle ended up applying in sextuplet for his residence permit the day before he was due to finish his 9-month contract.

The Ministry of Education, which must approve the appointment, now considers the following as sufficient qualifications for teachers: BA, MA or research degree, preferably in English or education, PGCE or Diploma in Education, or a teacher's certificate. You must have your diploma officially translated and notarized, and this is much cheaper if you can arrange to do this at the Greek Consulate before you leave home; the Department of Foreign Affairs in Athens (ld Voukourestiou Street) charges a substantial fee. You also need to submit your c.v. plus a certificate of good health (either officially translated or issued by a Greek state hospital such as the Evangelismos Hospital at 45-47 Ipsilantou, Kolonaki, Athens) and a signed contract in order to qualify for the teacher's licence. With this you can apply for a residence permit from the local police or in Athens the Aliens Bureau at 173 Alexandras Avenue. US citizens are required to obtain a work permit as well, in order to be eligible for a residence permit. Normally this must be obtained outside Greece.

A residence permit is normally valid for 6 months in the first instance and then for 5 years once it has been renewed. Some teachers who are not intending to stay long simply extend their tourist visa (as long as they can provide plenty of currency exchange slips to prove that they are self-supporting) or leave the country every 3 months to renew their tourist stamp. (Weekend trips to Yugoslavia are popular for this purpose.)

Although strict currency controls are placed on tourists, anyone with a work permit can charge up to 160,000 drachmas into sterling or dollars.

National Insurance

Frontisterion owners are legally obliged to pay IKA, Greek national insurance. Employers pay 22% and employees $11\frac{3}{4}$%. It is worth making sure that this is paid, not least because private health care in Greece is very expensive. You should go with your employer to the local IKA office in order to apply for an IKA book 60 days after starting to pay contributions; thereafter you are entitled to free medical treatment on production of the book, though you have to pay for prescriptions.

CONDITIONS OF WORK

Standards very enormously among *frontisteria*. The sole motive for their existence is profit. In general the large chains like *Strategakis* are better, probably for no other reason than that they have a longer history of employing native English speakers. Many of the small independently owned schools are cowboy outfits. Some of the owners passed the Proficiency exam more than 20 years ago and have had little contact with the English language since, apart from shouting (usually in Greek) at their students and getting them to recite English irregular verbs parrot fashion.

Teaching unions have negotiated some reasonable conditions, though not all schools offer them. Single teachers are entitled to a minimum hourly wage of 720 drachmas and married ones 790 drachmas. Bonuses, holiday pay and health insurance are all stipulated, plus employers may not fire teachers during the school year. The majority offer 8 or 9 month contracts from September/October and allow two paid fortnight holidays at Christmas and Easter (remember that the Greek Easter is usually later than elsewhere). The basic salary (net of tax and insurance) falls in the range of 80,000-120,000 drachmas per month, with 100,000 drachmas being average.

This is considerably augmented by compulsory bonuses and index-linked rises. All employees in Greece are legally entitled to Christmas and Easter bonuses which are based on the number of days they have worked. For every 9 days you have worked before Christmas you get one day's pay (i.e. 5 hours). For every 13 days worked between January 1st and April 30th you get 2 days pay.

You also get a lump sum at the end of your contract which is not in fact a bonus. It is 2 weeks holiday pay and 2 weeks severance pay (both tax-free). Beware of employers who pay for your accommodation out of your gross salary and then try to calculate your bonuses as a percentage of your net salary. This is illegal.

Approximately every 4 months, the government issues a figure for ATA which is a cost of living linked rise. Even though you have signed a contract, you are entitled to this rise and it is likely to be substantial as inflation is currently running at 22%. In fact one of the teachers' unions recommends that teachers *not* sign any contracts which could be limiting their negotiated rights. (For further details, contact the Greek Association of Foreign Language Teachers — "Vironas," 48 Triti Septemvriou St., Athens.)

The working week in a *frontisterion* is longer than in most countries averaging 28-30 hours per week. Split shifts are less common than usual, however, since most young students pursue their English studies after school (which in many cases is not until 7pm!). It is not unusual to be expected to teach in 2 or more "satellite" sites of the main school in villages up to 10 miles away. Local bus services are generally good and cheap but you could find yourself spending an inordinate amount of (unpaid) time in transit and standing around at bus stops.

Despite the fact that he found his working hours of 4-9pm agreeable, Andrew Boyle was very dissatisfied with his salary of 53,000 drachmas (in 1989) and decided to press for a 23% increase. His boss reluctantly agreed to this, since it would have been virtually impossible to fill the position at that time of year (i.e. February). Andrew was pleased with his success but does not recommend this tactic to anyone of a nervous disposition.

There is already a union for employees of *frontisteria* attached to the Federation of Secondary School Teachers. Be sure to contact them if you think you are being paid less than the legal minimum since a letter from them is often enough to bring a *frontisterion* into line.

Pupils

Most native English speakers are employed to teach advanced classes, usually the 2 years leading up to First Certificate. Because of the Greek style of education, pupils won't show much initiative and will expect to be tested frequently on what they have been taught. Andrew Boyle found the prevailing methodology of "sit 'em down, shut 'em up and give 'em lots of homework' was moderately successful.

Accommodation

Since most schools provide accommodation — for example all but two of the schools listed in this chaper offer a free flat or help in finding a flat — teachers need not be too concerned about their living arrangements. Although Athens rents are high, accommodation generally is not unreasonably priced. A group of 4 could rent a decent house for 25,000 drachmas a month in most areas. Of course there are exceptions. Andrew Boyle describes his flat in Tripolis as a "particularly vile, subterranean cavern with an almost non-existent window and stomach-turning plumbing" but found that anything more congenial was ridiculously expensive. Leah White solved her accommodation problem in Athens by approaching managers of blocks of flats to see whether they could arrange for her to have a rent-free flat in exchange for teaching their children. (This way she avoided the problem which plagues live-in tutors, a lack of privacy.)

If your employer provides your accommodation, it is definitely worth checking which (if any) utility bills are included in the rent. If you are living in a modern block of flats — little else is available in many towns — your central heating bill can be extortionate and you have no control over when it is on. Often it will be on in the early evening when you are out teaching and the early morning when you are in bed. Other inconveniences you may encounter include an unreliable water supply, since Greece has a chronic water shortage.

LEISURE

Outside Athens, the social order in Greece is still fairly conservative. A further problem is the enormous language barrier in a country where it will take some time to learn how to read the alphabet. Watching Greek television is a good way to learn the language plus Greek lessons are run free of charge in many locations. Set against the famed hospitality of the Greeks is their inevitable impatience with foreigners, who have swamped many parts of their country, at least in the summer. A few teachers have found the communities in which they worked rather insular and have even detected a whiff of xenophobia. But on the whole Greeks are extraordinarily friendly, at least on a superficial level.

As anyone who has visited Greece knows, the country has countless other attractions, not least the very convivial and affordable tavernas. Cafés (*kafeneions*) are a largely male institution in which women teachers may not feel comfortable. Travel is relatively cheap and a pure delight out of season.

When people think of Greece they automatically think of sun-soaked Mediterranean beaches, but it is quite a different story in the inland towns of northern Greece in the winter. Be sure to pack accordingly, and take a warm coat, stout shoes and a hot water bottle (bearing in mind that heating costs are very high). You can even go skiing, and very inexpensively.

LIST OF SCHOOLS

AGAPIDOU SCHOOL OF ENGLISH
10 Pindou Street, PO Box 75, 59100 Veria, Greece. Tel/Fax: (331) 26416.
Number of teachers: 4-5.
Preference of nationality: UK.
Qualifications: BA, TEFL qualification and, preferably, some experience.
Conditions of employment: 8-9 month renewable contracts. 28-30 45-minute teaching sessions per 5 day week. Pupils aged 8-16.
Salary: above government standard plus holidays and bonuses.
Facilities/Support: accommodation provided. No training.
Recruitment: adverts in *Guardian*. Interviews are essential and are held in UK.

ALPHA ABATZOGLOU ECONOMOU
10 Kosma Etolou St., 54643 Thessaloniki. Tel: (31) 830 535.
Number of teachers: 6.
Preference of nationality: none.
Qualifications: BA.
Conditions of employment: 1 academic year renewable contracts. 25 h.p.w. in the morning and evening. Pupils from age 10.
Salary: varies according to experience.
Facilities/Support: assistance with accommodation. Training provided.
Recruitment: adverts in *TES*. Mostly UK interviews.

ATHENS COLLEGE
PO Box 65005, 15410 Psychico, Athens. Tel: (1) 671 4621/8.
Number of teachers: 32.
Preference of nationality: US, etc.

Qualifications: MA/MEd in ESL and at least 3 years certified teaching experience.
Conditions of employment: 3 year contracts, 18-21 h.p.w. Pupils range in age from 8-18.
Salary: starting at 180,000 drachmas per month (August 1990).
Facilities/Support: no assistance with accommodation. Some training provided.
Recruitment: through direct application. Interviews are essential and take place in Greece and sometimes in UK or US.

ENGLISH, C, PETALAS
5 Kassopitras St., 47100 Arta. Tel: (681) 24414.
Number of teachers: 2.
Preference of nationality: Australia, Ireland.
Conditions of employment: 9-10 month contracts. 28 h.p.w. Pupils range in age from 9-16.
Salary: 80-90,000 drachmas per month plus bonuses and two paid 15 day holidays at Christmas and Easter.
Facilities/Support: free accommodation provided. Training given.
Recruitment: adverts in *TES.* Interviews not essential but sometimes held outside Greece.

GNOSSI ELS
25 G. Sxina St., 19100 Megara. Tel: (296) 23322/29656.
Number of teachers: 3.
Preference of nationality: UK.
Qualifications: BA/BEd. TEFL qualification and 1 or 2 years experience; however, recent graduates will also be considered.
Conditions of employment: 9 month contracts initially. 28 h.p.w. Pupils range in age from 7-16.
Salary: as specified by labour regulations and collective agreements.
Facilities/Support: accommodation provided free of charge. Training provided.
Recruitment: through *TES.* Interviews held in London.

HOMER ASSOCIATION
52 Academias St., 10677 Athens. Tel: (1) 362 2887.
Number of teachers: an average of 20 at each of the Association's 110 schools in Greece.
Preference of nationality: none.
Qualifications: BA or teacher's certificate and experience of TEFL.
Conditions of employment: 8-10 month contracts. 24-28 h.p.w. Pupils range in age from 9-16.
Salary: £400 per month plus Christmas, Easter and vacation bonuses.
Facilities/Support: assistance with accommodation mostly provided. Training given.
Recruitment: adverts in Athens newspapers. Local interviews only.

INSTITUTE OF ENGLISH, FRENCH, GERMAN AND GREEK FOR FOREIGNERS — ZAVITSANOU SOPHIA.
13 Joannou Gazi St., 31100 Lefkada. Tel: (645) 24514/25567.
Number of teachers: 2-3.
Preference of nationality: UK.

Qualifications: BA, RSA Cert., TEFL experience.
Conditions of employment: minimum 1 year contract, preferably longer. 21-28
h.p.w. Pupils aged from 6 upwards.
Salary: average £280 per month, negotiable.
Facilities/Support: assistance with accommodation. Training provided if
required.
Recruitment: adverts in *Guardian.* Local interviews essential.

INSTITUTE OF FOREIGN LANGUAGES — G. KARANTZOUNIS
41 Epidavrou St., 10441 Athens. Tel: (1) 514 2397.
Number of teachers: 5.
Preference of nationality: UK, US.
Qualifications: BA.
Conditions of employment: 1 academic year contracts from September to June.
20-25 h.p.w. mainly evening work. Pupils range in age from 8-16.
Salary: 100-120,000 drachmas per month.
Facilities/Support: assistance with accommodation. Training provided.
Recruitment: interviews essential, carried out in Athens or London.
UK contact: c/o 23 Ladbroke Road, London W11 (tel: 071-721 5614).

D. KOUTOUGERA KORRE
**4 Smyrnis St, Nea Philadelphia, 14341 Athens. Tel: (1) 251 1657/252
0854.**
Number of teachers: 3.
Preference of nationality: UK.
Qualifications: BA/Higher diploma in English/TEFL qualification.
Conditions of employment: minimum 8½ month contracts. 25 h.p.w. Pupils aged
from 8-18.
Salary: 80,000 drachmas per month plus holiday bonuses totalling 146,000
drachmas.
Facilities/Support: 1 bedroom furnished flat available as accommodation.
Training provided.
Recruitment: adverts in *TES.* Interviews not essential but sometimes carried
out in UK.

A. LYMBEROPOULOS ENGLISH LANGUAGE INSTITUTE
29 Pindarou St, 32200 Thebes. Tel: (262) 29191.
Number of teachers: 2.
Preference of nationality: UK.
Qualifications: TEFL certificate.
Conditions of employment: 9 month contracts (September-May). Approximately
28 contact h.p.w. Pupils aged 9-17. Private lessons easy to obtain and can increase
salary by nearly 50% if desired.
Salary: 90,000 drachmas per month (net).
Facilities/Support: free accommodation provided. Training given if necessary.
Recruitment: through adverts and teacher training colleges. UK interviews
possible.

MAKRI'S SCHOOL OF ENGLISH
2 Parados G Olympion St, 60100 Katerini. Tel: (351) 22859.
Number of teachers: 2-3.

Preference of nationality: UK, Ireland.
Qualifications: BA, TEFL qualification.
Conditions of employment: usually 1 year contracts. 30 h.p.w. Pupils range in age from 8-18.
Salary: 80,000 drachmas per month (1990).
Facilities/Support: assistance with accommodation. Training provided sometimes.
Recruitment: adverts in *Guardian*. Interviews sometimes possible in UK.

M. PERDIKOPOULOU-NEARCHOU
20 Av. Eleftheriou, 67100 Xanthi. Tel: (541) 25055/29454.
Number of teachers: 2.
Preference of nationality: UK, Ireland.
Qualifications: experienced TEFL teachers.
Conditions of employment: 1 academic year contracts from September to May. 30-32 h.p.w. Pupils range in age from 8-17.
Salary: according to cost of living.
Facilities/Support: assistance with accommodation. No training provided.
Recruitment: through *TES*. Interviews not essential.

SCHOOL OF FOREIGN LANGUAGES — LINDA LEE-NIKOLAOU
12 P. Isaldari St, Xylokastro, 20400 Korinth. Tel: (743) 24678/617276.
Number of teachers: 12.
Preference of nationality: UK, Ireland.
Qualifications: BA and RSA Cert, or equivalent; previous experience not essential but an advantage.
Conditions of employment: 1 academic year renewable contracts. 20-21 h.p.w., maximum 24 h.p.w. Hours of work 3-8pm weekdays.
Salary: 100-130,000 drachmas per month.
Facilities/Support: free flat provided. Training provided.
Recruitment: adverts in UK newspapers. Interviews usually essential and take place in UK in June/July.

SKOURAS SCHOOL OF FOREIGN LANGUAGES
AG Triados — Zalokosta 2, 54640 Thessaloniki. Tel: (31) 820866.
Number of teachers: 2.
Preference of nationality: UK.
Qualifications: BA, previous TEFL experience.
Conditions of employment: 8 month contracts. 32 h.p.w. Pupils range in age from 10-20.
Salary: £300-£400 per month plus holiday bonuses.
Facilities/Support: free furnished apartment provided. Training given.
Recruitment: through adverts in *TES*. Interviews essential and are held in UK.

PETER SFYRAKIS' SCHOOL OF FOREIGN LANGUAGES
21 Nikiforou Foka St., 72200 Ierapetra, Crete. Tel: (842) 28700.
Number of teachers: 1.
Preference of nationality: none.
Qualifications: BA or primary school teaching experience.
Conditions of employment: 20th June-20th September or 1st October-30th May.

Hours of work: 9am-12pm and 4-8pm. 30-40 h.p.w. Pupils mainly aged 8-18, adult groups occasionally.
Salary: 800-900 drachmas per hour plus bonuses, £150 deposit required to cover training expenses.
Facilities/Support: accommodation provided for 40/60,000 drachmas per month. Training given.
Recruitment: through adverts. Interviews are not essential.

THE STRATEGAKIS SCHOOLS OF LANGUAGES
24 Proxenou Koromila St., 54622 Thessaloniki. Tel: (31) 264 276.
Number of teachers: 50 in 100 schools all over Greece.
Preference of nationality: none.
Qualifications: BA/MA, PGCE (or equivalent). TEFL qualifications welcomed but not required.
Conditions of employment: 1 academic year renewable contracts. 26 h.p.w. Pupils mainly aged 9-17 although there are also some adult groups.
Salary: 100-130,000 drachmas per month (1990/1991).
Facilities/Support: assistance with accommodation. Training provided.
Recruitment: through advertising and UK agencies. Interviews essential and are held in UK.

THE A. TRECHAS LANGUAGE CENTRE
20 Koundouriotou St., Keratsini. Tel: (1) 432 0546. Also 34 Argostoliou St., Egaleo. Tel: (1) 561 7263.
Number of teachers: 4-5.
Preference of nationality: UK, Canada, Australia.
Qualifications: BA (English) or equivalent.
Conditions of employment: 9 month extendable contracts. Morning and afternoon work. Pupils aged between 9-24.
Salary: £350 per month plus £350 summer bonus.
Facilities/Support: assistance with accommodation. Training sometimes given.
Recruitment: through newspaper adverts and TEFL training centres. Interviews essential and are held abroad.

UNIVERSAL SCHOOL OF LANGUAGES
66 M.Alexandrou St., Panorama, 55200 Thessaloniki. Tel: (31) 941014.
Number of teachers: 1.
Preference of nationality: UK.
Qualifications: BA, TEFL qualification and experience.
Conditions of employment: 9 month contracts (September-June). 20-25 h.p.w. Monday to Friday. Pupils aged 7-18.
Salary: depending on qualifications, approximately 1,300 drachmas per hour or 100-120,000 drachmas per month.
Facilities/Support: training and help with accommodation.
Recruitment: through adverts in *TES*. UK interviews.
UK contact: C. Kondoyiannis, 484 Finchley Road, London NW11 8DE.

XENES GLOSSES XINI
98 Academias St., 10677 Athens. Tel: (1) 364 5115/6.
Preference of nationality: UK, US. Also Australia and Canada.

Conditions of employment: 8 month contracts (October-June), or part-time. School hours 8am-10pm, 3-9 hours work per day. Pupils from 18 years.
Salary: 1,200-1,800 drachmas per hour.
Facilities/Support: no assistance with accommodation. Training provided.
Recruitment: through local adverts and direct application. Local interviews only.

ZOULA LANGUAGE SCHOOLS
Sanroco Square, Corfu. Tel: (661) 39330/35894.
Number of teachers: 5.
Qualifications: BA (English), PGCE or TEFL qualification.
Conditions of employment: 9 month contracts. 28 h.p.w. Pupils range in age from 8-18.
Salary: 120-140,000 drachmas per month plus 1 month bonus.
Facilities/Support: much assistance with accommodation. Training provided.
Recruitment: through adverts in *TES*. UK interviews essential.
UK contact: 081-889 3646.

Italy

Learning English is almost as much a 1990s obsession in Italy as it is in Spain. Enrolment in language schools has increased by a fifth in the past year or two. Among young people there is an enormous interest in British and American music and "pop culture" generally. It is not just the sophisticated urbanites of Rome, Florence and Milan who long to learn English. Small towns in Sicily and Sardinia, in the Dolomites and along the Adriatic all have more than their fair share of private language schools and institutes. In fact of the jobs advertised in the *Guardian* and the *Times Educational Supplement* over a period of a few months in 1990, there were more in Sicily than in any other region. English teaching in the state system is generally acknowledged to be inadequate (pupils are taught English for an average of only 3 hours a week). So private schools flourish and are constantly on the lookout for educated English speakers.

Prospects for Teachers

There is an enormous range of language schools in Italy, as any *Yellow Pages* will confirm. At the elite end of the market, there is the handful of schools (about 30 but increasing) who belong to AISLI, the Associazione Italiana Scuole di Lingua Inglese, which is located at Via Campanella 16, 41100 Modena. Very strict regulations exclude all but ultra-respectable schools. A list of their members can be obtained from the Education Advisor at the Italian Institute in London (39 Belgrave Square, London SW1X 8NX). The majority of schools listed at the end of this chapter are members of AISLI. They demand advanced qualifications of their teachers and in return offer attractive remuneration and conditions of employment. Contracts with these schools are normally open-ended.

At the other end of the spectrum, there is a host of schools which some might describe as cowboy operations. For a job in one of these, TEFL qualifications are not always necessary, though even here the RSA Certificate is widely recognized and respected. (US qualifications are much less well known for the simple reason that work permits are virtually impossible for non-EEC citizens to obtain).

International organizations like Linguarama, Berlitz and inlingua are major providers of English language teaching in Italy, and regularly feed their "graduates" to their tied schools. Ian Abbott's experience is typical:

> *I signed up for a short TEFL course with inlingua in Birmingham. What rocked me was that after 4 days of being on this course, we were asked where we were hoping to teach. I was asked if I would consider a 12-month contract in Milan (which paid £700 a month).*

FIXING UP A JOB

In Advance

There is no compendium of the estimated 750 language school addresses in Italy. The British Council offices in Rome and Milan are not particularly helpful to aspiring teachers and at best will send the list of AISLI members and a letter explaining that British Council teachers are recruited in London for the DTOs in Milan and Naples. The Council office in Naples does have a rather out-of-date list of 15 or 20 language schools in the Naples area. Another possible source of language school addresses is the Associazione Italo-Britannica in the city where you want to work. International House has 18 affiliated schools, while the Bell Trust has schools in Bolzano, Trento and Riva.

The Connor TEFL Register in Milan specializes in matching teachers with language schools throughout Italy. Interested teachers (whether British or American) should send their c.v., a photograph and contact telephone number to Linda Kavanagh (Connor Register, Via Settembrini 1, 20124 Milan; tel: 2-670 0774/670 1192). The placement service is free to teachers. Many of their client schools turn to the Register when they have urgent vacancies especially in September and October but also throughout the year.

There are several Italian-based chains of language schools which you might try, such as the British Schools Group (Viale Liegi 14, 00198 Rome) which has about 75 branches and sometimes recruits through *English Worldwide*. The group of Cambridge Schools is represented in the UK by Cambridge Schools (Italy), 11 Cherry Orchard, Oakington, Cambridge. Other chains include Oxford Institutes, Oxford Schools, Wall Street Institutes and British Institutes; the latter's head office is at Piazzale Cadorna 9, 20123 Milan (tel: 2-720 0974). Recruitment organizations which occasionally advertise vacancies in Italy are *ELT Banbury, Anchor Language Services, Language Exchange, Language School Appointments* and *Nord-Anglia*. It might also be worth trying the Butler School (170 Victoria Street, London SW1E 5LB; tel: 071-834 0606), A. G. Harvey & Co. (36 Chesterfield Road, London W4 3HQ; tel: 081-995 2996) and Ruskin School Services Ltd. (40 Ardrossan Gardens, Worcester Park, Surrey KT4 7AU).

On the Spot

If the adverts in the Education *Guardian* and the *TES* do not turn anything up, the heading *Scuole de Lingua* in the Yellow Pages is the best source of possible employers. (These are available for public inspection and photocopying at the Italian Institute in London, 39 Belgrave Square, London SW1X 8NX). Or you can wait until you get to Italy, as Bruce Nairne and Sue Ratcliffe did:

> *Rather unimaginatively we packed our bags and made for Italy in the middle of the summer holidays when there was no teaching work at all. Nevertheless we utilized*

the Yellow Pages *in the SIP office (equivalent to British Telecom) in Syracuse and proceeded to make 30 speculative applications, specifying our status as graduates who had completed a short course in TEFL. By the end of September we had received 4 job offers without so much as an interview.*

Unfortunately the jobs in Bari which they chose to accept never materialized and so they once again resorted to the Yellow Pages, this time in Milan railway station, where they managed to secure the interest of 3 or 4 establishments for part-time work. Scouring adverts in English language newspapers in Italy usually yields nothing.

Without any kind of TEFL qualification, a speculative job hunt can be discouraging as Laurence Koe discovered. He visited all the language schools in Como and Lecco, some of them on several occasions, and was told that he needed a qualification or that he was there at the wrong time (October). After 3 weeks of making the rounds he was asked to stand in for an absent teacher on one occasion, and this was enough to secure him further part-time work. After a few more weeks he found work teaching an evening class of adults. He began to attend the weekly English Club and was offered a few thousand lire to answer questions on the plot after the showing of a James Bond film. Most towns have an English Club which may offer conversation classes and employ native speakers.

If you don't manage to sign a contract by early October, you will probably have to piece together part-time work for several employers. Although there is no job security this way, most people find that the longer they stay, the more hours they get.

Another posssibility is to set up as a freelance tutor, though a knowledge of Italian is even more of an asset here than it is for jobs in schools. You can post notices in supermarkets, tobacconists, primary and secondary schools, etc. As long as you have access to some premises, you can arrange both individual and group lessons, and undercut the language institutes significantly. The going wage for private tutors is 20,000-30,000 lire an hour in Rome, less elsewhere. The ever-enterprising Laurence Koe presented himself to a classroom teacher who asked her class of 12 and 13 years olds if they would like to learn English from a native. They all said Yes and paid Laurence the equivalent of 50p each for a class after school.

Whatever way you decide to look for work, remember that life grinds to a halt in August, just as in France. Competition is keenest in Rome, Florence and Venice, so job-seekers without an RSA qualification would be advised to bypass the major cities. On the other hand, Milan is known as a promising destination for the unqualified and also for Americans.

If you are in Rome, check the notice board at International House's training centre in Rome (Accademia Britannica, Viale Manzoni 57, 00185 Rome). As the major RSA teacher training institute in Italy (see page xx), they are often contacted by schools looking for teachers. Having decided that 5 days of training in Birmingham was not sufficient preparation for becoming an English teacher, Ian Abbott signed up for the RSA Certificate course in Rome and while there fixed up a summer job at a lakeside language camp. His conclusion after studying the notice board and keeping his ear to the ground was that only small schools in the sticks, who have been looking for a teacher for a long time without success, would welcome applications from unqualified teachers.

Universities throughout Italy employ foreigners as *lettori* (readers/lecturers). Although personal recommendation often plays a part in getting this work, it may be worth contacting various faculties directly and asking for work, preferably in September/October. There are probably around 1,000 *lettori*, on yearly contracts earning about the same as EFL teachers in private institutes. The rules were recently changed so that *lettori* are limited to a 3-year tenure, thereby pushing some long-term *lettori* out of the universities and creating increased competition for jobs in the private sector.

REGULATIONS

As mentioned above, non-EEC citizens have very little chance of getting their papers in order. Even EEC nationals are bedevilled by bureaucratic difficulties. According to a (fairly confusing) leaflet from the Italian Consulate in London, *General Information Regarding Living and Working in Italy,* there are three situations for EEC nationals wishing to work in Italy, though the *Ufficio Stranieri* of the *Questura* in Rome (Via Genova 2) indicates that the third requirement has been dropped:

1) For seasonal work or work which is not intended to last for more than 3 months, no permit is needed beyond the police registration within 8 days of arrival, which is compulsory for all foreigners including tourists, who normally have it done by their hotels.

2) If you prearrange a job in Italy, you apply in Italy for a *permesso di soggiorno* (residence permit) from the *questura* (police) and a *libretto di lavoro* (work permit) from the local *Anagrafe.* This normally takes between one and two months, though it can take up to 4 months.

In all cases you need documented proof of a contract of employment. Most schools are willing to provide a contract, though many are for just 8 months (October to May). This way the employer avoids having to pay the very high social security contributions which can cost him or her half as much of your salary again.

If you prearrange a job, you can smooth your way by asking the Italian Consulate to authenticate your degree and TEFL certificate before departure. The majority of language schools play by the rules and will guide you through the bureaucratic maze.

CONDITIONS OF WORK

Salaries are not as high as might have been expected because of the high cost of compulsory national insurance, social security and pension contributions mentioned above. But you may find your salary supplemented by various perks. Gross monthly salaries are normally between 1,400,000 and 1,600,000 lire (1,000,000 lire net). Perks can include free or subsidized housing and air fares, bonuses, luncheon vouchers (typically 100,000 lire a month) and generous holidays. Upmarket schools may offer free Italian tuition, and a subsidy to study for the RSA Diploma.

Help with accommodation is an especially valuable perk in the main cities where affordable accommodation is very scarce. Teachers in Rome, Milan, Bologna, etc. have had to reconcile themselves to spending up to half of their salaries on rent. Salaries tend to be substantially higher in northern Italy than in the south to compensate for the much higher cost of living.

After accepting a job, always insist on a detailed signed contract. There are many stories of disappointed teachers who turn up at a school which has hired them at the beginning of term only to be told that they are surplus to requirements.

Obviously the schools are trying to protect themselves against "no-shows", though this is small consolation if you find yourself jobless in some Calabrian town. This happens throughout the world, but it seems to happen more frequently in Italy.

LEISURE TIME

Italian culture and life style do not need to have their praises sung here. A large number of teachers who have gone out on short-term contracts never come back —probably a higher proportion than in any other country. While rents are high, eating out is cheap and wonderful and public transport is quite affordable. Women teacher should be prepared to cope with some Mediterranean *machismo*.

LIST OF SCHOOLS

ACCADEMIA BRITANNICA (INTERNATIONAL HOUSE)
Via Bruxelles 61, 04100 Latina. Tel: (773) 491 917.
Number of teachers: 3.
Preference of nationality: UK.
Qualifications: minimum RSA Cert. (grade 'B').
Conditions of employment: 9 month contracts from mid-September. 25 h.p.w. in the afternoons/evenings. Pupils aged between 8-60.
Salary: 1,100,000 lire per month (according to national contract).
Facilities/Support: assistance with shared accommodation (at a cost of about 250,000 lire a month). Training is possible.
Recruitment: through IH London. Interviews essential.

BLENHEIM SCHOOL OF ENGLISH
Borgo Pieve 88, 31033 Castelfranco Veneto (TV). Tel: (423) 494282.
Number of teachers: 2.
Preference of nationality: UK.
Qualifications: BA/RSA Cert. (or equivalent) plus 1-2 years experience.
Conditions of employment: 8 month renewable contracts (October-May). 24 contact h.p.w. Afternoon and evening work. Pupils aged from 8.
Salary: 1,000,000 lire per month.
Facilities/Support: free accommodation in a shared flat. No structured training given. This is a small school where individual contribution counts.
Recruitment: through adverts in *Guardian*. Interviews are essential and are held in London, usually at the end of July.

THE BRITISH INSTITUTE OF FLORENCE
Palazzo Feroni, Via Tornabuoni 2, Florence. Tel: (55) 298 866/284 033.
Number of teachers: 20.
Preference of nationality: none.
Qualifications: RSA Dip. plus at least 2 years experience, preferably including ESP.
Conditions of employment: 2 year contracts in first instance. 35 h.p.w. of which 23 are contact hours. Pupils from age 8.
Salary: from £8,500 per year (net).
Facilities/Support: excellent library. Italian tuition available. Assistance given with accommodation. In-house training provided.
Recruitment: interviews compulsory, occasionally held in UK.

THE BRITISH LANGUAGE CENTRE (INTERNATIONAL HOUSE)
Via Piazzi, Angolo Largo Pedrini, 23100 Sondrio. Tel: (342) 216 130. Fax: 513 236.
Number of teachers: 3-4.
Preference of nationality: UK.
Conditions of employment: minimum RSA Cert. with a good grade. Sense of humour necessary.
Salary: 1,100,000-1,400,000 lire per month (net) 14 times per year.
Facilities/Support: assistance with accommodation and training given. All contributions, health, tax, pension also paid.
Recruitment: through trade publications and IH London. Interviews carried out locally and in London.

BRITISH SCHOOL
Via Cottolengo 9, 13051 Biella. Tel: (15) 849 2566.
Number of teachers: 5.
Preference of nationality: UK.
Qualifications: BA plus RSA Cert.
Conditions of employment: open-ended contracts. 23 contact h.p.w. Pupils aged 7-70.
Salary: 1,000,000 lire per month.
Facilities/Support: assistance given with finding accommodation. In-house training given.
Recruitment: newspaper adverts in UK. Interviews available in UK.

BRITISH SCHOOL
Via dei Servi 2, 50122 Florence. Tel: (55) 218 252/3.
Also: Galleria Nazionale 21, 51100 Pistoia. Tel: (573) 367 317.
Number of teachers: 11.
Preference of nationality: UK.
Qualifications: RSA Dip. (or equivalent) plus 2 years experience.
Conditions of employment: open-ended contracts. 20 contact h.p.w., mainly in evenings. Pupils aged 17+.
Salary: 1,600,000 lire (gross).
Facilities/Support: in-house training and help with finding accommodation provided.
Recruitment: through direct application. Interviews are essential and are sometimes conducted in Britain.

BRITISH s.r.l.
Via XX Settembre 42, 16121 Genoa. Tel: (10) 593 591/562 621/587 469.
Also: Via Niella 6/1, 17100 Savona. Tel: (19) 827 830.
Number of teachers: 20.
Preference of nationality: EEC only.
Qualifications: BA plus RSA Cert. and minimum experience. Italian useful.
Conditions of employment: open-ended contracts after 4 month trial. 26-28 h.p.w. in afternoons and evenings. Most pupils aged 18-30.
Salary: 1,300,000 lire × 13 months plus severence pay for giving 3 months notice. 13th month paid holiday.

Facilities/Support: assistance given with finding accommodation and training provided.

Recruitment: adverts in *TES*. Interviews not essential, but usually take place in Italy.

CAMBRIDGE CENTRE OF ENGLISH
Via Campanella 16, 41100 Modena. Tel: (59) 241 004.
(Same address as AISLI.)

Number of teachers: 8.

Preference of nationality: UK.

Qualifications: BA plus TEFL certificate and 2 years experience.

Conditions of employment: open-ended contracts. 24 contact h.p.w. No overtime. Pupils are all ages.

Salary: from 1,500,000 lire gross per month. 14 months pay. 9 weeks paid holiday. Increments for higher qualifications and experience. All social security payments made.

Facilities/Support: furnished accommodation provided at low rental. Assistance given with RSA Dip. course.

Recruitment: through recommendation and direct applications, often via other AISLI schools. Interviews sometimes held in UK.

THE CAMBRIDGE SCHOOL
Via Mercanti 36, Salerno. Tel: (89) 228 942.

Number of teachers: 5.

Preference of nationality: none.

Qualifications: TEFL qualification/experience.

Conditions of employment: 2 year contracts. Hours of work 4-9pm. Pupils aged 8-25.

Salary: negotiable.

Facilities/Support: assistance with accommodation. Training provided if necessary.

Recruitment: through adverts. Interviews can take place in UK or locally.

CENTRO DI LINGUE MODERNE
Via Pozzo 30, 38100 Trento. Tel: (461) 981 733.

Number of teachers: 15.

Preference of nationality: UK.

Qualifications: BA/PGCE plus RSA Cert./Dip.

Conditions of employment: permanent contracts. 21 contact h.p.w. Pupils aged from 5 upwards.

Salary: 1,000,000 lire per month.

Facilities/Support: assistance given with finding accommodation. Training provided.

Recruitment: through newspaper adverts abroad. Interviews are essential and take place in UK.

IL CLUB DI LINGUA INGLESE
Corso Trieste 215, 81100 Caserta. Tel: (823) 326 225.

Number of teachers: 6-8.

Preference of nationality: UK, US.

Qualifications: BA and TEFL experience.
Conditions of employment: contracts run from October-June. Hours of work 3/4-8/9.30pm, with some morning classes. Pupils aged from 5.
Salary: £9 per hour (gross).
Facilities/Support: assistance with accommodation whenever possible. No training.
Recruitment: local interviews essential.

THE ENGLISH CENTRE
Via Dei Mille 18, 07100 Sassari, Sardinia. Tel: (79) 232 154.
Number of teachers: 8/9.
Preference of nationality: none.
Qualifications: BA, RSA Cert., 2/3 years experience abroad.
Conditions of employment: 2 year contracts. Mainly afternoon and evening work. Pupils aged 6-60.
Salary: based on the national contract.
Facilities/Support: assistance with accommodation. Training given.
Recruitment: adverts in *Guardian*. Interviews are essential and can be held in UK.

THE ENGLISH INSTITUTE (INTERNATIONAL HOUSE)
Via S. Martino 261, 98123 Messina. Tel: (90) 2935444.
Number of teachers: 3/4.
Preference of nationality: UK.
Qualifications: RSA Cert. and teaching experience.
Conditions of employment: permanent contracts. 25 h.p.w. Pupils aged from 11.
Salary: 1,000,000 lire per month (net).
Facilities/Support: assistance with accommodation. Training given.
Recruitment: through IH London. Interviews essential.

THE ENGLISH INSTITUTE
Corso Gelone 82, Siracuse, Sicily. Tel: (931) 60875.
Number of teachers: 4.
Preference of nationality: UK.
Qualifications: TEFL qualification/experience.
Conditions of employment: 1 academic year contracts. 25-27 h.p.w. Pupils aged 23-35.
Salary: varies according to experience.
Facilities/Support: assistance with accommodation. Training given.
Recruitment: through newspaper adverts. Interviews not always required.

ENGLISH LANGUAGE SCHOOLS ASSOCIATED
Corso Botta 36, 10015 Ivrea (TO), and schools at Aosta and Alessandria.
Preference of nationality: UK.
Qualifications: qualified teacher/TEFL qualification/experience and knowledge of Italian preferred, but intelligence and enthusiasm without qualifications will also be considered.
Conditions of employment: minimum 9 month contracts (September-June). 25 contact h.p.w. Pupils aged from 7, with the largest age group being 16+.
Salary: 1,300,000-1,500,000 lire per month (gross) plus Christmas bonus and end-of-contract gratuity.

Facilities/Support: single flats provided at Aosta and Alessandria at 350,000 lire per month and a shared flat available in Ivrea at 225,000 lire per month.
Recruitment: applications should be sent to Jennifer Hughes at A. G. Harvey Ltd, 36 Chesterfield Rd., London W4 (tel: 081-995 2968). Interviews held in London in the summer.

ENGLISH LANGUAGE STUDIO
Via Antonio Bondi 27, 40138 Bologna. Tel: (51) 347394.
Number of teachers: 5 full-time, 15 part-time.
Preference of nationality: none.
Qualifications: at least 1 year's experience, BA and TEFL qualification preferred.
Conditions of employment: 8 month contracts (October-June). Maximum 25 h.p.w., mainly evening work. Pupils mostly aged 30-50.
Salary: from 1,000,000 litre per month (net).
Facilities/Support: assistance with accommodation and training given.
Recruitment: local interviews if possible, if not then by phone. Also through Language Specialists International, Portsmouth (see page 60).

INTERNATIONAL HOUSE (CAMPOBASSO)
Via A. Grandi 7, Campobasso. Tel/Fax: (874) 63240.
Number of teachers: 10-15 (for summer camp in Campitello in the Dolomites).
Preference of nationality: UK.
Qualifications: TEFL qualification essential, and experience on summer camps.
Conditions of employment: contract for month of July. 6 hours work per day. Pupils aged 6-16.
Salary: approximately £500-£600.
Facilities/Support: accommodation provided. No training.
Recruitment: through IH London. Interviews essential.

INTERNATIONAL HOUSE (LIVORNO)
Piazza 1850 Rgt. Art. Folgore, 57100 Livorno. Tel: (586) 508 060.
Number of teachers: 4-5.
Preference of nationality: UK.
Qualifications: RSA Dip. and 2 years experience essential.
Conditions of employment: 8-12 month contracts. 24 contact h.p.w. Pupils are all adults.
Salary: 1,300,000 lire per month (net).
Facilities/Support: assistance with accommodation and training given.
Recruitment: through IH London. Interviews essential.

INTERNATIONAL HOUSE (TURIN)
Via Saluzzo 60, 10125 Turin. Tel: (11) 683 245.
Number of teachers: 20.
Preference of nationality: EEC only.
Qualifications: RSA Cert. minimum.
Conditions of employment: open-ended contracts. 24 contact hours per week. Pupils aged 8-80.
Salary: 1,500,000 lire per month.
Facilities/Support: help given with finding accommodation. Training seminars held once a month.
Recruitment: through IH, London.

LANGUAGE POINT (INTERNATIONAL HOUSE)
Via Balbo 4, 10023 Chieri (TO). Tel: (11) 942 4558/7001.
Number of teachers: 4.
Preference of nationality: none.
Qualifications: RSA Cert./Dip.
Conditions of employment: 1 year renewable contracts. 24 h.p.w. Pupils range in age from 4-12 and 16+.
Salary: 1,050,000 lire per month after tax.
Facilities/Support: assistance with accommodation. Some training provided.
Recruitment: through IH London, or (occasionally) locally in Turin. Interviews essential.

LORD BYRON COLLEGE
Via Sparano 102, 70121 Bari. Tel: (80) 232686.
Number of teachers: 15.
Preference of nationality: EEC.
Qualifications: BA, RSA Cert., 1 year's teaching experience abroad, knowledge of a foreign language and single status.
Conditions of employment: 5-10 month renewable contracts. 24-26 h.p.w. Pupils aged 7-70, most are in the 20-30 age group.
Salary: approximately 1,000,000 lire per month (net).
Facilities/Support: furnished, subsidized flat provided. Training given.
Recruitment: adverts in *TES*. Shortlisted candidates receive free travel to Bari for orientation and contract signing.

MODERN ENGLISH SCHOOL
Via Giordano Bruno 6, 45100 Rovigo. Tel: (425) 200266.
Number of teachers: 2 full-time, 2 part-time.
Preference of nationality: UK, US.
Qualifications: BA, TEFL qualification and 1-2 years experience.
Conditions of employment: 8 month contracts. 22 h.p.w.
Salary: 1,500,000 lire per month (net).
Facilities/Support: assistance given finding accommodatioin. Informal training provided.
Recruitment: adverts in *TES* and local newspapers. Interviews are essential and are carried out in UK if necessary.

MODERN ENGLISH STUDY CENTRE
Via Borgonuova 14, 40125 Bologna. Tel: (51) 227 523.
Number of teachers: 6.
Preference of nationality: UK.
Qualifications: minimum 3 years experience; RSA qualifications preferred.
Conditions of employment: open-ended contracts. 20-24 contact h.p.w. Pupils aged between 9-65.
Salary: according to AISLI i.e. from 1,500,000 lire per month (gross).
Facilities/Support: no help given with accommodation. Occasional seminars and workshops.
Recruitment: through direct application. Interviews in Italy essential.

OXFORD INSTITUTES ITALIANI
Via Don Bosco 22, 73100 Lecce. Tel: (832) 25571/45165.
Number of teachers: 7.
Preference of nationality: UK preferred, also Australia/New Zealand with a British passport.
Conditions of employment: 9 month contracts. Hours of work 3-9pm weekdays. Pupils aged 5-60.
Salary: approximately £900 per month (net).
Facilities/Support: free, furnished flat for 4 teachers provided (for females only). Training given.
Recruitment: through newspaper adverts. Interviews are essential and are held in London.

OXFORD SCHOOL
Via Degli Aranci 187, Sorrento (NA). Tel: (81) 878 3606.
Number of teachers: 5-6.
Preference of nationality: UK only.
Qualifications: 'A' Levels (minimum).
Conditions of employment: at least 1 year contracts. Hours of work vary from 2.30-9pm, 5/6 days per week. Pupils aged 7-60.
Salary: £7.50 per hour plus holidays, a month's bonus, pension contribution and paid sick leave.
Facilities/Support: assistance given finding accommodation if necessary. Training provided.
Recruitment: through direct application. Local interviews essential.

OXFORD SCHOOL OF ENGLISH
San Marco 1513, 30120 Venice. Tel: (41) 521 0288. Fax: 521 0785.
Number of teachers: 50-60 in the organization's 15 schools throughout Italy.
Preference of nationality: none.
Qualifications: BA or TEFL qualification.
Conditions of employment: 4-month trial period after which contract becomes permanent. 22 h.p.w. Pupils aged 6-60.
Salary: in accordance with the national contract.
Recruitment: adverts in UK. Interviews essential and usually held in London.

REGENT SCHOOL (INTERNATIONAL HOUSE)
Via Uguccione da Pisa 6, 20145 Milan. Tel: (2) 46 92 419.
Number of teachers: 6.
Preference of nationality: UK.
Qualifications: RSA Cert. (grade 'B') minimum.
Conditions of employment: open-ended contracts. 25 contact h.p.w. Pupils aged from 6.
Salary: 1,250,000 lire per month, 14 times per year.
Facilities/Support: assistance with accommodation and training given.
Recruitment: locally and through IH London. Interviews essential.

REGENT SCHOOL (INTERNATIONAL HOUSE)
Corso Italia 54, 21047 Saronno. Tel: (2) 960 9696.
Number of teachers: 6.
Preference of nationality: UK.

Qualifications: minimum RSA Cert. plus experience.
Conditions of employment: open-ended contracts, 24-28 contact h.p.w. Classes for adults, children and company members.
Salary: 1,175,000 lire per month plus 100,000 lire in luncheon vouchers.
Facilities/Support: guidance provided by full-time Director of Studies with regular workshops and encouragement to attend outside seminars.
Recruitment: adverts in *Guardian*. Interviews carried out by IH, London.

STUDIO LINGUISTICO FONEMA
Via Marconi 19, 50053 Sovigliana-Vinci (FI). Tel: (571) 500551.
Number of teachers: 2.
Preference of nationality: none.
Qualifications: BA, some teaching experience preferable.
Conditions of employment: 9-10 month renewable contracts. 18-24 h.p.w. in the afternoons and evenings. Pupils aged 6-60 in classes of maximum 8.
Salary: 12,500 lire per hour (net).
Facilities/Support: assistance with accommodation. Training given.
Recruitment: local interviews required.

UNIVERSAL SCHOOL
Via A. Manzoni 9, Trav, XXV Aprile, 88079 Crotone (CZ).
Tel: (962) 22159.
Number of teachers: 1.
Preference of nationality: none.
Qualifications: BA, TEFL qualification and relevant experience.
Conditions of employment: 9 month contracts. 25 contact h.p.w. afternoon/evening work weekdays. Pupils aged 8-40.
Salary: approximately 1,200,000 lire per month.
Facilities/Support: assistance with accommodation and training given. Income tax and insurance paid.
Recruitment: adverts in *Guardian*. Interviews are essential and can be held in UK.

WALL STREET INSTITUTE
Corso V. Emanuele 30, 20122 Milan. Tel: (2) 76013959.
Number of teachers: 40-50.
Preference of nationality: EEC countries or those from elsewhere who already have work permits.
Conditions of employment: contracts run until 30th June of each year. 25 h.p.w. Pupils range in age from 17-65.
Salary: from 1,300,000 lire (net) per month.
Facilities/Support: 2 school flats are available, otherwise assistance is given finding accommodation. A limited amount of training is available.
Recruitment: through direct application, agencies and adverts.

Portugal

Portugal offers an attractive alternative to the rat race of teaching and visa-chasing in Spain. Relations between Portugal and Britain have always been warm and there is a continuing strong demand for English tuition especially among children (or at least parents on behalf of their children). Most schools cater for anyone over the age of 7, so you should be prepared to teach little ones. In fact one of the schools in the directory, *Euritmia,* has mounted courses in Oporto's nursery schools for children from the age of 4.

Although the vast majority of British tourists go to the south of Portugal and you would therefore expect Portuguese people on the Algarve to want to learn English, the demand for English teachers is mostly in the north. Apart from in the main cities of Lisbon and Oporto, both of which have British Council offices, jobs crop up in historic provincial centres such as Coimbra (where there is also a British Council) and Braga and in small seaside towns like Aveiro and Póvoa do Varzim. These can be a very welcome destination for teachers burned out from teaching in big cities.

FIXING UP A JOB

Most teachers in Portugal have either answered adverts in the educational press or are working for one of the major organizations like International House (which has 7 affiliated schools in Portugal) or Linguarama (which own the chain of Cambridge Schools in 6 locations). Of course schools are willing to hire native speakers locally, though outside the cities where there have traditionally been large expatriate communities, they cannot depend on English speakers just showing up and so must recruit well in advance of the academic year (late September to July). Newspaper adverts are much more commonly used than recruitment agencies. One exception is the Bristol Schools Group (of which the *Instituto de Linguas da Maia* is a member) which recruits through South West English (Pill, Bristol BS20 0AA; tel: 027-581 3814) as well as directly. This is the only possibility of which we have heard for working in the Azores, so if you want to work in the most isolated islands in the Atlantic Ocean (760 miles west of Portugal) this is your chance.

Small groups of schools, say six schools in a single region, is the norm in Portugal. A number of the 17 schools listed in the directory at the end of this chapter belong to such mini-chains. English Schools in Portugal (ESP) at Apartado 102, 2100 Coruche (tel: 43-63977) runs an employment service as well as various other services for Portuguese language schools such as importing teaching materials and providing English language entertainment.

The British Council in Oporto is helpful and will send a list of about 50 English language teaching schools in Northern Portugal. Speculative enquiries to these addresses may well succeed if sent in plenty of time, though many schools are small family-run establishments with fewer than 10 teachers, so opportunities are not endless. The British Council in Lisbon runs courses at the Instituto Britanico (Rua Luis Fernandes 3) and may be able to advise on English schools in and around Lisbon.

As is true anywhere, you might be lucky and fix up something on the spot. Call at the *British Council* and also check the English language weekly newspaper

Anglo-Portuguese News which occasionally carries adverts for private tutors. The RSA Prep. Cert. is widely requested by schools and in fact can be obtained after 4 weeks of study at International House in Lisbon (see page 33). But a number of schools (especially those advertising vacancies in June, July and August) seem willing to consider anyone with a BA plus a promising c.v. and photo. A few chains offer their own intensive training, for instance the schools group seen advertising in the *EFL Gazette* and *TES* in 1990, at P.O. Box 2965, 1124 Lisboa Codex, Portugal.

REGULATIONS

Like Spain, Portugal joined the European Community in 1986 but the free exchange of labour will not be allowed until January 1993. Until then, teachers must obtain a work permit, which is more straightforward than it is in Spain. The teacher must contact the Portuguese Consulate or Embassy in his or her home country and sort out some preliminary documentation. After arrival the teacher takes the contract of employment to the *Serviço de Estrangeiros* (Aliens Office) in Lisbon at 18 Avenida António Augusto de Aguiar or to the local police. The permit obtained here is sent off together with the contract of employment to the Ministry of Labour. The final stage is to take a letter of good conduct provided by the teacher's own embassy to the police for the work and residence permit. Although all of this sonds very complicated, most schools claim that it does not take long and involves little bureaucratic hassle.

No employment permits are needed for private English teachers or governesses. EC passport holders do not need a visa for visits of up to 60 days. You can extend this twice at the Serviço de Estrangeiros but thereafter must prove to the authorities that you have some means of support.

Deductions for tax and health insurance are about 25% of your salary.

CONDITIONS OF WORK

The consensus seems to be that wages are low, and the cost of living is not as low as it once was. On the positive side, working conditions are generally relaxed. Some schools base their salary scale on local state school salaries which usually represent the legal minimum for teachers, approximately 80,000 escudos a month with a subsidy for accommodation amounting to about 20,000 escudos. International House pays a starting salary of 93,000 escudos in small towns and 120,000 escudos in Lisbon. Teachers working part-time and being paid on an hourly basis should expect to earn between 1,100 and 2,000 escudos an hour.

Contracts are for a minimum of 9 months though some are for a calendar year. A few schools will pay for your flights (from the UK) and for at least part of your accommodation, though this is not usual. The only school we have heard of which has its own accommodation for teachers is the IH-affiliated school in the small inland town of Viseu. They offer furnished 2-person flats for 17,000 escudos a month (each) plus bills of about 6,000 escudos. This represents less than quarter of the salary, which is quite a favourable percentage. Elsewhere you should expect to pay at least 20,000 escudos for a room in a shared house.

LIST OF SCHOOLS

AMERICAN LANGUAGE INSTITUTE
Av. Duque de Loulé, 22-1⁰, 1000 Lisbon. Tel: (1) 521535.

Number of teachers: 30
Preference of nationality: US.
Qualifications: BA.
Conditions of employment: 1 year renewable contracts. School open from 8am-9pm. Pupils range in age from 16-70.
Salary: average US$800 per month.
Facilities/Support: assistance with accommodation given. Training provided.
Recruitment: interviews take place in US.

AMERICAN LANGUAGE INSTITUTE
Rua José Falcão 15, 5⁰, 4000 Oporto. Tel: (2) 318127.
Number of teachers: 15.
Qualifications: minimum RSA Cert, or equivalent.
Conditions of employment: 1 year contracts. Hours of work 5-9.30pm. Pupils range in age from 16 upwards.
Salary: between US$750-1,050 per 18hr week depending on experience.
Facilities/Support: no assistance with accommodation. Training provided.
Recruitment: interviews held at TESOL convention.

BRISTOL SCHOOL
Instituto de Linguas da Maia & Ermesinde, Rua Dr. Carlos Pires Felgueiras, No. 12-3⁰, 4470 Maia. Tel: (2) 9488803.
Comprises a group of 6 small schools: 3 near Oporto, 2 in the Azores Islands and 1 in Castelo Branco.
Number of teachers: 14.
Preference of nationality: UK.
Qualifications: BA and TEFL qualification.
Conditions of employment: minimum period of work October-June, 25 h.p.w. Pupils aged from 8 upwards.
Salary: 90,000 escudos net per month plus end of contract bonus.
Facilities/Support: assistance with accommodation given. No training.
Recruitment: through advertising in *TES*, etc. and via South West English, Pill, Brisol BS20 0AA (tel: 027 581 3814).

CIAL CENTRO DE LINGUAS
Av. da Republica, 14-2⁰, 1000 Lisbon. Tel: (1) 533733. Fax: 3523096.
Number of teachers: 10-20.

Preference of nationality: UK, US.
Qualifications: BA, TEFL qualification and experience.
Conditions of employment: 9 month contracts (October-June). Pupils aged 24-50.
Salary: 100,000 escudos per month.
Facilities/Support: advice given on finding accommodation. Training provided.
Recruitment: through direct application and TEFL institutes. Interviews essential and usually held in UK.

ENCOUNTER ENGLISH
Av. Fernao de Magalhaes, 604, 4300 Oporto. Tel: (2) 567916.
Number of teachers: 12.
Preference of nationality: UK.
Qualifications: RSA Cert., degree, and minimum 1 year's TEFL experience.
Conditions of employment: 9 month contracts. 32 h.p.w. total work time. Pupils of all ages.
Salary: up to 1,500,000 escudos for 9 months plus return air fare.
Facilities/Support: assistance with accommodation given. Training provided.
Recruitment: local and UK adverts. Interviews normally in UK.

ENGLISH CENTRE
Rua Eng. Custodio Vilsboas, 4740 Esposende. Tel: (53) 961373.
Number of teachers: 2.
Preference of nationality: UK.
Qualifications: TEFL qualification.
Conditions of employment: 9 month contracts. 15 h.p.w. Pupils range in age from 10 upwards.
Salary: based on local rates and increase annually.
Facilities/Support: no assistance with accommodation. No training.
Recruitment: through local advertising. Interviews held in Portugal.

THE ENGLISH CENTRE
Apartado 73, 5001 Vila Real Codex. Tel: (59) 71236.
Number of teachers: 4.
Preference of nationality: UK.
Conditions of employment: 9 month contracts. Hours of work 6-9pm. Pupils range in age from 8-45.
Salary: paid on an hourly basis at approximately £7 per hour.
Facilities/Support: assistance with accommodation given. No training.
Recruitment: through local adverts. Interviews held in UK.

THE ENGLISH SCHOOL OF CORUCHE
Rua dos Guerreiros 11, 2100 Coruche. Tel: (43) 63977.
Number of teachers: 4.
Preference of nationality: UK.
Qualifications: BA, PGCE, 1-2 years TEFL experience. Should be lively, smiley and efficient.
Conditions of employment: 1 academic year contracts. Minimum 20 h.p.w. Pupils aged between 7-65.
Salary: hourly pay which varies according to experience.

Facilities/Support: accommodation provided. Training given if necessary.
Recruitment: through newspaper adverts. Interviews held in UK.

EURITMIA INTERNACIONAL
Rua de Gondarém. 577 R/C Dto., 4100 Oporto. Tel: (2) 677292.
Number of teachers: up to 1º.
Preference of nationality: none.
Qualifications: at least 2 years teaching experience plus TEFL qualification.
Conditions of employment: 1 year renewable contracts. 20-25 h.p.w. Pupils
range in age from 4-60.
Salary: varies from 100,000-125,000 escudos per month depending on experience.
Facilities/Support: assistance with accommodation given. Training provided.
Recruitment: through advertising locally and in the *TES*. Interviews are held
locally, otherwise over the phone.

IF-INGLES FUNCIONAL
Av. do Vidreiro, 95, 1º, dto., 2430 Marinha Grande. Tel: (44) 503977.
Number of teachers: 6.
Preference of nationality: Ireland.
Qualifications: TEFL qualification, degree, and 1 year's experience teaching
abroad.
Conditions of employment: 9 month contracts. 22-24 h.p.w. Pupils aged from
8 years to adults, the latter tending to be of a poor standard.
Salary: 80,000 escudos per month plus accommodation costs.
Facilities/Support: training provided. Strong emphasis on computers and videos.
Recruitment: through newspaper adverts. Interviews not essential; good
references are.

INSTITUTO AUDIO VISUAL
**Praça Mouzinho Albuquerque, 127-1º Esq., 4100 Oporto.. Tel: (2)
696744/6000252.**
Number of teachers: approximately 7.
Preference of nationality: UK.
Qualifications: TEFL qualification and teaching experience.
Conditions of employment: flexible working hours; mostly evening work. Pupils
aged 12 upwards.
Salary: dependent on qualifications and experience.
Facilities/Support: no assistance with accommodation is given. Training
provided.
Recruitment: through direct application. Local interviews essential.

INSTITUTO BRITANICO
Rua Conselheiro Januário, 119, 4700 Braga. Tel: (53) 23298.
Number of teachers: 7.
Preference of nationality: UK, US, Canada, Australia, South Africa.
Qualifications: RSA Cert.
Conditions of employment: 1 year contracts. Hours of work 9am-9pm. Pupils
from age 8.
Salary: £406 per month.
Facilities/Support: no assistance with accommodation. Training provided.
Recruitment: through adverts. Local interviews essential.

INSTITUTO SUPERIOR DE ASSISTENTES E INTÉRPRETES
Rua António Pedro, 24, 4000 Oporto. Tel: (2) 316465/316566.
Number of teachers: 3.
Preference of nationality: none.
Qualifications: BA, TEFL qualification and experience.
Conditions of employment: 1 year renewable contracts. 22 h.p.w. Pupils range in age from 19-25.
Salary: varies according to qualifications. BAs earn 2,000 escudos per hour.
Facilities/Support: no assistance with accommodation. No training provided.
Recruitment: through direct application. Local interviews essential.

INTERNATIONAL HOUSE
Rua dos Chaos, 168, 4700 Braga. Tel: (53) 74279.
Number of teachers: 7.
Preference of nationality: UK.
Qualifications: BA plus RSA Cert. (Grade 'B').
Conditions of employment: 9 month contracts. 24 h.p.w. Pupils range from 7-60 years.
Salary: 102,000 escudos per month.
Facilities/Support: assistance with accommodation. Training provided.
Recruitment: interviews take place through IH, London.

INTERNATIONAL HOUSE
Rua Antero de Quental 135, 3000 Coimbra. Tel: (39) 22971/34009.
Number of teachers: 11.
Preference of nationality: UK.
Qualifications: BA, RSA Cert.
Conditions of employment: 9 month contracts. 22 contact h.p.w. Pupils aged from 8.
Salary: 136,500 escudos per month.
Facilities/Support: assistance with accommodation. Training given.
Recruitment: through IH, London. Interviews required.

INTERNATIONAL HOUSE
Rue Marqués Sá Da Bandeira 16, 1000 Lisbon. Tel: (1) 571496.
Number of teachers: 21.
Preference of nationality: none.
Qualifications: RSA Cert. minimum.
Conditions of employment: standard length of stay 9 months. Flexible working hours to include evening work. Pupils range in age from 8-80.
Salary: 136,800 escudos per month for 1st year teachers.
Facilities/Support: assistance with accommodation. Training provided.
Recruitment: through local adverts and by IH, London.

INTERNATIONAL HOUSE
Rua dos Casimiros 33, 3500 Viseu. Tel: (32) 27720/27819.
Number of teachers: 7.
Preference of nationality: EEC passport-holders preferred.
Qualifications: minimum RSA Cert. (grade 'B'), BA/PGCE.
Conditions of employment: 9-12 month contracts. Maximum 24 contact h.p.w. Pupils aged 8-50.

Salary: from 110,000 escudos per month.
Facilities/Support: assistance with accommodation. Training given.
Recruitment: through IH, London. Interviews required.

IPFEL
Edith Cável 8, 1900 Lisbon. Tel: (1) 814 8864/5.
Number of teachers: 4.
Preference of nationality: none.
Qualifications: RSA Cert. and minimum 1 year TEFL experience.
Conditions of employment: full-time work rarely available. Hours of work 6-9pm and Saturdays 8am-2pm or 2-8pm. Pupils range in age from 13-40.
Salary: payment is on an hourly basis from 1000 escudos.
Facilities/Support: no assistance with accommodation. Training provided.
Recruitment: through adverts and RSA contacts in Lisbon. Local interviews essential.

LANCASTER COLLEGE
Praceta 25 de Abril, 35-1° Esq., Vila Nova de Gaia. Tel: (2) 306495/307201.
Number of teachers: 11.
Preference of nationality: none.
Qualifications: RSA Cert. Evangelical Christian teachers preferred.
Conditions of employment: 1 year renewable contracts. Approximately 22 h.p.w. Pupils range in age from 7-70.
Salary: £4.50 per hour.
Facilities/Support: assistance with accommodation. No training provided at present.
Recruitment: through recruitment agencies. Interview is not essential.

LINGUACULTURA
Largo Padre Francisco Nunes Silva, Santarem. Tel: (43) 24981.
Number of teachers: 15-20 total in group of 5 schools.
Preference of nationality: none.
Qualifications: RSA Cert. plus minimum of 1 year's TEFL experience.
Conditions of employment: period of work from September - June, 21-27 h.p.w. Hours vary from morning to late evening work.
Salary: 1,100-1,500 escudos per hour.
Facilities/Support: assistance with accommodation. No training at present.
Recruitment: advertising through *TES*. Interviews occasionally held in UK. Linguacultura is a group of 5 schools located in Santarem, Abrantes, Torres Novas, Vila Nova de Ourem, and Leiria.

LINGUAGEM
Rua Almirante, Candido Dos Reis, No. 8-10, 2870 Montijo. Tel: (1) 2313611.
Number of teachers: 10.
Preference of nationality: UK.
Qualifications: TEFL experience essential.
Conditions of employment: 1 year contracts. 16-25 h.p.w. Pupils range in age from 5-65.
Salary: 900 escudos per hour.

Facilities/Support: assistance with accommodation. No training.
Recruitment: through advertising in newspapers. Interviews are not essential.

MANITOBA
Avenida Mousinho de Albuquerque, Centro Commercial Premar, 4490 Póvoa de Varzim. Tel: (52) 683014.
Number of teachers: 4-5.
Preference of nationality: UK, US, Canada.
Qualifications: BA and TEFL experience.
Conditions of employment: 1-2 year contracts. 24 h.p.w. Pupils range in age from 7-50.
Salary: above average for Portugal.
Facilities/Support: assistance with accommodation. Training sometimes provided.
Recruitment: adverts in UK, US and Canadian newspapers. Interview not essential, but sometimes held in UK and US.

THE NEW INSTITUTE OF LANGUAGES
Urb. da Portela Lt. 197-5° B/C, 2685 Sacavém. Tel: (1) 943 52 38 38.
Number of teachers: 15.
Preference of nationality: UK.
Qualifications: BA, RSA Cert. or equivalent, or successful completion of the organization's own course.
Conditions of employment: period of work September-July. 4-5 hours per day between 3-9pm. Pupils range in age from 8 upwards but 80% are teenagers/young adults.
Salary: £600 per month plus cost of return flight.
Facilities/Support: assistance with accommodation. Training provided.
Recruitment: through adverts in the *TES*. Interviews held in UK.

PEC — PROFICIENCY ENGLISH CENTRE
Rua Sá da Bandeira, 538-5°, 4000 Oporto. Tel: (2) 2005077.
Number of teachers: 12.
Preference of nationality: UK, but also US, South Africa, Southern Ireland, etc.
Qualifications: RSA Cert.
Conditions of employment: 1 year renewable contracts, 22 h.p.w. Age range of pupils from 7 upwards.
Salary: negotiable.
Facilities/Support: assistance with accommodation. Training provided.
Recruitment: through adverts in newspaper. Interviews held in UK.

Scandinavia

Certain similarities exist in EFL throughout Scandinavia (apart from teachers in northern towns finding the long winter an ordeal). The standard of English teaching in state schools is uniformly high, as anyone who has met a Dane or a Swede travelling abroad will know. Yet many ordinary Scandinavians keep up their English by attending evening classes, if only for social reasons. Sweden, Denmark and Norway have excellent facilities for such people, which are variations on the theme of "folk university", a state-subsidized system of adult education. Classes at such institutions are the ideal setting for enthusiastic amateur teachers.

But things are changing as everywhere in Europe and the market for the English language is now located more firmly in business. Enthusiastic amateurs tend to be less in demand in this setting than more mature professional teachers. Yet Scandinavia is not a very popular destination for such teachers, despite its unspoilt countryside and efficient public transport. So there is scope for most kinds of teacher to work in Scandinavia, particularly in Finland, whose language schools frequently advertise in the British press.

None of the Scandinavian countries except Denmark is a member state of the EEC, and therefore American teachers are equally popular.

FINLAND

Although Finland's second language is Swedish, English runs a close second. English is taught in every kind of educational institution from trade and technology colleges to universities, but especially in commercial colleges (*Kauppaloulu*) and in Civic and Workers' Institutes. Private language schools flourish too and traditionally have not been too fussy about the paper qualifications of their native speaker teachers.

Fixing up a Job

The Finnish Embassy in London will send an up-to-date list of 16 language schools which hardly overlaps with the British Council's list of 20 private language schools in Helsinki. One of the key organizations in Finland is the Federation of Finnish-British Societies (Puistokatu 1 b A, 00140 Helsinki; tel: 639625) which takes on a substantial number of staff for its busy teaching centre and off-site contracts. In-company teaching is generally very popular in Finland and becoming more so.

Another major employer which advertises at regular intervals is *Linguarama*. Graduates of Linguarama's introductory training course in Britain are often encouraged to consider Finland for their posting abroad; the Linguarama office at King's Court, The Broadway, Winchester SO23 9JX handles vacancies in Finland. A typical advert placed by an independent Finnish language school might read "BA and TEFL preferred", a suitably vague requirement to encompass most university graduates. A recent advert for a Lektor at Joensuu University asked for no higher qualifications than these. A surprisingly high percentage of adverts are for schools outside Helsinki, presumably because there are not many residential expatriates in towns like Tampere or Hameenlinna.

One agency which recruits teachers to teach executives and professional people in Finland is Richard Lewis Communications plc, 107 High Street, Winchester, Hants. SO23 9AH.

Finding work after arrival in Finland would not be too difficult were it not for the problem of work permits (see below). As long as you were prepared to leave the country while your visa application was being processed, this would be fine. Vuorikatu, a major street in Helsinki, is a good hunting-ground since it houses several language schools (for example at numbers 8A, 16A and 22A). There is also demand for private tutoring which you could fix up by advertising in the usual way.

Regulations

Before you can work, you must obtain both a residence and work permit from outside Finland. The rules are seldom flouted since both employer and employee become subject to steep fines and possible imprisonment. The Embassy leaflet on work permits explains the application procedures, which are that the contract of employment, certificates of qualifications and photos must be forwarded to the Ministry of the Interior who alert the Embassy of their decision after 4-6 weeks. The permit will be for an initial period of 3 months, with the possibility of renewal.

Conditions of Work

The usual contract is for 9 months from September. A teaching unit of 45 minutes is the norm, with less evening work than elsewhere. Unexpectedly, a number of schools, including the Finnish-British Society, pay travel expenses and arrange furnished accommodation. Rents are calculated according to floor areas; reckon on roughly 70 markka per square metre (which includes heating). Wages are high, but so is the cost of living. Gross monthly salaries are often about £1,000. Teachers paid by the lesson can expect between 100 and 150 markka for 45 minutes. Tax will be at a rate of between 20% and 28%. It should be possible to save a certain amount on such a salary in order to finance trips into the unspoiled environment of Finland's interior and into neighbouring Soviet republics (though weekend excursions of Finns into the Soviet Union are famous mainly as drinking binges).

SWEDEN

The Folkuniversity of Sweden has a long-established scheme (since 1955) by which British teachers are placed for one or two years in its network of adult education centres all over the country. There are 5 university extension departments (called Kursverksamhet or KV), located in Stockholm, Gothenburg, Lund, Uppsala and Umeå, though they have branches throughout Sweden. The scheme is also referred to as the "British Centre" which is slightly confusing since there is no single Centre. KVs traditionally teach general English to a wide range of Swedes. Paul Greening was a British Centre teacher who taught "coffee and cake classes to housewives" as well as teaching "teenagers, businessmen, old aged pensioners and out-of-work semi-alcoholics". It is perhaps regrettable that business people are coming to dominate this varied list, and light-hearted conversational evenings, known as "study circles" in Sweden, are turning into something more earnest. It is probably more fun to teach people who are there for an evening outing of socializing than people who want to be able to swing better business deals.

Anyone interested in teaching in Sweden should obtain the admirably clear and informative brochure put out by International Language Services (36 Fowlers Road, Salisbury, Wilts. SP1 2QU; tel: 0722 331011), the UK representative of the Folkuniversity recruitment scheme. The fact that their brochure looks as though it might have been produced by the tourist board, complete with photos of Swedish forests, lakes and folk dances, is a good indication that the scheme is not wildly oversubscribed. Neither are International Language Services so well known that they do not need to advertise occasionally in the *TES*.

Fixing up a Job

With at least 20 jobs a year, mostly from September but also from January, the Folkuniversity offers the best chance to anyone aged 22-40 of fixing up work in Sweden. There are two levels of job in the Folkuniversity. The majority are Type B and are open to anyone with a BA and initial TEFL qualification (such as an RSA Certificate). Type A are more highly paid senior posts open only to RSA Diploma holders, preferably with some business English experience. The British Centre energetically encourages the "embryonic EFL teacher" to apply and promises to provide a good career start, which it generally does. Paul Greening found that his interviewer in London was more concerned to establish that he would be willing to stick it out in Sundsvall (northern Sweden) for a year and then Umeå the second year than to see his TEFL qualifications (which were nil though Paul did have a teaching qualification).

Anyone who does not want to work through the British Centre can request a list of language schools from the British Council in Stockholm, though this consists mostly of the individual Kursverksamheten addresses for which International Language Services recruit and also all the departments of English at Swedish universities. The British Council also refers enquirers to the British Institute at Hagagatan 3, 11348 Stockholm, which is associated with the Bell Educational Trust and therefore has its own internal source of teaching staff.

As in Finland, it would prove easy to fix up work, including lucrative freelance work, once you have arrived in Sweden, were it not for the difficulty over work permits. Apparently many British Centre teachers do teach privately to supplement their incomes, though technically this is forbidden by the terms of their visa.

Regulations

Anyone accepted as a British Centre teacher does not have to worry unduly about obtaining a work permit. Participating institutes apply collectively for their appointees' permits to a granting body which includes representatives from the two teaching unions to which the Folkuniversity is affiliated. All the paper work must be done outside Sweden, and it takes up to 6 weeks. The work permit will be valid for 9 months, and renewable up to a maximum of 2 years.

Other people who want to settle in Sweden may be able to obtain permission to teach, provided they can persuade the authorities that they are in a stable relationship (which need not be marriage) with a Swedish citizen.

There used to be a reciprocal tax agreement between Britain and Sweden; however it was rescinded in 1985 and now teachers must pay the full amount of the fixed state tax plus the municipal tax which varies from place to place. This will probably amount to about a third of your gross earnings.

Conditions of Work

One reason why teachers are not queuing to work in the Folkuniversity of Sweden is the low pay. The negotiated wage for 1990 was 92.15 krona per 45 minute lesson, which is about half of the going rate elsewhere in Scandinavia. Paul Greening found it difficult to make ends meet:

The accommodation which was provided was good but expensive. The poor wages were a problem. I always had to think about prices and look for the cheapest. I was able to save money only because I started a large number of teenage courses for which I was paid extra. In the summer there was a 3-month unpaid holiday which was difficult.

The Folkuniversity guarantees 720 hours of work over the 9 month contract. Hours in excess of this figure of 80 hours per month are paid extra. The teaching schedule is not normally onerous, though it may involve some travelling, perhaps even to neighbouring towns. It may also include some promoting of KV courses to increase enrolment.

The outgoing journey from Britain to Sweden by rail and boat is paid for and, if you stay 2 years, the return is paid as well. International Language Services also organize a free orientation course at the Salisbury School of English in Salisbury which covers not only teaching methods but life in Sweden and a smattering of the language.

Even people who learn some Swedish find it difficult to make friends. Most find Swedes fairly reserved, a problem that is not helped by the fact that there are few places to meet the locals outside the classroom, since drinking and eating out are so expensive. You should be willing to put up with your own company for long periods, especially in the north of the country during the 7 months of the winter when the locals either hibernate or devote all their leisure to skiing. Anyone who enjoys outdoor activities will probably enjoy a stint in Sweden, especially hill-walkers and other hikers, who take advantage of the *Allemannsrätt*, the law which guarantees free access to the countryside for everyone.

DENMARK

Because of Denmark's membership in the European Community, you might have expected a larger presence of British EFL teachers than in the other Scandinavian countries. But this does not seem to be the case. There is little recruitment of English teachers outside Denmark, apart from the *Cambridge Institute Foundation* which is Denmark's largest EFL institution and specializes in English for business. Many schools expect their teachers to speak Danish, and there seem to be enough fully bilingual candidates resident in Denmark to satisfy this requirement. If Britons do go to Denmark to look for work at least they will have no trouble regularizing their status. Having qualifications is essential.

The British Council in London publishes one of its £20 *Surveys of English Language Teaching and Learning* for Denmark. There is a strong emphasis in Denmark on preparing candidates for the Cambridge exams, and the list of schools supplied by the British Council in Copenhagen is simply a list of the 31 centres offering courses leading to UCLES and LCC (London Chamber of Commerce) exams.

In Denmark, all wages are set by law and teaching English is no exception. The range is 161.50-207.60 kroner, though most pay at the lower end of the range. Denmark has among the highest taxes in the world, i.e. 50%.

NORWAY

The trend in Norwegian EFL is similar to that in Denmark, and most schools rely on a pool of native speakers already resident in Norway. Most jobs are for part-time work and of course do not offer accommodation or help with the very strict Norwegian labour laws. The British Council in Oslo can send an up-to-date list of about 30 addresses including banks and insurance companies which have their own English language training departments. The Folkuniversity of Norway is less extensive than in Sweden and has no recruitment representative in the UK. There are branches in Stavanger, Skien, Kristiansand and Hamar, but again they normally offer only occasional teaching.

LIST OF SCHOOLS

Finland

HABIL OY (INTERNATIONAL HOUSE)
Mariankatu 15 B 7, 00170 Helsinki. Tel: (0) 135 7104. Fax: 135 7881.
Number of teachers: 5.
Preference of nationality: none.
Qualifications: minimum RSA Cert. (grade 'B').
Conditions of employment: 1-2 year contracts. 25 contact h.p.w. Pupils aged 25-50.
Salary: from 6,500 markka per month.
Facilities/Support: assistance with accommodation. Training given.
Recruitment: through IH, London. Interviews essential.

IWG KIELI-INSTITUUTTI
Näsilinnankatu 27D, 33200 Tampere. Tel: (31) 123519/147573.
Number of teachers: 15.
Preference of nationality: UK, US.
Qualifications: BA and TEFL qualification.
Conditions of employment: 9-10 month contracts. 6 hours work per day. Pupils aged 6-70.
Salary: 7,000 markka per month.
Facilities/Support: accommodation provided. No training.
Recruitment: through adverts. Interviews essential and can be held in UK.

KIELIPISTE OY
Vuorikatu 22 A 12, 00100 Helsinki. Tel: (0) 90177 266.
Number of teachers: 2-5.
Qualifications: RSA Cert., experience teaching adults and preferably a business background.
Conditions of employment: freelance work only. Hours of work 8.30am-4.30pm. Pupils range in age from 20-60.
Salary: from 100 markka per 45-minute lesson.
Facilities/Support: no assistance with accommodation. Training given.
Recruitment: local interviews essential.

LINGUABELLE
Fredrikinkatu 63 A 12, 00100 Helsinki. Tel: (0) 694 5177. Fax: 694 5578.
Number of teachers: 6-8.
Preference of nationality: UK, US.
Qualifications: BA in relevant subject (or commercial degree) plus TEFL qualification. Must be aged between 25-45, have good manners and be of business-like appearance.
Conditions of employment: 9 month contracts (September-May, sometimes August-June) with 3 month trial period. 26-28 45-minute lessons per week. Pupils are all business people.

Salary: negotiable.
Facilities/Support: furnished flat available in city centre for fair rent from school. Training given.
Recruitment: through UK newspaper adverts and LEXEL. Interviews are essential and can be held in UK.

LINGUARAMA SUOMI OY
Annankatu 26, 00100 Helsinki. Tel: (0) 649404. Fax: 603118.
Number of teachers: 50-60.
Preference of nationality: UK, US.
Qualifications: BA/TEFL/RSA.
Conditions of employment: 9-12 month contracts. 30 lessons per week. Hours of work 8.30am-5-30pm. Pupils aged 20-50.
Salary: varies according to experience.
Facilities/Support: assistance with accommodation. Training given.
Recruitment: through adverts. Interviews held in London.

MARKKINOINTI-INSTITUUTTI
Töölöntullinkatu 6, 00250 Helsinki. Tel: (0) 904 7361.
Number of teachers: 10 (part-time).
Preference of nationality: UK, USA.
Qualifications: BA plus TEFL qualification (or equivalent) and experience teaching adults.
Conditions of employment: only part-time work available. Hours of work 9am-4pm. Pupils aged 20-50.
Salary: 132-154 markka per 45-minute lesson.
Facilities/Support: no assistance with accommodation. Training given.
Recruitment: through direct application and personal recommendation. Local interviews essential.

Sweden

HOFER'S SPRAK-OCH KONTORSSERVICE AB
Bygatan 21, S-17155 Solna. Tel: (8) 834750.
Number of teachers: 2.
Preference of nationality: none.
Qualifications: as much experience and as many qualifications as possible in language and education.
Conditions of employment: contract lengths vary. 40 h.p.w. Pupils aged from 20 upwards.
Salary: negotiable.
Facilities/Support: accommodation negotiable with school. Training given.
Recruitment: through adverts. Interviews required and held in Stockholm.

Denmark

CAMBRIDGE INSTITUTE FOUNDATION
Vimmelskaftet 48, 1161 Copenhagen K. Tel: 33 13 33 02.
Number of teachers: 53 in various schools.
Preference of nationality: UK, Ireland.

Qualifications: BA, TEFL qualification and at least 1 year's TEFL experience abroad.
Conditions of employment: 8 month renewable contracts (October-May). Minimum 17.5 h.p.w. Pupils aged 18-70.
Salary: approximately £15 per lesson.
Facilities/Support: assistance with accommodation. Training given.
Recruitment: through adverts in UK newspapers.

FOF (Folkeligt Oplysnings Forbund)
Sønder Allé 9, 8000 Arhus C. Tel: 86 12 29 55.
Number of teachers: 5.
Preference of nationality: UK.
Qualifications: knowledge of adult education and Danish required.
Conditions of employment: 9 month contracts (September-April). 2-30 lessons per week between 9am-10pm.
Salary: approximately 200 kroner per lesson.
Facilities/Support: no assistance with accommodation. Training given.
Recruitment: through direct application and local interviews.

FOF
Farum Hovedgade 9, 3520 Farum. Tel: 42 95 18 14.
Number of teachers: none at present.
Preference of nationality: none.
Qualifications: experience in teaching necessary.
Conditions of employment: 20-50 hour contracts. Both day and evening work. Pupils aged from 14 years.
Salary: from 161.5-207.6 kroner per hour.
Facilities/Support: no assistance with accommodation. No training.
Recruitment: through adverts. Local interviews essential.

FOF
Lyngby Hovedgade 15D, 2800 Lyngby. Tel: 42 88 25 00.
Number of teachers: 8.
Preference of nationality: none.
Qualifications: teaching experience, especially with adults.
Conditions of employment: contracts run from October-April. Pupils are all adults.
Salary: from 161.5 kroner per hour.
Facilities/Support: no assistance with accommodation. Subsidized training available outside the school.
Recruitment: through direct application. Local interviews only.

FRIT OPLYSNINGSFORBUND
Vestergade 5, 1, 5000 Odense C. Tel: 09 13 98 13.
Number of teachers: 3.
Preference of nationality: none.
Conditions of employment: 8 month contracts. Pupils range in age from 18-100.
Salary: 170 kroner per hour.
Facilities/Support: no assistance with accommodation. Training given.
Recruitment: through Danish universities.

Norway

FOLK UNIVERSITY ROGALAND
Nytorget 8, 4013 Stavanger. Tel. (4) 52 85 75.
Number of teachers: 12, part-time only.
Preference of nationality: UK, US.
Qualifications: minimum RSA Cert, and business English experience.
Conditions of employment: minimum 1 year contracts. Part-time day and evening work. Pupils aged 16-60.
Salary: 190-220 kroner per teaching hour.
Facilities/Support: no assistance with accommodation. Training given.
Recruitment: through local adverts. Local interviews essential.

FRIUNDERVISNINGEN
Nedre Vollgt. 20 (P.B. 496 Sentrum), 0105 Oslo 1. Tel: (2) 11 41 60.
Number of teachers: 18, part-time only.
Preference of nationality: none.
Qualifications: TEFL experience and qualifications preferred. Prefer native speakers already resident in Norway.
Conditions of employment: no contracts. Pupils aged between 18-65.
Salary: varies from course to course.
Facilities/Support: no assistance with accommodation. Some training given.
Recruitment: local interviews only.

KOMMUNIKE
Seilduksgt. 6, 0553 Oslo 5. Tel: (2) 37 40 48.
Number of teachers: 5, part-time only.
Preference of nationality: US, UK.
Qualifications: education in business administration, law, computers.
Conditions of employment: no full-time contracts. Both day and evening work. Pupils aged 15-85.
Salary: negotiable.
Facilities/Support: assistance given with accommodation if necessary. Training provided.
Recruitment: local interviews essential.

PROFESSIONAL LANGUAGE SERVICE
HM Gaukrodger, Gamle Forusvei 43 (Boks 289), 4033 Forus. Tel: (4) 57 65 76.
Number of teachers: 2 full-time, plus other part-timers.
Preference of nationality: UK.
Qualifications: TEFL diploma and industrial experience.
Conditions of employment: minimum 1 academic year contracts. Flexible hours of work. Pupils aged 16-60.
Salary: minimum 140,000 kroner per year plus free air fares and baggage allowances.
Facilities/Support: assistance with accommodation. Training given.
Recruitment: adverts in *EFL Gazette* and *Guardian*. Interviews held in UK.

Iceland

MIMIR SCHOOL OF LANGUAGES
Ananaustum 15, 121 Reykjavik. Tel: (1) 911 0004.
Number of teachers: 2.
Preference of nationality: none.
Qualifications: BA plus TEFL experience.
Conditions of employment: 1 year contracts. Both day and evening work available. Pupils range in age from teenagers to 65 year olds.
Salary: approximately 1,300 kronur per hour.
Facilities/Support: no assistance with accommodation. No training given.
Recruitment: through local adverts. Local interviews required. (Residence and work permits can be obtained after arrival.)

Spain

The decade of the 1980s was one of unprecedented economic growth in Spain, as business and industry forged ahead. Under Franco, French was the first language taught in schools, which means that few people above early middle age know English, the very people who now find themselves as captains (lieutenants, sergeants, etc.) of industry in a Europe on the brink of economic unification. Nowadays in Spain, few job interviews fail to include the question, "Can you speak English?".

The growth in the market is not confined to business people. Children are being enrolled in private English lessons at a great rate, as parents try to supplement what most people acknowledge is inadequate language teaching in the state education system. Schools which have dealt more or less exclusively with company personnel for a decade are suddenly asking their teachers to organize sing-songs and games for young children.

Although estimates vary, there may be as many as 20,000 foreigners teaching English in Spain; there are several hundred language institutes in Madrid alone plus a further 150 in Barcelona and hundreds more scattered all over the country from the Basque north (where there is a surprisingly high concentration) to the Balearic and Canary Islands. The British Council has its biggest teaching operation in Madrid plus teaching centres in Barcelona, Bilbao, Granada, Las Palmas, Palma de Mallorca and Valencia. At the other end of the EFL spectrum almost every back street in every Spanish town has an *Academia de Ingles*.

Spain has always been a popular destination for EFL teachers whether qualified or not. Who can fail to be attracted to the climate, scenery, history and culture? And yet, many new arrivals in Spain soon realize that Spain and the Spanish people of their imagination bear little relation to what they find, at least in the major cities. All this economic expansion and increased prosperity has not only led to pollution and over-development, it has perhaps corrupted the people to some extent and made them more greedy and self-interested; certainly there are plenty of greedy people involved in the running of language schools.

Another myth which is soon exploded is that life in Spain is cheap. Although it is still possible to enjoy a 3-course meal with wine for £1.50 and to travel on the Madrid metro for a few pence, Madrid is considered to be one of the most expensive cities in the world, and Spain as a whole suffers from high inflation and expensive accommodation. Teaching wages rarely allow more than a tolerably comfortable lifestyle. These are points to bear in mind when visions of *paella* and Rioja dance before your eyes as you read the columns of adverts in the Education *Guardian* and *TES*.

Prospects for Teachers

There is no shortage of schools advertising for teachers, mostly between March and June but also into September. Obviously schools would prefer to hire experienced and qualified teachers with an RSA Certificate but there are simply not enough to go around, i.e. there aren't 20,000 of them. According to an article in the *Observer* in May 1990, perhaps about one in ten EFL teachers in Spain has a qualification. Although adverts usually inflate the qualifications they will accept, a great many adverts in the UK press ask simply for "graduates with some Spanish" or "dynamic, motivated and preferably qualified EFL teachers". One even stated that a job in their evening institute would suit a "student on a year out". Because the demand for teachers outstrips supply, it is always worth answering an ad for Spain, even if you lack the requested qualifications. For the jobs in Madrid which Bruce Nairne and Sue Ratcliffe landed, Linguarama was asking for holders of the RSA Prep. Cert. who were Spanish-speaking and had an interest in business English. Not only did Bruce and Sue lack all three, but so did most of their colleagues in Madrid.

This is the situation for schools which bother to advertise and recruit abroad, which generally occupy at least the middle rank of English institutes. There are also a great many less reputable schools which do not want to spend any money on foreign advertising nor for the services of a recruitment agency. They depend on word-of-mouth and local walk-ins for their staff requirements. There are even stories of buskers and other native speakers passing through being dragooned into teaching positions. A good word put in for you by someone already teaching usually works, as Marta Eleniak discovered:

> A friend got a job because a contact simply described him to the Director as the "best English teacher you'll ever find". (He is 29, has never taught and has no teacher training.)

If there is a dire shortage of teachers, the recommendation may not have been a lie, technically speaking.

Anyone with some relevant qualifications need have no worries. With the RSA Certificate you can walk into almost any job short of the British Council. With a knowledge of Spanish, you can usually find work teaching children (with whom the total immersion method is not really suitable). There is more resistance to being taught in English in the provinces.

The bias in Spain is towards Great Britain and also Ireland, with whom Spain has always enjoyed close ties, partly because of the shared religion. But other English-speaking nationals are welcome too. Officially EEC nationals will continue to require work/residence papers until 1993 (at the end of the 7-year transitional period from when Spain joined the Common Market), so they have no legal advantage over other nationalities at present. Americans make up half the teaching staff at many schools and the majority of schools who notified us of their teacher requirements expressed no strong preference of nationality. Other nationalities are at a bureaucratic disadvantage however, since they are supposed to apply for their permits and, months later, collect their permits at the Spanish Consulate nearest their place of residence, which is prohibitively expensive for North Americans (not to mention Antipodeans).

FIXING UP A JOB

Because schools run the whole gamut from prestigious to cowboy, every method of job-hunting works at some level. The big chains like inlingua (with 40 schools in Spain), Berlitz and Linguarama hire both through their central offices in Britain and locally. They are probably a good bet for the novice teacher on account of the stability of hours they can offer.

In Advance

To obtain a list of language schools you can use the usual method of consulting the Yellow Pages (*Las Paginas Amarillos*) at specialist libraries in your home country or you can get a more selective list of FECEI members (*Federacion Española de Centros de Enseñanza de Idiomas*), the professional body of private teaching establishments, from the Spanish Labour Office (20 Peel Street, London W8 7PD). The Spanish Institute (102 Eaton Square, London SW1W 9AN) also sends out a list of addresses in Spain. The most comprehensive and up-to-date list is contained in a fat volume put out by the Madrid British Council at the fat price of £50, *The Directory of English Studies in Spain*. (It is not known whether this can be freely consulted at Council offices in Spain.) The 8 Council offices in Spain all maintain lists of language schools in their region. For example the Seville office has one list for Seville and one for the whole of Andalusia, totalling more than 50 schools, and the Palma de Mallorca office has a list of 34 schools in Mallorca and Minorca.

Anyone with a TEFL qualification might want to make use of a recruitment agency, whether a general one or one which specializes in Spain such as English and Spanish Studies (Recruitment Consultants, 26-40 Kensington High Street, London W8 4PF; tel: 071-938 2222) and English Educational Services (Alcala 20-2, 28014 Madrid; tel: 531 4783). Both of these are highly respectable and warn teachers against accepting a job without an interview and against leaving home without a signed pre-contract. A surprisingly high proportion of Spanish language schools which advertise abroad are able to arrange interviews with a representative in England, usually in the summer months. The big ones might invite all comers to an open day at an agency office or hotel. Many of the recruitment agencies described in the Introduction (see page 55) deal with Spanish schools. One who has a branch office in Madrid is *Language Matters*.

Americans should contact ELS (57621 Buckingham Parkway, Culver City, California 90230) who have a new intake of teachers for their Madrid school every 3 months. Jobs are available for any native speaker with a degree in English and a year of teaching experience, and conditions are generous, including free air fares.

On the Spot

Most teaching jobs in Spain are found on the spot. Taking up a patch of pavement as a busker will probably not gain you entry to a language school. Although the demand for teachers is strong, there is also a considerable amount of competition, and you will have to exert yourself to land a decent job. The best time to look is at the beginning of September, after the summer holidays are ended and before most terms begin on October 1st. November is also promising, since that is when teachers hand in their notice for a Christmas departure. Since a considerable number of teachers do not return to their jobs after the Christmas break and schools are often left in the lurch, early January is also possible. There are a few language teaching jobs in the summer at residential courses for children and teenagers, but on the whole, the beginning of summer is the worst time to travel out to Spain to look for work. Therefore the temptation of all those early season cheap charters should be avoided. For voluntary work as an English assistant on summer camps, try Relaciones Culturales, a youth exchange organization at Calle Ferraz 82, 28008 Madrid (tel: 479 64 46), who also place native speakers with Spanish families who want to practise their English in exchange for providing room and board.

Michael Frost describes his successful job hunt in Barcelona:

I flew to Spain just before the start of the new term on a cheap last minute ticket with nothing fixed up in advance. I got a list from a helpful British Council; and then dutifully "did the rounds". Most schools were closed between 2 and 4 in the afternoon and directors were invariably out. At all the schools, I left the phone number of my pension in case anything came up. (Pensions don't usually mind doing this but ask first.) The person to see is obviously the director or principal but they can be hard to track down.

After one week I got lucky — right place, right time — and went for an interview. This was short and cursory, more of a "look-over" than an in-depth probe. I was asked if I had any experience of teaching and I untruthfully said that I had done a month of summer teaching at a fictitious UK school, using newspapers as the basis for a conversational class. I think that gave me an advantage but a serious director could easily have probed and seen if this story was bogus or not. I didn't have any training but I did have a degree. I think they were really checking to see that I wasn't a complete dud, and I found out that they needed someone in 3 days' time. My in-house training consisted of sitting in on a couple of lessons by other teachers.

Other sources of job vacancy information include the Madrid daily *El Pais* which usually have a few relevant classifieds under the heading *Trabajo — Idiomas*. Also try *Segundamano*, The Madrid British Council, whose notice board has proved so helpful to aspiring teachers in the past, is reported to be moving in the same direction as the Council office in Paris, i.e. they are becoming fussy about whom they allow to advertise and enter. Turner's English Language Bookshop (Calle de Genova, Madrid, near the Metro Alonso Martinez) have a very active notice board, so active that notices of teaching jobs etc. are often buried under other notices 6 deep.

Although the majority of job-seekers head for Madrid, other towns may answer your requirements better. There are language academies all along the Catalonian coast and a door-to-door job hunt in September should pay off. This is the time when tourists are departing so accommodation may be available at a reasonable rent on a 9-month lease.

Freelance Teaching

As usual, private tutoring pays much better than contract teaching because there is no middle man. According to Glen Williams in October 1990, the going rate in Granada was between 1,000 and 1,500 pesetas for individuals and 2,000 pesetas for 3 or 4 people. Freelance rates in Madrid were much higher (3,000 pesetas) but travelling time had to be taken into consideration.

It is difficult to start up without contacts and a good knowledge of Spanish; and when you do get started it is difficult to earn a stable income due to the frequency with which pupils cancel. Spaniards are fond of their *punte*: the bridge between a midweek holiday and the weekend. Getting private lessons is a marketing exercise and you will have to explore all the avenues which seem appropriate to your circumstances. Obviously you can advertise on the notice boards mentioned above as well as at universities, corner shops and wherever else you think there is a market. Send neat notices to local state schools asking them to pin it up broadcasting your willingness to ensure the children's linguistic future. Compile a list of addresses of professionals (e.g. lawyers, architects, etc.) as they may need English for their work and have the wherewithal to pay for it. Try export businesses, distribution companies, perhaps even travel agencies. Make the acquaintance of language teachers who will know of openings. It is not uncommon for teachers' contracts to stipulate that if the teacher wants a break, he or she must find and reimburse a substitute, so they may have work they want to farm out to someone on the spot. Place adverts in free papers (like *El 18*) and in advertising papers (like *Almoneda*, also in Granada).

Because private classes are so much better paid than institute teaching, they are much in demand, including by contract teachers, most of whom are engaged in some private tutoring. The ideal is to arrange a school contract with no more than 15 or 20 hours and supplement this with private classes which are lucrative though unstable.

REGULATIONS

Ninety per cent of all teachers are forced to work illegally because of the unbelievably sluggish and capricious bureaucracy. Marta Eleniak, writing from Madrid, says "never mind red tape — there's red ribbon and bows too; Spain is a bureaucratic nightmare." A foreigners' law (*ley de extranjeria*) was brought in just before Spain's entry into the EEC (which seems to have made matters worse rather that better) making the formalities both time-consuming and expensive in the extreme. The task of applying for a combined work/residence permit calls to mind any number of figures from classical mythology from Sisyphus to Tantalus, Theseus in the labyrinth to (perhaps most apt) Hercules and his 12 labours.

There are three possible work visas: Type A, B, and C. The majority of legal teachers have Type A which entitles them to work in one specific job and only for the duration of the contract, normally 9 months. Although the official waiting time from submitting the necessary documents (which itself takes months) is 2 months, it is more likely to be 5 or even 7, only to expire a couple of months later. The time taken apparently varies from place to place: much shorter in Zaragoza than in Barcelona. A handful of teachers get a Type B visa and virtually none gets a 5-year Type C permit.

Serious schools and recruitment organizations offer as much guidance as possible and will pay for all or part of the expenses incurred, for example £50 for the visa application, return fare to your home country to collect the visa when ready, etc. A number of schools send out detailed instructions to applicants; we reproduce the worthy stab which English Educational Services in Madrid have made at making sense of the muddle:

PART A *(FOR THE LOCAL SPANISH CONSULATE/EMBASSY)*
— *Copy of contract or letter of offer employment from the employer.*
— *Copy of current valid passport which will not run out in the next 180 days together with four photocopies of first few pages.*
— *4 passport photos.*
— *Fill in 4 application forms for "Special Visa," three of which will stay with the Consulate/Embassy.*
— *Medical certificate plus copy issued by local Doctor.*
— *Your degree certificate stamped as authentic by a solicitor. One copy must also be stamped by the Foreign Affairs Dept. Go to 70 Petty France Street in London and pay for an "Apostille" (Hague Convention of 5/10/61).*
— *Proof of local residence if you are not in your country of birth/origin.*

PART B *(FOR YOUR FUTURE EMPLOYER)*
— *Send copy of your application for "Special Visa".*
— *Send Medical Certificate.*
— *Send 4 passport photos signed by you on the back.*
— *Certified copy of your degree/diploma.*
— *Two copies of your passport (stamped by Consulate/Embassy).*
— *Sign and return a copy of contract or letter confirming your acceptance of the job offer.*

Actually this makes it sound easier than do some sources which describe what is necessary if you cannot return home and must apply by power of attorney. Americans need a further document, an *antecedents penales* (police certificate) stating that they do not have a police record.

Although the Spanish authorities take months to process all this, you are expected to send off documents as quickly as possible, by courier if necessary. English Educational Services go on to urge applicants to be patient with consular officials and not to be abusive, probably easier said than done once you are embroiled in the sordid business. It creates a bad situation all round, since some schools (understandably) don't think the effort is worth it for their 9-month contract teachers who in turn suspect that the employer is wanting to duck out of paying social security and tax on the teacher's behalf (which is no doubt true in some cases). Stuart Britton, who taught for a year in a tourist resort-cum-fishing port near Salou, lamented that common sense was not allowed to prevail over politics and concluded that "Spain is a lovely country in which to live and work but the pointless bureaucracy spoils it for many people".

In a country where the TEFL industry is so unregulated, it is ironic that such a ridiculous assortment of regulations is applied to the poor teacher. All of this should become easier from January 1993 (not to be confused with 1992 when the single European market will come into effect). Some say that the situation has improved recently, and that there is a straightforward quota of 2 foreigners for every Spaniard employed on staff.

But a huge black market in EFL teachers persists. Enforcement of the rules is patchy and deportations of teachers rare; schools are occasionally inspected by the authorities and fined if they are found to have illegal teachers on the payroll. Depending on your point of view, working without a permit might not be so bad after all. Not only will you save yourself all the frustration of doing battle with the bureaucracy, you may actually get a higher wage, since the school is paying no tax or social security. Without a contract you run a minute risk of ending up with a "con-trick school", one which does a bunk after collecting pupils' fees and failing to pay teachers. But most are honest third-rate schools.

Based on his year and a half teaching for a cowboy school in Barcelona, one veteran teacher expresses a laid-back attitude to the official line:

> *There was no red tape as I wasn't bothered by it and nor were they. I had no contract and in point of fact the school was operating illegally. I didn't give them any problems and they didn't give me any: I had a job teaching which was what I wanted.*

If you do work on a tourist visa it will be necessary to leave the country every 3 months to get your passport stamped on returning to Spain. Most teachers organize weekend trips to France or Portugal (whichever is nearer).

CONDITIONS OF WORK

The salaries in Spain would not lead anyone to assume that it is a teacher's market. This is no doubt attributable to the fact that Spain has always been one of the least prosperous countries of Europe, so teachers of English would not expect to earn as much as in Finland or France. A further problem is that there is no significant difference between salaries in the big cities where the cost of living has escalated enormously and salaries in the small towns. High inflation has added to the teacher's financial woes. British Council teachers in Madrid felt so aggrieved that they went on strike in 1990, a fairly unusual state of affairs. The minimum net salary is 80,000-90,000 pesetas per month. As mentioned above, the majority of teachers supplement this with private teaching at anything from 1,000 pesetas an hour. Compulsory social security payments of 8% will be deducted. Tax deductions are paid in arrears and do not normally affect teachers on 9-month contracts.

A writer in the *Guardian* recently accused Spanish TEFL of offering "low pay, long hours and sheer exploitation". This is probably true of some English schools in all countries and Spain is certainly no exception. Wages in Barcelona are said to be particularly low, since it is such a popular and trendy destination at present. However it does not take into account the broad sweep of schools, some of which offer quite the opposite. Certainly many schools expect their teachers to work long hours: 25-30 per week is average, and many teach up to 37. Considering that preparation adds about half as much again, plus travelling time which is considerable in Madrid where much of the teaching is off-site, teachers are looking at a gruelling schedule. Dennis Bricault refers to the notoriously uncongenial timetable of most EFL teachers (and not just in Spain) as a "bookend schedule", whereby you might have to teach between 8 and 10am, then again through the evening. Most teachers put up with the late finishing time without too many murmurs because they are not deprived of Spanish nightlife even if they have to work until 10pm.

Obviously teachers with a contract feel more secure than teachers without one. Yet a contract has no legal weight as long as a teacher does not have a work permit. (Usually this is a problem only for teachers of a nervous disposition.) Teachers without a contract wrongly assume that they have no power to insist on any rights. But there is the power of the *denuncio*, which involves informing the authorities (either in person or via a union, such as the Commissiones Obreros) that your school is not complying with tax and social security rules or fire regulations or whatever. The *denuncio* can effectively close a school if it is taken seriously and if the school does not have the proverbial friends in high places. In fact the procedure is complicated and time-consuming but the mere mention of it *might* improve your working conditions.

Holiday allowances are particularly ungenerous in Spain, usually no more than a week or ten days at Christmas and Easter. According to Spanish law, workers are not entitled to paid holiday until they have been working for 12 months, hence the near-universality of 9-month contracts. Most teachers find it impossible to save enough in 9 months to fund themselves abroad for the rest of the year.

For reasons which remain obscure, Spaniards have the reputation for being hopeless at languages, possibly as a result of unreasonable expectations. This is more tolerable in the adults who are fairly well motivated, but often hard-going with children (unless you are especially fond of kids). Regional differences are important, too, as Stuart Britton discovered in Catalonia:

> *There is a strong anti-Spanish feeling here. They claim that this part of Spain is not Spain but Cataluña (even though my map clearly states that the international frontiers are only with Portugal, France and Andorra). The Catalan language is very different from Spanish and most of the locals speak it all the time. I have some students who like to get into political discussions, which can be disturbing for an innocent bystander-teacher.*

Catalan is also the dominant language of Barcelona.

Accommodation

As mentioned in passing above, accommodation is frequently cited by teachers as a major headache. If you are lucky, your school will help by phoning potential landlords (who are invariably Spanish-speaking only). Rents usually swallow up at least a quarter of a teacher's income. The problem is much more serious in the big cities (though no worse than a newly arrived Spaniard trying to find cheap accommodation in London) than in small towns, where it is not uncommon for schools to arrange accommodation for its teachers. In smaller towns you can expect to pay about 18,000 pesetas a month if you're sharing with a couple of others, and 30,000 pesetas if you rent a small flat on your own. Many Spanish students want to live with English students so check university notice boards for flat shares, especially in the *Facultad de Filosofia y Letras* which includes the Department of English.

LEISURE TIME

Eating, drinking, smoking, entertainment and transport (including taxis) are all wonderfully cheap, though this advantage is cancelled out for some by the high cost of other things such as clothes, cars and electrical items, not to mention contraceptives, standard chemists' products and dental care. Spain is a good country for wine-drinking film-goers and tourists but not so good for gadget-addicts with poor teeth.

If you're looking for traditional Spanish culture, don't go to Madrid; Seville, Granada, Valencia are better bets. If you're looking for an idyllic Mediterranean climate don't go to northern Spain in mid-winter. But most teachers have little fault to find with the climate. Stuart Britton, who paints, was thrilled by the glorious blue light in which to paint historic castles and colourful narrow streets lined with gorgeous balconies.

Glen Williams describes his spare time activities in Madrid, a city he was clearly enjoying to the full:

> *Madrid is a crazy place. We usually stay out all night at the weekend drinking and boogying. During the gaps in my timetable (10-2 and 4-7) I pretend to study Spanish (I'm no natural) and just wander the back streets. I suppose I should try to be more cultural and learn to play an instrument, write poetry or look at paintings, but I never get myself in gear.*
>
> *I think most people teach English in Spain as a means to live in Spain and learn the Spanish language and culture. But there is a real problem that you end up*

living in an English enclave, teaching English all day and socializing with English teachers. You have to make a big effort to get out of this rut. I am lucky to live with Spanish people (who do not want to practise their English!).

Some schools offer free or subsidized Spanish lessons as a perk to teachers.

There are so many people teaching English in different situations that there is no average profile. While one teacher finds the locals cold and hostile and money-grubbing, another finds them warm and supportive. If the idea of teaching in Spain appeals at all, it is almost always a rewarding and memorable way of people with limited work experience to finance themselves as they travel and live abroad for a spell.

LIST OF SCHOOLS

There is simply not enough space to include full details of the teacher requirements for the 136 language schools from which we have heard during the research for this book. Besides, there would be an unacceptable level of repetition in such an exercise. Instead, we have provided a skeletal list of names and addresses of schools eager to receive applications, followed in brackets by the number of native speaker teachers which they employ. Most schools prefer their teachers to have a BA, RSA Certificate (or equivalent) and knowledge of Spanish, though may well be prepared to consider less. Net salaries are almost always in the range 90,000-120,000 pesetas with a steady average at the lower end of that scale. The best plan is to pick out the schools in the city or province which appeals to you, and write off for details (preferably enclosing an impressive c.v.).

In and Around Madrid

LA ACADEMIA DE INGLES: Avda. de Moratalaz 139, 28030 La Lonja (Madrid) Tel: (1) 430 5545. (20)

ACHNA: (American Language Program): San Bernardo 107, 28015 Madrid. Tel: (1) 447 1900. (90)

ALBION: Noria 14, 28807 Alcalá de Henares (Madrid) Tel: (1) 881 1312. (4)

ALBION: Juan de Cardona 3, 28805 Alcalá de Henares (Madrid) Tel: (1) 881 4686. (5)

BERLITZ: Gran Via 80, 4°, 28103 Madrid. Tel: (1) 542 3586. (200 approx. throughout Spain)

CAMBRIDGE HOUSE: Lopez de Hoyos 95, 1°A, 28002 Madrid. Tel (1) 519 4603/228 1335. (12) Also: c/ Mendez Alvaro 2, 1°A, Madrid.

LA CASA INGLESA: Principe de Vergara 45, 28001 Madrid. Tel: (1) 435 6223. (40)

CHESTER SCHOOL OF ENGLISH: Jorge Juan 125, 28009 Madrid. Tel: (1) 402 5879. (10)

ENGLISH CENTRE: Núñez de Balboa 17/Velazquez 18, 28001 Madrid. Tel: (1) 577 9122/577 9111. 2 schools which employ 35 teachers altogether.

ENGLISH LANGUAGE PROJECTS: Caleruega 11, 28033 Madrid. Tel: (1) 202 8945/46. Fax: 730 8943. (30) RSA Dip. and 5 years experience are required to teach corporate clients, and general TEFL qualifications for other teaching.

ENGLISH STUDY GROUP: Velazquez 40/Jorge Juan 16, 28001 Madrid. (15)

ESCUELA OFICIAL DE IDIOMAS CENTRAL DE MADRID: Jesús Maestro, s/n 28003 Madrid. Tel: (1) 253 7579. (5)

BERLENGUA: Torpedero Tucuman 26, 28016 Madrid. Tel: (1) 458 8257. (6-8)
DIOMAS DE LA COMMUNIDAD EUROPEA: Hileras 4, 4°-11a, 28103 Madrid.
Tel: (1) 248 4026. (4)
NLINGUA IDIOMAS: Arenal 24, 28013 Madrid. Tel: (1) 541 3246. (25-30)
NSTITUTO DE IDIOMAS MODERNOS: Universidad Pontificia Comillas,
Alberto Aguilera 23, 28015 Madrid. Tel: (1) 715 0696. Fax: 248 6569. (30)
NTER-COM ENGLISH: Paseo General Martinez Campos 19-4° Izqda, 28010
Madrid. Tel: (1) 445 4751. Fax: 447 4201. (30) Employs 50% North Americans.
KURSOLAN: Maria de Molina 32, 28006 Madrid. Tel: (1) 261 3100. (30-40) Runs
2 summer camps outside Madrid for Spanish boys and girls.
THE LANGUAGE HOUSE: Avda. Brasilia 7, 28028 Madrid. Tel: (1) 256 1844.
(7+)
LIVERPOOL, CENTRO DE IDIOMAS: Calle Libreros 11-1°, Alcalá de Henares,
28801 Madrid. Tel: (1) 881 3184. (20)
PAIDOS ENGLISH SCHOOLS: Arturo Soria 328, 28033 Madrid. Tel: (1) 202
3093/730 6066. (20) A group of 4 small schools; staff will teach at different
schools on different days. Part of English Language Projects (q.v.)
SAGASTA, CENTRO DE IDIOMAS: Sagasta 27-3° Izq, 28004 Madrid. Tel: (1)
446 6979. (7-10)
SHEFFIELD LANGUAGE SERVICES: Calle de la Reina 15-3°, 28004 Madrid.
Tel: (1) 532 9495. (8) Specializes in preparation for competitive examinations
fro the Spanish Public Service; knowledge of Spanish at degree level required.
THAMESIS, ASESORIA LINGUISTICA: Calle Castello 24, bajo Dcha, 28001
Madrid. Tel: (1) 575 8949. (20)

In and Around Barcelona

UNIVERSITAT DE BARCELONA, Escola d'Idiomes Moderns: Gran Via de les
Corts Catalanes 585, 08007 Barcelona. Tel: (3) 318 4266 ext 2500. (25)
BARNA HOUSE: Rambla de Catalunya 112, 1°, 08008 Barcelona. Tel: (3) 237
0536. (18-20)
THE BRITISH CENTRE: Valldoreix 22, Sant Cugat del Vallès, Barcelona. Tel:
(3) 675 1923. Fax: 675 5602. (12)
CAMBRIDGE SCHOOL: Plaça Manel Montañà 4-1° 08400 Granollers
(Barcelona) Tel: (3) 870 2001. (14)
CLARENCE HOUSE: Jovellanos 91, 08201 Sabadell (Barcelona). Tel: (3) 727
0663. (3)
EDIEPE: Via Augusta 10 pral., 08006 Barcelona. Tel: (3) 218 0962. Fax: 218
3711. (14) Specialization in business English.
ENGLISH CENTRE: Argenters, 17-1°, 08500 Vic (Barcelona) Tel: (3) 889 0578.
(22) This group comprises 2 schools in Vic and Igualada, and also recruits
teachers and sports monitors for children's summer courses near Barcelona.
EUROLOG: Travessera de Dalt, 38 entlo, 2a, 08024 Barcelona. Tel: (3) 218
7449. Fax: 415 3342. (7)
FIAC BADALONA: Calle León 19-2°, Badalona, (Barcelona) Tel: (3) 389 3005.
(2-3)
FIRST CLASS ENGLISH CENTRE: Elisa 15, ent. 2°, 08023 Barcelona. Tel: (3)
418 7087. (3+)
INLINGUA IDIOMAS: Rambla Cataluña 33, 08007 Barcelona. Tel: (3) 318 2338.
Fax: 318 1015. (43)

KINGSBROOK ENGLISH SCHOOL: Trav. de Gracia 60, 1º-3ª, 08006 Barcelona. Tel: (3) 209 3763. Fax: 202 1598.
LANGAGE: Enrique Granados 149 Pral., 08008 Barcelona. Tel: (3) 200 8741. Fax: 200 8947. (25)
WINDSOR SCHOOL: Diagonal 319, pral. 4º, 08009 Barcelona. Tel: (3) 257 9567. (7) Summer courses also offered.

The Rest of Spain (towns in alphabetical order)

LANGUAGE CENTRE: Convento 5, 46970 Alaquas (Valencia). Tel: (6) 150 6760. (1)
ENGLISH INSTITUTE: Carre La Mar 38, Denia, 03700 Alicante. Tel: (6) 578 1350. (6)
PADDINGTON: Calle Bailen 18-1ºD, 03001 Alicante. Tel: (6) 521 8673. (2-3)
STANTON SCHOOL OF ENGLISH: Colon 26-1º dcha., 03001 Alicante. Tel: (6) 520 7581. (4)
ENGLISH CENTRE, College of Languages: Artés de Arcos 34, 04004 Almeria. Tel: (51) 23 45 51. (9)
ESCUELLE CASTELLANA/CENTRO FRANCES: Arias de Miranda 24, 09400 Aranda de Duero (Burgos) Tel: (47) 50 76 82. (8)
THE AVILA CENTRE OF ENGLISH: Bajada de Don Alonso 1, 05003 Avila. Tel: (18) 21 37 19. Fax: 21 36 31. (5)
DAVID SCHOOL OF ENGLISH: Virgen de Covadonga 17, 05005 Avila. Tel: (18) 22 23 62. (5)
CENTRE CULTURAL: Passeig de 1 Estaciò 25, 25600 Balaguer. Tel: (73) 44 54 29. (2)
BRITANNIA CENTRO DE INGLES: Telesforo Aranzadi 3-6º, 48008 Bilbao. Tel: (94) 443 6642. (3)
LANSER LANGUAGE SERVICES: Colon de Larreategui 26-3º, 48009 Bilbao. Tel: (4) 424 0988. (10) Industrial and commercial experience preferred. Free accommodation.
SECOND LANGUAGE ACQUISITION SERVICE: Egaña 6-2ºC, 48010 Bilbao. Tel: (4) 444 8062/444 8066.
THE ACADEMY, CENTRO DE IDIOMAS: Paseo Alfonso XIII 47-49, Apto, 426, 30203 Cartagena (Murcia) Tel: (68) 52 09 42. Fax: 52 19 88. (12)
SKILLS CENTRO DE IDIOMAS; Trinidad 94-1º, Castellon. Tel: (64) 24 26 68. (8)
NUMBER NINE ENGLISH LANGUAGE CENTRE: Sant Onofre 1, 07760 Ciutadella de Menorca (Baleares) Tel: (71) 38 40 58. (2)
OXFORD HOUSE: Apto. 271, 43700 El Vendrell. Applications from certified teachers preferred; walk-ins and speculative phone calls not welcome.
ENGLISH COLLEGE: Empedrat 4, 03023 Elche (Alicante) Tel: (6) 545 8401. (5)
LENGUAS ATTIKA: Mariano Benlliure 6, Entlo, A, 03201 Elche (Alicante) Tel: (6) 544 2691. (2-3) Knowledge of Spanish required and those also able to teach French or German preferred.
INSTITUT BRITANIC: c/ Joan Maragall 16, 17600 Figueres. Tel: (972) 50 43 60. (3)
MANGOLD INSTITUTE: Calle Santo Duque 5-1º, 46700 Gandia (Valencia) Tel: (6) 287 3116/287 0599. (8)
EXETER ENGLISH SCHOOL: Uria 15, 33202 Gijón (Asturias) Tel: (85) 33 00 70. Also at Reina M. Cristina, 2-1ºA, 33430 Candas. Tel: (85) 87 17 0202. (30+ in 3 schools: 2 in Gijón and 1 in Candas.)

INLINGUA IDIOMAS: Menéndez Pelayo 2, 33202 Gijón. Tel: (85) 33 00 87. (4)
DUNEDIN COLLEGE: Recogidas 18-1º izq, 18002 Granada. Tel: (58) 25 50 18. (5) Under the same ownership as Lord Byron schools.
INSTITUTE OF MODERN LANGUAGES: Puerta Real 1, 18009 Granada. Tel: (58) 22 55 36. (10-12)
ENGLISH LANGUAGE INSTITUTE; Sant Roc 10, 1er, 08400 Granollers. Tel: 870 03 02. (7)
SAN ROQUE SCHOOL OF ENGLISH: Paseo de San Roque 1, 19002 Guadalajara. Tel: (11) 21 74 45. (4) Occasionally requires staff for summer camps.
CORINNE IDIOMAS: Paseo Santa Fe 7, 2º Dcha, 21003 Huelva. Tel: (55) 24 30 23. (3) Knowledge of Spanish essential.
ENGLISH LANGUAGE STUDIES: Edificio Edimburgo, Plaza Niña, 21003 Huelva. Tel: (55) 26 38 21. (18-20)
TEC ENGLISH CENTRE: Pedro Francés 22A, 07800 Ibiza (Baleares) Tel: (71) 31 58 28. (10) Also at: Guzman el Bueno 7, 28015 Madrid. Tel: (1) 243 9271 (3), and del Sol, Es Mercat, Sta. Eulalia, Ibiza. Tel: (71) 33 20 70. (3)
THE BRITISH CENTRE: Obispo Stuñiga 1-1º, 23007 Jaen. Tel: (53) 22 19 29. (4) TEFL Diploma training available.
TRINITY ENGLISH CENTRE: Apto. 9, Cazorla, Jaen. (2) Prepares students for the Trinity College (London) exams.
TEN: CENTRO DE INGLES: Caracuel 24, 11402 Jerez de la Frontera (Cadiz) Tel: (56) 32 47 07. (3)
CAMBRIDGE ENGLISH STUDIES Avda. de Arteijo, 8-1º, 15004 La Coruña. Tel: (81) 27 75 32. Fax: 26 76 25. (25)
TRELAND ANGLO-WORLD: Barria 1, 48930 Las Arenas (Vizcaya) Tel: (4) 463 1926/464 8989. (9)
INLINGUA IDIOMAS: Paseo de Tomás Morales 28, 35003 Las Palmas de Gran Canaria. Tel: (28) 36 06 71. Fax: 36 86 64. (10) Also recruits teachers for inlingua schools in Playa del Inglés, Tenerife, Lanzarote and Fuerteventura.
OXFORD SCHOOL; Aleixandre s/n, 33400 Las Vegas (Corvera de Asturias) Tel: (85) 57 75 75. (1)
NICOLAU'S LANGUAGE SCHOOL: Valenti Almirall 14, 25004 Lerida. Tel: (73) 24 82 35. (6)
LORD BYRON CENTRO BRITANICO: Canalejas 3-1º, 23700 Linares (Jaén) Tel: (53) 69 95 26. (3)
SAM'S ACADEMY; Juan XXIII, 11-1º Izda, Logroño (La Rioja) Tel: (41) 24 57 51. (4) Also General Franco 61-1º, Logroño.
VICTORIA ENGLISH CENTRE: Gran Via 3, Entreplanta D, 26002 Logroño, (La Rioja). Tel: (41) 24 20 38. (3)
BRITANNIA SCHOOL: Centro de Idiomas: Leopoldo Lugones 3, 33420 Lugones, (Asturias) Tel: (85) 26 28 00. (3)
THE AMERICAN CENTER: Manuel Llaneza 26, 33600 Mieres. Tel: (85) 46 14 54. (10)
AHIZKE: Avda. de Alava Nº4, 20500 Mondragon (Guipúzcoa) Tel: (43) 79 01 32. (11)
LORD BYRON CENTRO BRITANICO: Avda. Rodriguez Acosta 6-1º, 18600 Motril (Granada) Tel: (58) 60 26 87. (3-6)
APPLE IDIOMAS; Agüera 2, 30001 Murcia. Tel: (68) 21 10 38 (17). Also in Valencia.
BILINGUE NORMINGTON: Calle Vinadel Nº11, 30004 Murcia. Tel: (68) 62 84 39. (2)

ALCE — AUDIOVISUAL LANGUAGE CENTRE: Pasaje de los Nogales 1, 33006 Oviedo. Tel: (85) 25 45 43. (5)

BRIAN SCHOOL I: Magdalena 19, 33009 Oviedo. Tel: (85) 22 04 08. (2)

BRIAN SCHOOL II: Saturnino Fresno 2, 33011 Oviedo. Tel: (85) 29 85 19. (4)

YORK SCHOOL: Muñoz Degrain 9, 33007 Oviedo. Tel: (85) 24 13 41. (8)

THE BRITISH INSTITUTE: Carrer de Goethe 1, 07011 Palma de Mallorca (Baleares) Tel: (71) 45 47 12. (12) RSA Diploma needed.

POLIGLOT: Llinàs 2-1º, 07014 Palma de Mallorca (Baleares) Tel: (71) 45 72 60. (1-2)

PROGRESO CENTRO DE IDIOMAS: Plaza del Progreso 12B, 07013 Palma de Mallorca (Baleares) Tel: (71) 23 45 55/23 80 36. (15)

AMBRIT INGLES: Pintor Asarta 8-1º, 31007 Pamplona. Tel: (48) 24 74 92. (6)

INEL ENGLISH ACADEMY: Plaza del Castillo 17-1º, Pamplona (Navarra) Tel: (48) 22 69 45. (4)

LEAP: Inigo Arista 18 Entreplanta, 31007 Pamplona. Tel: (48) 27 79 04. (6)

ENGLISH CENTRE DE PONTEVEDRA: c/Cruz Gallastegui 2, 36001 Pontevedra. Tel: (86) 84 36 52. (6)

ENGLISH STUDIO; Salvador Moreno 4-3º, Pontevedra. Tel: (86) 86 05 86. (4)

NEW CASTLE ACADEMY: F. Juan de Navarrete 8-1º, Pontevedra. Tel: (86) 84 31 30. (5) Also 3 other schools in Sangenjo, Cambados and Vigo.

VILLAGE HILL SCHOOL OF ENGLISH: Apto. 61, El Grove, Pontevedra. Tel: (86) 73 22 28. (4) Knowledge of Spanish essential.

COLLIN'S ACADEMIA: Alameda de Gamón 7-3ºA, Renteria. Tel: (43) 52 76 81. (5)

INTERNATIONAL HOUSE; Llovera 47, 43201 Reus (Tarragona) Tel: (77) 30 35 62. (14)

LORD'S LANGUAGE CENTRE: Poeta Alfonso Camin, 33900 Sama de Langreo (Asturias) Tel: (85) 68 20 50. (4)

THE BRITISH CENTRE: B. Txirrita, 23-2º Bajo, 20017 San Sebastian. Tel: (43) 40 03 16. (6-9)

INLINGUA IDIOMAS; Hernani 29, 20004 San Sebastian/Larramendi 23, 20006 San Sebastian. Tel: (43) 46 36 36/42 37 27. (18)

INTERNATIONAL HOUSE, ACADEMIA LACUNZA: Urbieta 14, 20006 San Sebastian. Tel: (43) 42 77 07. (60)

THE SMITHS' SCHOOL: Maestro Guridi s/n, 20008 San Sebastian. Tel: (43) 21 10 28. (10) Bus fare from London paid.

CLIC — CENTRO DE LENGUAS E INTERCAMBIO CULTURAL: Santa Ana II, 41002 Seville. Tel: (5) 438 4703. (8)

LONDON SCHOOL OF ENGLISH: Calle Numancia 3, Santa Cruz (Tenerife) Tel: (22) 28 17 23/27 34 72. Fax: 24 47 60. (33)

NELSON ENGLISH SCHOOL: Jorge Manrique 1, Santa Cruz (Tenerife) Tel: (22) 21 89 19. Fax: 20 15 55. (5)

RAPIDIDIOM, ESCUELA DE IDIOMAS: Calle Castillo 15, Santa Cruz (Tenerife) Tel: (22) 24 21 01/77. Fax: 24 24 28. (2)

INLINGUA IDIOMAS: Rualasal 23, 39001 Santander. Tel: (42) 22 34 66. (12) Occasionally have short summer vacancies.

SCHOOL OF ENGLISH: Jenaro Oraá 6, 48980 Santurce (Vizcaya) Tel: (4) 461 9555/461 9756. Fax: 461 5723. (8-9)

KENT IDIOMAS: Tejedores 28, El Carmen, 40004 Segovia. Tel: (11) 43 44 23. (2)

ENGLISH SCHOOL MACARENA: Dr. Jimenez Diaz 20, 41008 Seville. Tel: (5) 435 6134. (19)

EPICENTER: Niebla 13, 41011 Seville. Tel: (5) 427 9540. (20)
ESCUELA UNION PACIFIC: Virgen de Luján 30A, 41011 Seville. Tel: (5) 445 5515. (50+) Mostly part-time work in 5 centres located in Madrid (2), Barcelona, Bilboa and Seville.
ESCUELA OFICIAL DE IDIOMAS: Alonso Velazquez, s/n, 42004 Soria. Tel: (75) 22 86 52. No full-time teachers, only conversation assistants who are employed through the Ministry of Education.
THE BRITISH SCHOOL — TARRAGONA: Prat de la Riba 6, 43001 Tarragona. Tel: (77) 21 16 05. (9)
ESCOLA ANGLO-FRANCESA: Carnicer 1, 25300 Tarrega (Lleida). Tel: (73) 31 12 45. (3) Also in Agramunt, Bellpuig, Artesa de Segre and Balaguer.
ANGLO CENTRE: Apto. 208, Toledo. Tel: (25) 22 20 67. (5)
INLINGUA IDIOMAS: Teodoro González 11, 1ºA, 43500 Tortosa (Tarragona). Tel: (77) 44 66 11. (2) Also has schools in Amposta (Tarragona) and Vinaroz (Castellón)
AMERICAN INSTITUTE: El Bachiller 13, 46010 Valencia. Tel: (6) 369 6168. (3-5)
LIVE CENTRES — CENTRO INGLES LUZ: Pasaje Residenciales Luz, 8 bajo, 46010 Valencia. Tel: (6) 361 4074/369 9590/274 2782. (20)
SANTA ANA CENTRO DE IDIOMAS: Pasión 10, 47001 Valladolid. Tel: (83) 35 82 42. (4)
EUROSCHOOLS: Regueiro 2, 36211 Vigo. Tel: (86) 291 7 48. (17)
CAMBRIDGE SCHOOL: Zurita 21, 1º Izda. 50001 Zaragoza. Tel: (76) 21 19 09. (6)
IDIOMAS CAMPO: Torrenueva 32, 50003 Zaragoza. Tel: (76) 29 11 21/39 40 42. (6)
MOD-LANG: Celso Emilio Ferreiro 10-1ºA, 50010 Zaragoza. Tel: (76) 33 34 33. Fax: 31 22 11. (12-15)
OXFORD CENTRO DE IDIOMAS: San Miguel 16, 50001 Zaragoza. Tel: (76) 22 18 10/21 11 20. Fax: 21 20 10. (25)
STEVENSON SCHOOL OF ENGLISH: Gran Via 11, esc. C-1º, puerta 5, 50006 Zaragoza. Tel: (76) 22 63 61. (3)
TECHNICAL COLLEGE OF ENGLISH: Francisco de Vitoria 13, 50008 Zaragoza. Tel: (76) 22 79 09. (12) Runs summer courses in the Pyrenees. Spanish to university level and an interest in children and sport only qualifications required.
TRINITY SCHOOL OF ENGLISH: Pº Ruiseñores 5, 50006 Zaragoza. Tel: (76) 27 65 77. (6)
YES ENGLISH SCHOOL: Zigordia 50, 20800 Zarautz. Tel: (43) 83 40 60. (4)

Switzerland

The teaching situation in Switzerland is similar to that of Germany, but the restrictive immigration regulations mean that very few native speakers are recruited abroad, except at a very advanced level. Very occasionally an advert appears in the educational press, such as one spotted on September 1990: "£200 Plus Per Day for top English teachers in Germany, Austria, Switzerland" for people with experience teaching business English to foreign executives. Similarly the agency Lexel (5 Percy Street, London W1P 9FA) recruits experienced EFL teachers for 12 or 18 month in-company contracts to teach general, business and banking English.

Surprisingly, the 9 Berlitz schools in Switzerland do not insist on very advanced qualifications, but the catch is that they mostly hire only people who already have a residence permit for Switzerland. The same is likely to hold true for Migros Language Schools in Zurich, Geneva and Lausanne, whose addresses are given out by the Swiss Embassy.

Switzerland is the only country in Europe which puts bureaucratic obstacles in the way of native-speaker English teachers. Because of a very strict quota system — numbers vary from canton to canton — most schools do not try to recruit abroad. In order to get permission to hire a foreigner, they have to prove (as in the US) that there is no one in Switzerland capable of doing the job. According to some sources, a special agreement between Ireland and Switzerland makes it easier for holders of Irish passports to get a work permit. If you did find a school which wanted to hire a native speaker for a few months, it might be possible for them to obtain a *Permis A* on your behalf. These are for seasonal work lasting up to either 9 months (which are subject to quotas) or 3 months (which are outside the quota system)

Vacation Work

As in Austria there are more possibilities for teaching English at summer camps than in city language institutes. The following organizations hire people between June and September as teachers or monitors (or some combination of the two):

Eurocentres, Head Office, Seestrasse 247, 8038 Zurich. Summer centres in Lucerne and Neuchatel.

The Summer Camp, Institut le Rosey, 1180 Rolle. Qualified or experienced EFL teachers for coeducational summer camps on Lake Geneva. Teachers must be capable of carrying out boarding school duties.

TASIS Summer Programs, Coldharbour Lane, Thorpe, Surrey TW20 8TE. Posts involve teaching on an intensive language programme, plus sports and general chaperoning. Late June to late August.

Village Camps SA, 1296 Coppet. Tel: (25) 776 20 59. Summer address: Chalet Seneca, 1854 Leysin. American company which has a summer camp for 13-17 year olds near Lake Geneva in French-speaking Switzerland. Salary for teachers is SFr400 per week and for monitors SFr100-160 per week plus full board and lodging and accident insurance. Camp also in Austria.

ETR Group, 15 King Street (4th Floor), London SW1Y 6QH. Needs EFL teachers for children aged 8 to 17 at international summer schools in Switzerland and Austria.

There are a number of international schools in Switzerland, some of which run EFL summer schools such as the Institut Alpin, 1837 Chateau d'Oex. Unfortunately the Embassy no longer sends out a list of private schools, ever since the Swiss Association of Private Schools (Zeughausgasse 29, Postfach 3367, 3000 Bern 7) requested that they stop to prevent an inundation of job applications. Watch for occasional ads or, if you are in Switzerland, make local enquiries. Susanna Macmillan hitch-hiked from Italy to Crans-Montana in the Swiss Alps in the autumn and within 3 days had arranged a job as a *monitrice* at the International School there. The job, which was to teach English and sport, came with room and board and paid an additional SFr850 per month. (Perhaps one reason the job was so easy to get was because of the 60-hour weeks and compulsory overtime with no compensation.)

BASILINGUA SPRACHSCHULE
Birsigstrasse 2, 4054 Basel. Tel: (61) 281 3954.
Number of teachers: 3.
Preference of nationality: none.
Qualifications: BA.
Conditions of employment: no fixed contract length. Hours of work between 7.30am-9.45pm. Hours per week will depend on demand at the time. Pupils range in age from 20-60.
Salary: £10 per 45-minute lesson.
Facilities/Support: no assistance with accommodation. Training provided.
Recruitment: local advertising and recruitment. Interviews essential.

BERLITZ
14 Rue de l'Ancien-Port, 1201 Geneva. Tel: (22) 738 3200.
Also at 1 Carrefour de Rive, 1207 Geneva. Tel: 786 1476.
Number of teachers: 11.
Preference of nationality: none.
Qualifications: BA.
Conditions of employment: minimum 1 year contracts. Flexible hours of work. Pupils range in age from 35-45.
Salary: 30 francs per hour.
Facilities/Support: no assistance with accommodation. Training given.
Recruitment: newspaper adverts and through universities. Interviews are essential and can be held in UK/US if necessary.

BERLITZ
Münzgasse 3, 4001 Basel. Tel: (61) 256360.
Number of teachers: 4.
Preference of nationality; UK.
Qualifications: BA or professional experience, e.g. business, banking.
Conditions of employment: no limit on contract length. Flexible hours of work. Pupils are adults whose average age is between 30-40.
Salary: 20.80 francs per 40-minute lesson plus 10-20% supplements for some programmes.
Facilities/Support: no assistance with accommodation. Training provided.
Recruitment: through adverts. Local interviews essential.

BRILLIANTMONT ECOLE INTERNATIONALE
Av. Secrétan 12-18, 1005 Lausanne. Tel: (21) 312 47 41.
Number of teachers: 4.
Preference of nationality: UK.
Qualifications: TEFL qualification plus 1 year's experience.
Conditions of employment: minimum 1 year contracts. 25 contact h.p.w. in the day school, and 25 h.p.w. in boarding school of which 16 are contact hours. Pupils aged 14-18.
Salary: 2,400 francs per month.
Facilities/Support: priority given to teachers resident in Switzerland. Staff sent to regular training workshops. Work permits will be applied for.
Recruitment: through ECIS in Hampshire. Interviews essential and held in UK.

Austria

The market for EFL in Austria is considerably smaller than in Germany, though there are some possibilities. The Austrian Institute in London (28 Rutland Gate, SW7 1PQ) can supply a list of 25 private language schools in the country including several Berlitz and inlingua addresses. There is one International House affiliated school in Vienna, the Interlanguage Center. Advertisements for teaching jobs in Austria almost never appear in the *TES* or the *Guardian*.

American students of German may be interested in the Austrian-American Educational Commission's teacher exchange (in association with the Fulbright Commission). Applications, preferably from prospective German teachers, must be received before March for an 8-month contract as an English assistant starting in October. The salary is AS14,000 per month less social security deductions of 16%. Further details are available from the Commission at Schmidgasse 14, 1082 Vienna.

One possibility for people who want to teach English in Austria is for vacation work. The organization Young Austria (Alpenstrasse 108a, A-5020 Salzburg) recruit about 30 teachers and monitors to work at summer language and sports camps near Salzburg. For about 3 or 4 hours of each day of the 3-week camp, children receive English tuition from teachers (who must have teaching experience). Monitors help the teachers with the social and outdoor programme as well as with the lesssons. Teachers receive about AS5,200 for a 3-week camp and monitors receive AS4,200 along with board and lodging and a lump sum payment of AS2,000 for travel expenses. Applications should be in by mid-March since compulsory interviews and briefing are held in London in May/June.

Similarly the organization Village Camps SA run a language summer camp at Zell-am-See. And the ETR Group also run an international summer school in Austria which employs EFL teachers. For addresses and further details, see Switzerland chapter above.

The hourly rate at reputable institutes starts at AS2,000, which sounds generous until you encounter the cost of living. Vienna is a very expensive city, though life in the provinces is considerably cheaper.

Austria is not a member of the EEC, so a work permit must be applied for from outside Austria, never an easy procedure.

INLINGUA
Landstrasse 24, 4020 Linz. Tel: (732) 281969.
Also at Neuer Markt 1, 1010 Vienna which hires locally.
Number of teachers: 5.
Preference of nationality: none.
Qualifications: RSA Cert. or equivalent.
Conditions of employment: no limit on contract length. Hours of work 5-9.30pm with some morning/afternoon work. All pupils are adults.
Salary: approximately 16,000 schillings per month.
Facilities/Support: assistance with accommodation. Training given.
Recruitment: through inlingua Teacher Service, Birmingham.

SPIDI (Spracheninstitut der Industrie)
Lothringer Strasse 12, 1031 Vienna. Tel: (1) 752506/71141.
Number of teachers: 50 part-time staff.
Preference of nationality: none.
Qualifications: BA. 2-3 years experience and Prep Cert./Dip. preferred.
Conditions of employment: 1 term renewable contracts. 6-8 h.p.w. Pupils range in age from 18-70, mostly 25-40.
Salary: from 208 schillings per hour.
Facilities/Support: no assistance with accommodation. Training given.
Recruitment: through personal recommendation. Local interviews essential.

Cyprus

A visitor to Cyprus will be struck by the similarities with Greece — cuisine, architecture, landscapes and culture — but then surprised at the relative prominence of English. Signs are printed both in Greek and English, many local people even outside the cities speak some English, and the British influence can be noticed everywhere. This is because the English language is given a much higher profile in the state educational system, which means that there is not the proliferation of *frontisteria* found in Greece. Nor does the British Council have an English teaching operation.

Still there is a certain number of language schools, many of whom hire native speakers, the majority of whom are drawn from the large pool of expatriates (most of them British) who have settled in Cyprus. But there is always a chance of a vacancy, and any EFL teacher eager to spend some time in the country which, according to some meteorologists, has the ideal climate, should obtain from the British Council in Nicosia the list of 24 language institutes in the Greek part of the island. Half are in Nicosia, while the others are in Limassol, Larnaca and Paphos, all along the south coast of Cyprus.

The Cypriot authorities require teachers in private institutes to have a university degree. The RSA Certificate (courses are occasionally offered by the *English Institute* in Nicosia) is not an acceptable substitute. For proper contract jobs, a work permit should be obtained outside the country. The English Institute is probably the most prestigious purveyor of English and occasionally advertises in the *TES*. Other centres might be prepared to hire a native speaker teacher with lesser qualifications on a more casual basis at an hourly rate of between 3 and 5 Cypriot pounds.

Finding out about opportunities in Turkish Cyprus is much more difficult. There is no British Council representative and few reports of TEFL activities. (One exception is the Eastern Mediterranean University in Famagusta, which was recently advertising for high level English teaching staff.) Since the demand for English is so great in mainland Turkey, it is not obvious why this would not be the case in Turkish Cyprus (except that there is much less need for English to participate in the tourist industry). Since so few English speakers go to northern Cyprus even as tourists, perhaps an enterprising EFL teacher would be able to create a demand, at least for private tuition.

MASSOURAS PRIVATE INSTITUTE LTD
1 Liperti St., Flat 103, Paphos. Tel: (61) 237192/244288.
Number of teachers: 1
Preference of nationality: unspecified.
Qualifications: BA.
Conditions of employment: 1 academic year contracts. Hours of work 2-7pm.
Pupils range in age from 8-18.
Salary: C£4 per hour.
Facilities/Support: no assistance with accommodation. Training provided.
Recruitment: through newspaper adverts. Local interviews essential.

THE ENGLISH INSTITUTE
c/o The English School, Nicosia. Tel: (2) 493300.
Number of teachers: 6 (mostly local residents).
Preference of nationality: UK, Canada, US, Australia, Cyprus, etc.
Qualifications: BA/MA (English) plus RSA Cert. or PGCE (or equivalent).
Conditions of employment: 1-2 year contracts. Hours of work 2.30-8pm plus
8 hours per week at any other time. Pupils range in age from 9-18+.
Salary: C£7-10,000 per year.
Facilities/Support: no assistance with accommodation. Training provided.
Recruitment: through local adverts and *TES.* Interviews will only be held in
UK and US if local applicants cannot fill vacancies.

Malta

Although somewhat off the beaten track, Malta has not escaped the EFL boom.
According to an article in the *EFL Gazette,* a number of cowboy language schools
have recently been set up in Malta, much to the annoyance of the more reputable
government-recognized schools. Their interests are represented by FELTOM,
the Federation of English Language Teaching Organisations in Malta (c/o English
Language Academy, 9 Tower Lane, Sliema, Malta; tel: 356-310427). The
Secretary of the Federation should be able to supply a copy of FELTOM's policy
on recruitment of English teachers from abroad and a list of member schools.
The British Council in Valletta does not recruit teachers nor advise on local
employment prospects. It is safe to assume that if there are indeed so many not-
so-reputable language institutes opening up, there would be vacancies for native
speakers on-the-spot. An average salary would be 3,000 Maltese pounds less
30% for tax and insurance. Work permits should be arranged before departure
if possible.

The language schools of Malta are not just for the benefit of Maltese language
learners. The NSTS English Language Centre (220 St. Paul Street, Valletta,
Malta; tel: 356-624983) markets its English courses in conjunction with sports
holidays for young tourists to Malta. NSTS run weekly vacation courses from
June to August, and it might be worth approaching them for a job, particularly
if you are a water sports enthusiast.

Yugoslavia

As a very popular tourist destination, one would have expected a considerable demand for English in Yugoslavia. But the TEFL industry seems to be in its infancy, probably for the same reason as it was in Eastern Europe until so recently — a shortage of finance. Advertisements rarely appear in the British press and the few which do are for summer courses. For example the following appeared in the *Guardian* in June: "Qualified teachers of English required for summer months. Tel: 081-451 5368". Two UK agencies which have been known to advertise summer vacancies in Yugoslavia are English Language Services (70 Oakington Avenue, Wembley Park, Middlesex) and the London Ryan Organisation (68 Franklyn Road, Willesden, London NW10 9TE). According to the one organization listed in the directory, a BA in English or a TEFL qualification with a year's experience is sufficient to gain a 9-month contract, earning free air fares, free accommodation and £100 per week. According to the *Language Study Centre* in Sombor, a small town in the north, work permits are not a problem.

A sample of one is not enough to generalize about conditions. Perhaps the change of political climatge in Europe will result in an increase in the number of opportunities in Yugoslavia, but there is little indication of this happening at present.

LANGUAGE STUDY CENTRE
Brace Miladinov 16a, 25000 Sombor. Tel: (25) 34213/37666 ext 19.
Number of teachers: 2.
Preference of nationality: BA (English)/TEFL qualification and at least 1 year's experience.
Qualifications: BA (English)/TEFL qualification and at least 1 year's experience.
Conditions of employment: 9 month contracts. 20-25 h.p.w. Pupils mostly aged 7-16, but there are also classes for adults.
Salary: £100 per week.
Facilities/Support: accommodation and return air fare provided free of charge. No training.
Recruitment: through adverts. Interviews are essential and are held in UK.

EASTERN EUROPE

English language teaching in the countries of Eastern Europe is in a state of flux, as Michael Frost discovered on an extensive visit to these countries in the summer of 1990. Political change has provoked a linguistic revolution. Countries which once taught Russian as the first foreign language have committed themselves in principle to a great expansion of English teaching, and there is a tremendous need for native English speakers. Demand is greatest in Hungary, Poland and Czechoslovakia, though all the countries of Eastern Europe (bar Albania) have opportunities in both state schools and emerging private language schools. Russian is out; English is in. It's currently as fashionable in the cities of Eastern Europe to be seen carrying a Western English langue textbook as it used to be to strut around with Levis and a Sony Walkman.

Why do people want to learn English? English is seen as the language of the West and as a necessary accompaniment to eonomic and political development. Ordinary people see it as a passport to a better way of life as they can expect higher salaries if they can speak it to some degree, and it gives a chance to experience Western popular culture which is now freely available. Educationalists and governments see the English language as a way of tapping into the knowledge and skills of the West which will be vital for development; it is the language of science, of business, of diplomacy and of conferences, and it is therefore essential for linking up with the West and effecting lasting changes in societies which had ossified under decades of Communist rule. The comment of Professor Hanna Komarowska, who has been advising the Polish Education Ministry on English teaching, applies equally to all the countries of the region: "There is a huge demand. For us English means access to civilization, technology, thinking — absolutely everything. It is as if when we stop teaching English we stop teaching people to read and write. We see it as an education for democracy".

The local educational systems simply cannot produce enough local teachers of English for state schools. The best local teachers are very often drawn into private sector teaching where salaries are much greater, or go into banking or tourism. In all the countries of the region there are acute shortages of teachers, as training establishments cannot produce new teachers and retrain ex-Russian teachers to meet the demands of all their schools. Hence many state schools will welcome teachers especially volunteers with little or no experience for conversation classes to supplement grammar taught by local school staff.

Opportunities for native speakers, then, are such that anyone interested in teaching in Eastern Europe should be able to find work with little difficulty. Jobs can either be arranged in advance or fixed up on the spot; even for the latter, there's usually no problem sorting out work permits. As there are real shortages of local teachers of English, native speakers cannot be accused of poaching other people's jobs. Those with qualifications and experience are obviously in the best position, though anyone with native-speaker status and the desire to experience life in this rapidly changing part of the world should find few problems.

The main drawback is the pay: generally fair to good by Eastern European standards but appalling by those of the West. A monthly salary of £120-£140 is standard. The problem is made worse by galloping inflation and sudden price rises which will eat away at a salary that was marginal to begin with. Even when accommodation is provided, teachers often only break even.

In a few cases a teacher's salary will be in excess of his or her needs A further problem is that it is likely to be paid in a non-convertible currency. Poland made the zloty freely convertible in January 1990 but restrictions still exist in Hungary and Czechoslovakia. Sometimes contracts will have special provisions to allow the conversion of local currencies into a hard currency, so check the small print beforehand.

Inevitably funds are in short supply, so there is a burgeoning demand for volunteer teachers, including opportunities for shorter teaching stays of 1-3 months. Although the pay will be minimal, help with accommodation is usually given. Voluntary organizations such as Education for Democracy in Czechoslovakia (see below) have sprung up to meet the demand. Also *VSO* and the *Peace Corps* have been asked to provide volunteer teachers (on the usual 2-year contracts) even though these organizations normally deal exclusively with developing nations. Ironically "volunteers" with the major agencies are comparatively wealthy since they benefit from the standard package which includes free travel, insurance and other benefits.

Ministries of Education and national educational establishments in the countries of Eastern Europe are also trying to attract qualified and experienced teachers. The very low pay offered, however, makes these jobs only marginally better than volunteer work. As more funds become available from the West for language projects, more qualified native-speaker teachers may be attracted: the EEC, for example, has proposed the establishment of multilingual training centres in Poland. Increasingly, UK newspapers carry adverts for Eastern European employers, some of which are placed by agents in Britain such as *English Worldwide,* the *Language Exchange* in Edinburgh and CILC (see page xx). One recent advert placed by the University of Gdansk read, "Idealistic recent graduate? Urgent need for energetic EFL teachers."

The now-redundant teachers of Russian are being retrained to teach English and fill the gaps, but this process takes time and will not lessen the demand for native speakers in the forseeable future. It is estimated that it takes between 3 and 5 years to retrain a Russian language teacher from scratch, and in the meantime there will be a huge demand for English. (Pessimists have predicted that inadequately trained ex-Russian teachers will be allowed to misteach a whole generation.) This process of retraining will in itself provide opportunities for native speakers, since high level teacher trainers are needed to impart both the language and the methods of teaching it.

It should not be surprising to learn that there is considerable uncertainty and confusion on the EFL front. In the words of an English lecturer in Budapest writing about Eastern Europe in the *EFL Gazette,* "there is a boom and a mess". The dire shortage of English teaching facilities through the past decades cannot be reversed instantaneously. The emergence of these countries into the "real world" will be attended by problems and pitfalls such as an absence of coordinated educational policies and the possibility of shoddy or exploitative working conditions for teachers, not to mention price rises, unemployment and a dramatic increase in crime.

While opportunities vary from place to place and while the future is uncertain due to the speed of change, it is true to say that there will be a great demand for native EFL teachers for many years ahead. And though these may not be the best paid EFL jobs in the world, Eastern Europe can offer historic and beautiful cities, genuinely friendly people and a unique chance to experience life in the "other Europe" before it turns into just another free-market democracy.

Here follows what Michael Frost calls a "snapshot circa summer 1990" of the EFL situations in Hungary, Czechoslovakia and Poland, with brief sections on the rest of Eastern Europe.

Hungary

EFL in Hungary is undergoing a boom, since the very popular decision in October 1989 to abandon compulsory Russian in schools and offer Western languages instead. Candidates for college and university entrance now have to pass an English language test, and both Arts and Science students at university take courses in English. Apart from Russian, the second language of Hungary has traditionally been German, a legacy of the old Austro-Hungarian Empire. But this is being overtaken by English and, of all the countries in the Eastern Bloc, Hungary offers the greatest range of opportunities. Estimates of teachers needed vary from 5,000 to 15,000 as the Hungarians set about teaching English in primary and secondary schools, as well as in the emerging private language schools. Private institutes have mushroomed in the past 2 years to teach the generations that missed out on English and now want to catch up, and parents are keen for their children to supplement the English teaching of the state schools.

"The need for teachers is so great," reports an English language administrator in Budapest, "that people are literally being hired off the street. Teaching credentials are practically irrelevant as long as you are a native speaker." However, teachers are very poorly paid in Hungary, aside from the top-notch private schools and the British Council. It is not uncommon for teachers to hold down 2 or 3 jobs just to make ends meet. Rents in Budapest are high and take a major proportion of salary; some schools help by subsidizing accommodation, or it may be possible to arrange accommodation in return for English lessons. Many foreign teachers claim that they can only hope to break even at best, though salaries may improve if the economy develops quickly. Although salaries are low by comparison with those of their Western counterparts, native speakers can console themselves with the thought that they are usually better paid than Hungarian university lecturers in English. And as many teachers have discovered, Hungary is a great place to spend a year.

FIXING UP A JOB

State Schools

Native English speakers are eagerly sought by all state schools. English is currently available for pupils in the Dual Language Secondary Schools (less than 1% of the total number of schools), in the Gimnazium schools (more academic "grammar schools", with 20% of total pupils) and, if plans go ahead, in secondary schools all over Hungary. The British Council recruits some staff for the handful of bilingual schools and also for some universities, usually via adverts in the *TES* or *Guardian* between April and June.

The English Teachers' Association of the National Pedagogical Institute (Bolyai u.14, 1023 Budapest) recruits native speakers for schools outside the capital, while the Budapest Pedagogical Institute (Horvéth Mihály Tér 8, Budapest 8) recruits for the capital itself. In Budapest alone there are 500 schools which need at least one teacher. At the time of writing many were without EFL staff due to teacher shortages. The retraining of ex-Russian teachers will provide only some 800 teachers per year (and of this figure only a fifth are predicted to stay on in state sector teaching). Another possibility is to contact the Oxford University Press representative, Mrs. Ilona Jobbagy, who will contact schools at teachers' behest; her address is Tarcali Utca 20, 113 Budapest.

Opportunities for interested native speaker teachers are thus great at present. Salaries, alas, do not equal the range of opportunities, and teachers interested in working in the Hungarian state sector will have to accept that their fortunes will not be made from EFL work in these schools. Help is usually obtainable with accommodation (which is much easier to find outside Budapest) and there is no problem with obtaining work permits, which are a legal requirement for being paid. These should be processed in less than a month, even if you arrived on a tourist visa.

Inexperienced teachers are used for language and cultural enhancement through conversation classes, while the nitty-gritty teaching of grammar and reading is usually done by Hungarian teachers. This team-teaching approach, while not always a success, gives an interim solution until more seasoned teachers are attracted to work in Hungary.

A recent visitor to Hungary estimates that American teachers outnumber Brits by 8 to 1. The Peace Corps currently has 61 EFL volunteers in Hungary and plans to increase this to 200. The Fulbright Program provides volunteer teachers for some state schools and offers a round trip from the US to Hungary plus salary and housing. Most teachers break even and can supplement their income by giving private lesssons. George Washington University (PO Box 2298, Washington DC 20057) provides internship teachers. A variety of other American organizations are funding US teachers in Hungary.

The University English departments take some native speakers through the British Council and USIS (c/o the American Embassy) or hire individually as their needs arise. There are also some exchange programmes for university staff. The pay in universities is not the highest in the land by any stretch of the imagination. There may also be work with the Ministry of Foreign Trade which offers special English classes to its officials, and also work with other Ministries; check things out on the spot.

Recruitment in the state sector will probably change as needs become more sharply focused and funds become available. At present there are staff shortages, exacerbated by the absence of coordinated recruitment and well-prepared programmes to attract EFL teachers. Many educationalists are bitter over the government's failure to tackle this problem effectively and are pressing for greater recruitment efforts and for higher salaries for EFL staff. If proposed World Bank loans for language education and suggested EEC assistance come about then more resources may be available to pay EFL staff making the state sector a more attractive option. For those altruistic enough, Hungarian schools offer one way of sampling life in the land of the Magyars.

Private Schools

The inefficiency of the state sector has allowed private language schools to flourish. The boom is further fuelled by the desire to learn among people who missed out under the Communist regime. Professional and relatively prosperous parents ensure that the private sector is never short of pupils. It is estimated that there are over 100 private language schools in Budapest alone, and new schools are constantly opening to cater for the seemingly insatiable demand for English. Many use native speakers as live commercials for the schools and some will take almost anyone, with or without experience or qualifications.

Prospects are excellent for anyone with an RSA Certificate or some experience. The larger Western-type schools which demand qualifications, such as *International House* and, more recently, the *Bell School* are establishing a niche in the quality end of the market and more are likely to follow. British and American accents are both in demand. International House, with 3 affiliated schools in Budapest plus provincial operations in Győr, Debrecen and Eger, hires both through its London headquarters and also locally as needs arise. It offers one-year contracts for qualified teachers of both adults and children and (according to Dennis Bricault) "a wonderful social and professional atmosphere". In addition to a salary of around 23,000 forints, a cash subsidy for accommodation is available. If the contract is renewed for a second year, air fares are paid. Short-term summer work for up to 6 weeks is sometimes available at the Bimbo Street IH in Budapest. This pays at the rate of 350 forints per period. *Living Language Seminar* also offers 3 month or longer contracts for experienced staff, useful for those interested in shorter stays. English language summer camps use qualified teachers and student assistants recruited in the UK by the Central Bureau, Seymour Mews House, Seymour Mews, London W1H 9PE (tel: 071-486 5101 ext. 24).

The British Council in Budapest can provide a list of private language schools, though others exist which are not on the list. Check out the small ads in the local press, e.g. *Magyar Nemzet* which contains adverts for courses of *Angol* at *Nyeliviskola* (language schools). Salaries vary, but currently teachers can expect between 13,000 and 25,000 forints for 15-20 hours, more at good schools. Assistance with accommodation is sometimes given, which is especially useful in Budapest where there is an acute shortage.

Private classes provide one way of supplementing a meagre salary and are usually easy to obtain. These pay anything between 200 and 600 forints per hour. Freelance teachers may find a developing market for their linguistic expertise in companies. Many executives need English for business as Hungary seeks to integrate with the economies of the West and attract foreign investors. The Department of Commerce, for example, employs teachers to train bankers, traders and top electrical engineers. Many professionals now need English as part of their work and are both able and prepared to pay for it.

As more and more Western businesses set up joint ventures, they may provide some of this missing language expertise. For example ABB Power Ventures Ltd. (PO Box 8131, CH-8050, Zurich, Switzerland) was recently advertising one year English teaching vacancies in their Hungarian and Polish joint ventures.

Teachers in private schools must expect to teach everything from grammar to conversation, with variable materials. You may find yourself explaining the cartoon antics of "Muzzy in Gondoland" (a popular BBC video) to a group of school kids or discussing the Oil Crisis with executives (though probably not vice versa). Pupils are generally keen and no problem to teach. They recognize that English is a big plus in the job market and are enthusiastic about learning. Dennis Bricault, who taught at IH in Budapest for a year, describes pupils as a "teacher's dream: hard-working, generally competent and with a good idea of what it takes to learn languages". Some pupils may find modern teaching methods strange as they are used to a more teacher-centred approach, and more creative techniques may take some getting use to.

English language materials vary, with some very old and dated texts being used alongside newer books. More and more authentic resources are becoming available in Hungary, including radio, English language television (even satellite TV), newspapers and modern textbooks, though teachers would be advised to take along some of their own back-up material (if they have any); favourite texts may not always be available, and often Western EFL books are expensive. The Hungarian journal *Nagyvilaq* regularly carries reviews of English books and translated extracts, and the *New Hungarian Quarterly* covering educational and cultural matters, is published in English.

LIST OF SCHOOLS

BELL SCHOOL
Bell Iskolák Kft., Tulipán u.8, H-1022 Budapest. Tel: (1) 115 5068/165 9683. Fax: 165 9683.
Number of teachers: 3.
Preference of nationality: UK.
Qualifications: BA/RSA Cert./Dip. and several years teaching experience.
Conditions of employment: 1 year contracts. Approximately 15 h.p.w. Pupils include young children, secondary school students and adults.
Salary: 25,000 forints per month.
Facilities/Support: accommodation provided free of charge. Training given.
Recruitment: through the Bell Trust, Cambridge. Local or UK interviews.

INTERNATIONAL HOUSE LANGUAGE SCHOOL (IHLS)
Bimbó út 7, 1022 Budapest. Tel: (1) 115-5275.
Also: 1HB, Cukor u.4, 1053 Budapest; and ILS, PO Box 64, 1363 Budapest.
Number of teachers: 14.
Qualifications: RSA Cert. (grade 'B').
Conditions of employment: 1 year contracts but minimum 6 weeks for summer work. 20 lessons per week. Pupils range in age from 16 during the summer, and from 8 for the rest of the year.
Salary: 23,000 forints per month (gross) for 1 year contracts; 350 forints per lesson (gross) for short term contracts.
Facilities/Support: assistance given finding accommodation plus 4,000 forints per month housing allowance. Training given, though less available during summer months.
Recruitment: through direct application and IH, London. Interviews essential.

KARINTHY FRIGYES GIMNÁZIUM
Thököly út 7, 1183 Budapest. Tel: (1) 787-383.
Number of teachers: 3-4.
Preference of nationality: none.

Qualifications: MA (English) or BA plus TEFL experience.
Conditions of employment: 1 academic year contracts. Hours of work from 8am-2pm. Pupils aged 14-19.
Salary: average for Hungary. Some candidates with PGCE earn tax free sterling subsidies of £5,500.
Facilities/Support: free accommodation provided plus heating/ electricity costs. No training given.
Recruitment: through the British Council and the Fulbright Commission.

KATÓNA JOZSEF GIMNÁZIUM
Dózsa György u.3, 6000 Kecskemét. Tel: (76) 21283.
Number of teachers: 4
Preference of nationality: UK, US.
Qualifications: Mathematics/Physics/Biology/English teachers qualified to teach in secondary schools.
Conditions of employment: 1 academic year renewable contracts. Pupils aged between 14-18.
Salary: 20,000 forints per month.
Facilities/Support: free furnished flats available. No training.
Recruitment: through adverts. Interviews not essential.

LIVING LANGUAGE SEMINAR
Fejér György u.8, 1053 Budapest. Tel/Fax: (1) 135-6154.
Number of teachers: 1-3
Preference of nationality: UK, US.
Qualifications: a great deal of ESL teaching experience.
Conditions of employment: contracts from 3 months. Negotiable hours. Pupils aged 10-14 and adults.
Salary: high to local standards.
Facilities/Support: no assistance with accommodation at present.
Recruitment: through adverts. Interviews required.

STUDIUM PRIVATE LANGUAGE SCHOOL
Döbrentei 8, 1013 Budapest. Tel: (1) 167-3218.
Number of teachers: 3-4
Preference of nationality: UK, US.
Qualifications: qualified English teachers.
Conditions of employment: 1 term contracts. Hours of work in the evening and Saturday mornings. Pupils are all adults.
Salary: 500 forints per 45-minute lesson.
Facilities/Support: no assistance with accommodation. No training given.
Recruitment: through personal contacts. Local interviews essential.

Czechoslovakia

The "Velvet Revolution" of 1989 has been followed by an EFL revolution to match it. Russian has ceded ground to Western languages and there is a clamour to learn English. The apparatus for teaching English is still developing to meet demand: some private schools run by locals are beginning to get off the ground, as are English language kindergartens. Western-backed language schools have already joined the scene and volunteer organizations are placing teachers in increasing numbers. As with most things in Czechoslovakia, there is considerable confusion while policies are being developed, and it will be some time before the exact structures of EFL are firmly established and operating. Czech students have had even less exposure to English than those in the rest of Eastern Europe, which has left the level of ability at a low general standard. One head teacher in a secondary school summed up the problem:

Very few people can speak English well here. They have been taught badly by bad teachers and with bad books. We have to create a brand new atmosphere for English teachers. Our accents are poor because we have not had any chance to travel abroad or to speak to English people.

Even pupils who have studied English have been taught complex words to do with trade union structures or the evils of British and American colonialism, from books featuring critical and exploited African exchange students. Yet students often lack simple words like "table" and "chair", and are thus at a loss when it comes to practical communication.

The general picture is that EFL in Czechoslovakia does offer opportunities for teaching, especially outside Prague where it has become difficult to obtain either employment or accommodation. The capital seems to have no problem in attracting native teachers. According to Graham Johnston, who has taught in Prague since 1988, "I doubt that people will simply be able to turn up and walk into a job. At least here in Prague, the party is over".

Cities like Bratislava, Brno, and Ostrava have much to offer interested teachers as do some of the smaller towns away from the tourist-clogged capital. All in all, EFL in Czechoslovakia offers the aspiring EFL teacher beautiful architecture, eager students and a memorable opportunity to bridge the East-West gap.

CONDITIONS OF WORK

Accommodation is generally in short supply. There are waiting lists for ordinary Czechs, though Western teachers are usually given assistance by employers. One point to remember is that the Czech currency (the crown) is not yet convertible, so teachers will have either to spend all they earn or risk the black market. Only those teachers coming under mutual agreements (e.g. via the British Council) receive their salaries in a hard currency. Teachers can expect about 4,000 crowns per month, which is as much as a Czech doctor or head teacher earns. Private tutoring should bring in between 40 and 80 crowns.

The cost of living, though, is extremely cheap: metro tickets cost 1 crown and a meal out is between 20 and 60 crowns. You could buy an awful lot of the truly excellent Czech beer out of a wage of 4,000 crowns.

Teachers would be well advised before setting out to check on the availability of materials in the school where they are going to teach and to take along their own favourites and all necessary back-up materials. According to the Director of the new ILC School in Brno (see below), the nearest photocopier (as of October 1990) was in Vienna. The British Council in Prague has a well-stocked library which is of some use, and Education for Democracy (see below) operates a "Books for Democracy" programme to obtain English-language books of all kinds for the country.

FIXING UP A JOB

State Schools

Qualified teachers are being recruited to teach in Czech secondary schools, usually on a one-year contract with free accommodation and a salary of about 4,000 crowns per month. Travel expenses have to be met by applicants, since state-run organizations do not have a hard currency budget. Recruitment for the Prague region is being carried out at present by the Pedagogicky Ustav Prahy (PUP), Na Poříčí 4, 11000 Prague 1, whose director is Dr. Libuše Hoznauerová. PUP also arranges teacher exchanges.

Other institutions which recruit teachers are the Ministry of Education, Karmelitska 9, 11000 Prague 1 (where the contact is Dr. Stasa Zavitkovska) and the Slovak Ministry of Education's International Relations Department at Suvororova 12, 80000 Bratislava.

The Academic Information Agency (AIA) at Senovazne Namesti 26, 10000 Prague 1 also recruits qualified staff for primary and secondary schools. Applicants are sent a questionnaire which AIA then circulates among schools who contact teachers directly when they need staff. AIA also recruits for the 3 major state-run language schools in Prague (such as *Prague 8*) which took their first native-speaker teachers in 1989. Salaries from all these recruiting organizations should be adequate to live on by local standards, and there should be opportunities also for private classes to supplement your income.

Private Schools

Private schools are in a real state of infancy. Schools run by locals are gruadually appearing. They advertise locally for staff and sometimes take on native speakers. The British Council in Prague may be able to provide information on these. Anyone who is well qualified or experienced should have few real difficulties in finding a job on the spot and obtaining a work permit. Those without qualifications or experience may find it harder, though it is still possible for people who can present themselves well.

Western-backed schools are also beginning to establish themselves. For example Language International (c/o Barbara Maxson, 630 West Alabama St, Suite 1, Houston, Texas 77006; tel: 713-528-2853) welcomes applications from professional ESL teachers on an ongoing basis for a new adult language school. *Aspect International Schools* recruits teachers and course developers for its Czech schools, and advertises in the *TESOL Bulletin* and *New York Times*. Teachers receive a salary equivalent to US$1,000 per month plus housing, return air fares, medical insurance and paid vacations.

From the UK, International Language Centres (ILC) of 1 Riding House Street, London W1A 3AS opened a school in Brno in October 1990. Teachers must have a degree and the RSA Prep. Cert. They also plan to open a smaller school in Prague in the near future. Other UK organizations have been recruiting on behalf of Czech private schools, e.g. Pro English, 90 Higher Trayne, Ilfracombe, Devon (tel: 0271 863321) and IAL Bailbrook College, London Road West, Bath BA1 7JD.

Local schools set up and run by Czechs occasionally advertise abroad but more often recruit only within Czechoslovakia. One note of caution: it seems that at present literally anyone can set up a language school, with or without any business or educational experience, and teachers should be wary of cowboy operators. It is reported that some school directors use dubious (or non-existent) teaching materials and methods, treat their teachers badly and are only out to make as much money as quickly as possible. Teachers would be advised to make sure that they know exactly what they're letting themselves in for and get a clear written contract whenever possible. In the last resort, teachers can register complaints with the British Council, the AIA or the Embassy of their country.

Here is a tentative list of private language schools in Czechoslovakia in addition to the ones in the Directory:

Anglictina Express (address not available). Prefers to hire Americans.

Et Cetera, PO Box 53, 13000 Prague 3. Tel: 89 44 84. Was recently advertising for native speaker teachers with some pedagogic experience to teach 4 hours per day Monday to Thursday for a monthly salary of 4,000 crowns.

IPC Language Centre, PO Box 21, 14300 Prague 412 (tel: 401 8320; evenings only). Part-time teachers needed (native and non-native) willing to work flexible hours for 80-100 crowns per hour.

London School, Belgicke Ulice 25, 12000 Prague 2 (tel: 2-256859). Advertised in the *Guardian* (summer 1990).

Porta Linguaram Praha, Starometske Nam. 8, 11000 Prague 1.

Slovaktourist, c/o Gabrila Movka, Head of Department, 01130 Zilina. Seen advertising in the British Council for staff to work at an English summer camp.

Voluntary Organizations

One of the most straightforward ways of arranging to teach in Czechoslovakia is through one of the voluntary organizations which are placing teachers all around the country. They recruit from the UK, US and Canada and have representatives on the spot; participants usually receive orientation, accommodation and a living allowance, but have to pay their own air fares. All have received a very warm welcome, though there have been some complaints that an element of North American volunteers are "undercover missionaries" who do things like ask questions about the Holy Trinity in a class of English for Engineers.

The main clearing house for volunteers is the organization Education for Democracy which was set up in Canada shortly after the historic events of late 1989 and was quickly established in Britain too. In the UK the organization can be contacted c/o Dr. Vera Dalley, 12 Pembroke Square, London W8 6PA (tel: 071-937 2122) or c/o Dr. John Marks, 2 Melbury Road, Harrow, Middlesex HA3 9RA (tel: 081-204 7336). In Canada, Education for Democracy is based at the City Hall, 100 Queen St. W., Toronto M5H 2N2 (tel: 416-463-3745). Volunteers can also apply from inside Czechoslovakia by turning up at EFD's Prague office, currently located at 16 Revolucni,

Education for Democracy currently has over 300 volunteers in place and plans to extend this to 600 in schools and universities and in government and commercial enterprises where there is a recognized need for native speakers. Volunteers currently teach conversation classes to supplement existing English teaching, though this will be extended shortly into providing "master" teachers to help retrain Czech and Slovak teachers of English. Volunteers typically spend between 1 and 6 months in Czechoslovakia, teaching for 4 hours a day. Students are reported to be "a delight to teach, alert, intelligent, fun-loving, keen and interested". Teachers of university students stay in the student dormitories; otherwise accommodation is usually provided with Czech families. An allowance is paid by the Ministry of Education and starts at around 1,200 crowns a month, though the average is about 2,000 crowns.

Another organization involved in helping Czechoslovakia with its educational needs is the Jan Hus Foundation (4 Offord Road, London N1 1DL; tel: 071-609 2703) also with a representative in Czechoslovakia (Nadia ana Husa, Radnická 4, 66223 Brno; tel: 5-25149). Although the Foundation does not have the staff to manage a teacher recruitment programme, they do put interested volunteers in touch with schools, institutions and summer school projects needing teachers. In Prague, their main contact is a teacher called Zdenka Kriskova, Zakladni skola, Horachova 11000, Prague 4 (tel: 2-4531 92 68) and in Brno, Jan Hus works through Ales Kvapil, appointed by the Town Hall at Zelny trh 12, Brno 1 (tel: 5-26028). In 1990, the Foundation arranged for a number of volunteers to teach for a full year in exchange for board and lodging and a specially negotiated salary of 4,000 crowns.

Students for Czechoslovakia, c/o Dum Zahraničnich Styků, Ministerstva Školstvi, ČSR, Naměsti M. Gorkého 26, 11121 Prague 1 (tel: 267077 or in Bratislavia 333010) is an organization which was set up at the request of Czech students who accompanied President Havel on a visit to Georgetown University in the spring of 1990. The volunteer teaching programme is backed (though not funded) by the Czech Ministry of Education and is run by American students for American students and graduates who have "some educational experience" to teach in academic and business settings. In 1990-91 Students for Czechoslovakia had over 50 teachers in place. Screening takes place in the US and hopeful candidates who present themselves at the office in Prague will join the end of an ever-growing waiting list. The programme is expected to run for at least another 3 years.

The Education for Democracy literature sums up the voluntary programmes:

> *It is a major and important decision to devote 6 months of one's life to a noble cause. It requires great enthusiasm and dedication. But the reward offered by participation of experience of life in a quickly-changing country where everyone is more than willing to improve the quality of life is enormous.*

LIST OF SCHOOLS

ASPECT INTERNATIONAL LANGUAGE SCHOOLS
26 Third St., San Francisco, CA 94103, US. Tel: (415) 777-9555.
Number of teachers: 20-30 staff in school in Prague.
Preference of nationality: US.
Qualifications: MA in TESL preferred, 2 years experience or 1 year's overseas experience desirable.
Conditions of employment: 1 year contracts. 25-30 h.p.w. Pupils aged 18-40.
Salary: equivalent of US$1,000 per month plus free return air fare, medical insurance, paid holidays.
Facilities/Support: free accommodation. Orientation only, no training.
Recruitment: through adverts in *NY Times* and *TESOL Newsletter.* Interviews essential and are held in US.

BELL SCHOOL
Janovského 29, 17000 Prague 7. Tel: (2) 804 003.
Number of teachers: 2
Preference of nationality: UK.
Qualifications: RSA Dip,/MA, plus minimum 5 years teaching experience.

Recruitment: exclusively though Bell Educational Trust, UK. Interviews essential.

PRAGUE 8 LANGUAGE SCHOOL
Lindnerova 3, 18200 Prague-Liben. Tel: (2) 820 583. Also at Narodni 20 and in Pankrac, Prague.
Number of teachers: 10.
Preference of nationality: none.
Qualifications: BA TEFL qualification and/or teaching experience abroad.
Conditions of employment: 1 academic year contracts (September-June). 19 lessons per week. Extra lessons are remunerated accordingly. Pupils aged between 16-60.
Salary: 3,500 crowns per month for graduates (who must be able to provide copy of degree certificate).
Facilities/Support: assistance with accommodation. Training programme imminent.
Recruitment: through private contacts and local agencies. Interviews preferred but not essential.

Poland

Demand for English is intensifying in Poland. In a country which feels itself to be part of Western Europe, there has always been a lively interest in English, an interest which recent political changes have brought to the fore. After the collapse of the Communist Party in early 1990 many CP buildings were vacated; the first priority for many town authorities was to use these buildings for English language teaching. Poles now want English to help modernize a moribund economy and to allow access to intellectual influences from which they have been shut off for 50 years. The fact that many Poles are now free to visit relatives in the US and the UK is a further incentive.

As Paul Coverdell, Director of the US Peace Corps, comments, "Poland needs an enormous amount of assistance. The Poles have a shortage of 10,000 English teachers and there is a critical need for trained EFL teachers to help the Poles improve their economic base." Opportunities for voluntary and paid work are numerous and likely to increase as Poland tries to attract foreign experts.

Private language schools catering for all kinds of English teaching are springing up everywhere following the changes which have allowed private enterprise. The success of these schools, however, is linked to the state of the economy, which can best be described as parlous. Recent austerity measures have cut living standards by a third in 6 months to fight inflation, and many economists predict a rough ride ahead (as indeed with all of Eastern Europe). What effect this will have on the private EFL market remains to be seen; with an average national income of US$80 per month, the man on the street usually has little left to pay for expensive private classes. As one teacher says, "When the going gets tough, whatever people would like, there is no way that an English course will get preference over a loaf of bread or some shoes". Many Poles resort to ad-hoc measures; for example, the editor of a respected Polish business journal teaches

English to local children free of charge after Sunday church services to supplement their English in school.

Teachers are sure to find Poles unfailingly friendly, open and keen to learn more about life in the much-admired West. Discussion classes are likely to be informed and lively, with students well up to date on developments and very well motivated to practise their English. Real live English speakers are something of a rarity in Poland and the level of conversational ability may not always match the level of grammatical awareness because of this lack of contact. But students make up for this with their enthusiasm.

There is normally little problem in obtaining work permits for teachers who have arranged employment outside Poland or for those who look for work after arrival. Levels of pay are low by Western standards but sufficient to live on. Modern textbooks are in short supply, as are many of the small luxury items of the West; teachers would be well advised to stock up on such items for their personal use before setting out.

FIXING UP A JOB

Private Schools

Private schools are just beginning to appear in Polish cities to meet the rising demand; at least 60 have opened since the advent of political reform. The big-name Western schools have yet to arrive on the scene in force, so the current situation is one of many local Polish-run schools with some offering employment to native speakers. The private language school market is not as developed as in, say, Hungary, but recent economic reforms aimed at stimulating the growth of private enterprise may change this.

The *Langhelp* school is typical of the Polish-run schools; it offers one-year contracts to native speakers (preferably American or British) and advertises in Polish newspapers. Qualifications and experience are not absolutely necessary; work permits, the school reports, are not always required either. Business English is an area of growth in Polish EFL, with the Polanglo School Prywatny Zaklad Nauczania Jezykow Obcych (ul. Zurawia 24A, Warsaw; tel: 21 11 61) having a long waiting list of businesses trying to arrange instruction for their staff. For every Pole learning business English, it is estimated that there are 3 more in the queue.

Most of the local language schools hire on the spot. The British Council in Warsaw can provide a list of schools in the capital, and would-be teachers should dutifully "do the rounds" of the *Dyrektors*. Most will arrange accommodation for you.

The situation is changing and developing at a great rate, as shown by the recent affiliation of the Lektor School (ul. Lisa Witalisa 24, 60195 Poznán) to International House, and the fact that Pitman Education & Training (154) Southampton Row, London WC1B 5AX) was advertising in November 1990 for experienced teachers of business English and offering £12,000 per year plus a range of perks. Meanwhile the Bell Educational Trust and many other UK-based schools are showing an interest. This is a trend that will continue. The future for private language schools appears promising, with consequent opportunities for native speakers, always bearing in mind that Poland faces an uncertain economic future which may affect the success of the private schools. Quite how

EFL will develop is one of the many imponderables of Poland's future — as indeed it is for the whole of Eastern Europe.

Freelance Teaching

Business English may prove one of the more lucrative areas for those familiar with the needs of businesses. The recruitment of teachers for Poland by a subsidiary of an international electro-technical group of companies, ABB Power Ventures Ltd., is mentioned in the section on Hungary above. One indication of the increasing importance of business English is the British Council's funding of an "English for Management Project". Try contacting firms directly to see if they need lessons or are prepared to pay an in-house teacher. It would be worthwhile taking along a stock of specialist business English materials as these are not readily available in Poland, particularly not outside Warsaw.

State System

Only a small proportion of school children have access to proper English language tuition, a situation which educationalists hope to alter radically. Poland at present has only 1,200 teachers of English compared to 18,000 teachers of Russian. At the current rate it would take the teacher training colleges 67 years to retrain them to meet today's needs. Hence opportunities abound in both the short and long term for native speakers wishing to come to teach in ordinary schools; those interested should contact the Ministry of National Education at ul. I Armii Wojske Pol. 25, Warsaw.

VSO is sending about 20 volunteers to the Ministry. They will be used as "assistants" to help Polish staff develop new teacher-training courses in the provinces of Gdańsk, Bydgoszcz, Szczecin, Legnica, Bialystok, Zielona Gora, Przemysl, Tarnow, Kielce, Trzebinia, Wroclaw and Slupsk.

As with all VSO positions, volunteers must be well qualified and must sign a contract for two years. The Peace Corps is also going to become increasingly active in Poland over the next few years. Meanwhile *WorldTeach*, the Harvard-based voluntary organization, is sending students to teach for one academic year (September to June) in Polish high schools. Volunteers live with families.

Studia

For many years the British Council has recruited qualified and experienced native speakers for its *Studia* operations, an institution unique to Poland. They are attached to a university or polytechnic and teach English to academic staff and research assistants. They currently operate in Wroclaw, Gdańsk, Kraków, Lódź, Poznán and Warsaw. Conditions are the same as for Polish teachers — salaries are paid in zloties and are sufficient to live on by local standards. "Money," Studia director says, "should not be considered the prime motivator by applicants!" In the spring of 1990, the director of the English Language Centre in Wroclaw (Skewska 48, 50-139 Wroclaw) advertised in the *Guardian* on behalf of some (or all) of the others.

The British Council continues to recruit for the posts of "Lektor" at English Philology Institutes in Poland. Contracts are usually for 12 months i.e. 540 hours during the academic year, with accommodation provided.

Summer Camps

Holiday language camps in 3 locations in Poland (and set to increase) are run by UNESCO who use the Central Bureau for Educational Visits and Exchanges (Seymour Mews House, Seymour Mews, London W1H 9PE) to recruit staff. Typically, 10 experienced teachers are employed along with 10 assistants who are sixth-formers or university students; participants receive free board and lodging. The camps last for 3 weeks, followed by one week for travelling. Judy Kendall enjoyed her 1989 camp, even if most of the other British participants used the teaching materials she had brought and although the accommodation was provided at a truckers' hostel in the middle of nowhere.

There are also some opportunities for short-term holiday courses which require native speakers in Krakow. *Optimum* for example, run 2 to 3 week "Holidays with English" in the countryside. For about 4 hours of teaching a day, teachers earn 1.5-2 million zloties in total. For longer-term contracts. Optimum pays 30,000-40,000 zloties per hour.

LIST OF SCHOOLS

AMERICAN ENGLISH SCHOOL, S.A.
ul. Kordeckiego 15/17, 04-143 Warsaw. Tel: (2) 610 4040.
Number of teachers: 1.
Preference of nationality: none.
Qualifications: no experience or qualifications necessary, just a positive attitude.
Conditions of employment: minimum 9 month contracts (September-May). Afternoon work minimum 4 days per week. Pupils aged from 8-12.
Salary: US$3-3.50 per hour.
Facilities/Support: free housing provided. Training given.
Recruitment: through adverts and direct application. Local interviews not essential.

ENGLISH LANGUAGE CENTRE
University of Silesia, ul. Warszawska 5, Katowice. Tel: (32) 538 526.
Number of teachers: 2-3.
Preference of nationality: none.
Qualifications: BA, RSA Cert., or TEFL experience.
Conditions of employment: 1 year contracts. 540 hours per year.
Salary: high for Poland.
Facilities/Support: free accommodation provided. Training given.
Recruitment: adverts in *Guardian*. Interviews are usually required and are held in London.

LANGHELP
Al. Jerozolimskie 23/34, 00-508 Warsaw. Tel: (22) 214434/396144.
Number of teachers: 6.
Preference of nationality: UK, US.
Qualifications: teacher qualification and experience preferred but 'A' Level holders acceptable.
Conditions of employment: 1 year+ contracts. Mostly evening work between 5-6pm with some mornings. Pupils aged from 6 upwards.
Salary: payment per hour with increases 2 or 3 times per year.

Facilities/Support: assistance given finding accommodation. Training given as of 1991.
Recruitment: local interviews essential.
Contact in UK: Ilona Pawlicka, 7 Rosemont Road, Acton, London W3 9LT.

MODERN ENGLISH SCHOOL
ul. Boni Fraterska 6/3, 00-213 Warsaw. Tel: (22) 311 887.
Number of teachers: 1.
Preference of nationality: none.
Qualifications: TEFL experience.
Conditions of employment: 9 month contracts. Hours of work 3-7pm, teaching both children and adults.
Salary: on application.
Facilities/Support: assistance with accommodation. Training provided.
Recruitment: local newspaper adverts. Interviews not essential.

OPTIMUM
Al. 29 Listopada 41B/21, 31-425 Kraków. Tel: (12) 110129.
Number of teachers: 1.
Preference of nationality: none.
Qualifications: must be patient for conversational groups and have a flair for teaching.
Conditions of employment: 2-3 week stays and longer contracts possible. 4 hours per day; longer hours for longer contracts. Pupils aged 16-40.
Salary: 1,500-2,000,000 zloties plus paid accommodation for 2-3 weeks. 30-40,000 zloties per hour for longer contracts.
Facilities/Support: assistance with accommodation. No training given.
Recruitment: through adverts. Interviews not essential.

Bulgaria

Specialist English and foreign language secondary schools in Bulgaria are being provided with native speaker teachers on one-year contracts from August by the Central Bureau (address above) on behalf of the Bulgarian Ministry of Education (18 Boulevard Stamboliski, Sofia). All teaching positions in the country are supposed to be organized by the Ministry, precluding the possibility of signing a private contract (at least officially). English teachers are paid 420-440 levs per month, plus assistance with accommodation and free heating. In some cases a sterling supplement of £3,000 will be paid, or else a portion of the salary, usually half, will be paid in pounds sterling at the official bank rate.

The Ministry of Education also recruits *lektors* for schools, as does the Ministry for Higher Education at Chapaev 55a, Sofia. The British Council is responsible for recruiting *lektors* for 2 universities in Bulgaria.

LIST OF SCHOOLS

"CHRISTO BOTEV" ENGLISH LANGUAGE SCHOOL
19 Komsomolska St, Kardjali 6600. Tel: (361) 24434.

Number of teachers: none at present.
Preference of nationality: UK, US.
Qualifications: BA (English), experience in teaching history and geography, at least 3 years experience in TEFL.
Conditions of employment: 1-3 year contracts. 18 lessons per week working 5 half-days. Pupils range in age from 14-18.
Salary: 600 levs per month.
Facilities/Support: fully-furnished flat provided with free maintenance. No training.

"CHRISTO KABAKCHIEV" ENGLISH LANGUAGE SCHOOL
Complex Chaika, Spirka Pochivka, 9005 Varna. Tel: (52) 883 784.
Number of teachers: 1.
Preference of nationality: UK.
Qualifications: TEFL qualification or teaching certificate: experience not essential.
Conditions of employment: 1-2 year contracts. 18-20 45-minute lessons per week plus other optional duties. Pupils range in age from 14-16.
Salary: 440 levs per month (half in sterling).
Facilities/Support: flat provided. No training given.

ENGLISH LANGUAGE SCHOOL
Timok St. 97, 6300 Haskovo. Tel: (38) 25222.
Number of teachers: none at present.
Preference of nationality: UK.
Qualifications: teaching qualifications.
Conditions of employment: 1 year contracts. 20 lessons per week. Pupils aged 14-18.
Salary: standard for Bulgaria.
Facilities/Support: assistance with accommodation. Training provided.

"ERNST THÄLMANN" ENGLISH LANGUAGE SCHOOL
5500 Lovech. Tel: (68) 23830.
Number of teachers: 1-2.
Preference of nationality: UK, etc.
Qualifications: must be able to teach English and American literature as well as EFL.
Conditions of employment: 1-2 year contracts. 18 h.p.w. Pupils aged 14-19.
Salary: 420 levs per month.
Facilities/Support: assistance with accommodation. No training given.

"GEO MILEV" FOREIGN LANGUAGES SCHOOL
Lenin Boulevard 1, Tolbukhin. Tel: (58) 25587/25421.
Number of teachers: 1.
Preference of nationality: none.
Qualifications: teaching qualifications and experience preferred.
Conditions of employment: 1 year renewable contracts. Hours of work from 8am-1pm or from 1pm-7pm. Pupils aged 14-19.
Salary: standard for Bulgaria.
Facilities/Support: full accommodation provided. Training sometimes given.

"IVAN VASOV" ENGLISH LANGUAGE SCHOOL
Lenin Bul.4, 4700 Smolyan. Tel: (301) 23328.
Number of teachers: 1.
Preference of nationality: UK, US.
Qualifications: qualified teachers in English, Geography, History, Biology, Chemistry.
Conditions of employment: pupils range in age from 14-19.
Facilities/Support: assistance with accommodation.

THE LANGUAGE SCHOOL OF BERTOLT BRECHT
Pirdop Str. 1, Pazardjik. Tel: (34) 28376/22795/22895.
Number of teachers: none at present.
Preference of nationality: UK.
Qualifications: BA.
Conditions of employment: 2-3 year contracts. 20 lessons per week. Pupils aged between 13-19.
Salary: unspecified.
Facilities/Support: assistance with accommodation. No training given.

"LILIANA DIMITROVA" ENGLISH LANGUAGE SCHOOL
Vidin. Tel: (94) 22125.
Number of teachers: 1.
Preference of nationality: none.
Qualifications: qualified teachers with some experience.
Conditions of employment: 1 year contracts. 18 lessons per week between 8am-1.30pm daily. Pupils aged 14-19.
Salary: 420 levs per month.
Facilities/Support: a fully-heated, rent-free apartment is provided. No training given.

"MLADA GVARDIA" SECONDARY LANGUAGE SCHOOL
9th September quarter, Pernik. Tel: (76) 28079.
Number of teachers: 1.
Preference of nationality: UK.
Qualifications: fully qualified teachers or TEFL qualification with at least 3 years experience.
Conditions of employment: 1 year contracts. 18 lessons per week. Pupils aged 13-18.
Salary: 420 levs per month.
Facilities/Support: fully-furnished flat provided, electricity and heating bills paid. No training given.

"ROZA LIUKSEMBURG" ELS SCHOOL
Mihailovgrad. Tel: (96) 23240/25235/29309.
Number of teachers: 1.
Preference of nationality: UK, US, Canada.
Qualifications: BA, teaching experience not necessary.
Conditions of employment: 1-2 year contracts. 20 h.p.w. Pupils range in age from 14-19.
Salary: 500 levs per month.
Facilities/Support: furnished flat provided. Training given.

Recruitment: through direct application. Interviews essential and held in UK or Sofia.

"ZAHARI STOYANOV" FL SCHOOL
Dimitar Polyanov St 1, 8800 Sliven. Tel: (44) 27010/26966.
Number of teachers: 1.
Preference of nationality: UK.
Qualifications: BA (Philology).
Conditions of employment: 1-2 year contracts. 18 lessons per week. Pupils aged 14-19.
Salary: 420 levs per month.
Facilities/Support: accommodation provided, including central heating and electricity. Training given.

"N.Y. VAPTSAROV" ENGLISH LANGUAGE SCHOOL
Bul. Tolbukhin 16, 9700 Shoumen. Tel: (54) 60153/60861.
Number of teachers: none as yet, since the school only opened in 1990.
Preference of nationality: UK, US.
Qualifications: BA (English) or qualified teachers of Geography, History, Biology, Chemistry or Physics.
Conditions of employment: 2 year contracts. 18 teaching periods per week. Pupils aged 14-19.
Salary: usual rates plus bonus.
Facilities/Support: accommodation provided. Training given.

ELM SCHOOL "VASSIL LEVSKI"
Pravets 2161. Tel: (7133) 2282.
Number of teachers: 1.
Preference of nationality: UK.
Qualifications: BA, TEFL qualification.
Conditions of employment: 1 academic year contracts. 18 h.p.w. Pupils aged 14-19.
Salary: 420 levs per month.
Facilities/Support: assistance with accommodation. No training given.

ROMANIA

Before the Christmas 1989 revolution the British Council maintained just 2 *lektors* in Romanian universities and English teaching was accorded an insignificant place in education. The politics of Romania continue to be volatile and unpredictable. Backwardness on the EFL front is one of the countless unfortunate legacies of the ruinous Ceausescu regime. According to the British Council in Bucharest at the time of writing there were no private language schools and no demand for EFL teachers. There are hints of change though, in Bucharest, Timisoara and Cluj. For example the BBC programme "Follow Me" is now being broadcast. It is expected that teachers of Russian will be retrained at some time in the future, but no one knows how long any of this will take.

SOVIET UNION

At the end of 1990 there were plans for the imminent opening of an International House school in Moscow and where IH leads, others are sure to follow. Other organizations such as *GAP* and *AFS* International/Intercultural Programs in the US are also making tentative moves in the direction of sending English teachers to the USSR. Six young GAP participants were sent to a town in the northern Caucasus to teach English (plus sport and drama) at a primary school for 6 months in 1990/91. Meanwhile the British Council was recruiting a team of EFL/ESP specialists for Estonia.

Various organizations are busy trying to set up teaching schemes in the Soviet Union. For example the Centre for Youth Initiative (c/o MIR Initiative, PO Box 28183, Washington, DC 20038-8183) was advertising at the end of 1990 for English teachers to work in Eastern Siberia for a salary of 500 roubles a month; the catch was that the candidates had to speak Russian. An offbeat travel organization called Poor Farms Unlimited run by an American in China is also trying to arrange English-teaching sponsored visa positions in the USSR; details from Box 9012, I.c.P.O., Beijing, China 100600.

So far only a handful of organized opportunities have been made known, but anyone with contacts in the Soviet Union might be able to arrange something on an individual basis. After completing a successful stint as an EFL teacher in Jakarta in the summer of 1990, Colin Boothroyd went caving in the Pamir Mountains with a university caving club from Siberia. He was taken aback at the end of the visit to be presented with a contract for teaching at the cavers' institute. The salary was 500 roubles a month, equivalent to a professor's salary, plus housing and meals. The contract, which was initially for $2\frac{1}{2}$ months plus 2 weeks paid vacation and with the possibility of renewal was officially for scientific research into karst (limestone topography) in which the institute specialized, since the university was not able to release funds for English teaching but it was for Western scientific staff.

He showed the contract to the British Council in Moscow (two offices at the back of the Embassy) but they said that they couldn't provide any support, financial or otherwise. Although Colin was tempted to accept, he next discovered that he was to become a father and decided that Siberia would have to wait. He reckons that anyone who can forge a link with an academic institution in the Soviet Union could arrange something similar if he or she was prepared to live on local wages (e.g. $50 a month). It may well be that in a few years time, the situation in the Soviet Union will be similar to that in China during the 1980s with the greatest demand for English coming from academic institutes.

MIDDLE EAST

Until the events of August 1990, the Middle East was as safe a destination for qualified teachers as it was lucrative. Prior to Iraq's invasion of Kuwait there were up to 1,000 English teachers in Kuwait (though most of them were out of the country at the time of the invasion, since it was the summer vacation). At the time of writing there seemed little imminent prospect of these teachers returning to their jobs. As an independent oil state, Kuwait spent a large proportion of it wealth on education including English language instruction. As a province of Iraq, there would be no such investment and probably as few English teachers as there have been in Iraq for many years.

Things have not changed so drastically in the other nations of the Middle East, though many teachers would prefer not to be anywhere near a possible war zone. At the time of writing, language schools were still functioning throughout Saudi Arabia including in the city of Dhahran, an important air base not far from Kuwait, where English teacher were promptly declared "essential staff" and issued with chemical warfare suits. Schools in Bahrain, Oman, Jordan, the United Arab Emirates, etc. seemed to be relatively unaffected by the crisis. This chapter has been written in a spirit of optimism, assuming that "normality" can be restored to the region within the lifetime of this book. We have even included in the directory details of some Kuwaiti schools, received not long before the debacle.

The Middle East includes more than the oil rich Gulf states of course, but common sense will tell you that Lebanon is not a possibility. (Released hostage Brian Keenan was an EFL teacher.) Neither is Iran, where representatives of Western culture are officially reviled, a far different situation from when teaching jobs could easily be found in Tehran by perusing the notice board of the travellers' favourite Amir Kabir Hotel and when the British Council's biggest operations were in Iran.

Teachers who undertake contracts in a strict Islamic country often do so with clenched teeth. People spend a year or two of their lives in Saudi Arabia for the money not for the fun (certainly) nor for the experience (unless they are students of Arab culture). When the amount of money accumulating back home is the principal or only motivation, morale can degenerate. An article in the *Daily Telegraph* referred to members of the expatriate community in the Gulf as "the cretinous flotsam of British society", though this description is unlikely to do justice to many English teachers.

And yet not everyone is gasping to get home to freely available alcohol *et al*. A surprisingly high percentage of teachers is recruited locally from a stable expatriate community. For example of the 17 teachers working at the British Council's DTO in Kuwait in 1990, only one was recruited from London.

Prospects for Teachers

Oil wealth has meant that many of the countries of the Middle East have been able to afford to attract the best teachers with superior qualifications and extensive experience. A number of teachers in the region are employed by large corporations to fulfil a government requirement that trading partners supply training as well as equipment, as in the case of British Aerospace in Saudi Arabia. Such employers

:an afford to hire only professionals yet there are some opportunities for the less well qualified. Advertisements placed by the Saudi government in September 1990 listed the qualifications sufficient to be considered for EFL contracts, and a humble BA appeared on the list, alongside "MA plus TEFL plus Diploma of Education".

Single women, no matter how highly qualified, are at a serious disadvantage. The majority of adverts specify "single status male" or, at best, "teaching couples". Another requirement often mentioned in job details which excludes many candidates is experience of the Middle East, in acknowledgment of the difficulty which many foreigners encounter in adapting to life under Islam.

FIXING UP A JOB

Unless you are more or less resident in the Middle East, it is essential to fix up a job in advance. Casual teaching is not a possibility for a number of reasons, including the difficulty of getting tourist visas, the prohibitively high cost of staying without working and, of course, the whole tradition of hiring teachers.

Job adverts abound in the *TES*, the *Guardian* and the *TESOL Bulletin*. The largest display ads in the British education press are quite often for Middle East vacancies, many placed by recruitment agencies on behalf of high-spending Saudi clients. The advantage of working through an agency is that they can provide some protection against what happened to Peter Feltham:

> *I am an Arabist and have worked in Bahrain, Oman, Saudi Arabia and Egypt on a "creative job-search" basis, sometimes with extreme success but mostly with disastrous consequences. For example, in Bahrain, I found that about two-thirds or three-quarters of all job offers had not been thought through, and were bogus. I spent between £1,000 and £2,000 in air fares following up bogus job offers and came to the conclusion that this was partly due to the lack of moral implications of failing to tell the truth within Islam.*

In a land where wealthy car drivers have been known to abandon a Mercedes when the oil needed changing, it is not too surprising to learn that English teachers are sometimes left in the lurch.

Here is an unedited list of agencies, organizations and corporations which recruit EFL teachers for the Middle East:

Arabian Careers Ltd. 115 Shaftesbury Avenue, London WC2H 8AD. Tel: 071-379 7877. To Saudi Arabia.

Arabian Oil Co. Ltd., 61 Brook Street, London W1Y 1YE. Tel: 071-499-3238.

ARA International Ltd. Recruitment Consultants, 6th Floor, Carolyn House, Dingwall Road, Croydon, Surrey CR0 9XF (tel: 081-686 9511). To Saudi Arabia.

Bell Educational Trust: Redcross Lane, Cambridge CB2 2QX. Tel: (0223) 246644. To Saudi Arabia, Qatar, etc.

British Aerospace Military Aircraft Ltd., Warton, Preston, Lancs. PR4 1LA. Tel: (0772) 634317.

Chemsult Ltd., International Recruitment Consultants. 135 Notting Hill Gate, London W11 3LB. Tel: 071-727 9278. To Saudi Arabia.

English Worldwide, 17 New Concordia Wharf, Mill St., London SE1 2BB. Tel: 071-252 1402. To Saudi Arabia.

ESO Ltd., 13 Gladwyn Road, London SW15. To Oman's state schools.

Ian Marshall Staff Recruitment Ltd., 11 Great Russell Street, London WC1B 3NH. Tel: 071-255 1696. About 10 male teachers per year to Saudi Arabia.

ILC Recruitment: 1 Riding House St., London W1A 3AS. Tel: 071-580 4351. To Kuwait.

Mentor Ltd., 21 Holly Road, Fairfield, Liverpool L7 0LH; or PO Box 36, Liverpool L13 2HB. To Saudi Arabia.

Middle East Christian Outreach, 22 Culverden Park Road, Tunbridge Wells, Kent TN4 9RA. Recruit volunteer teachers solely through church channels.

PACES Recruitment Consultants, 6b Eccleston Gardens, St. Helens WA10 3BN. Mainly for English medium schools in the Middle East.

Professional Communication Services, "Ashdown", 26 Corkran Road, Surbiton, Surrey KT6 6PN. Tel: 081-399 1097. To Bahrain, Qatar, Abu Dhabi, Oman and Kuwait.

Recruitment International Ltd., 2nd Floor, Copthall Tower House, Station Parade, Harrogate, North Yorkshire HG1 1TS. Tel: (0423) 530533. Fax: 530558. To Saudi Arabia (on behalf of the oil company Saudi Aramco).

STATS: Milton Keynes (0908) 271660. To UAE.

The British Council has Direct Teaching Operations in Bahrain, Iraq, (Baghdad), Jordan, (Amman), Oman (Muscat and Salalah), Qatar, Saudi Arabia (Jeddah, Riyadh and Dammam), Abu Dhabi, Dubai and Al Ain in the United Arab Emirates, and Yemen. The only International House-affiliated school is in Oman: Capital Institute, PO Box 3936, Ruwi, Oman. As mentioned above, the Saudi Embassy in London recruits directly, as does the Omani Embassy on behalf of the Ministry of Education. The representatives of the UAE and pre-invasion Kuwait supply lists of English medium schools, most of which have substantial EFL departments. Managed Institutes in Kuwait had several English teaching centres including the *Institute for Private Education* in Hawalli. Their "Recruitment Information Booklet" provided detailed information on teacher contracts and life in Kuwait, which makes rather sad reading now ("Almost anything can be bought in Kuwait . . . ").

As well as scouring the adverts in the TESOL *Bulletin*, American teachers might like to consult the book *Teaching Opportunities in the Middle East & North Africa* published by AMIDEAST (1100 17th Street, NW, Washington, DC 20036), though the majority of jobs are in international English-medium schools or colleges rather than in language institutes. There are bi-national centres in Iraq, Jordan, Syria and Yemen only.

LEISURE TIME

The majority of teachers live in foreigners' compounds provided by their employers. The principal pastimes are barbecues, reading out-of-date copies of the *International Herald Tribune* and complaining about the terrific heat and the lack of alcohol. Others of course try to learn some Arabic and make local friends, always taking care not to offend against Islam. The constraints of living under Islam are well known. For example in some countries anyone found drinking or smoking in a public place during the month of Ramadan could face a jail sentence, large fine and/or deportation. In some locations, such as Jubail in Saudi Arabia, water sports are a popular diversion.

Contracts often include two free leave tickets per year, which need not be to your home. (Apparently Bangkok is a popular destination for expats seeking R & R.) This is therefore a good chance to see the world at your employer's expense.

SAUDI ARABIA

Philip Aston, who has taught English in some unlikely places including Pakistan and Yugoslavia calls Saudi Arabia the "blackest of black holes". Furthermore the decline in oil prices during the 1980s meant that fabulously high salaries were no longer available. But even with a huge tax-free salary of £12,000-£18,000 per annum, free air fares and accommodation plus generous holidays and other perks, many teachers conclude that it isn't worth it. Teaching in a naval academy or petrochemical company while living in a teetotal expatriate ghetto is not many people's idea of fun. The rare woman who gets a job as a teacher may live to regret it when she finds that she is prohibited by law from driving a car and must not appear in public without being covered from head to foot. It is possible that the prolonged presence of the US military may lead to some concessions to Western habits but this will take a long time if it happens at all.

Among the documents required for a work permit are an AIDS-free certificate and a baptismal certificate (since atheism cannot be countenanced).

ISRAEL/PALESTINE

Because of the large number of English-speaking Jews who have settled in Israel from the US, South Africa, etc. there are many native speakers of English working in the state education system and no active recruitment of foreign teachers. One might have expected some volunteers on kibbutzim to be involved in teaching English to Hebrew-speaking kibbutzniks, but in fact this never seems to happen. The British Council's language teaching centres in Tel Aviv and Jerusalem recruit qualified EFL teachers from the local English-speaking population.

There is also a British Council teaching centre in East Jerusalem serving the West Bank and Gaza. It reports that because of the Intifada, opportunities in EFL are extremely limited. The Council office does keep a list of local schools and c.v.'s of TEFL teachers who are resident in the area. Commitment to working for the Palestinian people is essential in a place where curfews, strikes and low wages are the norm.

The charity UNIPAL (Universities Educational Fund for Palestinian Refugees) at 12 Helen Road, Oxford OX2 0DE, places British graduates as volunteers to teach English in the Occupied Territories and Palestinian villages inside Israel, as well as in Jordan and Egypt. Volunteers are needed for short-term placements lasting 4-8 weeks in the summer, or for one-year positions requiring an RSA Certificate and offering free air fares.

LIST OF SCHOOLS

Jordan

SIGHT AND SOUND
PO Box 739, Amman. Tel: (6) 661136/7. Fax: 722147.
Number of teachers: none at present.
Preference of nationality: none.
Qualifications: BA (English).
Conditions of employment: 1 year renewable contracts. 6 hours work per day, 6 days per week. Pupils aged from 17-25, mostly studying typing, computing and secretarial courses.

Facilities/Support: no assistance with accommodation. No training given.
Recruitment: via University of Jordan. Local interviews essential.

YARMOUK CULTURAL CENTRE
PO Box 960312, Amman. Tel: (6) 680726.
Number of teachers: 20 (summer), 12 (winter).
Preference of nationality: UK, Australia.
Qualifications: BA and TEFL/TESL qualification.
Conditions of employment: part-time, hourly payment system. 12-24 h.p.w. Pupils are both children and adults.
Salary: 4 dinars per hour.
Facilities/Support: assistance with accommodation sometimes given. Training provided.
Recruitment: locally and through adverts. Local interviews only.

Kuwait

AL NOURI ENGLISH SCHOOL
PO Box 46901, 64020 Fahaheel. Tel: 3911039.
Number of teachers: 24.
Preference of nationality: UK, Ireland.
Qualifications: UK teacher qualifications, plus primary school teaching experience.
Conditions of employment: 1 year renewable contracts. Hours of work 7.30am-1pm. Pupils are expatriate children aged $3\frac{1}{2}$-$11\frac{1}{2}$.
Salary: 340-460 dinars per month.
Facilities/Support: free accommodation plus electricity, water bills.
Return air fare paid. Training given.
Recruitment: adverts in *TES*. Interviews essential and are held in UK.

ARABIC & ENGLISH
Al-Ahli Technical Studies Institute, PO Box 3156, 22032 Salmeya. Tel: 5737533.
Number of teachers: 2 (part-time).
Preference of nationality: Arab.
Qualifications: BA plus 2 years experience.
Conditions of employment: 1 year contracts. 9 hours work per week. Pupils aged 18+.
Salary: 200 dinars per month.
Facilities/Support: assistance with accommodation. Training given.
Recruitment: local interviews required.

INSTITUTE FOR PRIVATE EDUCATION
EFL Department, PO Box 6320, 32038 Hawalli. Tel: 5737022.
Affiliated to Pitman Education and Training (154 Southampton Row, London WC1B 5AX).
Number of teachers: 40+.
Preference of nationality: UK, Ireland, US, Canada, Australia.
Conditions of employment: 3 month, 1 or 2 year contracts. 40 h.p.w. of which

0 are contact hours. Pupils are normally young adults and adults but also children
f 5-18 in the summer.
Salary: 370-750 dinars per month plus benefits.
Facilities/Support: shared, furnished, air-conditioned accommodation provided.
Training sometimes given.
Recruitment: through press adverts. Interviews are essential and are held in
JK, Ireland, Australia. Detailed *Recruitment Information Booklet* available.

Saudi Arabia

ELC KFUPM
PO Box 1004, 31261 Dhahran. Tel: (3) 8602393.
Number of teachers: 75-80.
Preference of nationality: US, UK, Canada, New Zealand, Australia.
Qualifications: MA in Applied Linguistics.
Conditions of employment: 2 year contracts. 20-25 h.p.w. Pupils aged 17-20.
Facilities/Support: accommodation provided. A little training given.
Recruitment: through adverts. Interviews essential.

ADMAN S. KAZELLY EST.
**PO Box 9004, 21413 Jeddah. Tel: (2) 665 0051/665 2462. Fax: 666
3493.**
Qualifications: BA in a relevant field. TEFL qualifications and at least 2 years
experience. PGCE and overseas experience also desirable. Adaptability to work
and live in Saudi important.
Conditions of employment: 2 year contracts preferred with a 90-day probationary
period. Teachers must be male, and should preferably be in the 25-45 age group.
Staff will work in the training centres of the Saudi national oil industry.
Salary: varies according to qualifications and experience. Tax-free.
Facilities/Support: accommodation, transportation, and medical insurance
provided plus an end-of-contract bonus.
Recruitment: through direct application. Interviews essential and are sometimes
held in London. C.v.'s will be kept on file in event of emergency requirements.

Turkey

This chapter, like so many others, must begin by proclaiming an amazing
expansion of English as a Foreign Language. Turkey's ambition to join the
European Community, together with a remarkable boom in tourism during the
1980s, means that the Turkish middle classes are more eager than ever to learn
English and for their children to learn English too.

The boom in English is not confined to private language schools *(dershane)*
which have mushroomed in the past couple of years. There are dozens of private
secondary schools *(lises)* and a few universities (both private and public) which
use English as the medium of instruction, something one expects to find only
in former British colonies like India. In order to prepare students for an English

language engineering, commerce or arts course, many secondary schools hire native speakers, not all of whom are trained teachers.

Prospects for Teachers

A rough count of the advertisements for teaching jobs abroad in the Tuesday *Guardian* and *Times Educational Supplement* over an extended period will reveal that Turkey outnumbers all but Spain. Furthermore many of the adverts promise a range of attractive perks including free air fares on completion of a one year contract and free accommodation. Virtually all of these employers want to see an RSA Certificate (or equivalent) as do the majority of schools listed at the end of this chapter. This is not simply to guarantee the standard of teaching, but is a requirement of the Turkish Ministry of Education before it will grant a work visa (see *Regulations* below).

The vast majority of schools do not of course advertise abroad. It is much quicker and cheaper for them to depend on word of mouth or to post notices in hotels frequented by budget travellers, eager to earn some money to extend their stay in Turkey. Among this kind of school, a degree and RSA Certificate are not a pre-requisite through usually a commitment to stay for a year is (unless they are filling a vacant post part way through the academic year which runs from October to June).

Unqualified teachers with a university degree who decide to do a TEFL course in Turkey can do so through ITBA (Istanbul Turco-British Association, Süleyman Nazif Sokak 68, Nişantaşi, 80220 Istanbul) and *English Fast* also in Istanbul, plus also the *Cinar School* in Izmir (see page 49 for details of these courses). Graduates are usually guaranteed a job at the end and may have their air fares reimbursed and their living expenses paid.

The bias in favour of British English over American is not particularly strong. Many schools claim to have no preference and yet because they advertise in the UK press and are more familiar with British qualifications, there is a predominance of British teachers (apart from the schools with specific American links; see entries for the *Fabsit Foundation* and *Turkish American University Association*). Schools which undertake to pay air fares have an obvious reason for preferring Brits.

FIXING UP A JOB
In Advance

The English Language Promotion Unit of the British Council publishes *A Survey of Language Teaching and Learning in Turkey* which contains a list of 60 private language schools. Unfortunately the Survey costs £20 and furthermore cannot be consulted at the Council office in London. You could try writing to the British Council in Ankara and Istanbul and ask them to send a photocopy of the relevant 6 pages (28 addresses in Istanbul, 18 in Ankara, 7 in Izmir and 7 elsewhere). In fact the very efficient and helpful British Council in Istanbul has its own computerized list, frequently updated which has even more addresses of schools in and around Istanbul plus nearly 50 *lises* with the name of the Head of English at each school.

Among the main indigenous language teaching organizations in Turkey are *English Fast* (who employ about 150 native speakers), *Kent English* and *English Centres* all with branches in Istanbul, Ankara and Izmir. English Fast opened a private high school in Istanbul in September 1990 for which teachers were recruited by their London representative (see entry). ITBA mentioned above recruits RSA-trained teachers throughout the year, both in Britain and locally and offers the best pay and conditions of any school in Istanbul. One year contracts from September 1st are available at Bilkent University in Ankara, a private English-medium university which recruits at least 35 EFL teachers annually through the *Centre for British Teachers.*

Other agencies which recruit for Turkish schools are: *Anchor Language Services, ELT Banbury, Nordanglia, English Worldwide* and *IES* (Suite 1, Alexander House, 1 Milton Road, Cambridge CB4 1UY). Again one of the main advantages of fixing up a job in advance is the possibility of having your air fare paid, worth about £250, though some schools will pay the return part of the fare to teachers whom they recruit in Turkey. Americans should contact the *TESL Recruiting Service* which has an office in Istanbul and promises to help its client teachers get settled.

On the Spot

If you begin the job hunt after arriving in Turkey, you should be able to find an opening somewhere. Although Istanbul is not the capital, it is the commercial, financial and cultural centre of Turkey, so this is where most of the EFL teaching goes on. On the negative side, there may be more competition from other travelling teachers here and also in Izmir than in Ankara or less obvious cities like Mersin and Diyarbakir. The best starting place in Istanbul is undoubtedly the British Council as Stephen McKeown discovered:

> *The helpful British Council near the Hilton will give you a list of English schools in Istanbul. The addresses read like chemical formulae but you soon get used to them. We were offered jobs by every school we went to and were promised wages of between 2 and 4 times the national average. The catch? You must be prepared to commit yourself for at least a year and to prove this you must have accommodation with the rent paid for 3 months in advance. All the schools insisted on this.*

You may find yourself drawn back to the British Council after you have landed a job as well. The modest joining fee of 20,000 Turkish lira entitles you to use the Council's Teaching Centre with a reference collection of ELT books, video cassettes, seminars, etc.

You may not even need to go as far as obtaining a list of schools. It is quite common for adverts to be posted in the most popular cheap hotels of Sultanahmet, the area of Istanbul around the Blue Mosque. Wages and working conditions are unlikely to match those of the more established schools, typically a million lire a month and no accommodation. Ian McArthur describes the problem often encountered by "teacher-travellers":

> *I often had problems with my wages (then £75 per week). My employer tried to make me feel guilty about asking for them on the day that they were due. If I hadn't demanded them several times every pay day, I don't think I would have seen them. When they tried to postpone my pay rise (inflation was running at 60%), it was the last straw. The final sanction of threatening to leave — I hinted at it — is effective due to the inadequate supply of foreign English teachers over the winter.*

Freelance

More informal teaching possibilities may present themselves even without your seeking them out. Mary Jelliffe heard of a traveller who, while lazing on the beach, was asked by a man to teach English to his two sons in return for board and lodging. University English departments might be a place to look for private pupils. Also check adverts in the English language *Daily News* which quite often advertises teaching positions and usually gives only a contact phone number.

REGULATIONS

The ideal way to regularize your status is to have your employer obtain pre-confirmation of your appointment before your arrival. This is done by sending copies of your degree and teaching certificate (which must be from a 100-hour course) to the Ministry of Education in Ankara. A few weeks later, you collect your work visa (which allows multiple entry to Turkey) from the Consulate in your home country. The fee for this work visa is £60; try asking the school to refund the money if they don't offer.

A separate residence permit *(ikamet tezkeresi)* must be obtained after arrival, for which you will need the originals of the same documents as above and a number of passport-sized photos. Without a teaching qualification it will not be possible to get the work permit and virtually impossible to get a residence permit unless you can prove that you have sufficient funding from outside Turkey. Those who work on tourist visas must leave the country every three months (normally across the border to Greece though a trip to Northern Cyprus is more pleasant). If you do this too many times the border officials may well become suspicious.

If the school makes social security contributions on your behalf, you will have medical cover from your first day of work. The scheme pays all your doctor's bills and 80% of prescriptions.

Currency restrictions have been lifted so you can buy foreign currency over the counter in banks and bureaux de change. (In Istanbul the Marko Polo travel agency near Sultanahmet has been recommended.)

CONDITIONS OF WORK

The burgeoning of language schools means that professional standards and working conditions vary tremendously. Salaries range from £2 an hour to £750 per month. (Because of inflation, it's a waste of time quoting salaries in Turkish lira.) In many cases a quoted salary may sound deceptively low, since free flights and accommodation bolster the value of the monthly pay cheque considerably. Also the cost of living is quite low and £500 a month is enough to live on comfortably if not luxuriously.

Inflation is very high in Turkey at the moment. Although the official rate (on which pay rises are calculated) was around 70% in mid-1990, unofficial estimates put it nearer 170%. The exchange rate is falling but more slowly. This means that before you accept work you must check whether your salary is to be inflation-linked or pegged against a foreign currency and how often it will be adjusted; October and March pay reviews are common. You will almost certainly be paid in Turkish lira in cash; luckily there are relatively few pickpockets in Turkey.

Before accepting a job you must check that the salary you are being offered is net and not gross. Not only are Turkish income tax rates fairly high, they also have a rather bizarre way of fixing them which results in the deductions from your salary increasing progressively throughout the financial year. This is a fairly unacceptable state of affairs for ex-pats — it's not something the Turks are exactly wild about either but they have no choice but to live with it — so most employers contrive to juggle the figures and top up teachers' salaries so that what they receive is actually the same each month, unless they have worked especially long hours and earned some overtime.

The Pupils

The major schools are well equipped with TVs, videos, language labs and course materials. But better than the back-up facilities is the enthusiasm of the pupils who are usually motivated, conscientious and well-behaved, and enjoy role play and group discussions. The friendly openness of young Turks may cause a foreign teacher to forget that Turkey is still an Islamic country where dress is conservative and women, no matter how promising do not normally go on to higher education. Dick Bird, a veteran EFL teacher in Turkey and elsewhere, describes some of his female and other pupils:

I have found women students defer to a far higher level of male chauvinism than would be acceptable anywhere in the West. Turkish women also seem to have exceptionally quiet voices and I can't help feeling that this irritating characteristic is somehow related to their role in society — a case of being seen but not heard until you are very very close perhaps? Sometimes my students know too much grammar to be able to express themselves freely. As their own language is radically different to Indo-European languages they have a lot of difficulty adapting to the sentence structure of English: they regard relative clauses as a perversion and are baffled, if not mildly outraged, by the cavalier way English seems to use any tense it fancies to refer to future actions but is puritanically strict about how one may describe present and past events. Another difficulty Turks have is that we EFL teachers like to use a lot of words in our meta-language (i.e. language about language e.g. adjective, verb) which do not have cognates in Turkish as they do in other European languages, for example a teacher may inform their students that " 'will' expresses probability, not intention"; this will be readily understood by an elementary level Spaniard but is total gibberish to a Turk (as I suspect it is a great many native speakers of English).

Dick's analysis of Turkish EFL students ends with a light-hearted description of their irrepressible energy and enthusiasm:

Whenever the class is asked a question they would fain prostrate themselves at their teacher's feet were it not that years of instilled discipline keep them penned by invisible bonds within the confines of their desks until the ringing of the bell whereat pandemonium breaks loose as a thousand berserk adolescents fling themselves across the (highly polished) corridor floors and down the (marble) steps headlong into the playground. (This phenomenon may help to explain why fire drills are not a regular feature of Turkish school life.)

One undesirable aspect of Turkish education which dints student morale is an artificially high failure rate imposed by schools eager to prove to the world what high standards they maintain. In fact, many *lises* are too strongly oriented to exam preparation and university entrance for many EFL teachers.

Hours and Holidays

Contracts are usually for a full 12 months since Turkish schools do not try to wriggle out of paying their teachers over the summer. Private language schools will expect you to work the usual unsocial hours, while *lises* offer daytime working hours plus a number of onerous extracurricular duties as Dick Bird recounts:

Major gripes include writing and marking the "common tests" which are imposed once a month, only to see the results overridden if the parents are of sufficiently elevated social status, then attending school ceremonies and staff meetings on one's day off at which a senior member of staff arrives two hours late and proceeds to castigate everybody for slackness. Any attempt to raise an issue of general teaching concern is then met with another rant. (The attitude of some people running the lises seems to be designed as a counterpoint to the generally high esteem accorded the profession by the rest of society.)

The standard holiday allowance for teachers is 4 weeks. At inferior schools, national holidays must be taken out of this annual leave, including Muslim holidays like Şeker Bayrami at the end of Ramadan and Kurban Bayrami, the festival of sacrifice (when, as Dick Bird would have it, Muslims celebrate Abraham's decision to have lamb that Sunday and not Isaac). Both of these festivals are 3 days and it's customary to make the bridge to a full week.

Accommodation

If accommodation is provided as part of your contract like a "tied cottage," it is usually located close to the school in a modern flat which you will have to share with another teacher. If you are on your own, it is usually possible to find an older and smaller furnished flat for yourself, though rents are high compared to a generally low cost of living, often accounting for up to 50% of your outgoing expenses.

The situation in over-crowded Istanbul is especially tight. Rural Turks are leaving the land where there is no opportunity to improve or change their way of life and coming to the big expanding industrial cities. In addition to internal migration there are the *gasterbeiter* forced out of Germany by reunification and the ethnic Turks who left Bulgaria.

If the school doesn't provide a flat they will certainly help you find one and act as go-between with the landlord. It is usual to bargain over the rent as if you were buying a second-hand car. They are advertised through *Hurriyet* newspaper or there are estate agencies called *emlak* but these tend to charge a month's rent. Rents are initially quite steep but this is on the understanding that they will not be increased for the first 12 months and then the rise will be about half the rate of inflation, so it becomes more worthwhile the longer you stay. It also means foreigners are an attractive proposition as they tend to be undemanding tenants who move out after a year or two.

The nicest flats are along the Bosphorus, the air is clean, the views stunning and a lot of the buildings are older properties with a lot of character; this is why they have been snapped up by well-heeled diplomats and multi-nationals. Rents are lower on the Asian side, the further you head into Anatolia the cheaper they get. The pollution is not as bad on the Asian side and although it has less charm (actually it has no charm at all), many people prefer it.

Ian McArthur chose the opposite situation; his school was in a suburb on the Asian side, but he chose to stay in a cheap hotel in Sultanahmet, partly for the social life:

I had to commute (from Europe to Asia in fact) for an hour in the morning and evening, but the marvellous views of the sunrise over the domes and minarets from the Bosphorus ferry whilst sipping a much-needed glass of strong sweet tea, made the early rise worth it.

Try to find out if the water supply is continuous because Istanbul has grown faster than its infrastructure. Whereas some areas have mains water gushing out of their lawn sprinklers 24 hours a day others have to make do with a niggardly trickle and the occasional tanker load into the storage tank. Wherever you end up staying in Turkey, you will have to learn to cope with erratic water and electricity supplies.

LEISURE TIME

Even if you are earning a salary at the lower end of the scale, you should be able to afford quite a good life. A loaf of bread costs less than 10p, taxi rides in Istanbul and a decent bottle of wine like Cankaya £1.50 and clothes are very cheap. Travel is also wonderfully affordable. The efficiency, comfort and low cost of Turkish bus travel put the coach services of most other countries to shame. There is very little crime in Turkey and women on their own need have no fear of serious harassment. Exposure to western ways (especially in the main teaching centres) has been sufficient for most Turks not to be too shocked by foreign customs.

A supply of duty-free cigarettes (preferably Marlboros) might go some way to repaying kindness. Take some foreign coins to give to children all of whom seem to collect foreign money. Companionable hours can be whiled away in cafés playing backgammon, Turkey's favourite game. Despite the fame of Turkish coffee, tea is the national drink, and coffee drinkers would be advised to take their own supply to avoid inflated coffee prices in the shops. Also take warm clothing if you are teaching over the winter since freezing conditions are not uncommon.

LIST OF SCHOOLS

ACTIVE ENGLISH
Atatürk Bulvari 127/701 Selcan Han Kizilay, Ankara 06640. Tel: (4) 1187973.
Number of teachers: 22-25.
Preference of nationality: UK, US, Canada, Australia.
Qualifications: teaching certificate in English preferable or any university degree plus RSA Cert.
Conditions of employment: 1 year contracts. 100 hours per month. Evening and weekend work. 2 days off per week if possible.
Salary: TL24,000 per hour (net).
Facilities/Support: accommodation provided, and training if necessary.
Recruitment: interviews in Turkey or with recruitment agency in London.

AKADEMI SCHOOL OF ENGLISH
Bahar Sokak No. 2, Diyarbakir 21000. Tel: (831) 17907/42297.
Number of teachers: 3-4.
Preference of nationality: UK.
Qualifications: minimum 4 year degree and RSA Cert. (or equivalent).
Conditions of employment: minimum 1 year contracts. 24 h.p.w.
Salary: TL3,000,000 per month net of all taxes, social security, etc. Free air fares are possible.
Facilities/Support: free furnished shared accommodation provided. Training given.
Recruitment: adverts in UK press and recruitment agencies.

BEST ÖZEL YABANCI DILLER KURSU
Ali Sami Yen Sk., Muhaddişoğlu Işhani, Kat 3-4, Gayrettepe, Istanbul. Tel: (1) 174 2890.
Number of teachers: 10-12.

Preference of nationality: UK.
Qualifications: BA essential, teaching qualification preferred.
Conditions of employment: 9 or 12 month contracts. 25 h.p.w. Pupils are all adults.
Salary: TL2,300,000 per month with accommodation, TL2,700,000 without. Salaries reviewed in March.
Facilities/Support: shared accommodation provided or assistance given. 2-week training course available.
Recruitment: locally or through agencies. Local interviews essential.

BOĞAZIÇI LISESI
Ayazağa Köyü Yolu Girisi, Maslak, Istanbul. Tel: (1) 764140.
Number of teachers: 5-10.
Preference of nationality: UK, US.
Qualifications: BA/MA (English).
Conditions of employment: 1-2 year contracts. 25 h.p.w. Pupils aged 12-18.
Salary: US$800-1,000 per month.
Facilities/Support: assistance with accommodation. No training given.
Recruitment: through adverts. Interviews sometimes held abroad.

BOĞAZIÇI OĞRETIM IŞLETIMESI
Gökfiliz Işhani Kat, 8 Mecidiyeköy, Istanbul. Tel: (1) 174 2070/71.
Preference of nationality: US, UK.
Qualifications: teaching certificate and decent appearance/behaviour.
Conditions of employment: 1 year contracts. 20-30 h.p.w. Average age of pupils is 20.
Facilities/Support: no assistance with accommodation. No training.
Recruitment: locally. Interviews required and may possibly be held abroad.

ÇINAR SCHOOL OF ENGLISH
860 Sokak 1/4, Konak, Izmir. Tel: (51) 137273/4. Fax: 411113.
Number of teachers: 15.
Preference of nationality: UK, New Zealand.
Qualifications: university degree and TEFL certificate. 26 h.p.w. maximum, mostly evenings. All details set out clearly in contract in English.
Salary: approximately £2.20 per hour.
Facilities/Support: free accommodation in furnished flats. Free flights, and training provided.
Recruitment: through newspaper adverts and interviews.

ÇIZAKÇA LISESI
Ihsan Çizakça Lisesi, Sirameşeler, Bursa. Tel: (24) 363 938.
Number of teachers: 7.
Preference of nationality: none.
Qualifications: BA plus teaching certificate (DES registration for Britons).
Conditions of employment: 1 year renewable contracts. 25 teaching periods (45 minutes) per week.
Salary: US$700 per month (paid in Turkish lira) after tax.
Facilities/Support: furnished flat provided, but no training.
Recruitment: through adverts and recruitment agencies abroad.

ÇUKUROVA UNIVERSITY FOREIGN LANGUAGES TEACHING CENTER
Balcali-Adana. Tel: (711) 133394/5/6/7 ext. 2923/4.
Number of teachers: 4-5.
Preference of nationality: UK, US.
Qualifications: degree in TEFL, Literature, Linguistics or Psychology.
Conditions of employment: 1 year renewable contracts. 12 h.p.w.
Salary: approximately TL2,000,000 per month.
Facilities/Support: no accommodation. Some training provided.
Recruitment: interviews held in Turkey.

DILKO ENGLISH CENTRES
PO Box 152, Kadikoy, 81300 Istanbul. Tel: (1) 338 0170/338 1070. Fax: 338 0170.
Number of teachers: 15-20 for 3 centres in Istanbul (Bakirköy, Kadiköy, and Şişli).
Preference of nationality: US, UK only.
Qualifications: minimum BA (English or related subject), RSA, PGCE or similar certificate plus 12 months teaching experience.
Conditions of employment: 9 month contracts (October-January). 24 h.p.w., mostly evenings and weekends, 6 days per week. Signing of agreement is compulsory.
Salary: £500-600 per month.
Facilities/Support: accommodation can be arranged at a DILKO residence and the cost deducted from salary. 2 week orientation provided plus in-service training programme throughout the year.
Recruitment: adverts in *TES* plus local interviews.

DILMER LTC
Unlu Cad, 7, Heykel, Bursa. Tel: (24) 214758.
Number of teachers: 10.
Preference of nationality: UK.
Qualifications: BA, RSA Cert. (or equivalent) and 1 year's experience preferred.
Conditions of employment: 1 year contracts. 26 h.p.w. Pupils aged 13 upwards.
Salary: TL1,300,000 per month with annual rise.
Facilities/Support: accommodation and training provided.
Recruitment: through adverts in *Guardian*. Interviews sometimes in London and if not, then by phone.

ENGLISH CENTRE
Selanik Caddesi 8, Kat 5, Kizilay, Ankara. Tel: (4) 135 3094/135 2397.
Number of teachers: 15.
Qualifications: BA, TEFL Certificate (preferably RSA or 110 hour equivalent).
Conditions of employment: 1 year contracts or sometimes 6 months. 24 h.p.w. Pupils aged between 18-40.
Salary: £310-400 per month.
Facilities/Support: accommodation provided. Training given.
Recruitment: through newspaper adverts. Interviews sometimes held in UK.

THE ENGLISH CENTRE
Rumeli Caddesi 92/4, Zeki Bey Apt., Osmanbey, Istanbul. Tel: (1) 147

0983/152 8271/152 8272.
Number of teachers: 14.
Preference of nationality: none.
Qualifications: BA and RSA Cert. (grade 'B' minimum) essential; RSA Dip. and experience preferred.
Conditions of employment: 12 month contracts. 24 periods of 50 minutes per week. 2 consecutive days off per week. Some company teaching in Istanbul.
Salary: Basic TL1,335,000 per month plus increments for qualifications. Twice annual salary reviews.
Facilities/Support: accommodation and free flights provided. Training available.
Recruitment: adverts in UK and *Turkish Daily News.* Interviews available in UK.

THE ENGLISH CENTRE
Şair Eşref Bulvari 30/3, Izmir. Tel: (51) 255673.
Number of teachers: 6-8.
Preference of nationality: none.
Qualifications: BA+TEFL Certificate.
Conditions of employment: 1 year contracts. 25 h.p.w.
Salary: approx £300 per month. Regularly revised for inflation.
Facilities/Support: free accommodation. Detailed lesson plans provided. Regular training sessions for teachers.
Recruitment: adverts in UK papers. Interviews not essential.

ENGLISH FAST
Head Office, Altiyol Yoğurtçu Sükrü Sokak No. 29, Kadiköy, Istanbul. Tel: (1) 338 9100/345 1440.
Language school group with 5 schools in Istanbul, Ankara and Izmir (addresses below).
Number of teachers: about 150.
Preference of nationality: none.
Qualifications: minimum BA and RSA Cert.
Conditions of employment: 12 month contracts. 26 h.p.w. Pupils are children and adults.
Salary: £4,500-7,500 (net) depending on qualifications and experience, paid monthly in local currency.
Facilities/Support: free accommodation and flights. RSA Cert, courses run in the autumn. Offer free 4-week training course to candidates with BA plus business background if they sign 1 year contract.
Recruitment: adverts in UK press. Interviews in London or Turkey.
Agent abroad: EF Group of Language Schools, 9 Denmark Street, London WC2H 8LS (tel: 071-497 8166/836 7693). Representative available Monday-Friday 4-6pm.
Branch addresses: Cumhuriyet Bulvari No. 36/3, Gumruk-Izmir (tel: 51-147793/255137).
Yüksel Cad. 19, Kizilay, Ankara (tel: 4-125 4442).
Taşocaği Cad. 2, Altan Erbulak Sok. 1, Mecidiyeköy, 80300 Istanbul (tel: 1-175 4398/9).

ENGLISH LAB
1720 Sokak No. 26/3, Karşiyaka-Izmir. Tel: (51) 118936.
Number of teachers: 2.

Preference of nationality: UK, US.
Qualifications: BA plus TESOL Cert.
Conditions of employment: 1 year contracts. Most teaching in evenings and at weekends. Most pupils aged 12-30.
Salary: TL1,000,000 per month.
Facilities/Support: assistance given with accommodation. Training provided.
Recruitment: interviews not essential.

EVRIM
Ozel Evrim Yabanci Dil Kurslari, Cengiz Topel Caddesi 8/2, Çamlibel, Mersin. Tel: (741) 21893/39541.
Preference of nationality: UK, US.
Qualifications: minimum 2 years experience of teaching, preferably to foreign students. Clear speech and colourful personality are important.
Conditions of employment: 1 year contracts. 30 h.p.w. between 8am-9pm.
Salary: minimum US$500 per month.
Facilities/Support: assistance with accommodation given. 15 days intensive training in September and also every Friday. Videos and language labs are used.
Recruitment: interviews in Mersin or in London (late June/early July).

FABSIT FOUNDATION
PO Box 4510, Greensboro, North Carolina 27404-4510, USA. Tel: (919) 292-9605.
Represents 3 schools in Turkey: Tarsus Americal School (PK 6, Tarsus), American Collegiate Institute (35290 Goztepe, Izmir) and Usküdar American Academy (Istanbul).
Number of teachers: 30+.
Preference of nationality: American/Canadian accents preferred.
Qualifications: BA in English (or similar) and valid teaching certificate. Teaching experience and advanced work preferred.
Conditions of employment: 2 year contracts. 24 periods per week of 45 minutes. Pupils aged 11-18.
Salary: US$410 net per month after all benefits provided and tax deducted. Reviewed every 6 months.
Facilities/Support: furnished accommodation plus utilities and medical insurance provided free. Training given.
Recruitment: interviews in US/UK held in February, mostly at recruitment fairs.

FONO PRIVATE ELEMENTARY SCHOOL
Gündoğdu Caddesi 49, Merter, 34016 Istanbul. Tel: (1) 575 5212/575 1352/554 3416. Fax:584 2742.
Number of teachers: 2.
Preference of nationality: UK.
Qualifications: must be qualified to teach elementary school.
Conditions of employment: 1 year contracts. 25 lessons per week. Children aged 7-12.
Salary: twice what local teachers are paid.
Facilities/Support: assistance given with accommodation. No training.
Recruitment: adverts in *TES*. Interviews not essential.

INTERNATIONAL SCHOOL
Kasap Sok., Eser Apt. A Blok, 16/7 Esentepe, Istanbul. Tel: (1) 759300/01.
Number of teachers: 6 full-time, 2 part-time.
Preference of nationality: none.
Qualifications: minimum BA, TEFL qualification; 2 years TEFL experience preferred.
Conditions of employment: 1 year contracts. 24 h.p.w. Pupils aged 16+, mostly aged 20-35.
Salary: TL3,000,000 per month reviewed every 6 months.
Facilities/Support: shared flats provided for 16% of basic salary. Training given.
Recruitment: through local and UK advertising. Interviews normally required and held locally or in UK.

KENT ENGLISH
Mithatpaşa Caddesi No. 46 Kat 3, Kizilay, Ankara. Tel: (4) 134 3833/133 6010.
Number of teachers: 15.
Preference of nationality: UK.
Qualifications: min. BA plus RSA Cert. or equivalent.
Conditions of employment: 1 year contracts. Week day hours between noon and 9pm. Weekend classes optional. Most pupils aged 20-35.
Salary: hourly rates from TL8,500 (inexperienced) to TL14,500.
Facilities/Support: free accommodation and utilities. Cost of work permit and flights are paid.
Recruitment: mostly local interviews, but some direct hiring from UK and also via recruitment agency in Cambridge.

NEW KENT ENGLISH
1472 Sokak No. 32, Alsancak, Izmir. Tel: (51) 632737.
Number of teachers: 7.
Preference of nationality: none.
Qualifications: BA plus RSA Cert.
Conditions of employment: 1 year contracts. Peak hours 5-9pm. Most pupils aged 15-35.
Salary: TL1,000,000 per month.
Facilities/Support: free accommodation. Reimbursed air fares. 4 weeks paid holiday. Social security payments made. Training given.
Recruitment: adverts and interviews (available in UK).

TEKDIL
45/A Meşrutiyet Caddesi, Kizilay, Ankara. Tel: (4) 134 3334/133 8474.
Number of teachers: 2-4.
Preference of nationality: US, UK.
Qualifications: BA/BSc plus teaching certificate and some experience.
Conditions of employment: 1 year contracts. 96 teaching hours per month. 1½ days off per week. Weekend work required. Pupils aged 16-40.
Salary: TL15,000 per hour.

Facilities/Support: teachers' flat provided. Pre-term orientation held and monthly meetings. Mackintosh computer programmes are used.
Recruitment: interviews held in Turkey or UK.

TURKISH AMERICAN UNIVERSITY ASSOCIATION
Language Center, Rumeli Caddesi No. 60-62, Titiz Building, Osmanbey, Istanbul. Tel: (1) 140 2607.
Number of teachers: 10.
Preference of nationality: US.
Qualifications: must have proven ability to teach EFL to adults.
Conditions of employment: minimum 3 semesters (1 year). Normal maximum of 20 h.p.w. between 10am-9pm. Pupils aged 18-45.
Salary: TL20,000 per hour (gross).
Facilities/Support: assistance given with accommodation. No training given.
Recruitment: through direct application and interview.

TURYAP INTERNATIONAL EDUCATIONAL CENTRE
Tarlabaşi Bulvari 60, Taksim, 80080 Istanbul. Tel: (1) 150 8556/153 6814. Fax: 146 9476.
Number of teachers: 10-14 (estimated since the school is new).
Preference of nationality: none.
Qualifications: minimum BA (Modern Languages/English), RSA Cert. or equivalent. Experience not essential.
Conditions of employment: 1 year contracts. 24 contact h.p.w. and 4 hours per month for social activities. Pupils aged 14-45.
Salary: from approximately TL3,650,000 per year plus bonus.
Facilities/Support: free accommodation and airfares provided. Training for RSA Dip. Course available in some cases.
Recruitment: locally and internationally through newspaper adverts. Interviews essential and can be arranged in UK if necessary.

UÇUK INTERNATIONAL LANGUAGE SCHOOL
Isik Han, Halep Caddesi, Malatya. Tel: (821) 12908.
Number of teachers: 1.
Preference of nationality: Ireland, UK.
Qualifications: TEFL Diploma necessary. Experience preferred. Friendly outgoing personality and good knowledge of grammar important.
Conditions of employment: 1 year renewable contracts. 20 h.p.w., mostly 6-8pm and weekend shifts 9-12am, 2-5pm and 6-8pm. Pupils from 13 years of age.
Salary: TL1,000,000 per month.
Facilities/Support: assistance given with finding and sometimes with paying for accommodation. No training provided.
Recruitment: mostly word of mouth and contacts. Interviews not essential.

AFRICA

Contradictions abound in a continent as complex as Africa, and one of them pertains to the attitude to the English language. On the one hand the emergent nations of Africa want to distance themselves from their colonial past. Hence the renaming of Leopoldville, Salisbury and Upper Volta to become Kinshasa, Harare and Burkina Faso. On the other hand, they are eager to develop and participate in the world economy and so need to communicate in English.

What makes much of Africa different from Latin America and Asia (vis-à-vis English teaching) is that English is the medium of instruction in state schools in many ex-colonies of Britain including Ghana, Nigeria, Kenya, Zambia, Zimbabwe and Malawi. As in the Indian subcontinent, the majority of English teachers in these countries are locals. But, unlike in India, there is considerable demand for native speakers in the secondary schools, especially in Zimbabwe and Kenya.

The drive towards English extends to most parts of the continent. In 1990 newly independent Namibia decided to make English its official language to replace the hated Afrikaans. A demand for hundreds of native speakers, mainly at the advanced teacher-trainer level, was created overnight, which organizations like VSO and the ODA were rushing to satisfy. Even in ex-colonies of France and Portugal, English is a sought-after commodity: a British Council teaching centre has just been opened in the Côte d'Ivoire, while the prestigious Institute of Foreign Languages in Maputo (capital of Mozambique) has been trying to recruit highly paid EFL teachers for 2-year contracts.

To balance the picture, it must be said that there has been some falling off in the urgent demand for English teachers in some countries such as Zambia and Nigeria, in favour of science, maths and technology teachers. And the Sudanese government, which once funded hundreds of native English speakers to teach in its schools, has stopped this programme partly because of continuing unrest but also because the new regime is decidedly less welcoming to Western influences.

Perhaps the reason that a salary of up to £15,000 was offered in Maputo was to counteract the disincentive of working in a country torn by civil strife. Partly due to turmoil in Mozambique, the government's teacher recruitment scheme which was administered through the Mozambique Information Offiice in London (7a Caledonian Road, N1 9DX) has been cancelled after 15 years of operation. Political instability has beleaguered a few of the countries where English either was or still is in demand, particularly the Sudan and also Liberia from which scores of foreign teachers, most of them American, were evacuated in 1990.

The situation is different in North Africa where there is relatively more stability and prosperity. Although Morocco is not a rich country by any means and although it is a former French colony, a number of commercial language schools employ native English speakers, a situation which is fairly uncommon in the rest of Africa apart from Egypt. In these countries it is possible to teach English on a casual basis, as in South America or Asia.

Prospects for Teachers

Africa is not a promising destination for the so-called teacher-traveller. The majority of foreign teachers in Africa are on one or two year contracts fixed up in their home country. Because a high proportion of opportunities is in secondary schools rather than private institutes, a teaching certificate is often a pre-requisite. Missionary societies have played a very dominant role in Africa's modern history, so many teachers are recruited through religious organizations, asking for a Christian commitment even for secular jobs. For example the majority of advertisements for jobs in Africa in the educational press are placed by voluntary or missionary organizations, particularly Christians Abroad and the Volunteer Missionary Movement.

But the image this evokes of religious zealots reading Bible stories in the jungle is quite out of place and will hardly do for the RSA Diploma qualified teacher who goes to work for a Libyan oil company on a Saudi-style salary. Nor will it fit the university student who does some informal teaching in a rural area of a tribal homeland like Bophuthatswana where schools have traditionally had trouble attracting qualified teachers. Making generalizations is always a dangerous pastime, and especially so when talking about Africa.

FIXING UP A JOB

In Advance

The following organizations recruit EFL teachers, often only on an occasional basis, for schools in Africa. These postings are normally regarded as "voluntary" since local wages are paid usually along with free housing and air fares. See page 62 for further details of the general agencies.

VSO, 317 Putney Bridge Road, London SW15 2PN. Tel: 071-780 1331. Sends teachers to Zimbabwe, Nigeria, etc.

Project Trust, Breacachadh Castle, Isle of Coll, Argyll PA78 6TB. Sends some school leavers (aged 17-19) to teach in schools (often science rather than English) for instance in Botswana and rural Zimbabwe. Participants must raise a proportion of the cost of the placement, usually almost £2,500.

Skillshare Africa, 3 Belvoir Street, Leicester LE1 6SL. Formerly known as IVS Overseas, this charity sends voluntary teachers on 2-year contracts to Lesotho, Botswana, Mozambique and Swaziland.

CIIR (Catholic Institute for International Relations), 22 Coleman Fields, London N1 7AF. Tel: 071-354 0883. Very occasionally sends professional teachers on 2-year contracts to Somalia and Zimbabwe. Positions are open to people of any or no religious belief.

WorldTeach, Harvard Institute for Int. Devt., 1 Eliot St, Cambridge, Mass. 02138, USA. Sends volunteer EFL teachers from North America to Kenya, Namibia (as of 1990) and possibly soon to Ghana. Participants must pay about $3,800 for travel, insurance and training.

Peace Corps, 1990 K Street NW, Washington, DC 20526, USA. Volunteers teach on 2-year assignments in many African countries.

The Embassies of some African nations such as Malawi may recruit teachers on behalf of their Ministry of Education. A teaching qualification is not always required, though a willingness to live on local wages is.

Commercial agencies occasionally recruit for North Africa; for example Management Training Services (39 Marsh Green Road, Marsh Barton, Exeter EX2 8PN; tel: 0392 72223) occasionally recruit qualified teachers to work on the Mediterranean coast of Libya for an oil company and Jawaby Oil Service

Recruitment (33 Cavendish Square, London WlM 9HF; tel: 071-499 0855) occasionally advertise.

The following missionary societies place teachers who are committed Christians in Africa:

Christians Abroad, 1 Stockwell Green, London SW9 9HP. Send teachers to Malawi and Zimbabwe.

Volunteer Missionary Movement (VMM), Shenley Lane, London Colney, St. Albans, Herts. AL2 1AR. Tel: (0727) 24853. VMM's adverts in the educational press often begin "Even Worse Pay. Teach in Africa". They cooperate with the churches in 7 African nations but most posts are in Zimbabwean and Kenyan boarding schools.

Africa Inland Mission, 2 Vorley Road, Archway, London N19 5HE. Tel: 071-281 1184. Have a few opportunities from time to time for English teachers in Kenyan secondary schools, and occasionally also in Zaire and the Comores Islands. Positions open to unskilled school leavers or graduates.

Baptist Missionary Society, PO Box 49, Baptist House, 129 Broadway, Didcot, Oxon. OX11 8XA. Tel: (0235) 512077. Very occasional openings in Zaire.

Red Sea Mission Team, 33/35 The Grove, Finchley, London N3 1QU. Tel: 081-346 1222. Occasional vacancies in Djibouti for French-speaking volunteers; teacher training not necessary.

The British Council has an English Language Officer in most African countries, who may be willing to advise on local opportunities. The *Centre for British Teachers* and *Worldwide Educational Services* occasionally advertise positions in Africa.

Americans might want to consult the book *Teaching Opportunities in the Middle East and North Africa* published by Amideast (1100 17th St NW, Washington, DC 20036 @ $14.95), though only a handful of addresses in Morocco, Tunisia and Egypt are provided. There are about 20 Binational Centers in Africa, several of which have entries in the Directory at the end of this chapter.

On the Spot

The best chances of picking up language teaching work on the spot in Africa are in one of the *American Language Centers* in Morocco, whose entries below acknowledge that they sometimes hire "walk-ins". Working as a private tutor or at a commercial language institute can also be arranged after arrival in Egypt and possibly the Sudan. Finally, the possibility of fixing up a job in Kenya after arrival cannot be ruled out, particularly in a *Harrambee* (non-government, self-help school in rural areas). These are all discussed under the relevant country headings below, along with information on regulations and conditions of work.

PROBLEMS AND REWARDS

If teachers in Spain and Hong Kong suffer from culture shock, teachers in rural Africa often find themselves struggling to cope. Whether it is the hassle experienced by women teachers in Muslim North Africa or the loneliness of life in a rural West African village, problems proliferate. Anyone who has fixed up a contract should try to gather as much up-to-date information as possible before departure, preferably by attending some kind of orientation programme or briefing (see Introduction). Otherwise local customs can come as a shock, for example finding yourself being bowed to (as Malawians do to anyone in a superior job). On a more basic level, you will need advice on how to cope with climatic extremes. Even Cairo can be unbearably hot in the summer (and surprisingly rainy and chilly in January/February).

A certain amount of deprivation is almost inevitable; for example teachers, especially volunteers, can seldom afford to shop in the pricey expatriate stores and so will have to be content with the local diet, typically a staple cereal such as millet usually made into a kind of stodgy porridge, plus some cooked greens, tinned fish or meat and fruit.

Health is obviously a major concern to anyone headed for Africa. The fear of AIDS-contaminated blood or needles in much of central Africa prompts many teachers to outfit themselves with a complete expat medical kit before leaving home (see Introduction). Malaria is rife and there is an alarming amount of mosquito resistance to the most common prophylactics, so this too much be sorted out with a tropical diseases expert before departure.

Currency regulations can present serious difficulties. Although your salary may be in excess of your spending requirements, savings are of little use if they cannot be taken out of the country at the end of your contract. Try to find out what the current situation is before you make any financial calculations.

If all that Africa could offer was a contest with malaria and a diet of porridge, no one would consider teaching there. But anyone who has seen movies like *Out of Africa* (romanticized as they no doubt are) can imagine how the continent holds people in thrall. A chance to see the African bush, to climb the famous peaks of Kilimanjaro or Kenya, to frequent the colourful markets, these are the pleasures of Africa which so many people who have worked there find addictive.

MOROCCO

Although Morocco is a Francophone country, English is increasingly a requirement for entrance to university or high ranking jobs. Like so many African countries, Morocco has sought to improve the standards of education for its nationals so that almost all teaching jobs in schools and universities are now filled by Moroccans. But outside the state system there is a continuing demand for native speakers, though there are fewer commercial institutes than might have been expected. The British Council in Rabat can supply a list of 15 (which includes its own DTO and the 7 American Language Centers) and is willing to give enquirers some idea of their chances of finding employment in Morocco in light of their qualifications and experience.

The Moroccan Ministry of Labour stipulates that the maximum number of foreign staff in any organization cannot exceed 50%. It also insists that all foreign teachers have at least a university degree before they are eligible for a work permit. Although a knowledge of French is not a formal requirement, it is a great asset for anyone planning to spend time in Morocco.

The International Language Centre in Rabat (2 rue Tihana) is one of the main centres of English but, like the American Centers, relies mainly on part-time staff. The hourly rate of pay is between $5 and $10. Net salaries for contract teachers are usually about 5,000 dirhams per month. A third of your net income can be exchanged into a hard currency and sent home.

There is one International House affiliated school, viz. The London School of English, 10 avenue de l'Armée Royale, Casablanca (tel: 261856), which recruits its teachers through IH London.

EGYPT

At one end of the spectrum there is the *American University in Cairo* and the three International Language Institutes affiliated to International House. At the other there are plenty of dubious establishments operating under such confidence-inspiring names as the BCC School (made to change its name from BBC though it retained the logo) and the Oxford School of English. Whereas you will need a professional profile for the former, back street schools will be less fussy.

Steve Smith taught for Cairo's BCC School for 2 or 3 months. He had been turned down by several schools he had visited since they wanted teachers who could speak Arabic. But at BCC he was interviewed by someone who was sufficiently impressed with his stumbling Arabic and "qualifications to an advanced level" (i.e. a few A levels) to hire him instantly. Women teachers may have even less trouble; Penny LeHeup was offered several teaching jobs while taking taxi rides.

Most language schools are not located in central Cairo but in one of the leafy prosperous residential areas like Heliopolis (where there is an IH school), Mardi or Zamalek. These are also the best areas to look for private clients as Ian McArthur found:

> In Cairo I sought to work as a private English tutor. I made a small poster, written in English and Arabic, with the help of my hotel owner. I drew the framework of a Union Jack at the top, got 100 photocopies and then meticulously coloured in the flags. The investment cost me £3. I put the posters up around Cairo, concentrating on affluent residential and business districts. I ended up teaching several Egyptian businessmen, who were difficult to teach since they hated being told what to do.

A simpler way of advertising your availability to teach might be to place an advert in the expatriate monthly *Cairo Today* or indeed to answer any ads for English tuition which appear.

It is not only Egyptian businessmen used to being in control who present problems to the teacher. Bryn Thomas describes his Egyptian pupils at the IH

The paper should flutter when you sound the letter 'p'

school (International Language Institute) in the northwest suburb of Sahafeyeen as "rowdy and sometimes a little over-enthusiastic". Having just obtained an RSA Certificate in London, Bryn went to visit some friends in Cairo and was immediately offered a 3-month summer contract at IH where they were desperate for a teacher. His pupils were not only Egyptians but Somalis, who are shy, quiet and industrious. Bryn describes his predicament with such a mixed class:

One of the problems I found in the class was the often quite shocking displays of racism by the Egyptians towards their dark skinned neighbours. Vast amounts of tact and diplomacy were required to ensure that enough attention was given to the Somalis without upsetting the Egyptians.

In fact it is the cultural differences not only between students but also between Western and local cultures that can put a teacher in a tricky situation. Different religions, different ways of thinking and (as I learnt in my first week at the school) different modes of dress must all be taken into consideration. One of the problems that English students in this area have difficulty with is hearing the difference between B and P. The exercise for this is to hold a piece of paper in front of the mouth and repeat the letters B and P. Since more air is exhaled during the sounding of the letter P than with B, the paper should fly up when P is said, and move only a little with B. The first time I made the students do this we went round the class, first Hamid the engineer from Alexandria, then Mona who was trying to get a job at the reception in the Hilton and then we came to Magda from Mogadishu (the capital of Somalia). All the Egyptians started to laugh — her whole face apart from her eyes was covered with a yashmak. I decided that this should not impede the exercise so if the yashmak moved it was a P, and not a B!

The reward for coping with all this is usually at least 1,000 Egyptian pounds a month with a small deduction (5-7%) for local taxes. Of course part-time teachers working on a casual basis cannot hope to earn this much, but living expenses are modest in Egypt. This may account for the fact that the RSA Certificate course offered by IH Sahafeyeen is the cheapest available (see page 34) and will get even cheaper for foreign candidates if Egypt's inflation continues to rise at its current disastrous rate.

Most teachers enter Egypt on a tourist visa (which can be purchased at the airport) and then ask their school to obtain a work permit for them from the Ministry of the Interior.

Advertisements for jobs in Egypt rarely appear in the UK or US press. *Worldwide Educational Services* annually recruit volunteer teachers on 2-year contracts for two colleges in Alexandria. The salary is based on local rates (360 Egyptian pounds per month in 1990) plus a modest supplement, housing allowance and bonuses.

SUDAN

The country which was known as the Anglo-Egyptian Sudan between 1898 and 1955 has a long-established bias in favour or Britain and the English language. For example there are (were?) a number of bilingual English/Arabic primary and secondary schools in Khartoum. Unfortunately the current political situation means that Khartoum is no longer an attractive or even a possible destination for aspiring teachers. Even the Sudan Cultural Centre in London (31 Rutland Gate, SW7 1PG; tel: 071-589 4481) cannot get reliable information about the educational situation. In the words of the Cultural Counsellor's Secretary in May 1990:

Sudan's political situation is now at rather a low ebb, and it is currently dangerous for foreigners to visit the country and nigh impossible to obtain a visa. We have been receiving very little information from Khartoum, and there have been no requests for teachers at all this year. I am sad to have to inform you that the recruitment office at the Cultural Centre has had to close down.

At the time of going to press the English teacher recruitment programme was "in abeyance" rather than "cancelled" and could be reactivated if circumstances in the Sudan change. You can ring the Cultural Centre for the latest information. (This experience may provoke a mild case of culture shock: the gentleman who answers the phone will probably apologize for the rather haphazard time-keeping of the staff, and will be heard struggling with faulty switchboard equipment. If you do succeed in being put through to the Cultural Counsellor, he may not be able to impart much hard information; in fact he may ask you to ring again another day after he has had a chance to "dwell upon your question".)

If the politics do stabilize, travellers may find that on-the-spot opportunities still exist, as they did a few years ago when Mike East spent 4 months teaching in Khartoum. He was approached in his hotel and asked if he would like to teach gifted 4 to 6 year olds part-time in a prestigious expat primary school. The pay was only pocket money, so he tried to find a supplementary source of income by arranging to meet the principals of the expat secondary schools and offering to tutor sixth formers for their exams. This evening work proved to be much more lucrative.

After his stint of teaching in Cairo, Steve Smith journeyed up the Nile to Khartoum where he put up a large notice in the local Institute of Further Education and was soon approached by a group of students eager to improve their English. They were particularly keen on learning technical vocabulary, which proved a bit of a challenge.

ZIMBABWE

When Zimbabwe became independent on 18th April 1980, it inherited an education system which was unfairly biassed towards the white population at the expense of the black. Since then the government has been working hard to redress this imbalance by building more schools and introducing "hot seating", whereby the same building houses two schools, one from 7am to 12pm and one from 12pm to 5pm. One feature which has remained the same is that English remains the principal medium of instruction.

In the last ten years the number of schools has increased dramatically. Because of this rapid expansion, Zimbabwe has a serious shortage of teachers, particularly at secondary school level. Despite the fact that the government has set up teacher training colleges in an effort to increase the ratio of home-produced teachers, many are still recruited overseas. Adult night schools have also been established and native speakers may be able to find part-time evening work to supplement their income.

Another possible new source of ELT opportunities is in the Mozambican refugee camp schools. The department in charge of this is the Non Formal Education Section, Ministry of Primary & Secondary Education, PO Box 8022, Causeway, Harare, though they are unlikely to reply to a general enquiry. The neighbouring countries of Mozambique, Angola and Namibia are looking to the private tertiary colleges of Zimbabwe for EFL training, so there may be increased demand for native speakers in that sector as well.

Fixing up a Job

Most of the hiring of English teachers for schools in Zimbabwe is carried out either by the Zimbabwean Government (through their diplomatic representatives overseas, primarily in London) or by voluntary agencies (see the introduction to this chapter). The Zimbabwe High Commission in London (429 Strand, London WC2R OSA) recruits a number of British teachers every year on 3-year contracts to teach English as well as the sciences, maths, geography, French (occasionally) and technical subjects. The main qualification is a degree in the subject to be taught, though naturally they prefer a teaching qualification as well. Air fares and a baggage allowance are paid, and up to two weeks paid accommodation on arrival. The salary is linked to local rates, but teachers can send home up to a third to fulfil financial commitments in the UK. As Zimbabwe is chronically short of hard currency, it is as well to bring proof of financial commitments to ensure that you get yor entitlement. Teachers can also apply to the Reserve Bank to take savings home when they leave at the end of their contract.

It is still feasible to go to Zimbabwe on a 3-month tourist visa and apply for a work permit as a teacher when you are out there. However, the red tape can be infuriating, especially if your holiday visa is rapidly running out. It is far better to fix up a job beforehand if possible.

Initial enquiries about the government recruitment scheme should be addressed to the Recruitment & Education Attaché at Zimbabwe House. If you are very serious about teaching in Zimbabwe, arrange an interview with the Attaché and be persistent. The academic year starts in April, though the majority of London-recruited teachers travel out in September.

British and American visitors do not need a visa for holidays in Zimbabwe, but in order to work they need a residence permit and a temporary work permit. These must be arranged either directly through the High Commission overseas, through the Department of Immigration in Zimbabwe or with the prospective employer. Overseas candidates who apply direct to the Ministry of Education need the following documents: birth certificate, marriage certificate where applicable, proof of qualifications and previous experience, satisfactory medical certificate including a radiologist's certificate of freedom from active pulmonary tuberculosis. The red tape may seem daunting, but perseverance will produce results. If you are married but separated or divorced, it is as well to keep this information private; there are stories of female applicants being turned down on the grounds that their estranged husbands might come to claim them at some future point.

As a teacher in the Ministry of Education, you can join the Public Service Medical Aid Society which provides health cover on the payment of a few Zimbabwe dollars a month; a separate payment also covers dental care. Income tax is high at 44% and you must pay your own national insurance contributions.

Conditions of Work

All government-recruited teachers must sign a 3-year contract. If the contract is broken (as very often happens) the teacher forfeits the return flight and some of their hard currency remittances.

In schools with "hot seating", hours can vary from half term to half term. Otherwise lessons usually finish by 2pm with some afternoon sports. Most teachers are expected to supervise some sporting activities.

In the rural areas, where most overseas teachers are now sent, the salaries are more than sufficient to live on, especially when accommodation is provided, mainly because there is so little to spend your money on. The cities, especially Harare the capital, are more expensive but the salaries are still adequate. There are increments for a BA, PGCE and teaching experience. Teachers get 3 months of holiday a year, as well as a November bonus consisting of an extra month's salary, tax-free for the first Z$1,100.

Secondary school students work towards the Cambridge Overseas Examinations (GCSE and A level). Although by secondary level all lessons are supposed to be in English, many pupils still have problems with it, especially in the rural areas where they may have had little exposure to the language and here the teaching often amounts to EFL. Unlike Britain there is no screening process for exam candidates, other than the ability to pay for the exam fee, so you may well find yourself taking a remedial student through a GCSE exam which they have no hope of passing. Adaptability is an essential quality for teachers. Yet students are much more enthusiastic and well-motivated than their British counterparts. Some remember the days when education was denied to a large proportion of the black population and are aware that their families are sacrificing a lot to send them to school. Often their main ambition is to get a good job to pay for their younger brothers' and sisters' fees. But with the high level of unemployment among school leavers, especially those who have studied the arts, there are the beginnings of discontent, and a growing emphasis on practical and scientific subjects at the expense of English.

Judy Fletcher worked in Zimbabwe for over 3 years and summarizes her experiences:

> *Zimbabwe is a very exciting place to be. It is a new country and things are changing and developing fast. The people are very friendly once you have shown that you are not a "Rhodi" (a white Zimbabwean who still wishes it was Rhodesia). The music scene is also very exciting, particularly in the township bars, and the landscape wherever you are is stunning. There is a very strong expatriate network, especially in the cities, but for anybody who really wants to experience Zimbabwe rather than an artificially British lifestyle, this should be avoided as much as possible. Venture into the townships and the rural areas, mix with the people who live there, and you will find Zimbabwe a difficult place to leave.*

Martin Goff, a school leaver who spent a year in Zimbabwe, echoes this enthusiasm:

> *Zimbabwe is a beautiful country; the people are 95% very friendly and $4\frac{1}{2}$ friendly, and they seem eternally pleased to see you. My time out there was easily the best of my life, and it was only a booked plane ticket that made me leave.*

MALAWI

Again there is a shortage of teachers both for government and mission-run secondary schools. However the Malawian government has a strong preference for certified teachers and it is not easy for an unqualified teacher to find work in a Malawian school. Christians Abroad, which is the main agency recruiting teachers for Malawi, insists that candidates be trained teachers with two years of classroom experience (not to mention a Christian commitment). Volunteers are paid a local salary plus a small expatriate bonus and are provided with free air fares and insurance. Advertisements appear in the new year for contracts starting in September.

Jayne Nash travelled extensively in East Africa and was struck by how progressive a country Malawi is and how helpful the expat community is. She suggests that a traveller who wanted to do some teaching only needs to ask around in Blantyre and Lilongwe and a short-term opportunity might well turn up.

Malawi's stodgy porridge is called *tsima*, and the local beer is called "green" (which apparently is exactly how over-indulgers are left feeling around the gills). Life in the rural areas is not easy, especially if you are unlucky enough to find termites building their giant hills in your garden or the killer African bee building a hive in your chimney, as happened to Tessa Shaw, a volunteer with VSO. Her solution to the problem was to build a fire in the fireplace in the hope of driving the bees out of the chimney. She came home to find her house deep in dead and dying bees. According to her account, she had to go outside and smoke 100 cigarettes before working up the courage to clean up the sticky mess.

KENYA

Kenya is another country which has a chronic shortage of secondary school teachers — 35,000 in 1990. The worst shortages are in Western Province. English is the language of instruction in Kenyan schools, so not knowing Swahili need not be an impossible barrier. However a 1988 announcement by the Kenyan Ministry of Education has limited the number of opportunities, at least in the state schools. In addition to a university degree, teaching certification and at least one year of professional teaching experience are now required. This is a major shift from the position a few years ago when many teachers hadn no more advanced qualification than a few A levels. Obviously each case is decided on its own merits and it seems that the Kenyan government does not always enforce this stipulation rigorously, especially in the case of science teachers. Apparently private language institutes — the British Council in Nairobi can supply a list of 4 addresses — are not subjecty to this restriction, since neither of the Nairobi schools in the Directory specified teacher certification as a requirement. The English Language Officer at the British Council should be able to offer informal advice to enquirers on their chances of local employment and on the current government position.

It is even less certain that these strict requirements would be applied to native English speakers looking for teaching work on the spot. Certainly in the mid-1980s it was possible to fix up a teaching job by asking in the villages, preferably before terms begin in September, January and April. The Harvard-based volunteer organization WorldTeach, which has sent hundreds of volunteer teachers to Kenya since 1986, cooperates with the Kenyan Christian Churches' Education Association. Anyone who could track down this organization in Nairobi might be put in touch with a school looking for a teacher. Be prepared to produce your c.v. and any diplomas and references on headed paper. Also ascertain before accepting a post whether or not the school can afford to pay a salary, especially if it is a *Harrambee* school. A cement or mud hut with a thatched or tin roof will normally be provided plus a monthly salary of 1,400-1,500 shillings, which is enough to live on provided you don't want to buy too much peanut butter or cornflakes in the city. Living conditions will be primitive with no running water or electricity in the majority of cases. The Kenya version of maize porridge is called *Ugali*.

People who choose to teach in Kenya do it for love not money. In the words of Ermor Kamara, Ph.D., Director of the *American Universities Preparation & Learning Centre:*

Candidates must view being in Kenya as a holiday with pay. The cost of living and corresponding local salaries sound quite low to foreigners. Consequently they must think of the opportunities to enjoy Kenya's beaches, mountains and game parks as well as experiencing a new and interesting culture. During weekends and holidays, one can travel the breadth of Kenya. Also the proximity to other countries in East and Southern Africa permits a traveller to see a good deal of our continent.

School vacations take place in December, April and August.

LIST OF SCHOOLS

Benin

AMERICAN CULTURAL CENTER (USIS)
B.P. 2012 Cotonou, Benin. Tel: 300312
Number of teachers: up to 10 (part-time only).
Preference of nationality: US, UK.
Qualifications: dynamic personality and some TEFL training/experience preferred.
Conditions of employment: no contrqacts; work paid per hour. Hours of work 7-9pm. Pupils range from teenagers upwards.
Salary: US$12 per hour.
Facilities/Support: no assistance with accommodation. Training provided.
Recruitment: through direct application. Interviews not essential, but sometimes held at TESOL convention.

Egypt

AMERICAN UNIVERSITY IN CAIRO
113 Sharia Kasr El Aini, PO Box 2511, Cairo, Egypt. Tel: (2) 357 6998.
Number of teachers: 11.
Preference of nationality: US.
Qualifications: MA (TEFL) and at least 2 years experience.
Conditions of employment: 2 year contracts. 15 h.p.w. over 5 days. Pupils aged 18-40.
Salary: 9-16,000 Egyptian pounds per year.
Facilities/Support: accommodation provided. Training given.
Recruitment: through TESOL and direct applications. Interviews not essential.

BRITISH LANGUAGE INSTITUTE
46 Hussein Street, DTE 12311, Dokki, Cairo, Egypt. Tel: (2) 345 9848/349 9202/71 8644.
Number of teachers: 8.
Preference of nationality: none.
Qualifications: BA, 1 year's teaching experience/RSA Cert.
Conditions of employment: 1 year contracts. 18-30 hours of work per month. Pupils aged 18-40, mostly in companies or hotel industry. Teachers my be asked to teach outside Cairo for up to a month; accommodation, transport and bonuses provided.
Salary: 25 Egyptian pounds per hour.
Facilities/Support: assistance given with finding accommodation.Training provided.
Recruitment: through adverts in the *Guardian*. UK interviews essential.

INTERNATIONAL LANGUAGE INSTITUTE
PO Box 13, Embaba, Cairo, Egypt. Tel: (2) 346 3087/346 8597.
Affiliated to: International House.
Number of teachers: 21.
Preference of nationality: none.
Qualifications: BA plus RSA Cert.
Conditions of employment: 1 year contracts. 25 h.p.w. Pupils aged 16-60.
Salary: 1,300 Egyptian pounds per month plus increments.
Facilities/Support: free flights and 8 weeks paid holiday. Some training provided.
Recruitment: through International House, London.

Gabon

AMERICAN CULTURAL CENTER (USIS)
B.P. 2237, Libreville, Gabon. Tel: 743332.
Number of teachers: 6.
Prefernce of nationality: US, UK.
Qualifications: MA in EFL or teaching qualification.
Conditions of employment: 9 month contracts. 20 h.p.w. afternoon/evening work weekdays only. Pupils from age 20.
Salary: from US$13 per hour.
Facilities/Support: no assistance with accommodation. Training provided.
Recruitment: locally and through direct application. Interviews preferable and can be held in US during the summer months.

Kenya

THE LANGUAGE CENTER
PO Box 14245, Nairobi, Kenya. Tel: 569531/2.
Number of teachers: 10.
Preference of nationality: none.
Qualifications: overseas teaching experience. TEFL/TESL qualification or other teaching certificates, and preferably aged 25-36.
Conditions of employment: 2 year contracts. Hours of work 8.25am-12.35pm plus afternoon/evening work. Pupils aged from 8.
Salary: approximately £2,500 for first year, rising by £250 second year.
Facilities/Support: no assistance with accommodation. Training provided.
Recruitment: through local newspaper adverts. Local interviews essential.

THE AMERICAN UNIVERSITIES PREPARATION CENTRE
PO Box 14842, Nairobi, Kenya. Tel: 741764/741652.
Number of teachers: 4.
Preference of nationality: US, Canada, UK, Australia.
Qualifications: BA (English)/TEFL qualification; experience is preferred.
Conditions of employment: minimum 1 year renewable contracts. Hours of work 8.15am-4pm. Pupils range in age from 16-40.
Salary: based on local rates.
Facilities/Support: accommodation provided but not paid for by school. Training provided.
Recruitment: mostly local. Interviews are essential and can sometimes be held abroad.

Morocco

THE AMERICAN LANGUAGE CENTER
1 Place de la Fraternité, Casablanca, Morocco. Tel: 277765/275270.
Number of teachers: 52 including part-timers.
Preference of nationality: none although mostly US at present.
Qualifications: BA essential, teaching experience preferred.
Conditions of employment: minimum 1 year contracts. Mostly evening work.
Pupils from 4 years.
Salary: depends on experience.
Facilities/Support: assistance given with finding accommodation. Training
provided.
Recruitment: Interviews are not essential. Some local hire and at TESOL
Conference.

THE AMERICAN LANGUAGE CENTER
2 Bd El Kadissia, Kenitra, Morocco. Tel: (16) 6884.
Number of teachers: 2.
Preference of nationality: none although only US to date.
Qualifications: BA in arts field essential. Knowledge of French/Arabic and
experience living abroad necessary; MA or TEFL qualification preferred.
Conditions of employment: 1 year renewable contracts. 20-25 h.p.w. full time.
Hours of work 5-9pm weekdays and Saturday 5-9pm. Pupils aged from 12 —
most aged 14-30.
Salary: US$5,900-9,500 per year (gross). Paid sick leave and medical insurance
provided.
Facilities/Support: free housing provided for 3-4 weeks while permanent
accommodation is being located. Training given.
Recruitment: through TESOL convention and some walk-ins. Interviews
generally required.

THE AMERICAN LANGUAGE CENTER
**4 Zankat Tanja, Rabat, Morocco. Tel: (7) 61016/61269/66121. Fax:
67447.**
Number of teachers: 20.
Preference of nationality: none although mostly US.
Qualifications: BA in arts field essential. Knowledge of French/Arabic and
experience of living abroad necessary. MA or TEFL qualification preferred.
Conditions of employment: 1 year renewable contracts. 20-25 h.p.w. full time.
Hours of work between 8am-9pm weekdays and 9am-5pm Saturdays. Pupils aged
from 5, mostly aged 14-30.
Salary: US$9,700-14,500 per year (gross). Paid sick leave and medical insurance
provided.
Facilities/Support: free housing provided for 3-4 weeks while permanent
accommodation is being located. Training given.
Recruitment: through TESOL convention and some walk-ins. Interviews
generally required.

THE AMERICAN LANGUAGE CENTER
1 Rue Emsallah, Tangier, Morocco. Tel: (9) 33616.
Number of teachers: 10.

Preference of nationality: none.
Qualifications: experience preferred but good teaching personality more important.
Conditions of employment: minimum 3 month commitment. Hours of work are negotiable, mostly evening work. Pupils aged from 4.
Salary: US$5-9 per hour.
Facilities/Support: no assistance with accommodation. A little training provided.
Recruitment: mostly walk-ins. Interviews essential and sometimes held at TESOL conference.

THE BRITISH COUNCIL
BP 427, Rabat, Morocco. Tel: (7) 60836.
Number of teachers: 7.
Preference of nationality: UK, Ireland.
Qualifications: minimum BA, RSA Cert. or equivalent and 2 years experience teaching, preferably abroad.
Conditions of employment: 1 year contracts. 36 h.p.w. of which 24 are contact hours. Pupils aged from 9.
Salary: minimum 9,000 dirhams per month plus 500 dirhams per month for transport costs.
Facilities/Support: no assistance with accommodation. Training provided.
Recruitment: locally or through British Council, London.

C.E.G.I.S. (Centre d'Enseignement Gestion Informatique Secretariat)
28 boulevard Girardot, Casablanca, Morocco. Tel: 308410/300437.
Number of teachers: none to date.
Preference of nationality: none.
Qualifications: BA (English).
Conditions of employment: 1 year contracts. Part-time work only. Pupils range in age from 18-30.
Salary: hourly rates.
Facilities/Support: no assistance with accommodation. Training provided.
Recruitment: adverts in newspapers.

INSTITUTION KHALIL JABRANE
Av. Bir Kacem, Souissi, Rabat, Morocco. Tel: (7) 52948.
Number of teachers: 10.
Preference of nationality: none.
Qualifications: minimum BA or equivalent, 2 years experience, ESL/EFL background and experience preferred.
Conditions of employment: 1 year renewable contracts. Hours of work 8.15am-3.45pm weekdays plus participation in school activities. Pupils at this elementary school range in age from 3-17.
Salary: approximately 4-6,000 dirhams per month.
Facilities/Support: limited accommodation available on premises, assistance in locating other accommodation given. Training provided.
Recruitment: locally or through university employment offices abroad. Interviews not essential but can sometimes be arranged in US or possibly UK.

INTERNATIONAL HOUSE
10 Av. des F.A.R., Casablanca, Morocco. Tel: 261856.

Number of teachers: 10-12.
Preference of nationality: UK, Australia, New Zealand, US.
Qualifications: BA, RSA Cert.
Conditions of employment: 9 month contracts (October-June). 25 h.p.w. weekdays. Pupils range in age from 12-40.
Salary: minimum net salary 5,000 dirhams per month (1990).
Facilities/Support: assistance with accommodation. No training provided.
Recruitment: through IH, London. UK interviews essential.

Niger

ENGLISH LANGUAGE PROGRAM
American Cultural Center (USIS), B.P. 11201, Niamey, Niger. Tel: 732920.
Number of teachers: 3.
Preference of nationality: US.
Qualifications: TEFL training and experience in a developing country are preferred.
Conditions of employment: no contracts, teachers hired per hour. Mostly part-time work. Pupils aged 18+ apart from one class of young teenagers.
Salary: approximately US$10-12 per hour.
Facilities/Support: accommodation provided within school. Very little training given.
Recruitment: only local hire with interviews.

Togo

ENGLISH LANGUAGE PROGRAM (USIS)
Amercian Cultural Center, B.P. 852 Lomé, Togo. Tel: 212166.
Number of teachers: 12.
Preference of nationality: US.
Qualifications: at least BA (English or Education) and one year's teaching experience.
Conditions of employment: 9 month-1 year contracts. Part-time morning and evening work 4 days a week. Pupils range in age from 17-65.
Salary: approximately US$11-12 per hour.
Facilities/Support: no assistance with accommodation. Training provided.
Recruitment: at TESOL conference and locally through adverts in US embassy newsletter. C.v. and 2 references required.

Tunisia

THE BOURGUIBA INSTITUTE OF MODERN LANGUAGES
47, Av. de la Liberté, Tunis 1002, Belvedere, Tunisia. Tel: 282418/282923.
Number of teachers: 5-10.
Preference of nationality: none.
Qualifications: MA/PhD (English Language), TEFL qualification, experience preferred.
Conditions of employment: 2 year contracts. 12-18 h.p.w. Pupils aged from 17 upwards.

Salary: depends on experience.
Facilities/Support: no official assistance with accommodation provided. Some training given.
Recruitment: through direct application to the Tunisian Ministry of Education. Interviews held locally but not essential.

Zimbabwe

RANCHE HOUSE COLLEGE (Adult Education Centre)
PO Box 1880, Harare, Zimbabwe. Tel: (4) 702198/9.
Number of teachers: 1.
Preference of nationality: none.
Qualifications: BA, TEFL qualification.
Conditions of employment: 6 month-1 year contracts. Hours of work 8am-12.30pm. Pupils all aged over 18.
Salary: $1,500 (Zimbabwean) per month.
Facilities/Support: no assistance with accommodation. No training given.
Recruitment: through adverts and personal contacts. Local interviews essential.

ASIA

China

One of the first signs of China's softening towards the West in the late 1970s was the welcome it extended to English language teachers. By the late 1980s there were thousands of native speakers teaching at academic institutions around the country. With the events of June 1989, the door of the so-called open door policy seemed to be on the brink of clanging shut. There was a mass exodus of foreigners either from fear for their security or from repugnance at the Tiananmen Square massacre and what it signified about the direction which Chinese politics were taking. Yet little seems to have changed from the Chinese point of view. The government is still committed to developing economic and cultural links with the West and is now eager to entice English teachers back to China.

The legacy of the Cultural Revolution, when access to foreign culture was forbidden, has left a great many Chinese with an absorbing fascination for the English language and all things Western. Since China is much more open now than it was, one might have expected a falling off of enthusiasm but this is not noticeable. English is now compulsory for school pupils from the age of 9. Yet their spoken ability remains poor into adulthood if they never have the opportunity to practise with a native speaker. A great many students and teachers are very keen to improve their English to Cambridge Proficiency standard in the hope (often vain) of being chosen to study overseas. Others are simply curious. But all are eager to learn, even if the style of learning to which they have become accustomed can be difficult for foreign teachers to cope with.

The other major problem which teachers encounter and which can wear down even the most enthusiastic China buff is the bureaucracy. It is top-heavy, all-powerful and often strikingly inefficient. All teachers admit that working in China is exhausting, but most also find the experience fascinating.

Prospects for Teachers

The Chinese government classifies teachers either as Foreign Experts (FEs) or Foreign Teachers (FTs). Foreign Experts are normally expected to have an MA in a relevant area (English, Linguistics, etc.) and either a TEFL qualification or some solid teaching experience. Foreign Teachers are normally less than 25 and have only a BA; it is unusual for non-graduates to be accepted unless they show wide experience and genuine expertise. Your designated status brings various privileges and conditions as described below.

There are a great many vacancies in both categories and often these go unfilled. A large proportion of foreigners are employed in Beijing but there are many opportunities in the provinces as well, especially for FTs. Specialist recruitment organizations such as ISIS in the US (see below) are notified of more positions than they are able to fill, explaining that "it is difficult to find enough qualified teachers to take these jobs due to low pay" (and yet the necessary qualifications are not very high). Similarly in recent years, 800 Peace Corps volunteers have been requested, but only 100 supplied.

Demand exists in the hundreds of universities, colleges, foreign language institutes, institutes of technology, teacher training colleges, etc. but it can be tricky making contact with an appropriate institution in order to set the recruitment wheels in motion. According to a China expert writing in the *EFL Gazette* (December 1989), "No effective national recruitment system is in operation". Unfortunately the mechanism for placing teachers can be subject to the same tendency to bureaucratic ineptitude as plagues teachers in China. The Chinese Embassy in London has a special Education Section (9 Birch Grove, Acton, London W3; tel: 081-752 0459) which screens applications for positions mainly as FTs but also as FEs. The co-ordinator of teacher recruitment, Mr. Tao, requests that enquirers enclose a resumé.

FIXING UP A JOB

It is worth persevering with the Education Section which is in a position to interview and recommend applications to individual institutions in China. Late winter and spring is the best time to be making enquiries for one or two year contracts starting in September. Adam Hartley (to whom this chapter is deeply indebted, along with Richard McBrien) heard about the scheme from the Careers Office at St. Andrews University and found that the interview in London was not too gruelling. After having satisfied his interviewer on why he wanted to go to China and how he would run his classes, he was assigned to a post at Shanxi Teachers' University in the provincial town of Linfen.

Residents of other English-speaking countries should contact the Education Division of the Chinese Embassy for further information. In the US, the address is 2300 Connecticut Avenue NW, Washington, DC 20008. In Australia the China Education Centre is located at Sydney University (tel: 02-692 3834).

Here are some other organizations which recruit teachers for China:

The Amity Foundation, 17 Da Jian Yin Xiang, Nanjing, China. Each year this independent Chinese church organization invites various missionary societies abroad such as the Baptist Missionary Society (PO Box 49, 129 Broadway, Didcot, Oxon. OX11 8XA) and the Church of Scotland Board of World Mission and Unity, (121 George Street, Edinburgh EH2 4YN) to recruit and select teachers of English for two year contracts beginning each August. "Enquiries welcomed from graduates and others suitably qualified (e.g. TEFL) to live and work in simple conditions." Applications are due in October.

The British Council continues to recruit for China but mostly for teacher training or lecturing positions rather than straight teaching.

GAP, 44 Queen's Road, Reading RG1 4BB. Tel: 0734 594914. Offer 6 4½-month attachments at secondary schools in Fuzhou, Hangzhou and Nanjing to school leavers.

Project Trust, Breacachadh Castle, Isle of Coll PA78 6TB. Send volunteers (aged 17-19) to work as teacher-aides in universities and training colleges.

VSO are active in China but require more than just a BA; in many cases they expect volunteers to have a PGCE.

Organizations of interest to Americans:

AFS International/Intercultural Programs, 313 E. 43rd Street, New York, NY 10017.

ISIS (International Scientific & Information Services), 49 Thompson Hay Path,

Setauket, NY 11733. Tel: (516) 751-6437. Place about 12 teachers with TEFL training and experience (preferably) plus experience (preferably in Asia) of travel or work abroad. One year contracts start in September or February.

WorldTeach, Harvard Institute for Int. Devt., 1 Eliot St., Cambridge, MA 02138. Tel: (617) 495-5527. College graduates are placed in one-year contracts all over China. Volunteers pay $3,200 for their air fares, insurance and orientation (and get paid the standard FT salary).

Direct Application

It is also possible to apply directly to institutions, since it is not compulsory that appointments be made by the Bureau of Foreign Affairs in Beijing working through Chinese Embassies abroad. A personal visit to a Chinese Embassy might overcome their reluctance to hand out lists of academic institutions to which you can write. If you know any Chinese academics or graduate students, ask them if they would be willing to put your name forward at the institute to which they were previously attached.

There are no private language schools in China although some hotel chains and large city companies have their own language training facilities.

On the Spot

Travellers in China have been approached and invited to teach English as Rachel Starling discovered:

> *Whilst travelling extensively in China (autumn 1988), I was offered several opportunities to teach English. There is an agency for English teachers in Beijing, which sends teachers all over the country. But if you want a place just ask at all the colleges, as it is likely that one school or college will require someone.*

The agency referred to is probably the Bureau of Foreign Affairs (Ministry of Education, Beijing 10086) which oversees recruitment, or possibly the office of the External Relations Secretary, Chief of Recruiting and Placement Division, Box 300, Beijing.

CONDITIONS OF WORK

Foreign Teachers are the poor relations of Foreign Experts and may end up out-of-pocket at the end of their contract. While FEs are paid by central government, FTs are funded by local education authorities who do not have large budgets. FTs must pay for their own air fares and shipping costs while FEs are paid travelling expenses from their home. Both have their accommodation provided by the host institution, either in on-site residences or in a foreigners' hotel.

FTs are paid 500-800 Yuan per month, while FEs are paid 900-1500 Yuan. There is a dual currency system in China. Renminbi (Rmb) and Foreign Exchange Certificates (FEC) are both issued in units of Yuan; the latter are available only to foreigners and can be converted into dollars at the end of their stay or used to buy imported goods, Western luxury items, international air tickets, etc. Although officially one FEC is equivalent to one Renminbi, there is a thriving black market due to their unequal purchasing power. High status jobs are rewarded with a higher proportion of FECs. Whereas 70% of an FE's salary is paid in FECs, only 30% of an FT's is convertible. Bear in mind at the outset that it is possible to change status from FT to FE, unless of course you have signed an FT contract for 2 years.

Conditions vary greatly from one institute to the next and it is vital to negotiate as much as possible before arrival. When you are first notified by your employer in China that you have a job, you should avoid the temptation to write back enthusiastically accepting it. Rather ask for more details such as your status, salary, timetable and other conditions. You could also ask for the names of any current foreign employees whom you can ask for inside information. What is agreed at this stage will set the terms of employment even though it is standard practice not to sign a contract until after 2 months probation (if at all).

Most foreign teachers are expected to teach between 12 and 16 hours a week, which sounds a light load until you find that there are up to 100 students in these classes. The administration's main ambition is often to maximize your exposure, which may have the effect of minimizing your usefulness. Hours of teaching are unpredictable and may be mostly in the evenings. If you want to keep your weekends free for travel and relaxation, firmly decline teaching hours on Saturday and Sunday.

Terms run from September 1st to February 4th and March 4th to July 31st. Foreign teachers can sometimes arrange to have longer breaks depending on their exam commitments.

The Pupils

"Big noses" (foreigners) are normally treated with great respect. In the early years of Western contact with China, English teachers in small towns found themselves lionized, unable to complete the simplest task in public without an enormous audience. But there are not many corners of China these days into which foreigners, whether teachers or travellers, have not penetrated, and as a consequence the Chinese are becoming more blasé.

"A tape recorder could have done as good a job"

With time, they may also adapt a little better to Western attitudes to pedagogy, but the learning habits of centuries are hard to undo. Role-playing and free discussion are quite alien to Chinese students, especially when there is a "political form monitor" sitting in on classes. A teacher must be very patient before he or she can expect lively class participation. Adam Hartley describes his frustration:

> *Politics are a complete no-no in class and yet politics are so central to life that you find yourself always coming up against a brick wall of silent faces. Class participation of any kind was hard enough to achieve. I was given a class of 100 people (of vastly different standards) for listening comprehension. I was an absolute monkey, playing, rewinding and replaying a cassette with obnoxious voices and muddled questions. I'd play it twice or thrice, ask if they were ready. "Yes." Okay, who thinks the answer is A? No one. Who thinks B? 2 people. Who thinks C? 3 hands. And who things D? No one. 5 responses out of 100. I'd try it again and again, and only ever got 27 hands in the air for any one question.*
>
> *I had another class of beginners, and spent two hours reading things very very slowly for them to repeat. Immensely dull, unstimulating and tiring work. Again a tape recorder could have done just as good a job as I did.*

A teacher's problems are exacerbated by the difficulty of obtaining materials. Textbooks may be dated. Even if there are photocopying facilities, they will probably be rationed to, say, 20 per week and will require a great deal of form-filling out before permission is granted. Even more basic problems crop up such as a shortage of desks, and no heating in the classrooms. If you try to initiate something new, such as teaching smaller groups of similar ability, the Foreign Affairs Office in your institute may make enthusiastic noises but do nothing to help you. Losing your temper will be counterproductive; patient persistence is sometimes rewarded. It is not easy to know when to prolong negotiation and when to admit defeat. Adam tried to persuade the authorities to let him teach smaller groups but in the end spent a month's salary on some chairs so that he could teach a small group of advanced pupils in his room over a glass of beer and without the presence of a form monitor. A feeling of being stifled by red tape and of uselessness is bad for teacher morale, and you should be prepared to contend with such feelings.

The enthusiasm of the students goes a long way to counteracting the gloom. They are genuinely keen to learn about life in the West. One of Adam's favourite duties was to give an open lecture on British culture and life. By 3pm every seat was taken for the 7.30 lecture. Chinese people are unfailingly polite and friendly outside official and observed situations.

Accommodation

Accommodation for FTs is normally in a purpose-built hostel, which will be spartan (at best) and often downright depressing, especially if electricity and heat are rationed. Adam describes his lodgings in Linfen:

> *A flat containing very little was provided. A fridge and TV were provided though never used. I wanted chairs, desks, lamps, and after weeks of pushing I got them. "Next week you shall have them." Then next week, "That man is away at a conference now" and so on. I got carpets put in and had a good set-up, except snow and dust managed to filter in through the windows. After a few weeks, the electricity blew, so I couldn't use the desk lamp (which I'd had to buy) or listen to music. It got depressing living under neon light, padding around on dusty carpets wrapped up in a coat to keep warm.*

Many of the deprivations may sound trivial but cumulatively they can be disheartening. On the other hand local Chinese teachers consider the foreigners' accommodation (like their salaries) to be luxurious compared to their own and it may strike you as churlish to complain too vociferously.

REGULATIONS

If the hiring body notifies the Bureau of Foreign Affairs sufficiently early, you might get a working visa before leaving home. But the bureaucracy is so convoluted and delays so commonplace that this is rare. If it does occur, you may not be sent the visa by the Chinese Embassy until days before your scheduled departure. It is more usual to enter China on a visitor visa and then the Foreign Affairs Office at your institute will arrange for an Alien Residence Permit. You will also be issued with a card which enables you to buy goods with Renminbi and allows discounts on trains, planes and hotels which are unavailable to Western tourists.

Free health care of a good standard is provided, so few people bother with medical or personal insurance.

LEISURE TIME

Foreigners who teach in Beijing can lead a standard expatriate life if they want to, attending Embassy films and discos and dining in expensive restaurants. Life in the provinces will be very different. There may be no restaurants even to rival the Chinese take-away in your home town; but the locals will be far more interested in you and perhaps even teach you to cook your own Chinese food. If there are several foreigners, communal dining facilities (often segregated) will normally be provided. Glutinous rice, soy beans and cabbage are staples and fresh produce may be in short supply in winter.

Learning Chinese is the ambition of many teachers and is a great asset especially outside cosmopolitan areas. Take a good teach-yourself book and cassettes, since these are difficult to obtain outside Beijing and Shanghai. Mastering Chinese characters is a daunting business, though the grammar is straightforward. Others prefer to study Tai Chi, Wushu or other exotic martial arts.

Be prepared for noise and air pollution even in small towns, though it is usually possible to escape into the countryside by bicycle or bus. Some universities with large contingents of foreign teachers organize excursions in the same way that Israeli kibbutzim do for their volunteers after a few months. Independent travel is now allowed and most of the country is open with the possible exception of Tibet. FEs can easily afford to travel, while FTs may find that extensive travels will leave them out-of-pocket.

Much of the time you will be responsible for your own amusement, so take plenty of reading matter, including if possible *China Through My Window* by Naomi Woronov, an American who went to teach English in China in 1979 (published by M. E. Sharpe in 1989).

Hong Kong

Like Korea, Taiwan and Thailand, Hong Kong is a country in which unqualified teachers have an excellent chance of finding work. Although the medium of instruction in Hong Kong's state schools is English, many students are keen to hone their conversation skills in extracurricular classes. According to one source there are over 10,000 fee-paying language students in Hong Kong. As 1997 and the hand-over of Hong Kong to China approaches, many Hong Kong residents are eager to emigrate to Britain, the US, Australia, etc. for which a good speaking knowledge of English is seen to be essential.

Prospects for Teachers

In a milieu where 3 months qualifies as a long stay for a teacher, prospects for casual teacher-travellers are excellent. Anyone who has any relevant qualification and is interested in staying in the colony for a longer period will have absolutely no difficulty fixing up a contract where the rewards will be considerably greater than for the part-time casual teacher, though still modest by the standards of the other prosperous nations of Asia, viz. Singapore, Taiwan and Japan.

Recruitment rarely takes place outside Hong Kong, except by the British Council (which, for example, was advertising for 15 EFL teachers in June 1990). In fact the *TES* and *Education Guardian* carried no adverts for Hong Kong language schools in 1990. Of the 70 or so schools circularized for this book from the Hong Kong *Yellow Pages* (which are available at the Hong Kong Government Office, 6 Grafton Street, London W1X 3LB), only two replied.

FIXING UP A JOB

Schools open as frequently as others close, so unless you are British Council material — and the Council has 80 teachers in its Hong Kong centre, which ties with Madrid as its biggest operation in the world — you will have to wait until arrival to look for work. The best source of job vacancies is the *South China Morning Post,* especially the bumper Saturday edition which has 150 pages of jobs. It tends to be the downmarket schools which advertise on a regular basis, but this may provide an acceptable starting point. Look for English Clubs which provide a cheap alternative to formal English classes where Chinese learners can drop in for conversation with a native speaker.

The place to which a great many travellers gravitate is Chung King Mansions at 40 Nathan Road in Kowloon. It is nearly as famous for its notice board as for its range of cheap (and grotty) accommodation. The notice board often carries easy-come easy-go job offers from schools at the bottom end of the market. According to Martyn Owens, who had a longer stint of teaching in Hong Kong than most, these job notices often come with scribbled footnotes warning other travellers about the drawbacks (usually low pay in the case of teaching jobs). In the Travellers' Hostel in Chung King Mansions and in that area generally, there will be no shortage of travellers willing to advise the newcomer. One of their pieces of advice is likely to be not to accept the first job which comes along. HK$25/30-an-hour jobs abound throughout the year and with a little perseverance, you should be able to do better than that. Always find out if you will be teaching classes (which are more difficult but better paid) or individuals.

If none of the advertised jobs in the paper or on the notice boards bears fruit, you will have to turn to the *Yellow Pages.* Phone calls within the city limits are free, so by phoning around you can easily get an idea of the possibilities. Although hiring is continuous, the summer months bring even more openings. You might also enquire about teaching opportunities in the Vietnamese Refugee Camps administered by the UN.

Your interview is unlikely to be a daunting experience as Martyn Owens discovered:

> *After ringing, I went to the school to have an interview with the Director. It was quite informal — she seemed to be most interested in my intended length of stay, after she realized I was "presentable" so to speak and asked also about my academic qualifications. She didn't expect me to have had any teaching experience and was most impressed when I presented my TEFL certificate (5-day introductory course at the Surrey Language Centre). I'm sure I would have got the job without it, merely on the basis of my willingness to work.*

Obviously in a school which had been through 4 foreign teachers in almost as many weeks, standards were not very rigorous. If you can present proof of a lengthy stay (particularly for the summer), you should find yourself in demand. Even dressing up is not essential, since teachers have been known to turn up for work wearing T-shirts and backpacks.

Freelance Teaching

One way to escape the generally low wages paid by Hong Kong language schools is to go freelance. The private tuition market appealed to Brett Muir not only because of the higher earnings but because as a New Zealander, he couldn't get a work visa. He describes the tactics he used to find clients:

> *My recommendation is to hire a paging device (really cheap by the month — major companies have offices in the big subway stations) and write an attractive advertisement for placing in the letter boxes of the ritzy apartment estates in Mid Levels, Jardines, Lookout and Causeway Bay suburbs. Although the gates are locked, the maids are constantly going in and out, so you just walk in with them to post your photocopied ads. In this way you are always on the phone. Generally it is housewives and businessmen who are looking for conversation practice.*

REGULATIONS

Until recently there were no visa or work permit requirements for UK citizens at all. A Hong Kong Identity Card could be obtained free of charge from the Immigration Office, 2nd Floor, Empire Centre, Tsimshatui East Kowloon. However as Hong Kong's change of status approaches, Brits who want to work in Hong Kong need to apply for a work visa from any UK passport office or Consulate.

Full-time teachers of other nationalities can be sponsored for a work visa by their employer; otherwise it is difficult for them to work except at unlicensed schools. Contract teachers normally have 15% deducted from their pay packets for tax and health insurance.

CONDITIONS OF WORK

Except for the highly qualified, privileged few who teach at the prestigious end of the market (and earn HK$12,000 per month), low wages and long hours are the norm. HK$40 an hour is about the best a part-time teacher can expect to earn. Anyone prepared to sign a contract for more than 3 months can expect to earn more. One possible justification for the meagre wage is that many schools hand out detailed lesson plans to their untrained teachers which means that lesson preparation time is minimal.

Erratic hours are also a problem, as Leslie Platt found out:

> *The Norton Institute (tel. 893 4945) was very vague as to what hours I should be working. I would arrive in the afternoon as instructed only to be informed that*

*no students had turned up but that I had better hang around for a few hours just
in case one did. Of course if none did, I didn't get paid.*

The life of the casual teacher can be unpredictable as Leslie found at his next
job, where he was horrified to be confronted with a classful of 7 and 8 year
olds whose main ambition was to torment the teacher, especially when he
unwillingly tried to conduct a sing-song. Among older students, the Chinese
respect for the printed word results in a rather inflexible attitude to textbooks.

It has to be said that the majority of young adults learning English are serious
about learning, indeed a little too serious for some. Their expectations are high
and they will boycott the classes of a teacher whose knowledge of grammar proves
shaky or whose conversation classes are as dull as ditchwater. This in turn will
alarm the school administration which sometimes decides to sack the teacher
responsible for the decrease in custom. Free market competition runs riot in
Hong Kong.

People with teaching qualifications can avoid these problems by working in
government schools where teachers sign contracts and wages are guaranteed.
According to the "English Teaching Profile" for Hong Kong (available free of
charge from the English Language Information Unit of the British Council at
10 Spring Gardens, London SW1) which was last updated in 1986, the Hong Kong
government became alarmed by a decline in standards of English and proposed
recruiting up to 200 native speaker teachers each year for secondary schools.
Ask the British Council about this. The government also runs adult education
institutes which might be prepared to hire foreign teachers. Another way of
avoiding exploitative conditions is to become a self-employed tutor. If you are
paying house calls, you should be able to charge HK$80-100 per hour.

Accommodation may be a problem unless you are prepared to stay in a hostel.
There are some single rooms in Chung King Mansions which start at HK$2,200
a month. Expect to spend a quarter to a third of your wages (assuming you are
working full-time) on a bed-sit or room in a shared house. According to Martyn
Owens, Chinese landladies and landlords are loath to rent out accommodation
to foreigners. If you are intending to stay in Hong Kong for some time, decent
accommodation is available more cheaply on the outlying islands, which can
be an attractive option in view of the cheap and plentiful public transport.
Needless to say, the kind of language school we have been describing does not
offer accommodation to its teachers.

LEISURE TIME

Not surprisingly, culture shock is kept to a minimum in Hong Kong by the
Western affluence and the British bias. Anyone who enjoys shopping will have
a marvellous time in Hong Kong. Food, clothing and travel are all cheap which
helps to alleviate the problem of expensive accommodation.

Martyn Owens describes the range of leisure activities:

*Hong Kong buzzes 24 hours a day and is like a film set! Consequently there is
much to do — bowling, movies, sports, restaurants, etc. all probably within walking
distance. I spent most of my spare time in restaurants with friends; eating out is
the most popular pastime among the locals. I also travelled around the New
Territories which is a beautiful place.*

Inevitably there is a large and flourishing expat community who tend to socialize
on Hong Kong Island at pubs like 1997 and Mad Dogs. An area for more sleazy
bars is Wanchai, which ironically is where the British Council is located.

LIST OF SCHOOLS

FIRST CLASS LANGUAGES CENTRE
22A Bank Tower, 351-353 King's Road, North Point, Hong Kong. Tel: (5) 887 7555.
Number of teachers: 30.
Preference of nationality: UK.
Qualifications: education to degree level preferred. Must have outgoing personality.
Conditions of employment: minimum stay normally 3 months. Very flexible working hours between 10.30am-9.30pm. Teachers can choose hours. Pupils mostly young adults. Group and individual tuition.
Salary: HK$30-100 per hour depending on type of student.
Facilities/Support: advice on accommodation given informally. No training provided.
Recruitment: usually by word of mouth and referral by friends. Local interviews essential.

HONG KONG ENGLISH CLUB
Ground Floor, 176B Nathan Road, Tsimshatsui, Kowloon. Tel: (3) 722 1300. Branches also at: 1/F, 190 Nathan Road (tel: 666 961) and 1/F, 487 Nathan Road (tel: 851 931).
Number of teachers: 40+.
Preference of nationality: UK.
Qualifications: university graduates preferred but others considered.
Conditions of employment: 6 month-1 year contracts. Evening hours. Pupils of all ages but mostly aged 16-30.
Salary: HK$6,000-7,000 per month.
Facilities/Support: assistance given with accommodation. Training provided.
Recruitment: mainly through university careers departments. Interviews not essential.

Indonesia

Indonesia is the fifth most populous nation on earth and it seems that a very high percentage of those 156 million people wants to learn English. Furthermore a booming oil industry has brought new wealth, especially to Jakarta, and a host of English schools has opened to cater to the desire of Indonesians to climb the business ladder. The vast majority of these schools are small private institutes employing only Indonesian teachers. The British Council in Jakarta estimates that there are several thousand language schools in Jakarta alone, many of them not particularly permanent. But there are enough big companies and rich people to support about a dozen large "native speaker" schools, which can afford to hire trained foreign teachers and pay them about ten times the local wage.

FIXING UP A JOB

Prospects are good for people who want to teach in Indonesia, and anyone with an RSA Certificate should be able to pre-arrange a 12 or 18 month contract in Jakarta, or possibly Surabaya and Bandung. (Although Yogyakarta has a population of over $2\frac{1}{2}$ million and is arguably the most interesting city in Indonesia, there aren't many openings for teachers.) Schools seem to be split between those which prefer British teachers and those which prefer North Americans with a slight bias in favour of Brits.

RSA or equivalent teaching qualifications are respected in Jakarta and the oil companies carefully scrutinize staff qualifications before investing their money. However beggars can't be choosers and even the most respectable schools do occasionally hire unqualified teachers with university degrees and/or teaching experience.

In Advance

Private schools with overseas contacts advertise and recruit internationally. For example the *British Institutes* in Jakarta and Bandung are affiliated with the Bell Foundation whose Overseas Division undertakes most of the recruitment of the 20 teachers in Jakarta and the 8 in Bandung. *International Language Programs* in Jakarta and Surabaya have 2 agents in the UK who place advertisements (usually in the Tuesday *Guardian*) and conduct interviews. Similarly *Executive English Programs* has a London-based recruiter. Colin Boothroyd, who has been teaching for EEP since July 1988, describes the way he arranged the job:

> *I answered an advertisement in the Education section of the* Guardian *immediately but did not get a response for a month. The response came in the form of a phone call requesting an interview with me. I was interviewed a few days later — a very relaxed affair in a South London pub — and was told on the spot that I would be recommended for a posting. Two weeks later I received a load of information from EEP welcoming me to the school. Three weeks later I was on a plane to Jakarta, having picked up a visa at thte Indonesian Embassy in London.*

The beauty of Colin's 18-month contract is that it includes free flights, an increasingly rare perk these days.

As usual, the British Council's English Language Centre in Jakarta represents the elite end of the market. Highly qualified and experienced ELT staff (who are recruited in London and Jakarta) specialize in training government employees for academic and occupational needs. But the Council office can provide a list of the established schools and advise teachers on local opportunities. They also maintain a register of teachers available for work in Indonesia, as does the Indonesian-Australian Language Foundation (Cipta Building, Jalan H. R. Rasuna Said, Kaveling C-10, Kuningan, Jakarta Selatan).

The volunteer agencies are fairly major employers of EFL teachers especially *VSO* who have 27 teachers working in various corners of the country. Both *GAP* and the *Project Trust* send school-leavers to teach in remote parts of Indonesia including Timor and Kalimantan. Commercial agencies which have been known to recruit for Indonesion schools include English Language Services, 70 Oakington Avenue, Wembley Park, Middlesex.

Fax machines seem to have caught on in a big way in Indonesia and you might impress schools with your professionalism by corresponding by fax.

On the Spot

Colin Boothroyd reports that more and more teachers are being hired on the spot which suits schools like EEP who then don't have to pay for air fares. Local recruits can negotiate shorter contracts, for example six months, unlike teachers recruited abroad who usually have to stay at least 18 months.

Most teaching jobs start in July or October. Interviews are compulsory for most schools, so if you don't manage to arrange a job through an agent/interviewer in your home country, you may have to fly to Jakarta and shop around.

With an RSA Certificate your chances of being offered a job are very high. Unqualified applicants would have to be extremely well presented (since dress is very important in Jakarta), able to sell themselves in terms of experience and qualifications and prepared to commit themselves for a longish spell or to start with some part-time work in the hope of building it up.

Local schools staffed by Indonesians present an entirely different situation. Travellers have stumbled across friendly little schools up rickety staircases, all over Indonesia, not only in the large cities but in small towns, particularly in Bali. If you stay in one place long enough to get to know the man who runs a school, he may invite you to take some conversation classes in exchange for free board and lodging and possibly a small wage. Teaching materials may be in short supply. Sue Nuttall noticed that the crib sheets at several Balinese English schools were riddled with errors, and declined to take up an offer to teach because she felt that without training or experience and without any back-up from the school, she would be worse than useless at imparting her native tongue. (She later returned to England to obtain an RSA Certificate and is hoping to return to Indonesia as a teacher.) One of the problems faced by those who undertake casual work of this kind is that there would be very little chance of obtaining a work permit (see below). It is also difficult for freelance teachers to become legal unless, like Paul Greening who has been teaching in Jakarta independently for more than 3 years, you have a contact who "knows who to bribe in the Immigration Office."

The problem of visas doesn't arise if you teach English on a completely informal basis as Stuart Tappin did:

> *In Asia I managed to spend a lot of time living with people in return for teaching English. The more remote the towns are from tourist routes the better, for example Bali is no good. I spent a week in Palembang Sumara living with an English teacher and his family. You teach and they give their (very good) hospitality.*

REGULATIONS

The work permit regulations are fairly rigidly adhered to in Indonesia and all of the established schools will apply for a visa permit on your behalf. To illustrate how seriously schools take the rules, EEP in Jakarta employs a full-time visa co-ordinator. You must submit your c.v., teaching certificate, photocopy of your passport and application form which the school sends off to the Indonesian Ministry of Education (Jalan Jenderal Sudirman, Senayan, Jakarta Pusat), the Cabinet Secretariat and the Immigration/Manpower Departments. Some schools request that you send on the necessary documents months in advance, but it is possible to apply after you arrive in the country. You should at least be in possession of a firm contract of employment or letter of agreement before leaving home. Anyone without the necessary qualifications is very unlikely to be granted the visa; one participant in the GAP scheme for school-leavers had his English-teaching job cancelled at the last moment since the school found that it could not get a visa for him.

The logistics of getting a *dinas* visa (which allows you to work as a teacher) are complicated and expensive, since a certain number of bribes (known locally as *pungli*) must be paid to hasten the bureaucratic procedures. Most schools will underwrite these expenses for you. Others, who have government contracts, may encounter no problems.

Tourists can stay for two months in Indonesia. It is possible to renew your tourist status by leaving the country every two months (e.g. flying to Singapore, or to Medan and then by ferry to Penang in Malaysia) but the authorities might become suspicious if you did this repeatedly. Anyone found working while on a tourist visa could be deported and blacklisted from entering Indonesia again. (Also, the employer would find himself in serious trouble.) Anyone planning to go to Jakarta to look for a job would be advised to enter Indonesia on a London-Jakarta-Singapore ticket. The onward part of the ticket will assure the Indonesian immigration authorities that you are an innocent tourist intending to leave their country within two months. And if your employer does apply for a work permit, you will have to leave the country at least once for lodging the application and collecting the visa; most people go to Singapore.

Health & Insurance

Some schools provide a medical scheme, usually in the Yayasan Medical Scheme to which most expatriates belong. The annual fee covers all treatment and prescribed medication. If your employer is not able to advise, you will have to make your own enquiries to the scheme which is located at the Setiabudi Building, Jalan H. Rangkayo Rasuna Said, Kuningan, Jakarta (tel: 515481).

Of the schools listed at the end of this chapter, only the Oxford Course Indonesia stipulated that it required an AIDS-free certificate. This may simply reflect the health-consciousness of the director who also prefers his teachers to be non-smokers.

CONDITIONS OF WORK

Salaries are relatively high at the "native speaker" schools, even after Indonesian tax of 10%-12% has been subtracted and despite the relative unreliability of the rupiah. Pre-tax salaries often approach two million rupiahs per month which results in a net salary of approximately £580/$900. Since the cost of living is low, many teachers are able to save considerable sums while enjoying a very comfortable lifestyle. According to Paul Greening, you are eligible for a 20% tax rebate if you complete a 2-year contract.

If you happen to work for a school which takes on outside contracts, you may have the occasional chance to work outside the school premises, possibly in a remote oil drilling location in Sumatra, for up to double pay. The majority of teachers, however, conduct lessons at their school through the usual peak hours of 3.30pm to 8.30pm with some early morning starts as well.

Many schools offer generous help with accommodation, ranging from an interest-free loan for initial rent payments to free housing complete with free telephone, electricity *and* servants. It is customary in the Jakarta housing market to be asked to pay the annual rent in a lump sum at the beginning of your tenancy, and so access to a loan from your employer is often essential.

The Pupils

Outside the big cities, the standard of English is normally very low, with pupils having picked up a smattering from bad American television. Classes also tend to be large, as many as 40 pupils, all expecting to learn grammer by the traditional rote methods. According to a VSO volunteer teaching in Western Java (as quoted in the *TES*), "If I want to do something interesting, the students say, 'but it's not in the exam'."

Pupils in Jakarta present fewer problems as Colin Boothroyd describes:

The pupils are incredibly enthusiastic and are genuinely appreciative of the opportunity to learn from native speakers. I have never once had a discipline problem whilst I've been teaching here. My classes have varied from 2 to 20 in size. The students are generally unfamiliar with our communicative form of teaching, since kids aren't really expected to think for themselves in Indonesian schools. Students are reluctant to speak about controversial issues (the issues that should really provoke loads of communication) because they are afraid that big brother may overhear something that doesn't suit. Otherwise the students are brilliant.

LEISURE TIME

Although Jakarta is a hot, dusty, overcrowded, polluted and poverty-stricken city, there is a great deal to see and do, and many teachers enjoy living there. Indonesia is a fascinating country and most visitors, whether short-term or long, agree that the Indonesian people are fantastic. Travel is cheap and unrestricted, and excursions are very rewarding in terms of scenery and culture. Travel by public transport can be time-consuming and limiting for weekend trips, so you might consider getting a motorcycle, although Jakarta's traffic problems make this too dangerous and unhealthy for many. Internal flights are also within the range of most teachers.

Predictably the community of expatriate teachers — estimated to comprise about 35 — participates in lots of joint activities such as football and tennis matches, chess tournaments, beach excursions, diving trips and parties. Most teachers have videos but occasionally go out to see an undubbed American film.

Eating out is so cheap relative to salaries that many teachers indulge themselves at restaurants most nights of the week. Breakfasting on tropical fruit is easy to get used to, too.

Bahasa Indonesian, almost identical to Malay, was imposed on the people of Indonesia after independence in 1949 and is one of the simplest languages to learn both in structure and pronunciation. Mastering a vocabulary of about one hundred words should be enough to get by.

LIST OF SCHOOLS

AMERICAN LANGUAGE TRAINING (ALT)
Jalan Panglima Polim Raya 100, Kebayoran Baru, Jakarta Selatan 12130.
Tel: (21) 720 0758/59/61.
Number of teachers: 22.
Preference of nationality: US, Canada.
Qualifications: MA in TESL/TEFL/Linguistics plus 3 years experience.
Conditions of employment: 18 month contracts. Hours of work 7.30am-5pm.
Most pupils are aged 16-30.

Salary: US$15,000-18,000 per year.
Facilities/Support: in-house training available.
Recruitment: some interviewing in US, although interviews are not essential.

THE BRITISH INSTITUTE (TBI)
Setiabudi Building, 2 Jalan H.R. Rasuna Said, Jakarta 12920. Tel: (21) 512044/516750. Fax: 520 7574.
Number of teachers: 20.
Preference of nationality: none.
Qualifications: RSA Cert./Dip./MA in Applied Linguistics.
Conditions of employment: 12-18 month contracts. Maximum 24 h.p.w. with no more than 10 hour span in one day. Mostly adult classes with some for children and teenagers.
Salary: on request. Housing loan repayable over 5 months.
Facilities/Support: no training.
Recruitment: adverts abroad. Interviews essential; can be carried out in UK by Bell Educational Trust.

THE BRITISH INSTITUTE BANDUNG
Jalan Martadinata 63, Bandung. Tel: (22) 436059.
Number of teachers: 8.
Preference of nationality: UK, Commonwealth.
Qualifications: RSA Cert. (minimum Grade 'B') and 1 year's experience essential.
Conditions of employment: 12-18 month contracts. 24 h.p.w. weekdays.
Salary: 1,639,375 rupiahs per month (net). Interest-free loan for housing.
Facilities/Support: training available when required.
Recruitment: interviews essential; can be carried out in UK by Bell Educational Trust.

ENGLISH EDUCATION CENTER (EEC)
Jalan Let. Jend. S. Parman 66, Slipi, Jakarta 11410. Tel: (21) 591144/548 6296.
Number of teachers: 30.
Preference of nationality: US, UK.
Qualifications: BA in relevant subject, RSA Cert./Dip., minimum 1 year's overseas TEFL experience.
Conditions of employment: 2 year contracts. Maximum 25½ h.p.w. Pupils from age 8.
Salary: 2,200,000 rupiahs per month.
Facilities/Support: assistance given with finding accommodation. Training provided.
Recruitment: adverts in education periodicals. Interviews not essential.

ENGLISH LANGUAGE SERVICES INTERNATIONAL
Jalan Tanjung Karang No. 7 C-D, Jakarta 10230. Tel: (21) 327376/333525. Fax: 520 7453.
Number of teachers: 15.
Preference of nationality: US, UK.
Qualifications: BA in English or humanities essential, RSA Cert. preferred.
Conditions of employment: 1 year contracts. 25 contact h.p.w.

Salary: 1,900,000 rupiahs per month plus housing allowance and medical scheme.
Facilities/Support: monthly workshops held for teachers.
Recruitment: usually local interviews.

ENGLISH LANGUAGE TRAINING INTERNATIONAL (ELTI)/GRAMEDIA
Complex Wijaya Grand Centre, Block F 83A, 84A & B, Jalan Wijaya II, Jakarta Selatan. Tel: (21) 720 2957/720 6653/720 6654. Fax: 548 6085.
Number of teachers: 18.
Preference of nationality: US, UK.
Qualifications: BA (English)/TEFL training/experience in oil and gas industry.
Conditions of employment: 12-18 month contracts. 26 h.p.w. Classes for adults and children (from 6 years).
Salary: US$1,000 per month, plus medical insurance, vacation pay and sick leave. Loans for rent payments.
Facilities/Support: in-house training planned for future.
Recruitment: positions advertised locally and interviews take place in Indonesia.

EXECUTIVE ENGLISH PROGRAMS (EEP)
Jalan Wijaya VIII/4, Kebayoran Baru, Jakarta Selatan 12160. Tel: (21) 770812/773 864. Fax: 773976. Also branch in Bandung.
Number of teachers: 50.
Preference of nationality: none.
Qualifications: RSA Cert./PGCE plus 1 year's experience.
Conditions of employment: 18 month contracts. 24 h.p.w. 8.30am-9pm with no more than $8\frac{1}{2}$-hour span in one day.
Salary: 1,925,000 rupiahs per month (less approx. 10% tax). Free accommodation for one month. Interest-free housing loans available.
Recruitment: newspaper adverts abroad. Interviews essential, and can be held in London.

INSTITUTE FOR THE DEVELOPMENT OF LANGUAGE TEACHING PROGRAMMES/INDONESIAN OPEN UNIVERSITY
Jalan Cilacap 6A, Jakarta Pusat 10310. Tel: (21) 370513/310 7823/310 7824.
Number of teachers: 3.
Preference of nationality: UK.
Qualifications: MA/PhD in Applied Linguistics (TESOL) with teaching, publishing and distance teaching experience.
Conditions of employment: 2 year renewable contracts. Hours of work 8am-5pm weekdays; 8am-2pm Saturdays. Adult classes only.
Salary: expatriate salary as set by ODA/British Council.
Facilities/Support: no training.
Recruitment: interviews take place in UK through British Council.

INTERNATIONAL LANGUAGE PROGRAMS (ILP)
Jalan Panglima Polim IX/2, Kebayoran Baru, Jakarta 12160. Tel: (21) 770 449.
Number of teachers: 20.
Preference of nationality: none.
Qualifications: BA, RSA Cert., and preferably some TEFL experience.

Conditions of employment: 2 year contracts preferably starting in July. 20 h.p.w. 4 hours per day, 5 days per week. Pupils range in age from 7-70, but are mostly aged 20-40.
Salary: from 1,500,000 rupiahs per month.
Facilities/Support: accommodation paid for. Training provided.
Recruitment: UK adverts followed by annual UK interviews.
Contact in UK: Martin Harper, 19 Longmeadow Drive, Ickleford, Hitchin, Herts. SG5 3TJ (tel: 0462 451723).
Contact in US: Lynne Guerrette, 143 Montello Street, Lewiston, ME 04240.

INTERNATIONAL LANGUAGE PROGRAMS (ILP)
Jalan Bengawan No. 10, Surabaya, Jawa Timor. Tel: (31) 67141. Fax: 595052.
Number of teachers: 10.
Preference of nationality: UK, Australia, New Zealand, US, Canada.
Qualifications: BA plus RSA Cert. or MA/PGCE in TEFL/TESL essential. Minimum 1 year's experience strongly preferred.
Conditions of employment: 1 year contracts. 25 hours per 5 day teaching week. Most classes are in the evenings until 9.15pm and also some morning classes.
Salary: £400 per month (net).
Facilities/Support: free accommodation with all utilities and air fares provided. Informal training provided.
Recruitment: carried out mainly by London agent who advertises in the *Education Guardian,* through adverts in Sydney and occasionally at TESOL conferences in the US. Interviews essential.
UK contact: Jocelyn Potter, St. Benets, Church Lane, Charlbury, Oxon. OX7 3PX.

OXFORD COURSE INDONESIA (OCI)
Jalan Samodra Oxford O1, Jakarta Utara 14230. Tel: (21) 828 2570/490 672/829 9969. 48 branches in 14 Indonesian cities.
Number of teachers: no foreign teachers at present.
Qualifications: minimum 'A' Levels, RSA qualifications/MA preferred.
Conditions of employment: 1 year contracts. 40 h.p.w. Third of classes are for 10-15 year olds; third for 16-21 year olds and rest for adults.
Salary: £3-£10 per hour.
Facilities/Support: no teaching materials/course outlines provided at present. Some in-house training available.
Recruitment: local interviews and test essential.
Miscellaneous: teachers must provide certificates of good health (including AIDS-free document). Non-smokers preferred.

SCHOOL FOR INTERNATIONAL TRAINING (SIT)
Jalan Sunda 3, Jakarta Pusat 10350. Tel: (21) 335671/336238/337240.
Number of teachers: 20.
Preference of nationality: US, Canada, UK, Australia.
Qualifications: BA/MA (TESOL or related subject) plus several years experience preferred. Experience in Asia or developing countries desirable.
Conditions of employment: 1 year renewable contracts. 25½ h.p.w. (8am-4.30pm

or 1.30-9pm plus Saturday mornings on rotating basis). Public classes in communicative English, ESP classes for business and government, etc.
Salary: varies with qualifications. 4 weeks annual leave, 12 days sick leave, hospitalization and accident insurance provided. Return air fare paid after completion of 2 years.
Facilities/Support: 3 months free accommodation in school-leaed housing if recruited abroad.
Facilities/Support: in-service training for first 3 months, bi-monthly workshops thereafter.
Recruitment: interviews held locally or by telephone. Local newspaper adverts, TESOL newsletter, foreign adverts and through graduate departments of some American universities.

TRIAD ENGLISH CENTRE
Jalan Purnawarman 76, Bandung 40116. Tel: (22) 433104/431309. Fax: 431149. Also in Jakarta: Jalan Gajah Mada 16 H, Jakarta. Fax: (21) 359835/431149.
Number of teachers: 8.
Preference of nationality: UK, US.
Qualifications: BA, RSA Cert./MA plus 2 years experience.
Conditions of employment: 1-2 year contracts. 25 h.p.w. 9-11am and 2-7.30pm. Classes for beginners, children, high school students and businessmen.
Salary: US$500-800 per month.
Facilities/Support: assistance with accommodation. Training given when necessary.
Recruitment: through direct applications and fax correspondence. Interviews sometimes held abroad.

Japan

Just as diplomats hope for a posting to New York not Nigeria and international bankers would prefer to work in Switzerland than Swaziland, travelling teachers dream of Japan. While considering themselves lucky if their modest earnings in dinars or pesos are actually handed over at the end of the working week, they imagine that their colleagues in Kyoto are reliably paid an unimaginable number of yen. Stories still circulate of Japanese businessmen so desperate to improve their English that they stop foreigners on the street proffering fistfuls of cash.

Alas, if this was ever the situation, it isn't now. Certainly there is an enormous demand for English, with some observers estimating that one in ten of all Japanese sign up for an English course at some point in their careers. But people who lack the appropriate qualifications will encounter difficulties: they cannot expect to step off the plane and into a teaching job. Yet if the waiting period is longer than about 48 hours, the expenses of living in Japan can become crippling.

The high wages are not a myth: few schools pay less than £10 an hour. But these quoted figures are meaningless without balancing them against the cost of living. In view of the astronomical setting-up costs (described later), most people say that it is necessary to arrive with at least £1,000 or $2,000 and that you can't expect to break even and begin to save before you've been in Japan a year. So anyone thinking of Japan as a place to get rich will have to be moderately rich at the outset and be prepared to stay for a long spell.

As long as your expectations are realistic, Japan may turn out to be an excellent choice of destination. Native speakers are needed in a surprising range of contexts: in-house language programmes in steel or electronics companies, hot-house crammers, "conversation lounges" where young people get together for an hour's guided conversation, vocational schools where English is a compulsory subject, in what are quaintly called "ladies' classes" where courses called "English for Shopping" are actually offered, and also in classes of children from as young as two, since it has become a status symbol in Japan to send children of all ages to English classes. In fact studying English for many Japanese is still a social thing, like playing golf. It doesn't really matter if their progress is less than spectacular.

Many schools operate on a huge scale, with many branches and large numbers of staff. Whether untrained and inexperienced foreigners will be welcomed by any of these establishments is a different matter. The Japanese press has in recent years focussed on the low life stratum of casual English teachers. They are perceived as sponging Westerners who arrive from Asia hoping to make a quick killing in order to set off again in their idle, nay degenerate, pursuit of pleasure. Nothing could be more unJapanese. The cliché about workaholic Japanese is not exaggerated and even moderately serious teachers may be taken aback by the level of commitment or, crudely, the number of hours employers and students will expect them to work.

This is only one source of the culture shock which grips most new arrivals to Japan. Incoming teachers are often so distracted by the mechanics of life in Japan and the cultural adjustments they have to make to survive that they devote too little energy to the business of teaching. Even participants in the government's Japan Exchange and Teaching (JET) Programme who are given extensive guidance both before departure and during their stay, often spend most of their year abroad feeling shell-shocked. On the other hand, anyone who has a genuine interest in Japan and who arrives reasonably well prepared may find that Japan does after all represent a Shangri-la for English language teachers.

Prospects for Teachers

Middle-ranking language schools in Japan are normally looking for native speakers with a BA in any discipline (which is a visa requirement in any case) and some TEFL experience. Even among the tiny minority of schools who advertise and recruit abroad, the qualifications requested are not very daunting, e.g. "College graduates. No teaching experience is needed" or "Cultural opportunity to teach English conversation with a smile". Many schools have no set intake dates and so serious applications are welcome at any time of the year (though the academic year begins in April).

With such a large selection of advertisements at a sub-professional level, it is often possible for university graduates to fix up a job before arrival. Most employers who recruit abroad sort out visas and help with initial orientation and housing. The disadvantage is that their salary and working conditions will probably compare unfavourably with those of teachers who have negotiated their job after arrival; but most conclude the trade-off is a fair one.

It has been claimed that the preferred accent is Canadian; the Japanese favour North American accents certainly, but nothing too stridently American. Ironically, few Japanese can distinguish a Scot from a Queenslander, or an Eastender from an Eastsider. What *can* be detected and is highly prized is clear speech. Slow precise diction together with a smart appearance and professional bearing are enough to impress most potential employers.

FIXING UP A JOB
The JET Programme

The prospects for people who wish to participate in the JET Programme are excellent and the requirements few. Provided you are a national of Great Britain (who contribute over 250 people to the scheme), Ireland, the US, Canada, Australia or New Zealand, under the age of 35 with a BA and an interest in Japan, you are eligible to apply. The programme has been in existence since 1987 and is responsible for sending hundreds of native speakers to teach for 12 months in secondary schools throughout Japan. In the UK the scheme is administered by The Council on International Educational Exchange (CIEE, 33 Seymour Place, London W1H 6AT; tel: 071-224 8896) though you can also obtain the JET literature from the Japan Information and Cultural Centre (part of the Japanese Embassy) at 101/105 Piccadilly, London W1V 9FN; tel: 071-465 6583). Americans should contact either the Japanese Embassy (2520 Massachusetts NW, Washington, DC 20008; tel: 202-939-6700) or one of the many Consulates across the country. Similarly, Irish people, Canadians, Australians and New Zealanders should request JET details from the Japanese Embassy in their countries.

The programme timetable is as follows:

mid-December: deadline for applications

February: screening and interviews

March/April: final selection

May: details of placements sent out, plus Japanese language cassettes and other preparatory material

July: orientation weekend at Japanese Embassy

end of July: departure on designated flight of jobs beginning in August

Often government-run exchanges of this kind do not offer generous remuneration packages; however pay and conditions on the JET scheme are reasonable. In addition to a free return flight, JET teachers receive 3,600,000 yen a year (over £14,000 or $27,000). The salary is standard for all JET participants, which is hard on teachers in Tokyo with its exorbitant cost of living and generous to people in smaller more manageable cities. There are other discrepancies which can lead to resentment or disappointment, since it is the luck of the draw which decides who goes where (although stated preferences will be taken into consideration). Whereas some district departments of education deduct pension and/or health insurance contributions from all salaries, others don't which can make a significant difference in take-home pay. But teaching loads are generally low, usually only 3 50-minute periods a day with the rest of your time taken up with preparing materials for future use by the school.

Teachers who are placed in private schools often get a better deal than teachers in the state system. Problems are inevitable in the first years of such a programme though a reference to JET'S "flagging fortunes" in a recent *EFL Gazette* is probably too harsh. Well over half of JET participants renew for a second year which is a sign of good health. Although Claire Wilkinson was not among those who extended her stay, she has little but praise for the programme and the way it was administered. She worked at a girls' private high school in the port of

Shimizu one hour west of Tokyo and was delighted to find about 60 JETs in her area, all of whom received a great deal of support from the scheme.

In Advance

There are many other ways to fix up a job in Japan ahead of time, though these will normally require more initiative (and possibly more qualifications) than signing on with JET. Many Japanese language schools have formed links with university careers departments, particularly in the US, so anyone with a university connection should exploit it. In fact there are more organized placement schemes for Americans than for Britons. For example the International Office for Asia of the YM/YWCA (909 4th Ave., Seattle, WA 98104) sends volunteer teachers to some of the 88 Japanese Ys which teach English. Canadians, Australians and New Zealanders should consider joining the SWAP Japan Programme; details from university travel offices.

In addition to the adverts in British papers and in the *TESOL Placement Bulletin* placed by individual schools, agencies occasionally make their requirements known, such as Japan Recruitment, 5 Sherwood St, London W1 (tel: 071-734 4421). Surprising for a country comprising mainly Buddhists and Shintos (lapsed or not), several missionary societies recruit teachers, for example the evangelical Japan Mission (42B Wilton Road, Salisbury, Wilts. SP2 7EJ) who can't begin to fill all the vacancies they are asked to fill.

Large Japanese companies often have their own language teaching programmes and it might be worth making contact with their local headquarters (though this

is a long shot). With ELT programmes in Tokyo, Yokohama, Atsugi, Osaka and Nagoya, Sony is a good bet, especially for Americans who should contact their New York address (9 West 57th Street, New York, NY 10019). Another good possibility for "friendly and adventurous" degree-holding Americans is with the American English Institute which has 24 locations mostly in rural areas. A low salary is balanced by furnished apartments, company car and paid holidays. Details are available from Robert Purcell, 7885 Makaqoa Place, Honolulu, Hawaii 96825, USA.

The polar opposite from teaching corporate executives is available at a farm in Hokkaido, the most northerly island of the Japanese archipelago, known as Shin-Shizen-Juku (Tsurui, Akan-gun, Hokkaido 085-12; tel: 0154 64 2821). The owner Hiroshi Mine welcomes international travellers who want to work on the farm and teach English in the community in exchange for board and lodging and pocket money. Guy Strijbosch wrote from Shin-Shizen-Juku that in his opinion this is a wonderful opportunity to meet Japanese people of all kinds: "We teach local farmers, students, housewives, doctors and dentists, and learn about their culture".

A speculative job hunt from abroad has some chance of success but not a very high one. The British Council in Tokyo sends a select list of about 100 private schools in the Tokyo area, though there are hundreds of others, while the British Council in London added Japan to its series of *Surveys of English Language Teaching and Learning* in 1990 which provides the Tokyo addresses of another 30 plus language schools in western Japan. The book *Jobs in Japan* published by the Global Press in Denver and distributed in Europe by Vacation Work (9 Park End Street, Oxford OX1 1HJ @ £9.95) has an appendix of hundreds of language school addresses. The book is written in both a lively and authoritative style and covers all the topics of relevance to those going to Japan to work, with much practical advice. Kodansha International in Tokyo published *The Job Hunter's Guide to Japan* in 1990. Although only one out of 16 chapters is on teaching, it is a useful and up-to-date book. It is available in the UK @ £9.95 from Biblios, Star Road, Partridge Green, Horsham, West Sussex RH13 8LD. In the US, contact Kodansha at 114 Fifth Avenue, New York, NY 10011 for a copy (@ $12.95).

On the Spot

Few things could be more intimidating for the EFL teacher than to arrive at Narita International Airport with no job and limited resources (i.e. less than £1,000). Given time, virtually every native speaker can get a job, but the longer it takes, the faster the finances dwindle and the more nerve-racking and discouraging the situation becomes. One way to lessen the monumentality of the initial struggle would be to get out of Tokyo straightaway. Although there are more jobs in the capital, there is also more competition from other foreigners, to the point of saturation. Enterprising teachers who are willing to step off the conveyor belt which takes job-seekers from the airport to one of Tokyo's many "gaijin houses" (hostels for foreigners) may well encounter fewer setbacks. Gaijin houses in Tokyo such as Okuba House (1-11-32 Hyakunin-cho, Shinjuku-ku) or the English House Ryodan (2-23-8 Nishi-Ikebukuro, Toshima-ku) will be full of new or nearly new arrivals chasing teaching jobs. The advantage of course is that they are good places to pick up information; some have notice boards which may have notices about jobs. Because it is so difficult to rent accommodation, some teachers continue living in gaijin houses (minimum £10 for a dorm bed) after they find work, and there is always the chance of inheriting their hours if they decide to move on.

Wherever you choose to conduct your job hunt, English language newspapers are the starting place for most. The *Japan Times* sometimes carries as many as 80 adverts for English teachers in one issue. The *Mainichi Daily News* and *Asahi Evening News* are also worth a look. (The publishers of the latter run a chain of cultural centres which teach English.) Once you do set up some interviews, a number of practical steps should be taken to outshine the competition. These should be taken even more seriously than when trying for teaching work elsewhere in the world if only because travelling to an interview in Tokyo is a major undertaking which can take up to 3 hours and cost £8; so it would be a shame to blow your chances because of a simple oversight.

Dress as impeccably and conservatively as possible, and carry a respectable briefcase. Inside you should have any education certificates you have earned, preferably the originals since schools are catching on that forgery is a widespread practice. Increasingly, a TEFL qualification and/or experience is expected. Your resumé (the American for c.v. is used in Japan) should not err on the side of modesty. Steven Hendry who spent 10 months in Japan supporting himself by teaching and saved £1,000 as well, suggests converting "travelling for two years" to "studying Asian cultures and languages" and describing a period of unemployment as "a chance to do some voluntary teaching with racial minorities". Apparently these are never checked.

This mention of racial minorities brings us to a regrettable feature of hiring practices in Japan. A native speaker who happens to have non-Caucasian features will be discriminated against. It is not uncommon and yet clearly absurd for a German to be hired to teach English over an American with Chinese parentage, purely on the strength of his Aryan complexion. Bryn Thomas, who happened to arrive in Tokyo just when a recently opened school in the heart of the city was hiring, enjoyed most aspects of his job as a conversation lounge facilitator, but was shocked by one incident. When the publicity photos were being taken for the company brochure, a qualified teacher from Hawaii was rudely asked to step aside from the staff portrait.

More professional teachers might make contact with JALT, the Japan Association of Language Teachers (Lions Mansion 111, Kawaramachi Matsubara-Agaru, Shimogyo-ku, Kyoto 600) which might be able to offer informal advice about job vacancies, though the Association is mainly for members who have been teaching in Japan for some time. JALT endorses a book called *A Guide to Teaching English in Japan,* a collection of essays published by the *Japan Times* and available only in Japan for 2,500 yen. This is not a job-hunter's manual but a survey of issues affecting English teaching in Japan, with some advice for classroom techniques.

REGULATIONS

The key to obtaining a work visa for Japan is to have a Japanese sponsor. This can be a private citizen but most teachers are sponsored by their employers. Not all schools by any means are willing to sponsor their teachers, unless they are persuaded that they are an ongoing proposition. The "fly-by-night" type of language school willing to hire untrained and inexperienced foreigners will seldom help with visas.

If you find a sponsor, you need to provide the original or notarized copy of your degree, resumé, 2 signed contracts and photos. The work visa is valid for 12 months and renewable annually. If your visa is to be processed before arrival, you should secure a job and a sponsor at least 3 months before arrival. Once a "Certificate of Eligibility" is received from Japan, the Embassy in London undertakes to issue the visa within one week.

Many people arrive on a tourist visa (valid for 6 months in the case of Britons, 3 months for Americans), find a job and sponsor and then apply for a work visa. Normally this must be done outside Japan (e.g. Seoul, Taipei, Hong Kong), though some people claim to have obtained the work visa while remaining in Japan. The visa regulations were being revised in 1990; current visa information should be sought from the Ministry of Foreign Affairs (Gaimusho), 2-2-1 Kasumigaseki, Chiyoda-ku, Tokyo 100 (tel: 3-580-3311). Ask other foreigners about the form. If you do have to lodge the application outside Japan, you will either have to spend several months in that third country or organize two trips, one to apply and the other to collect the visa. The visa will allow you to work only for the one employer (for tax reasons), though a great many teachers do unofficial freelance work.

Traditionally many people have worked on tourist or other visas without difficulty. However this may change with the passing of controversial legislation in June 1990. Employers who are caught employing illegal aliens are now subject to huge fines (2 million yen), while the employee will be fined 300,000 yen and both parties risk imprisonment. The law is not aimed at native speaker English teachers, but at large numbers of manual workers mainly from the poorer nations of Asia. According to most observers, it has been brought in for racial rather than economic reasons. How significant a change this will make to English language teachers remains to be seen and will depend on the extent to which the law is enforced at language schools. It is conceivable that the government will turn a blind eye as it does in so many countries where there is such a large demand for English.

You are permitted to work up to 20 hours a week on a cultural or student visa. To qualify for one of these you must be studying something Japanese such as the tea ceremony, shiatsu massage, martial arts or the Japanese language. At one time these study visas were liberally handed out but nowadays you must produce concrete evidence that you actually are studying.

Student participants (aged 18-30) on the SWAP scheme mentioned above are granted a working holiday visa which is valid for 6 months and renewable for a further 6.

The tax situation is normally favourable for teachers, provided they are exempt in their home countries. Deductions in Japan are never more than 12% in the first year. Legitimate schools accustomed to recruiting native speaker teachers provide comprehensive health insurance.

CONDITIONS OF WORK

According to an article in the *EFL Gazette* (October 1990), conditions are deteriorating for native speaker teachers in Japan with on average longer hours and actual pay cuts. The reason given for this is that conversation lounges, which are tremendously popular with adolescents (especially now that there is a listening component in the state exams), are depriving the private academies of business, causing them to stint on salaries, etc.

The longer you work in Japan the higher the salary and better working conditions you can command. Rank beginners outside Tokyo and Osaka can earn as little as 200,000 yen a month, which is considerably less than the steady average of 250,000 yen (about £1,000/\$1,900) quoted by schools listed in our Directory. This low figure can be increased by increments for higher qualifications, an end-of-contract bonus and various perks such as travel tickets. Some schools offer free Japanese lessons. Experienced and qualified teachers can earn upwards of 8 million yen a year. Mere mortals can normally calculate on earning from 2,500 yen per hour, and some teachers manage to subsist on only 15 hours of teaching a week.

Teaching schedules can be exhausting, especially if you work for a school which sends its teachers out to company premises. As usual, the timetable may be announced at the last minute, though it is more difficult to opt out in Japan than in other countries because of the dedication Japanese workers show to their firms. (At best a Japanese worker gets 10 days of holiday a year and few take their full entitlement for fear of seeming lazy or disloyal to the company.) Some schools remain open all weekend and on public holidays too. One of the advantages of working in state school (as JET teachers do) is that they close for holidays, usually 3 weeks at Christmas and 2 weeks in August between semesters. Several public holidays fall in the same week in May which allows another chance for a break.

The Pupils

Japanese pupils are usually as diligent as Japanese workers. They confer great respect on their teachers and in some out-of-the-way places you may enjoy celebrity status (or *not* enjoy as the case may be). All teachers are expected to look the part and most schools will insist on proper dress (e.g. suits and dresses).

"Akiko, tell us your views on love and marriage"

Adults will have studied English at school for at least 6 years, and their knowledge of grammar is usually sound. The difficulty comes in trying to get them to practise conversational English, and the so-called "communicative techniques" now in vogue simply do not work in a Japanese context. As well as being cripplingly prone to perfectionism, they are extremely shy in class, as Michael Frost discovered:

> It is very difficult for Japanese students to come out and express an individual opinion, which is the whole purpose of debates in EFL. Europeans will do it readily (sometimes too readily; try stopping a French speaker in full flow!) but we should not imagine that a Japanese speaker will respond in the way we would. Because their whole culture is group-based, as opposed to individually based, they are reluctant to venture opinions which may differ from anybody else's view or upset the group harmony. You won't get much of a real debate going from the Japanese — it's something they're trained not to do, and it makes them feel very ill at ease. (This gets even worse if the group is all female and the topic is in any way controversial.) Some Japanese visibly shake if you, the teacher and person in authority, ask them, the student, for an opinion.
>
> The best tactic is to get them in pairs, so that together they can work something out. They are more productive and open in pairs, and it takes the pressure off them. Then get the pairs into fours, to express a mini-group opinion, then work for a total group agreement. The thing to avoid at all costs is to stroll into class, saying, "OK, today we are going to discuss pollution. Tetsuya, you set the ball rolling: What do you think of pollution?" It will not work.

A book which could prove invaluable is *Teaching Tactics for Japan's English Classrooms*, a companion to *Jobs in Japan* mentioned above and available for $6.95/£5.95.

The Japanese are famed for their good manners and most adults in private language classes will be faultlessly polite. The same is not always true of secondary school pupils and JET teacher Claire Wilkinson found some of her classes surprisingly ill-disciplined. The job description booklet for JET contains a fascinating set of "What if . . ." mini-scenarios, which illustrate what they understatedly call "surprising or uncomfortable situations". Some of them sound downright diabolical, such as, "One of the students in your class hits another and your Japanese co-teacher doesn't react" or "You are a woman and a student asks you for your three sizes (i.e. body measurements)". Obviously Japanese students are not always meek and shy and polite.

Accommodation

It is not uncommon for teachers who are hired overseas to be given help with accommodation, which is a tremendously useful perk, even if the flat provided is small and over-priced. If you are on your own, you will be forced to use an English speaking rental agency (which will charge about one month's rent) and then pay a colossal deposit called "key money" which is often 6 months rent in advance. Unlike rent deposits in the West you can't expect to recoup it all. Assuming the range of rents is 60,000-85,000 yen per month in Tokyo, that means you might have to pay over £2,000 upfront. Well-established schools may be prepared to lend you the key money or (exceptionally) pay it outright. Rents outside Tokyo and Osaka should be nearer 50,000 yen, with an additional monthly payment of about 6,000 for utilities.

A further problem is the near total absence of furnished apartments, so you may have to go shopping for curtains and cookers on top of all your other expenses. Again, schools which have a steady flow of foreign teachers may keep a stock of basic furnishings which they can lend to teachers. In view of this, a bed in a dormitory may not sound so bad after all.

LEISURE TIME

According to some veteran teachers, leisure time and how to spend it will be the least of your worries. Depending on your circumstances, you may be expected to participate in extracurricular activities and social events which it would cause offence to decline — always a major concern in Japan. Although Bryn Thomas enjoyed the sushi which his school provided for teachers still at work at 9pm, he was less keen on the "office parties when teachers were required to dress up in silly costumes and be nice to the students". Most teachers are happy to accept occasional invitations to socialize with their Japanese colleagues or pupils, even if it does mean an evening of speaking very very slowly and drinking heavily.

A glut of Westerners in Tokyo means that your welcome may be less than enthusiastic. In fact non-Japanese are refused entrance to some Tokyo bars and restaurants. You are far more likely to be invited into people's homes in rural areas (which is true throughout the world). Any entertainment which smacks of the West such as going out to a fashionable coffee house or a night club will be absurdly expensive. However if you are content with more modest indigenous food and pastimes, you will be able to save money. A filling bowl of noodles and broth costs about £2, though you may never take to the standard breakfast of boiled rice and a raw egg. Staying home to listen to Japanese language tapes or to read a good book (e.g. *Pictures from the Water Trade,* a personal account of life in Japan) costs nothing. Obviously the more settled you become, the more familiar you will be with the bargains and affordable amusements.

Finding your way around is nothing if not a challenge in a country where almost all road and public transport signs are incomprehensible. What use is an A-Z if you can't read the alphabet? Japanese addresses are mind-bogglingly complicated too: the numbers refer to land subdivisions: prefecture, district, ward, then building. When in doubt (inevitable) ask a friendly informant for a *chizu* (map). It is also a good idea to get a Japanese person to write your destination in both *kanji* (Japanese script) and *roma-ji* (the Roman alphabet). Japanese people will sometimes go to embarrassing lengths to help foreigners. This desire to help wedded to a reluctance to "lose face" means that they may offer advice and instructions based on very little information, so keep checking. Young people in jeans are the best bets. Outside the big cities the people are even more cordial. Wherever you go, you don't have to worry about crime.

Travel is expensive. For example the bullet train from Tokyo to Sendai, a couple of hundred miles north, costs £60 one way. Yet the pace of a teacher's life in Tokyo or another big city can become so stressful that it is essential to get on a local train and see some of the countryside. Unfortunately hitch-hiking is not a recognized form of transport. The risk is not of being left by the roadside or of being mugged but of being taken unbidden to the nearest railway station (which might be a major detour for the hapless driver who feels obliged to do this out of courtesy).

The alienness of Japanese culture is one of the main fascinations of the place. It is foolish to become bogged down worrying about transgressing against one of their mysterious customs. Claire Wilkinson felt quite overwhelmed after reading the JET literature. One of the many prohibitions mentioned is "never blow your nose in public", and so the heavy cold with which she arrived made her even more miserable than it would have otherwise. But she soon discovered that the Japanese allow foreigners a great deal of latitude and that she could relax and be herself without causing grave offence.

LIST OF SCHOOLS

AMERICAN CULTURAL EXCHANGE
3123 Eastlake Avenue East, Seattle, Washington 98102, USA. Tel: (206) 726-0055.
Number of teachers: 50 in Asia University, Tokyo and possibly other locations throughout Japan.
Preference of nationality: US, UK.
Qualifications: recent TESL training and experience.
Conditions of employment: 1 year contracts. 20 contact h.p.w. Pupils aged between 18-30.
Salary: US$15-25,000 per year.
Facilities/Support: assistance with accommodation only if employee is hired overseas. Training given.
Recruitment: through adverts and personal contacts. Interviews essential and held in both US and UK.

ASA COMMUNITY SALON
ASA Staff Center, Tanaka Building, 2-11-12 Yoyogi, Shibuya-ku, Tokyo 151. Tel: (3) 320-8649/348-3333.
Number of teachers: 200+.
Preference of nationality: UK, US.
Qualifications: minimum BA plus teaching experience, and/or teaching qualification.
Conditions of employment: 1 year contracts with 3 month trial period. Hours of work 2-10pm. Pupils are mainly adult, professional people.
Salary: from 2,500 yen per hour with increments after certain number of hours worked.
Facilities/Support: assistance with accommodation given only if employee is hired overseas. Training and health insurance scheme provided.
Recruitment: interviews essential and held mostly in Japan but also in US/UK 2/3 times per year.

ASPECT INTERNATIONAL LANGUAGE SCHOOLS
26 Third St., San Francisco, CA 94103, USA. Tel: (415) 777-9555.
Number of teachers: 20-30.
Preference of nationality: US.
Qualifications: MA (TESOL) and 2 years' teaching experience or 1 year's overseas experience preferred.
Conditions of employment: 1 year contracts. 25-30 h.p.w. Pupils aged 18-40.
Salary: depends on location.
Facilities/Support: assistance with accommodation. Orientation only.
Recruitment: through adverts in the *TESOL Placement Bulletin* and *New York Times*. Interviews held in US.

ATTY LANGUAGE INSTITUTE
5F Osaka Ekimae Daiichi Building, 1-3-1 Umeda, Kita-ku, Osaka 530. Tel: (6) 346-2323.
Number of teachers: 170.
Preference of nationality: none.
Qualifications: BA required. TEFL experience preferred but not essential.
Conditions of employment: 1 year contracts. Hours of work 1.30-8.15pm weekdays. Pupils of all ages, majority aged 18-30.
Salary: 10-11,800 yen per day plus monthly bonus and transportation costs.
Facilities/Support: apartments and dormitory rooms available from school. Training given.
Recruitment: through direct application, overseas recruitment sessions and locally. Interviews not essential but sometimes held in UK.

BERLITZ SCHOOLS OF LANGUAGES (JAPAN) INC.
Kowa Bldg. 1, 5F, 11-41, Akasaka 1-chome, Minato-ku, Tokyo 107. Tel: (3) 589-3525.
Number of teachers: 550-600.
Preference of nationality: US first, but also UK, Canada, Australia, New Zealand.
Qualifications: some teaching experience helpful but not required. Must be available for training programme held in Japan.
Conditions of employment: 1 year contracts. Hours of work 4.45-9.10pm. Pupils of all ages, but mostly adults.
Salary: 235,000 yen per month for 20 h.p.w.; extra work available during the day.
Facilities/Support: school will act as guarantor for accommodation only. An 8-day training programme compulsory before beginning contract.
Recruitment: through personal contacts. Local interviews essential.

CALIFORNIA LANGUAGE INSTITUTE
Kouchi Bldg, 4F, Ohtemachi 1-1-27, Naka-ku, Hiroshima 730. Tel: (82) 242-4141.
Number of teachers: 40 in 9 branch schools.
Preference of nationality: US, Canada, UK, Australia.
Qualifications: training in TEFL/TESL and experience with children.
Conditions of employment: 2 year contracts. 30 h.p.w. Pupils aged 3-70.
Salary: 250,000 yen per month.
Facilities/Support: furnished apartments are provided and housing subsidies in some areas. Training given.
Recruitment: through newspaper adverts and overseas. Interviews are essential and take place abroad 1-2 times a year.

CLARKE CONSULTING GROUP
Three Lagoon Drive, Suite 230, Redwood City, CA 94065, USA. Tel: (415) 591-8100 Fax: 591-8269.
Preference of nationality: none.
Qualifications: MA (TESL), 3 years experience preferably in a Japanese company.
Conditions of employment: no standard contract length. Full-time work only. All pupils are adults.
Salary: competitive.

Facilities/Support: no assistance with accommodation. Training given.
Recruitment: through conferences and the *TESOL Placement Bulletin*. Interviews are essential and are conducted in US and Japan.

ECC FOREIGN LANGUAGES INSTITUTE
Shikata Building 2F, 4-43 Nakazaki-Nishi, 2-chome, Kita-ku, Osaka 530. Tel: (6) 359-5380.
Number of teachers: 200.
Preference of nationality: none.
Qualifications: minimum BA, TEFL qualification preferred.
Conditions of employment: 1 year contracts. Hours of work 5-9pm, 20 h.p.w. Pupils aged 18-30.
Salary: 240,000 yen per month.
Facilities/Support: assistance with accommodation. Training given.
Recruitment: through personal contacts. Local interviews essential.

ENGLISH ACADEMIC RESEARCH INSTITUTE
Maruyoshi Building 6-2-2, Higashi Ueno, Taito-ku, Tokyo 110. Tel: (3) 844-3104.
Number of teachers: 1-2.
Preference of nationality: US, UK, Canada, Australia, New Zealand.
Qualifications: college graduates; no teaching experience needed.
Conditions of employment: 1 year contracts. Hours of work 11am-8.30pm.
Salary: US$30 per hour.
Facilities/Support: no assistance with accommodation. No training given.
Recruitment: through newspaper adverts. Local interviews essential.

ENGLISH ACADEMY
2-9-6 Ichibancho, Matsuyama 790. Tel: (899) 31-8686.
Number of teachers: 20+.
Preference of nationality: none, but most are from US/Canada.
Qualifications: BA, teaching experience preferable, and enthusiasm essential.
Salary: 18 month contracts. Maximum 25 contact h.p.w. between 1-9pm. Pupils aged 5-70, but most are young adults.
Facilities/Support: apartment or house provided if available, if not then financial help is given. Training available.
Recruitment: through direct application. Interviews required but can be held over the telephone.

ENGLISH CIRCLES/EC INC.
President Bldg. 3rd Floor, West 5, South 1, Chuo-ku, Sapporo 060. Tel: (11) 221-0279. Fax: 221-0248.
Number of teachers: 40-50.
Preference of nationality: none.
Qualifications: BA preferably with TESL/TEFL qualification.
Conditions of employment: 1 year/18 month/2 year contracts available. 35 h.p.w. Pupils aged 16-60.
Salary: 260-290,000 yen per month, rising to latter sum after completion of trial period.
Facilities/Support: advance payments of up to 100,000 yen for accommodation offered plus school pays real estate agency's fee. Training given.

Recruitment: through newspaper adverts and universities. Telephone interviews are essential.

EVERGREEN LANGUAGE SCHOOL
21-18, 1-chome Yutenji, Megono Ku, Tokyo. Tel: (3) 713-4958.
Number of teachers: 20.
Preference of nationality: UK, US, Canada.
Qualifications: graduates under 35 years old.
Conditions of employment: 2 year contracts. Hours of work from 3-9.30pm. Pupils aged 5-50.
Salary: 280,000 yen per month.
Facilities/Support: assistance with accommodation. Training given. Subsidized Japanese lessons offered in the morning.
Recruitment: through former teachers. Interviews not essential.

INSTITUTE FOR INTERNATIONAL STUDIES & TRAINING
c/o G. Edward Reynolds, PO Box 1118, New London, New Hampshire 03257, USA. Tel: (603) 526-2247 (summer) or 8101 Connecticut Ave, Apt. N-189, Chevy Chase, Maryland 20815. Tel: (301) 652-6505 (November to May).
Number of teachers: 3-6 for school in Fujinomiya.
Preference of nationality: none.
Qualifications: BA, must be males aged 21-30.
Conditions of employment: 3 month contracts, to reside in dorms with young Japanese professionals and conduct classes. 3-4 hours teaching per day. Average age of pupils is 30.
Salary: 260,000 yen per month.
Facilities/Support: study/bedroom on campus provided free of charge. Training given.
Recruitment: through personal contacts. Interviews not essential.

INTERLANG SCHOOL
Bell Commons 7F, 2-14-6 Kita-Aoyama, Minato-ku, Tokyo 107. Tel: (3) 497-5451.
Number of teachers: 10.
Preference of nationality: US, UK.
Qualifications: BA preferably in education; or experience teaching Japanese students.
Conditions of employment: 6 month-1 year contracts. Varied work hours but mostly evenings. Part-time work available. Pupils are mostly adult, with some children occasionally.
Salary: 3-4,000 yen per hour.
Facilities/Support: assistance with accommodation. Training given.
Recruitment: local interviews required.

INTERNATIONAL LANGUAGE CENTRE
Iwanami-Jimbocho Building 9F, Kanda-Jimbocho 2-1, Chiyoda-ku, Tokyo 101. Tel: (3) 264-5935.
Number of teachers: 50-60.
Preference of nationality: UK, Canada, Australia, New Zealand.

Qualifications: RSA Dip., and at least 3 years full-time TEFL experience essential.
Conditions of employment: 2 year renewable contracts. Maximum of 24 teaching h.p.w. Pupils aged from 15 upwards with possibility of future children's courses.
Salary: 350-440,000 yen per month.
Facilities/Support: accommodation located and all refundable and non-refundable deposits paid. Training given.
Recruitment: through ILC London. Interviews held in UK. (see page 57).

ISS
1-6 Koji-machi, Chiyoda-ku, Tokyo 102. Tel: (3) 265-7103.
Number of teachers: 15, mostly part-timers.
Preference of nationality: none.
Qualifications: BA.
Conditions of employment: 6 month-1 year contracts. Mostly evening work. Pupils range in age from 18-50.
Salary: from 3,000 yen per hour.
Facilities/Support: no assistance with accommodation. Training given.
Recruitment: through adverts. Local interviews essential.

JAMES ENGLISH SCHOOL
2429 Middleton Beach Road, Middleton, Wisconsin 53562, USA. Tel: (608) 238-0712.
Number of teachers: 40, in Sendai and other cities in Northern Japan.
Preference of nationality: none.
Qualifications: teaching qualification, TESL preferred.
Conditions of employment: minimum 1 year contracts. 18 h.p.w., mostly afternoon/evening work. Pupils are mostly adults, but a few children's classes.
Salary: 250,000 yen per month.
Facilities/Support: assistance given finding accommodation. Training provided.
Recruitment: through adverts in the *TESOL Placement Bulletin*. Telephone interviews essential.

KOBE STEEL
Kobe Language Center, Personnel Department, 3-18 Wakinohamacho, 1-chome, Chuo-ku, Kobe 651. Tel: (78) 261-4316.
Number of teachers: 10, in Tokyo and Kobe.
Preference of nationality: none.
Qualifications: MA/RSA Cert. plus 3 years experience teaching adults, preferably in Japan.
Conditions of employment: 1 year contracts. $42\frac{1}{2}$ h.p.w. Pupils are all employees of Kobe Steel.
Facilities/Support: a housing allowance is allocated, and computer and Japanese language training provided.
Recruitment: through adverts in Japanese newspapers and through JALT and TESOL conferences. Interviews required.

LANGUAGE INSTITUTE OF JAPAN (LIOJ)
4-14-1 Shiroyama, Odawara, Kangawa 250. Tel: (465) 23-1677.
Number of teachers: 20.
Preference of nationality: none.

Qualifications: MA in TESL or Applied Linguistics/business experience.
Conditions of employment: 1 year contracts. 30 periods per week of which 20 are contact hours.
Salary: 329,300 yen per month.
Facilities/Support: assistance given finding accommodation and in paying initial costs. Training given.
Recruitment: through newspaper adverts and recruitment fairs. Interviews essential and can be held in UK/US.

MATSUDO ENGLISH CENTER
Serizawa Bldg. 2F, 17-11 Honcho, Matsudo-shi, Chiba-ken. Tel: (4723) 66-0987. Also: Kurokawa Bldg. 5F, 3-4 Sakuragaoka, Shibuya-ku, Tokyo. Tel: (3) 496-0555.
Number of teachers: 12.
Preference of nationality: US, UK.
Qualifications: college graduates; must be enthusiastic and motivated.
Conditions of employment: 1 year contracts. 30 h.p.w. Pupils aged from 2.
Salary: varies according to experience.
Facilities/Support: assistance with accommodation. Training given.
Recruitment: through newspaper adverts. Interviews essential and sometimes held in US.

MATTY'S SCHOOL OF ENGLISH
3-15-9 Shonan-takatori, Yokosuka 237. Tel: (468) 65-8717. Fax: 65-0406.
Number of teachers: 10-12.
Preference of nationality: US, Canada, UK.
Qualifications: teaching or linguistics degree and TESL qualification preferred. Must enjoy teaching pre-school children.
Conditions of employment: 1 year renewable contracts. 40 h.p.w. Pupils are pre-school to senior high school age. Majority are aged 5-11.
Salary: 1,470,000 yen per year plus one-way airfare and bonus; a care is also provided.
Facilities/Support: the school arranges and pays for Japanese homestays for all employees. Training given.
Recruitment: through colleges and universities. Interviews not essential but are held in Canada/America.

M.I.L. THE LANGUAGE CENTER
3F Eguchi Bldg., 1-6-2 Katsutadai, Yachiyo-shi, Chiba-ken 276. Tel: (474) 85-7555. Fax: 85-7875.
Number of teachers: 15.
Preference of nationality: Canada, US.
Qualifications: BA in relevant subject; teaching experience and TESL qualification preferred. Must be creative and flexible.
Conditions of employment: 2 year contracts. Maximum 40 h.p.w. of which 25 are contact hours, between 12-9pm weekdays. Pupils from 4 upwards.
Salary: 250-270,000 yen per month with 10% raise for 2nd year and bonus on completion of contract.
Facilities/Support: initial costs, furnishings and telephone provided towards accommodation. Training given.

Recruitment: through adverts and agencies. Interviews in US, but telephone interviews also possible.

MOBARA ENGLISH INSTITUTE
618-1 Takashi, Mobara-shi, Chiba-ken 297. Tel: (475) 22-4785/ 24-0194.
Number of teachers: 3.
Preference of nationality: US, UK.
Qualifications: BA/MA.
Conditions of employment: 1-2 year contracts. 32-33 h.p.w. Pupils range in age from young children to adults.
Salary: approximately 235,000 yen per month.
Facilities/Support: assistance with accommodation. Some training given.
Recruitment: through personal recommendation. Interviews not essential.

PLUS ALPHA (Agency)
2-25-20 Denenchofu, Ota-ku, Tokyo 145. Tel: (3) 721-3795. Fax: 721-1245. This organization places teachers in private English language schools throughout Japan and has offices in Tokyo, New York and London.
Number of teachers: 50.
Preference of nationality: Canada, US, UK.
Qualifications: BA in English, Japanese, Education or TEFL and teaching experience preferred.
Conditions of employment: 1 year renewable contracts. 20-25 h.p.w. Pupils range in age from 5-75.
Salary: 200-250,000 yen per month.
Facilities/Support: assistance with accommodation. Training given.
Recruitment: through adverts, universities and contacts. Interviews are essential and are regularly held in UK/US.

QE LANGUAGE SCHOOLS
3F Yuzuki Bldg., 7-14 Minamiyawata, 4-chome, Ichikawa, Chiba 272. Tel: (473) 77-1144. Fax: 79-6918.
Number of teachers: 12-15.
Preference of nationality: none.
Qualifications: BA, RSA Cert.
Conditions of employment: 1 year contracts. 23 contact h.p.w. Pupils from 4 upwards.
Salary: from 2,880,000 yen per year, plus 100,000 yen bonus and one-way airfare.
Facilities/Support: furnishings, deposit and agency fees for flat paid by school. Training given.
Recruitment: through adverts in UK newspapers. Interviews essential and are held in London or Tokyo.
UK contact address: 1 Blounts Court House, Potterne, Devizes, Wiltshire.

SHANE ENGLISH SCHOOL
4F Kimura Bldg., 4-14-12 Nishi Funa, Funabashi-shi, Chiba-ken 273. Tel: (474) 31-1220. Fax: 33-7185.
Number of teachers: 120.
Preference of nationality: UK, Ireland, North America.

Qualifications: BA, RSA Cert. (or equivalent) and some teaching experience preferred.
Conditions of employment: 1 year contracts. 25-30 h.p.w. Pupils aged from 3 upwards.
Salary: from 3,300,000 yen per year.
Facilities/Support: assistance with accommodation. Training given.
Recruitment: interviews essential and held in UK or Japan.
UK contact: Saxoncourt (UK) Ltd., 77A Station Road, West Wiickham, Kent BR4 0PX. Tel: 081-777 7358. Fax: 081-777 0434.

SIMUL ACADEMY OF INTERNATIONAL COMMUNICATION
Kowa Building 9, 2F, 1-8-10 Akasaka, Minato-ku, Tokyo 107. Tel: (3) 588-8061.
Number of teachers: 40 at various schools in Tokyo area.
Preference of nationality: none.
Qualifications: MA or equivalent in TESOL or related field, with a minimum of 2 years experience preferred.
Conditions of employment: 1 year contracts. Some evening and Saturday morning work. Pupils aged from 18.
Salary: from 320,000 yen per month.
Facilities/Support: assistance given finding accommodation. Training given.
Recruitment: through newspaper adverts. Local interviews essential.

SUNDAI ELS LANGUAGE CENTER
1-5-8 Kanda, Surugadai, Chiyoda-ku, Tokyo 101. Tel: (3) 233-2311. Fax: 233-2469.
Number of teachers: 19.
Preference of nationality: US.
Qualifications: BA English/Education/ESL, 2 years TESL/TEFL experience.
Conditions of employment: 1 year contracts (April-March), 15 90-minute units per week. Pupils either aged 19-22 or adult professionals.
Salary: 3,300,000 yen per yer with 6 weeks paid vacation.
Facilities/Support: assistance with accommodation if hired overseas. Some training given.
Recruitment: through the *TESOL Placement Bulletin* and ELS centres in US. Interviews essential; held locally or in US.

TOEFL ACADEMY
1-12-4 Kudankita, Chiyoda-ku, Tokyo 102. Tel: (3) 230-3500. Fax: 264-7960.
Number of teachers: 3-5 full-time, 4-8 part-time.
Preference of nationality: none, but mostly North America, UK.
Qualifications: some relevant teaching experience and some qualification in business/TESL/the sciences.
Conditions of employment: 1-2 year contracts for full-time and unlimited for part-time staff. 20-40 h.p.w. full time, 4-8 h.p.w. part time. Pupils mostly aged 25-30 although some are students. All are trying to raise their scores on standard TOEFL tests in order to study abroad; many are sponsored by their companies.
Salary: 6,000 yen per hour for part-time staff, 3-8, 100,000 per year for full-time staff.
Facilities/Support: dormitory available for approximately half the usual rent and without deposit. Training given.
Recruitment: through direct application, contacts and advertising. Interviews are required and rarely held in UK/US.

TOKYO FOREIGN LANGUAGE COLLEGE
7-3-8 Nishi-Shinjuku, Shinjuku-ku, Tokyo 160. Tel: (3) 367-1101.
Number of teachers: 140.
Preference of nationality: none.
Qualifications: minimum BA (English related); MA/RSA/TEFL qualification and 2 years experience preferred.
Conditions of employment: 1 year contracts. Hours of work 9am-4pm weekdays. Pupils range in age from 18-21 and are studying tourism, etc. at this vocational college.
Salary: 300,000 yen per month.
Facilities/Support: assistance with accommodation. Training given.
Recruitment: interviews essential and held locally and in UK/US.

TOKYO—YAMATE YMCA ENGLISH SCHOOL
18-12 Nishi-Waseda, 2-chome, Shinjuku-ku, Tokyo 169. Tel: (3) 202-0321.
Number of teachers: 9.
Preference of nationality: US, Canada, UK, Australia, New Zealand.
Qualifications: BA/MA in TESL or related fields.
Conditions of employment: 1 year contracts. 40 h.p.w. of which 22 are teaching hours. Pupils aged from 9 upwards.
Salary: 250-300,000 yen per month.
Facilities/Support: assistance with accommodation. Training given.
Recruitment: through adverts in UK newspapers. Interviews preferred but not essential if applicant is living outside Japan.

Korea

Anyone who has witnessed the early morning scramble by students and businessment to get to their English lessons before the working day begins in

Seoul, might be surprised to learn that the name for Korea is "Land of the Morning Calm". Because Korea's economy is so heavily dependent on export, English is a very useful accomplishment for people in business. Korean students are often looking to export themselves, mostly to the US to acquire a college education. Both these groups have probably studied English for many years at school but need to practise conversation with native speakers.

Although Korea does not quickly come to most people's minds as a possible destination, the demand for English and the ability of many to pay for tuition matches that of Taiwan. According to the British Council there are over 100 language schools in Seoul and nearly half that many in Korea's second city Pusan. As in Taiwan there is a definite American bias, though even schools which concentrate their recruitment drive in the US are very willing to hire British teachers as well.

Student strikes, some of them violent, have taken place over the past few years, highlighting the volatility of Korean politics. This together with the lower wages relative to Japan has done nothing to stem the flow of teachers to Japan while Korean schools are finding it increasingly difficult to hire native speaker teachers. But given the struggle facing would-be teachers in Japan, it is worth considering Korea as an alternative. The politics of South Korea seem more stable at present, and the lower wages are compensated for by the lower cost of living.

Although the regime in North Korea has made some tentative moves in the direction of the West, there is still no sign that they would welcome English teachers.

Prospects for Teachers

Native-speaker status matters far more to most schools than specialist qualifications and is normally sufficient to persuade a school to hire you. For those trying to fix up a job ahead of time, schools are often willing to hire a teacher without an interview, provided they have a university degree and some evidence of experience.

A few years ago the demand was so great that businessmen actually visited travellers' hostels looking for English speakers whom they could pay to hold conversations with them. But the government took a dim view of all these untrained, itinerant teachers and has made it difficult to get a teaching visa (see *Regulations* below) Still, in *hogwons* (language schools) at the lower end of the market, casual teachers can still find temporary jobs. With ELT approaching saturation point in Taiwan and Japan, Korea may no longer remain off the teachers' beaten track.

FIXING UP A JOB

In Advance

Few adverts appear in the British press for jobs in Korea, though both *ILC Recruitment* and *ELT Banbury* occasionally recruit teachers at an advanced level for clients in Korea. The *TESOL Placement Bulletin* is a better source of job vacancies in Korea, though the same schools tend to advertise regularly.

You can request the Seoul British Council's long list of language schools in Seoul and Pusan, which is preferable to spending £20 on the British Council's *Survey of English Language Teaching in Korea* which contains an almost identical list. The British Council is Seoul says that it will advise people who are not ufficiently well qualified to work in its own teaching centre on other local job opportunities.

Anyone with a BA and some TEFL experience has a reasonable chance of being hired by *ELS International* in Seoul. They hire new teachers every month and offer an attractive "total compensation package" worth about $20,000.

Another possibility for qualified or experienced teachers is to work for the language department of a Korean university (of which there are nearly 100). Serious teachers might enquire at their local Korean Embassy about jobs in universities.

As mentioned above, it is not unusual to arrange a job without an interview. One school suggests that would-be teachers send a cassette of their voices or, even better, a video of them teaching a lesson, which would certainly be more memorable and impressive than simply sending a c.v.

On the Spot

A personal approach to language schools in Seoul or Pusan will usually be rewarded with some work within a week or two. Daewon Yogwon, a small but long-established travellers' hostel in Seoul, has been the centre of teaching information for travellers for many years. To meet foreigners in the know, stay at Daewon (Dongju-dong, Chongro-gu; tel: 735 7891) or alternatively Dae-gee Yogwon. In fact the Chongro area of Seoul has a high concentration of language schools and would be a suitable area for a door-to-door job search. New schools are opening all the time though most of them in the suburbs rather than the city centre for the convenience of students. Seoul has an extensive subway system which makes it possible to attend interviews at far-flung schools and (if successful) to commute to work without too much difficulty. As always your chances are improved if you are conservatively-dressed, clean shaven and professional-looking.

If you make a good impression at a school which does not happen to have a vacancy, they may well advise you on alternatives. For example, John Valentine, the Program Director at *Jongro Foreign Language Institute* claims that he is in a position to "offer work to almost all applications" since other institutes often call him when they need a teacher.

There are two English language newspapers in Seoul. The *Korea Herald* and *Korea Times* if you want to advertise your availability to teach.

REGULATIONS

The 1988 Olympics in Seoul occasioned a crackdown on illegal immigrants of all kinds including teachers; and anyone working without a visa risks heavy fines and possible deportation. Similarly, the schools which hire freelance foreigners without permits can be closed down by the government. So, if at all possible, obtain a teaching visa.

It is much easier if this can be done before arrival. If you do find a school which wants to hire you, they will send you a contract and sponsorship document (valid for a minimum of one year). You must send these together with your c.v., references, photos, first page of your passport and copy of your degree certificate (plus transcripts for Americans) to your nearest Korean Embassy, who will take 6 to 8 weeks to process the visa. According to the information from *Yonsei University* the process can be reduced to a month or less by requesting that the documents be sent by telex (at your expense) rather than by diplomatic courier. You must collect your visa at the Embassy.

Alternatively, you can enter Korea as a tourist, find a job and then go to Japan, Hong Kong or Taipei for up to a month while the visa application is being dealt with. (British nationals don't need a tourist visa for stays of less than 60 days, while tourist visas for Americans are valid for 90 days.) If this is your intention buy an air ticket from your home to Hong Kong via Seoul. This is a good idea in any case if you want to travel around the Far East since air tickets are more expensive in Korea than in Hong Kong.

A teaching visa is also needed to tutor privately. Although schools are usually tolerant of their teachers doing free-lance teaching on the side, this is illegal. There is also a law which prohibits any foreigner from teaching secondary school pupils in any subject.

Once the tax-exempt period of two years expires, teachers are liable for very high rates of tax which results in most teachers leaving the country.

Taking out private medical insurance is advisable and will probably cost about $25 a month.

CONDITIONS OF WORK

One year contracts arranged in advance are often quite lucrative, typically comprising a gross monthly salary of a million won (tax-free for the first two years), subsidized accommodation, often free air fares and an end-of-contract bonus. Salaries are usually quoted in American dollars (even if advertised in the UK) and range from $12,000 to $20,000 per year, with increments for higher degrees and overtime payments. One possible perk is the ability to remit up to two-thirds of your salary to your home country. Part-time teachers are normally paid a round 10,000 won per hour, unless the school operates a percentage system whereby the teacher earns about half of the takings. This can be very lucrative if you are teaching business English to classes in companies, an area of TEFL which is rapidly expanding.

The quality of *hogwon* varies enormously. Some are run by sharks who may make promises at interview which they can't fulfil, and overfill classes to maximize profits. Many schools do not use recognized course books but rely on home-made materials of dubious usefulness. Despite Korea's reputation as a centre for high tech, some schools lack basic video and computer facilities. Few schools at this level offer any training and no RSA courses are available in Korea.

The average teaching schedule in Korea is 6 hours a day (2 in the morning and 4 in the evening), 5 days a week. Weekend work is less commonplace than in many other countries. The teaching load in universities is often lighter. For example Sogang University employs its native speakers for 4 terms of 10 weeks each, and pays them through the 12 weeks of vacation.

Teachers have no trouble motivating their students, some of whom attend 2-hour classes 3 or 4 times a week. The majority are serious about learning the language and want to be taught systematically and energetically. They also expect their teachers to direct the action and are not happy with a laid-back "let's have a chit-chat" approach.

Accommodation

As in Japan, a large deposit (known as "key money") must be paid before an apartment can be rented. The larger the deposit the cheaper the rent. If you don't hear about available flats from your school or other foreigners, check the English language newspaper or find an English-speaking rental agent. Boarding house accommodation costs about 150,000-200,000 won per month. It may also be possible to arrange to live with a Korean family in exchange for English conversation.

LEISURE TIME

Visitors are often surprised to discover the richness and complexity of Korean history and culture, partly because Japanese culture is far better known. Despite being a bustling metropolis of 10 million, Seoul has preserved some of its cultural treasures. Teaching schedules usually allow sufficient free time and vacations to explore the country and to study some aspect of Korean culture, such as the martial art Tae Kwon Do.

Anyone homesick for the West will gravitate to the area of Seoul called Itaewon, where all the fast food restaurants and discos are concentrated, not to mention a jazz club and other expatriate forms of entertainment. Korea is also a shopper's paradise especially for clothes and spectacles. Many teachers do not bother to ship many clothes, knowing that they can outfit themselves so reasonably after arrival, including the warm clothes they will need for winter.

LIST OF SCHOOLS

DONG-A FOREIGN LANGUAGE INSTITUTE
505-21 Hadan-dong, Saha-ku, Pusan. Tel: (51) 206-1633.
Number of teachers: 1.
Preference of nationality: US.
Qualifications: BA (English) minimum.
Conditions of employment: 1 year contracts. 25 h.p.w. Pupils are mostly college students.
Salary: varies according to experience.
Facilities/Support: no assistance with accommodation. Training given if necessary.
Recruitment: through direct application. Interviews essential.

ELS INTERNATIONAL
649-1 Yeoksam-dong, Kangnam-ku, Seoul 135-080. Tel: (2) 654-9191.
Number of teachers: 60.
Preference of nationality: none.
Qualifications: MA (TEFL/TESL/Linguistics), BA (TEFL/TESL/Linguistics) plus 1 year's experience or BA/MA in any discipline plus 2 years TEFL experience.
Conditions of employment: 1 year contracts. Hours of work 10am-12pm and 6-10pm. Pupils aged between 18-45.
Salary: 10,584,000 won annual salary plus one month's pay on completion of contract. 70% remittable overseas. Return air fare and US$300 shipping allowance each way provided.
Facilities/Support: furnished, shared housing is provided. Training given.
Recruitment: through ELS International, 5761 Buckingham Parkway, Culver City, California 90230. Interviews held in US and UK.

ESS LANGUAGE INSTITUTE
8, 1-ka Shinchang-dong, Jung-ku, Pusan 600-061. Tel: (51) 246-3251. Fax: 241-1988.
Number of teachers: 6.
Preference of nationality: US, UK.
Qualifications: TESL major, teaching experience preferred.
Conditions of employment: 1 year contracts. Hours of work, 6 hours per day, 5 days per week. Pupils aged 18-40.
Salary: US$16,000 for an MA and one month's paid vacation per year plus one-way airfare for 1 year's work, return airfare for 2.
Facilities/Support: half of the cost of rent paid by the school. Training given.
Recruitment: through adverts in the *TESOL Placement Bulletin*. Interviews not essential.

ETC (ENGLISH TRAINING CENTER)
646-22, Yoksam-dong, Kangnam-ku, Seoul 135-081. Tel: (2) 555-7771.
Number of teachers: 18.
Preference of nationality: US, UK, Canada.
Qualifications: MA plus 2/3 years TESL experience or BA plus 3 years TESL experience in a foreign country.
Conditions of employment: 1 year contracts. 5 hours work per day with a split schedule possible. Pupils aged 20-45.
Salary: 1,000,000 won per month.
Facilities/Support: furnished accommodation provided. Training given.
Recruitment: through the *TESOL Placement Bulletin* and Peace Corps Hotline.

INSTITUTE OF LANGUAGE RESEARCH AND EDUCATION
Yonsei University, Sodaemun-ku, Shinchon-Dong 134, Seoul. Tel: (2) 392-6405.
Number of teachers: 50 (1991).
Preference of nationality: none.
Qualifications: BA (preferably English or TEFL) minimum or MA, plus some TEFL experience preferred.
Conditions of employment: 3 months × 2, then 1 year renewable contracts. Hours of work 4.30-6pm and 6.30-9pm with Wednesdays and weekends off. Pupils are aged from 18.
Salary: from 750,000 won per month (gross).
Facilities/Support: assistance with accommodation. Training given. Paid vacations (12 weeks total).
Recruitment: through universities in US and Europe. Interviews not necessary.

JONG-RO FOREIGN LANGUAGE INSTITUTE
Jong Ro Ku, Kong Pyong Dong, 55 Bungi, Seoul. Tel: (2) 732-8383.
Number of teachers: 20-25.
Preference of nationality: US (majority).
Qualifications: easy-going personality with leadership qualities. No experience necessary.
Conditions of employment: part-time 1-3 month contracts or 1 year renewable contracts. Hours of work, part-time 2-4 hours per day, full-time 5-7 hours per day, 20 days per month.
Salary: 10,000 won per hour (April, 1990).

Facilities/Support: small advance given for accommodation which is, generally, not hard to find.
Recruitment: walk-ins or through direct application with cassette or video. Interviews not essential.

LANGUAGE ARTS TESTING & TRAINING
Choong Jong, PO Box 269, Seoul 120-013. Tel: (2) 363-3291/ 363-1277.
Number of teachers: 6.
Preference of nationality: none.
Qualifications: BA with TEFL course and/or 2 years experience.
Conditions of employment: 1 year contracts. Hours of work 7.30-10am and 7.30-9pm weekdays. All pupils are adults.
Salary: approximately 1,000,000 won per month.
Facilities/Support: advice given on accommodation and training provided.
Recruitment: through referrals. Interviews not essential.

LANGUAGE TEACHING RESEARCH CENTER
60-17, 1-ka, Taepyong-Ro, Chung-gu, Seoul 100-101. Tel: (2) 737-4641.
Number of teachers: 10-12.
Preference of nationality: US, UK, Australia, Canada.
Qualifications: BA, teaching qualifications/experience preferred but not essential.
Conditions of employment: 1 year renewable contracts. 4-5 hours per day in split shifts, 5 days per week. Pupils mostly aged 18-35 with some classes for children.
Salary: from 10,000 won per hour.
Facilities/Support: assistance given finding accommodation and help with loans for deposits. Training provided.
Recruitment: through adverts at colleges/universities in US/UK. Local interviews only; sometimes will hire through correspondence.

MINO FOREIGN LANGUAGE SCHOOL
Mido Sang-Ga Bldg., 3rd Floor 311, Dae-Chi Dong, Kang-Nam Ku, Seoul 135-280. Tel: (2) 562-6714/566-8972.
Number of teachers: 7.
Preference of nationality: US, UK.
Qualifications: BA and experience in teaching preferred.
Conditions of employment: 1 year contracts. 6 hours work per day. Pupils aged from 6-35.
Salary: from US$1,400 per month.
Facilities/Support: assistance with accommodation. In-house training given.
Recruitment: through newspaper adverts and contact with foreign universities and colleges. Interviews essential and held in UK/US.

PAGODA LANGUAGE INSTITUTE
56-6 2nd Street, Jong-Ro, Seoul. Tel: (2) 277-8257/274-4000.
Number of teachers: 20.
Preference of nationality: US.
Qualifications: TESL major or related fields.
Conditions of employment: 1 year renewable contracts. 4-6 hours work per day. All pupils are adults.

Salary: negotiable.
Facilities/Support: assistance with accommodation. Training given.
Recruitment: adverts in the *TESOL Placement Bulletin*. Interviews are essential and phone interviews are possible.

SHIM-BUN LANGUAGE INSTITUTION
416-5 Chang Jun 3-Dong, Kum Jung-Gu, Pusan 609-393. Tel: (51) 56-2928/513-4960.
Number of teachers: 3.
Preference of nationality: US.
Qualifications: at least 2 years of further education.
Conditions of employment: 1 year contracts. 6 hours work per day (2 hours morning, 4 hours evening). Pupils aged 17-45, 90% in early 20's.
Salary: from US$1,200 per month.
Facilities/Support: assistance given finding accommodation. Training provided.
Recruitment: through adverts in US. Interviews essential, but may be carried out over the phone.

SOGANG INSTITUTE FOR ENGLISH AS AN INTERNATIONAL LANGUAGE
Sogang University, CPO Box 1142, Seoul 100-611 Tel: (2) 714-5103/5104.
Number of teachers: 20+.
Preference of nationality: none.
Qualifications: MA and TEFL experience with adults preferred, but business or other experience also desirable.
Conditions of employment: 1 year contracts. 20 50-minute lessons per week. All pupils are college graduates.
Salary: approximately US$20,000 per year (plus overtime).
Facilities/Support: small loans for rental deposits available. Training given.
Recruitment: word of mouth and through newspaper adverts and TESOL conferences. Interviews are usually required and can sometimes be held abroad.

YOIDO FOREIGN LANGUAGES INSTITUTE
54 Yoido-dong, Young-dung-po-ku, Seoul. Tel: (2) 783-3804.
Number of teachers: 5.
Preference of nationality: US, Australia.
Qualifications: teaching experience.
Conditions of employment: 1-2 year contracts. 6 hours work per day. Pupils aged 25-35.
Salary: reasonable rates, hourly for part-timers and monthly for full-time contracts.
Facilities/Support: no training given.
Recruitment: through newspaper adverts. Interviews held in US/Australia.

South Asia

In contrast to Thailand and Indonesia with their strong demand for native-speaker English teachers, other countries between Pakistan and the Philippines (with a few exceptions) are not easy places in which to find work as an English teacher. The reasons for this vary. In former colonies of Britain, principally the Indian subcontinent, English is the medium of education and many members of the educated classes speak English virtually as a first language. There is therefore little call for foreign native speakers. Poverty is another reason why there is a very small market for expatriate teachers. Even if local Indians, Pakistanis, etc. (who had not had the benefit of an elitist education) wanted to have English conversation classes, few could afford them. Few Westerners could manage on the wages earned by ordinary teachers in India, Nepal, Sri Lanka and Pakistan. The small number who do teach in this region (for example a few *GAP* participants teach English, cricket, etc. in Indian schools and a few people teach English to Tibetan refugees) do so on a voluntary basis, or else they are part of a foreign-funded project such as the 3 opportunities listed in the Directory for Pakistan.

Visas can also be a problem since these countries understandably want to control the number of long-stay foreigners; for example, with very few exceptions, the Nepali government does not allow foreigners to stay for more than 3 months in any 12, so even the British Council depends mostly on permanently resident English speakers who are married to Nepalis.

The countries in which there is demand are the more wealthy nations of South Asia, namely Singapore, Malaysia and Brunei. The future may bring increased opportunities. For example some Sri Lankan politicians are in favour of giving English an enormous boost in order to defuse the destructive animosity between the Tamil and Sinhala languages. After decades of isolationism, Burma is now cautiously moving towards the West and may in time want to encourage more English teaching. Even Bhutan has opened a primary school which has been recruiting teachers whose mother tongue is English (though not EFL teachers). Finally, VSO has been energetically recruiting 2-year volunteers for specialized ELT projects in Laos and Cambodia.

MALAYSIA SINGAPORE

During the 1980s the Malaysian government implemented an ambitious and expensive programme. Foreign teachers are paid expatriate salaries to teach pre-university and university students in English and other subjects. Some students do 2 years of their degree in Malaysia and then complete their course abroad, especially at cooperating universities in the US. A great many Malaysian students also go to Australia. Intensive English language tuition is of course an essential part of these students' training. As Malaysia's economy declined towards the end of the decade, pressure was put on the Ministry of Education to try to spend less and to hire native-speaker teachers on a local basis, so anyone with a serious EFL profile might have success approaching the universities such as the International Islamic University and Institute Teknologi Mara in Kuala Lumpur. The Malaysian Ministry of Education (Pusat Bandar Damansara, Blok J, 50604 Kuala Lumpur) should be able to advise. Interested Britons should contact the *Centre for British Teachers* who have been recruiting teachers for Malaysia since 1979 and who now also supply RSA Certificate holders to the National Islamic University.

The British Council can send a list of 6 language schools in 6 Malaysian cities plus its own English teaching centres in Kuala Lumpur and Penang, though there are far more than this in the country. The market is in fact expanding as evidenced by the fact that *ELS International* opened their newest centre in Kuala Lumpur at the end of 1990, for which they were advertising for ESL teachers in the *TESOL Placement Bulletin.*

Wages are high by the standards of developing nations; for example ESP teaching could be rewarded with as much as 50 ringgits (£10) per hour. Obtaining a work permit requires the usual red tape of filling out forms, sending photos, medical certificates, etc. The Department of Education will have to approve your qualifications — Malaysia is not a promising destination for the unskilled or inexperienced — in order to satisfy the "Malaysianisation Secretariat".

One aspect of life in Malaysia which can be difficult to accept is that racial Malays are accorded special privileges over other citizens of Chinese, Indian or tribal origins. For example, places at the universities mentioned above are available exclusively to *bumiputeras* or *"bumis"*, which means "sons of the soil", i.e. ethnic Malays. Otherwise teachers normally suffer less from culture shock than they do in Thailand and Indonesia. Kuala Lumpur is a model of modernity and efficiency when compared to the neighbouring capitals of Jakarta and Bangkok.

Malaysia's tiny neighbour clinging to the tip of the Malay peninsula is a wealthy and Westernized city-state in which there is a considerable demand for qualified English teachers on minimum one-year contracts.

The Singapore Ministry of Education has very recently decided to upgrade the standard of spoken and written English at the secondary level and is recruiting English language and literature teachers through the Singapore High Commission in London (16 Kinnerton Street, London SW1X 8ES; tel: 071-235 4562). Candidates must have "suitable teaching qualifications" and at least 5 years experience. The 3-year contracts (to start June/July 1991) include everything from tax-free annual bonuses to education allowances for dependent children, plus a salary of up to S$5,000 a month.

International House, ILS and inlingua all have schools in Singapore:

Advanced Training Techniques (IH affiliate), 7th & 8th Floors, Tanglin Shopping Centre, Tanglin Road, Singapore 1024. Tel: 235-5222.

Language Services (ILS affiliate), 122 Middle Road, 03-01 Midlink Plaza, Singapore 0718. Tel: 338-5415. Occasionally advertise in the *TES* offering return air fares, initial help with accommodation and a salary of £9,000-£12,000.

inlingua, 424-430 The Cuppage Centre, Cuppage Road, Singapore 0922. Tel: 737-6666.

The British Council provides a list of several other language school addresses including a camp for Vietnamese refugees which can occasionally make use of volunteer teachers. As in Japan and Taiwan, the YMCA in Singapore (1 Orchard Road; tel: 336-6000) hires English teachers on location. Check adverts in the *Straits Times.*

If you have been doing some extended travelling take care to spruce up your appearance; after 6 months of wandering around India, it may be next to impossible to project an image which will impress a sophisticated Singaporean language school owner.

Bryn Thomas taught for inlingua, but broke his contract half way through the first year:

This was the only contract I broke, but then so did many of the other teachers. It wasn't just the school but the place. Singapore may be a great place for a short shopping spree but unless you like living in a shopping mall, the place isn't much

After 6 months of wandering around India, it may be difficult to present the right image

fun for an extended visit and certainly not for a 1½ year contract, unless the pay is on a par with the money you can earn in the Middle East or Japan.
If shopping malls and a repressive regime (for example there are signs threatening to fine you if you fail to flush the loo or eat on the underground) leave you cold, Singapore is perhaps best avoided.

BRUNEI

Few people can locate Brunei on a map of the world, let alone anticipate that there is an enormous demand for English teachers there. This wealthy oil state on the north shore of Borneo, in which the Sultan famously donated a television to every household in his tiny kingdom, can afford an expensive educational system for its population of 227,000. The Ministry of Education is in the process of implementing a bilingual educational system which "ensures the sovereignty of the Malay language while at the same time recognizing the importance of the English language". There are at present 250 British teachers working in primary and secondary schools, all of whom are hired through the *Centre for British Teachers* on 2-year contracts.

The CBT requirements are stiff: secondary school EFL teachers must have a PGCE and a minimum of 5 years teaching experience including 2 years of TEFL. Primary school EFL teachers must have a BEd (or a degree and PGCE) and a minimum of 2 years teaching experience, or alternatively a Cert. Ed., minimum of 5 years experience and an RSA Certificate (the latter will be funded by the Centre).

The terms of employment are generous in most respects, i.e. the job carries with it a tax-free salary of between £9,000 and £13,000 in addition to free air fares and free accommodation, plus other perks. One of the drawbacks is that the weekend consists of Friday and Sunday. Full details are readily available from the CBT.

LIST OF SCHOOLS

Malaysia

THE BANGSAR ENGLISH LANGUAGE CENTRE
3A Jalan Telawi Tiga, Bangsar Baru, 59100 Kuala Lumpur, Malaysia. Tel: (3) 255 2936/254 2408.
Number of teachers: 9.
Preference of nationality: UK, Australia, New Zealand, US.
Qualifications: minimum BA/BEd/teaching qualification; experience in TEFL preferred.
Conditions of employment: 1 year contracts. 15-20 h.p.w. mostly evenings. Pupils aged 10+.
Salary: 30-40 ringgits per hour.
Facilities/Support: accommodation easily found; no assistance given. No training available at the moment.
Recruitment: local adverts and local interviews essential.

THE ENGLISH LANGUAGE CENTRE
PO Box 253, 93704 Kuching, Sarawak, Malaysia. Tel: (82) 424126/426684.
Number of teachers: 5.
Preference of nationality: none.
Qualifications: RSA Dip./BEd/BA (English)/teaching experience.
Conditions of employment: 11 month renewable contracts (December-October), 20 contact h.p.w. with morning, afternoon and evening work. Pupils aged 6-60. Possibility of ESP work.
Salary: varies according to experience with a basic rate of 1,000 ringgits per month plus an 11% gratuity on completion of contract. ESP work pays 50 ringgits per hour.
Facilities/Support: assistance given with finding accommodation. Training provided.
Recruitment: through local adverts. Interviews essential and are held in UK between May-September.

IPOH LANGUAGE TRAINING INSTITUTE
6 Jalan Tambun, 30350 Ipoh, Perak, Malaysia. Tel: (5) 503067. Fax: 505489.

Number of teachers: 4.
Preference of nationality: none.
Qualifications: BA with solid TEFL experience.
Conditions of employment: 1 year renewable contracts. Hours of work 3-9.15pm weekdays. Pupils range in age from 4-60.
Salary: £500 per month.
Facilities/Support: assistance given with accommodation and limited training provided.
Recruitment: locally through contacts and adverts. Interviews essential.

Nepal

AMERICAN LANGUAGE INSTITUTE (USIS)
GPO Box 58, Kathmandu, Nepal. Tel: (1) 416745.
Number of teachers: 20.
Preference of nationality: US.
Qualifications: minimum BA, TEFL/TESL degree preferred.
Conditions of employment: 1 year contracts. Hours of work 7.20-11am or 3-6.30pm. Pupils aged 16-35.
Salary: US$3.50 per hour is the average.
Facilities/Support: no assistance with accommodation. Training given.
Recruitment: local interviews essential.

Pakistan

CENTER FOR INTENSIVE ENGLISH LANGUAGE STUDIES
US Agency for International Development, US Embassy, PO Box 1973, Islamabad, Pakistan. Tel: (51) 819511.
Number of teachers: 10.
Preference of nationality: US.
Qualifications: MA in Applied Linguistics or TEFL, minimum 2 years teaching experience. Overseas and EAP experience preferred.
Conditions of employment: 1 year contracts offered after 3 month trial period. 40 h.p.w. of which 20 are contact hours. The average age of pupils is 32, 98% are male.
Salary: approximately US$98 per day.
Facilities/Support: accommodation provided for short-term staff over the summer, and a food allowance given. Training is available.
Recruitment: mostly local recruitment but interviews possible in US.
US contact: Experiment in International Living, 1411 K Street NW, Suite 1100, Washington, DC 20005.

INTERNATIONAL RESCUE COMMITTEE
GPO Box 504, Peshawar, Pakistan. Tel: (521) 41845. Fax: 42283.
Number of teachers: 3-4.
Preference of nationality: none.
Qualifications: varies; sometimes need people with technical experience for curriculum development.
Conditions of employment: 6 month-1 year contracts. 8 hours per day between 8am-4pm. Pupils aged 15+ but mostly in 30's and 40's.

Salary: volunteers are paid US$300 per month and staff paid US$1,000 per month.
Facilities/Support: free accommodation provided. Training given.
Recruitment: local recruitment and IRC in New York. Interviews are usually carried out via the telephone.
US contact: International Rescue Committee, Inc., Overseas Programs, 386 Park Avenue South, New York, NY 10016.

TIPAN
NWFP Agricultural University, Peshawar, Pakistan. Tel: (521) 44490.
Number of teachers: 2-4.
Preference of nationality: US, UK only.
Qualifications: BA, TEFL qualification, at least 2 years teaching experience in a developing country.
Conditions of employment: 1 year contract offered after 3 month trial period. Part-time staff work 4 hours per day of which 2 are contact hours and full-time staff 8 hours per day of which 4 are contact hours. Pupils are aged between 26-40 and are all male.
Salary: US$10 per hour.
Facilities/Support: assistance with accommodation. No training given.
Recruitment: mostly local recruitment. Interviews are not essential but c.v. and references required.

Taiwan

The teaching scene in Taiwan is a dream for world travellers looking for a financial refuelling station, and a nightmare for serious EFL teachers. It is estimated that well over three-quarters of native speaker teachers in Taiwan have no training or experience whatsoever. Yet these teachers manage to save a staggering $3,000-$4,000 in 3 or 4 months. There are hundreds of private language institutes struggling to supply a seemingly insatiable demand for English conversation and English tuition. Few of these are run by educationalists. Rather they are run by businessmen looking for profit. Taiwan is a country in which free market capitalism has been allowed to run riot.

According to the operators of language schools *(buhsibans)*, Taiwanese consumers of English have a clear preference for the American accent because of strong trading and cultural links between Taiwan and the US. But the Taiwanese are increasingly looking towards Europe and this may change. Women are often preferred by the mothers of female pupils and also for teaching young children, since they are thought to be more patient and gentle. However, most language teaching establishments are so short of teachers that they are willing to accept Britons, Australians, etc. of any sex. It is not uncommon for a cowboy language school operator to hire a Swede or a German as a "native speaker" of English, in preference to a non-white Brit or an American with Asian features. (Taiwan is not a country strong on equal opportunity legislation.) The more disreputable schools might ask you to pretend to your pupils that you are American, a fiction which is virtually impossible to maintain once the students begin to ask where you are from, which university you went to, etc. Since very few Chinese can distinguish among accents in any case and they all learn to speak English with a pronounced Chinese accent no matter who teaches them, this requirement seems a little superfluous. Indeed non-American teachers usually find that once they confess their true country of origin, their pupils don't mind in the slightest.

Although almost anyone who wants to teach English in Taiwan can find some kind of job, the situation is not quite as rosy as it was in the late 1980s. The boom in the Taiwanese economy appears to be over, so money is not flowing quite as freely as it was. There has also been a large influx of foreigners, partly from mainland China after the events of June 1989 and partly as a result of Taiwan's spreading reputation as a paradise for teacher-travellers. So there is competition for the decent jobs; and salaries are not as high as they were. Still, the turnover of teachers is very high with dozens leaving the island every week, and passing on their pupils and teaching hours to newcomers. Few stay for more than 6 months (partly for tax reasons as set out below) and schools willingly put up with the transience of their teachers.

Old Taiwan hands identify four groups of teacher: the world travellers stopping for a few months to boost their travel funds, the relatively small number of serious EFL teachers, foreigners (mainly American) who go to Taiwan to study Chinese and do occasional English teaching to earn spending money, and finally the social misfits and men funding their vices. According to one language school director, the island "swims in degenerate Americana". This profile applies principally to the capital Taipei (population 5 million) though there are teaching opportunities both at *buhsibans* and privately in the other major cities of Taiwan, viz. Taichung, Tainan and Kaohsiung.

Prospects for Teachers

In 1990 travellers were still walking into jobs the day after arriving at Taipei International Airport. However it is more usual to have to spend a couple of weeks chasing jobs and gradually building up hours. This settling-in period is not nearly as traumatic nor as expensive as it is in Japan, though Taiwan is the second most expensive country in Asia outside Japan. The cost of living can be something of a shock if you have been travelling in Asia, as David and Greeba Hughes discovered:

> We have been here just over 3 weeks and have established around 30 hours teaching per week each. We have found everything very expensive. For example the cheapest dormitory accommodation is £3.50+ and eating out, even from street vendors, will cost about £1. Prices may sound OK by European standards, but if you have just come through India and Thailand and don't have any money, they're tough. There is work (and plenty of it) but bring every spare penny, rupee, cent and kopek to spend while you're looking for it.

The longer you stay, the more chance you will have of moving to the better paid more reputable jobs. Helen Welch arrived at Chinese New Year, a bad time to be looking for teaching work, and by the end of the year was assistant director of JJ-ELS, then one of the most prestigious schools in Taipei.

A high proportion of schools in Taiwan specialize in teaching young children, so anyone who is good with primary age children, i.e. likes to sing songs, play games and comfort little ones who miss their mums, will have no problem finding work. They generally provide such detailed lesson plans that no time is spent on preparation, which appeals to people who aren't really interested in teaching.

FIXING UP A JOB
In Advance

Almost no hiring takes place outside Taiwan, though schools would probably be very willing to offer contracts to TEFL-trained teachers who approached them. The only teaching job advertised in the British educational press in the first half of 1990 was placed by the Taiwan Trade Centre (Centric House, 391 The Strand, London WC2R 0LT). Serious teachers might enquire about possible future vacancies.

There can't be a British Council office in Taipei because there is already one in China (i.e. Beijing). The British Council manqué is the Anglo-Taiwan Education Centre, 9th Floor, Jen Ai Road, Sec.2, Taipei (tel: 02 322 4242) which won't be interested in helping anyone who is not a serious teacher.

The Free Chinese Centre (4th Floor, Dorland House, 14-16 Regent Street, London SW1Y 4PH; tel: 071-930 5767), which is Taiwan's diplomatic representative in the UK, does not handle recruitment, though it can advise on visas and send a list of the 3 English medium schools in Taipei. There is no British Council nor American Bi-National Centre in Taiwan. There is a British Council *Survey of English Langage Teaching and Learning in Taiwan,* though it is hardly worth investing £20 for the list of only 23 language school addresses.

Because of the strong bias in favour of American English, there are several addresses in the US which will be of interest to unqualified Americans wanting to fix up a job in advance. The largest language school for children in Taiwan, *Hess Language School,* employs some 300 teachers in various locations. The founder Donald Hess lives in the US and can send instructions on applying and further information (see page 282).

It is reassuring to know that not everyone who teaches in Taiwan is in it for the money. The YMCA of the USA arranges for about 30 American volunteers to teach for a year from July or October. Further details of this cultural exchange are available from the YMCA's International Office for Asia, 909 4th Avenue, Seattle, WA 98104.

On the Spot

The vast majority of people wait until they are in Taiwan before approaching potential employers. The best time is at the beginning of summer at the end of the school year, when Chinese parents enrol their offspring in English language summer schools. Late August is another peak time for hiring, though there are openings year-round.

By far the best way to find work is by word-of-mouth. Foreign teachers may be in a position not only to offer advice but actual hours if they need a deputy for some reason. The best places to meet these people are at the many budget hostels of Taipei, which Lee Coleman (who saved $4,800 in 3 months) describes as "cheerful and friendly grot-holes." Head for Taipei Hostel (6th Floor, 11 Lane 5, Linsen N. Road), Happy Family Hostel (3rd Floor, 2-2 Lane, Chung Shan N. Road), Amigo Hostel (4th Floor, 286 Chilin Road), Formosa Hostel (3rd Floor, 16 Lane 20, Chung Shan N. Road) or the Madonna Hotel (Chung Hsiao W. Road, Sec. 1 #41, 6F).

Some expat bars which might serve the same purpose of putting you in touch with teachers are Herbies, Roxy I-4, and Rick's American Café, which are on

Hoping E. Road near the university. Other towns have pubs frequented by foreigners such as DJ's, Dirty Roger's and Mad Dog in Tainan.

Since almost nothing in Taiwan is regulated, there is no association of recognized language schools. In fact it is impossible to get a list of language schools; there is no English language Yellow Pages. That is why word-of-mouth is so important. Always check the Positions Vacant column of the English language *China Post* and *The China News* where a number of language schools regularly advertise for teachers. A typical advert might read:

> *Just arrived! Don't speak any Chinese! No teaching experience! That's the kind of teachers we want. Call (02) 754 8406.*

There is a disproportionate number of advertisers outside Taipei, which reflects the relative shortage of native speakers who venture outside the capital.

One of the most regular advertisers is YES English Institute which hire about 5 new teachers every week. Their address is Room 2, 10th Floor, 213 Fu Hsin S. Road, Taipei; tel: 751-0259/773-1296. They operate as a home-study institute, i.e. teachers are sent out to give lessons in the clients' homes. David Hughes enjoyed this system of teaching on the whole:

> *Pupils with more advanced English mainly want a chat, either formal or informal. This is usually great as you get to become friends, make a social call and you get paid. Some are not so great — parents desperate for their children to excel at school and who want you to push their kid excessively. Home study has many advantages: you build a relationship with your students and they feed and water you, take you on trips and look after you. They often have useful contacts and will set up further private tuition.*

Spruce up your sock collection

Beware of agents who hire teachers for clients and take 20% of the first month's salary. Also don't count on too much spontaneous hospitality. According to Helen Welch, who has lived in Taipei for several years, "with any favour given in this country, there is a pay-back system; anything done under the guise of hospitality is done for a reason." Although not always the case, school-based teachers at the more respectable schools like JJ-ELS and ELS International tend to be more serious teachers.

Once you have collected some phone numbers from the *China Post,* various notice boards (especially the one at Taiwan Normal University) and other foreigners, it is a matter of persuading a school to hire you. First make contact by telephone. The best telephones to use are at the new Taipei Railway Station and the Telegraph Office at the Northgate G.P.O. where there are private cubicles. Next you must present yourself in person to the schools. In order to get around Taipei you should spend NT$100 on the invaluable English language *Taipei Bus Guide* available from Caves Bookshop (corner of Chung Shan Road and Minsheng E. Road) or Lucky Book Store in the university. Take along any certificates or qualifications. Although these won't be asked for nor expected, they can only help your cause. And take the trouble to look presentable. David Hughes specifically recommends paying attention to your feet:

> *Bring plenty of socks/tights. You have to leave your shoes at the door of Chinese homes, and it's difficult to appear serious and composed with a toe poking through.*

Arranging to be elegantly stockinged may be easier than passing yourself off as an American wanting to stay in Taiwan for at least 18 months, but most new arrivals learn to be "economical with the truth" in order to get a toe-hold (sic) on the English teaching ladder.

Freelance Teaching

In a country where foreigners are sometimes approached in bars or on trains and asked to give English lessons, it is not hard to set up independently as an English tutor. A helpful hint for getting started is to have name cards printed up, calling yourself "English consultant". After having investigated teaching possibilities in several cities, Adam Hartley concluded that you could go anywhere on the island, muster some pupils and teach them in groups of 4 or more at a rate of NT$200 per person. Women should find this easier to set up than men. The main problem is finding appropriate premises: those grot-hole hostels are hardly appropriate. It is also possible to exchange English lessons for free accommodation.

Once you are established, other jobs in the English field may come your way such as correcting business faxes, transcribing lyrics from pop tapes or writing c.v.'s and letters of application for Taiwanese students hoping to study overseas.

REGULATIONS

Although the official literature states that working without a work permit is illegal, it is a very widespread practice. A handful of professional teachers on long-term contracts do get work visas (which entitle the holder to health insurance) but the vast majority work on a visitor's visa. This is easily obtained provided you have an onward or return ticket. If you are buying your ticket in Hong Kong and intend to sell the return half after arrival in Taiwan, it is better to buy an open return valid for one year (HK$1,600 rather than a cheaper 60-day ticket) due to possible problems at the airport.

The visitor's visa is valid for two months in the first instance and is renewable twice for two months each time. Many people have reported that the situation has tightened up, but if you follow the accepted procedures there should be no problem, though the second renewal is usually a little trickier than the first.

The most common reason for wanting to renew your visitor's visa is to pursue your studies of Chinese (or Tai-chi or whatever). If you have a certificate testifying that you have been attending classes for at least 10 hours a week, your extension should be straightforward, provided you can supplement it with some currency exchange receipts. Many people staying in Taiwan genuinely do want to learn Chinese and there are plenty of legitimate places offering courses, such as the Mandarin Training Center (162 Hoping E. Road, Sec. 1, Taipei, which incidentally has a useful notice board). Others do not want to study nor to pay for lessons, so they turn to "visa schools", which are in business simply to help foreigners extend their visas and may not even have any Chinese teachers on their payroll. It is easy to find out about these visa schools from the hostels or from adverts in the *China Post*. The standard fee for this service is NT$1,500, though some advertise cheaper prices. Foreigners who have tried to bypass this racket and have gone to the police to apply for an extension in the approved manner have been known to fail.

The other requirement for visa extensions is proof of payment of tax. If you stay for 90 days, you must clarify your tax position at the tax office (547 Chung Hsiao E. Road, Sec. 4: tel: 763-1313 ext. 240-245). The flat rate of tax in Taiwan is 20%, all but 6% of which can be reclaimed if you stay in Taiwan for six months of the tax year which runs from January 1st to December 31st. To prevent you from repeating this annually, you are now asked to sign a statement that you will not return to work in Taiwan for 5 years before the rebate will be given. Many schools will deduct tax and issue a certificate at the request of the teacher and not otherwise. Other schools are very obliging and will declare far fewer hours than have actually been worked in order to reduce the tax bill. If your employer seems cooperative, you might make tactful enquiries in this direction.

One other possibility involves proof of currency transactions. The authorities are happy to renew the visitor's visa of anyone who is self-supporting. To prove this, you would need plenty of currency exchange documents, probably at least US$700 per month. David Hughes invented his own scheme for getting around the tax but didn't have a chance to try it out before leaving the country. His plan involved taking his New Taiwanese dollar earnings to a black market money dealer (e.g. in the gold shops on Yen Ping N. and S. Road) and exchanging them for US currency. He would then exchange the US currency back into Taiwanese currency at a bank and show his certificate of exchange to the tax man. You would have to calculate whether the commission paid on the exchanges would be more or less than the tax bill.

When the second renewal comes to an end you must leave the country and apply for a new visa. Most go to Hong Kong which can even be visited on a day-trip. Reports from Hong Kong indicate that there has been a clampdown. For example applicants who claim that they want to continue their Chinese studies have been given a spot test in Mandarin which they will certainly fail if they have been enrolled in a phoney Chinese school. The Taiwanese embassy in Bangkok is reputedly more lenient than in Hong Kong, though it too will expect documentation to back up your claims. The government decided late in 1990 to make an AIDS test mandatory for foreigners wishing to renew their visas, which met with vehement protest.

CONDITIONS OF WORK

Despite a recent weakening of the New Taiwanese dollar (which stands at 47 to the pound sterling and 27 to the US dollar), wages for English teaching are among the highest in the world. The majority of schools pay NT$350-400 an hour, though people who teach in companies can earn up to NT$800. (All rates are pre-tax figures.) It is not difficult to fix up 40 hours a week and earn US$3,000 a month, though this would leave no time for relaxation or enjoyment. Rates outside Taipei (where the cost of living is lower) tend to be slightly higher due to the relative scarcity of teachers.

Despite the general atmosphere of unscrupulousness in many of the schools, treatment of teachers is usually fair and considerate. For example, there are few complaints of schools not paying their teachers the promised rate on time. A bad school may try to cheat you if you break contract or haven't been specific when you sign on the dotted line, but this is not common. Many schools are shambolic when it comes to timetabling their teachers' hours. In a profit-driven atmosphere, classes start and finish on demand and can be cancelled at short notice if the owner decides that there are too few pupils to make it economic. When you are starting a new job, ask your employer to be specific about the actual number of hours you will be given. This problem also afflicts teachers who pay house calls. It is very common for pupils to cancel at short notice and unless you have access to a phone, it is impossible for you to be notified. It is prudent to explain to students gently but forcefully, that they will be liable to pay in these circumstances; most will not object. You can even request one month's fees in advance.

The usual problems which bedevil TEFL teachers occur in Taiwan, such as split shifts, often ending at 10pm, and compulsory weekend work, especially if you are teaching children. Few schools provide much creative training or incentives to do a good job. Pupils will respond to teachers with bubbly personalities more than those with carefully designed lesson plans. Although Taiwanese students do not present the problems which mainland Chinese or Japanese students present, namely a crippling reluctance to speak, it can be difficult to overcome their initial shyness. But like the educational system of China and so many other countries, Taiwanese state schools rely heavily on rote learning, making it difficult to introduce a more communicative approach, especially at the beginner level.

Whereas some schools offer no guidance whatsoever, others leave almost nothing to the teacher. What is termed a "training programme" often consists of a paint-by-number teaching manual. Here is an extract from the Teacher's Book of the *Hess Language School*, a large chain of children's schools:

> *How to teach ABCs (e.g. the letter K): Review A-J . . . Using the flash cards, say "A — apple, B — boy, C — cat . . . J — jacket". The whole class repeats after the teacher. Then say, "A-B-C-D-E-F-G-H-I-J" and have the whole class repeat. Show the letter K flashcard. Say "K" having the whole class repeat it each time you say it. Say "K" 4 or 5 times.*

And so on. This certainly makes the inexperienced teacher's job easier but possibly also very boring.

Accommodation

Many transient teachers stay in the budget hostels for the duration of their stay. Some have double rooms which are a little more civilized than living in a dorm on a long-term basis (the latter costs about NT$3,000 a month). Flats are predictably expensive in central Taipei so many teachers choose to commute from the suburbs, where living conditions are more pleasant in any case. There are so many foreigners coming and going, and the locals are so friendly and helpful, that it is not too difficult to learn of flats becoming vacant. You will have to pay a month's rent in advance plus a further month's rent as a deposit; this bond or "key money" usually amounts to about £300. With the help of a Chinese colleague, David and Greeba Hughes rented a room in a karate school and above a Presbyterian church for NT$6,000 a month, which is about the cheapest available.

LEISURE TIME

Having described at length the ease with which remunerative teaching work can be found, it is now time for the bad news. Not a single visitor to Taipei, which is one of the most densely populated cities in the world, fails to complain of the pollution, second only to that of Mexico City. Not only is the air choked with the fumes and noise of a million motorized vehicles, but apparently chemicals have infiltrated the water table contaminating locally grown vegetables. It is really horrific.

The weather is another serious drawback. The typhoon season lasts from July to October bringing stormy wet weather and mouldy clothes. The heat and humidity at this time also verge on the unbearable.

Although many foreign teachers resort to using a motorbike to get around, the traffic is at best unpleasant and at worst life-endangering. Most of Taipei's streets are being dug up at present to build a long overdue underground, so perhaps when this is completed in five years or so, the traffic congestion will be lessened. In the meantime, it's worse. At least you can avoid sweltering in a traffic jam by taking an "air-con" city bus (which costs NT$10 instead of NT$8). Some teachers stay in hostels near the central station and commute to work in a satellite city where wages are higher than in Taipei (e.g. Tao Yuan and Chung Li).

Taipei is not the only city to suffer from pollution; Taichung and Kaohsiung are also bad. Even Tainan with a population of about 650,000 (about the size of Sheffield) has some pollution; 100 new cars are registered here every day adding to the problem. (This is a statistic which rather detracts from Tainan's appeal as the most historic city on the island with many old temples, etc.) Kaohsiung on the south-west coast is a large industrial city with a high crime rate but has the advantage of being near the popular resort of Kenting Beach. The geographical advantage of Taichung further north is proximity to the mountains as well as a good climate and cultural activities. David and Greeba Hughes were attracted to the idea of Kang-Shan near Kaohsiung in the south, which they describe as a "nice city, with a semi-tropical banana-belt climate and friendly people." Unfortunately the Gwoyeu Ryhbaw Kang-Shan Language Center couldn't offer them enough hours.

Leisure Time

Taipei has a 24-hour social scene which can seriously cut into your savings. Heavy drinking is commonplace. The serious saver will follow David Hughes' example and join the local library. For the truly homesick there are some English-style pubs with pool tables and darts boards. A rather less traditional entertainment called *karaoke* is unlikely to appeal to many Westerners, though it is extemely popular in Taiwan as well as in Japan where it was invented. *Karaoke* bars allow their customers to sing along to electronic accompaniment. A favourite refinement in Taiwan is to watch yourself performing on television (called KTV). Some prefer MTV (rooms with music videos for hire) or plain ordinary discos and cinemas.

LIST OF SCHOOLS

BUSINESS EXECUTIVE ENGLISH ASIA PACIFIC
Rm 78-08 World Trade Centre, Hsin Yi Rd, Section 5, Taipei. Tel: (2) 725-2573.
Number of teachers: 3-6.
Preference of nationality: Canada, US, England.
Qualifications: TESL/TEFL qualifications essential.
Conditions of employment: teachers usually have to stay for 6 months. Up to 37 h.p.w. instructing 10 week courses in companies. Pupils are all business people. Classes vary in size but average 6-8 per class. Some private teaching.
Salary: NT$800 per hour for qualified teachers.
Facilities/Support: no assistance with accommodation. No training given.
Recruitment: through newspaper adverts. Interviews not essential.

ELS INTERNATIONAL
59 Chungking South Road, Section 2, Taipei. Tel: (2) 321-9005.
Number of teachers: 150 (6 locations in Taipei plus one in Kaohsiung and Taichung).
Preference of nationality: none.
Qualifications: relevant teaching degrees/qualifications (if hired abroad).
Conditions of employment: 1 year contracts (if hired abroad). Morning and evening work. Pupils range in age from 16-60.
Salary: approximately £8 per hour.
Facilities/Support: assistance given with temporary accommodation. Training provided.
Recruitment: mainly through direct application/walk-ins.

GRAM ENGLISH INSTITUTE
7F 402 Tun Hwa South Road, Taipei. Tel: (2) 741-0970.
Number of teachers: 50-75.
Preference of nationality: US.
Qualifications; BA, experience preferred.
Conditions of employment: minimum 8 week contracts. Mostly evening and weekend work. Pupils range in age from children to adults.
Salary: US$16-18 per hour.
Facilities/Support: assistance given finding accommodation. Training provided.
Recruitment: through direct application. Local interviews essential.

HESS LANGUAGE SCHOOL
51 Ho Ping East Rd., Section 2, 3F Taipei. Tel: (2) 703-1118.
Number of teachers: 300 in 23 branches in 6 cities in Taiwan.
Preference of nationality: none.
Qualifications: BA, enthusiastic, lively and genuine liking for children.
Conditions of employment: 3 months or 1 year contracts. Hours of work 4-8pm Monday-Saturday. Pupils aged from 6-15.

Salary: NT$360 per hour (gross).
Facilities/Support: assistance with accommodation. Training provided.
Recruitment: through newspaper adverts and US office at 105 Lower Dix Av., Glenns Falls, NY 12804, US (tel: 518-793-6128, fax: 518-793-6183). Interviews essential and can be held in US at above address.

JJ-ELS
9th Floor, 33 Chung Hsiao West Road, Section 1, Taipei. Tel: (2) 361-9100.
Number of teachers: 15-25 (seasonal).
Preference of nationality: none but prefer UK, Canada, Australia.
Qualifications: BA preferred.
Conditions of employment: repeatable 2 month courses. 14-28 h.p.w. Pupils aged from 15-45, but 70% are college students.
Salary: approximately US$13-15 per hour.
Facilities/Support: assistance given with finding accommodation. Training provided.
Recruitment: through direct application and walk-ins. Local interviews essential.

OXFORD LANGUAGE COMPUTER INSTITUTE
8th Floor, 240 Chung Shan 1st Road, Kaohsiung. Tel: (7) 231-7065/281-2315.
Number of teachers: 20-25.
Qualifications: BA, some teaching experience.
Conditions of employment: 6 months contracts. 20 hours per month. Pupils aged from 20 upwards.
Salary: US$14 per hour.
Facilities/Support: some assistance with accommodation. No training given.
Recruitment: through adverts. Local interviews essential.

TAIPEI AMERICAN SCHOOL
800 Chung Shan North Rd., Section 6, Shihlin 11135, Taipei. Tel: (2) 873-9900.
Number of teachers: 28.
Preference of nationality: US.
Qualifications: at least MA in teaching-related subject, and 2 years experience in a school. US teacher certification preferred.
Conditions of employment: minimum 2 year contract. Hours of work 8am-3.30pm plus after-school activities. Pupils range in age from 5-18.
Salary: US$36,000 plus 7% (tax free) per year for MA with 5 years experience.
Facilities/Support: housing allowance of US$11,500 p.a. Staff development program provided.
Recuitment: interviews carried out in February of each year in US; also possible in UK.

Thailand

Thailand prides itself on being the only Asian nation never to have been under foreign domination. A newly arrived visitor confronted with McDonalds, Pizza

Huts and 7-11 stores might find this hard to believe. A huge influx of foreign (mainly American and Japanese) investment, commercial development and consumer goods has created a huge demand for English, the language of international business success. A knowledge of English is eagerly sought by almost all urban young people and, in the context of Thailand, "urban" is almost synonymous with "Bangkok", which is 5 times larger than its nearest rival Chiang Mai. It sometimes seems that the (unrealizable) ambition of most young Thais is to go to UCLA, and English lessons from a native speaker are perceived as essential to bringing them nearer their goal.

The economic boom has also been fuelled by a surge of tourism rivalled only by the recent "discovery" of Turkey. It is estimated that 3 million tourists now descend on Thailand every year, the majority of whom are English-speaking and want to be able to communicate with waiters, souvenir sellers, etc. in English. So the demand for English instruction among Thais is enormous and increasing.

"They seem to value games above grammar."

Prospects for Teachers

The many English teaching opportunities in Thailand seldom appeal to the serious career-minded EFL teacher. Almost no recruitment takes place outside Thailand. Even Thai universities and teachers' colleges, as well as private business colleges which all have EFL departments, depend on finding native-speaker teachers locally. No doubt most would prefer a highly qualified and experienced EFL teacher but the fact is that they can't afford one.

This means that there is a preponderance of teacher-travellers on the Thai teaching scene, earning just enough money from part-time teaching to fund a longer stay or subsequent travels. Thais are exuberant and fun-loving people and their ideas about education reflect this. They seem to value games above grammar, and an outgoing personality above a teaching certificate. Of course there is a nucleus of professional EFL teachers working at the most prestigious institutes in Bangkok (living in some splendour), but the majority of teachers and tutors teach on a casual basis without formal contracts. So anyone determined to teach in Thailand is guaranteed some opportunities, provided he or she is willing to go to Thailand to seek them out.

FIXING UP A JOB

In Advance

The British Council has its own institutes in Bangkok and Chiang Mai; with three teachers the latter is the smallest of all the Council's Direct Teaching Operations. A small number of qualified teachers is recruited through London on 2-year renewable contracts. A local tax-free salary is paid together with air fare, medical insurance and housing allowance. In addition a few highly qualified advisors are required for ODA-funded projects. *VSO* hires language teachers on 2-year contracts.

As mentioned, job vacancies in other Thai language institutes are almost never publicized abroad, apart from *EEC* which does advertise in the *Guardian* and *TES* in order to fill its 120 vacancies in 10 branches. The only other exception spotted during the research for this book was for *Elite Language School*.

American readers should note that *AFS* International Teachers Programs and *WorldTeach* (see Introduction) recruit voluntary teachers for Thailand, and *ELS International* of California have a school in Bangkok which recruits locally as well as in the US (see entry below).

On the Spot

Finding a list of language schools to approach on spec should present no difficulties. The British Council has a list of private and public universities, institutes, teachers' colleges and international schools throughout the country which have English departments and therefore possible openings for a native speaker. The British Council list of private language schools is far from exhaustive with just five schools listed. They don't want to be seen to be endorsing institutions in what they describe as a "volatile ELT market".

The Bangkok Yellow Pages include about 40 addresses and are used by many speculative job-seekers. One such enterprising traveller was Laurence Koe whose initial contact by telephone with a selection of schools resulted in some degree of interest from all of them. He found that travelling around this city of 6 million was so time-consuming that he could visit only a couple of schools a day, and so plotted his interview strategy on a city map before making appointments. Within a few days he had secured work with *EEC* which involved some house calls and therefore plenty of time taken up in travelling; but he enjoyed the social contact with his pupils.

Another possible source of job vacancies is the English language press, viz.

the *Nation* and the *Bangkok Post*. Even Thai papers, 95% of which are in Thai, occasionally carry adverts in English for English teachers. Language institutes seem to hire teachers all year round, though there are more vacancies in June and November, since the academic year runs from June/July to March.

It may not be necessary even to do this much research to discover the schools with vacancies. Many of the so-called back street language schools (more likely to be on a main street, above a shop or restaurant) look to the cheap hotels of Banglamphu, the favourite haunt of Western travellers in the northwest of Bangkok. The noisy Khao San Road is lined with budget accommodation, many with notice boards offering teaching work or with other foreigners (known as *farangs*) well acquainted with the possibilities. They will also be able to warn you of the dubious schools which are known to exploit their teachers. There is such a high turnover of staff at many schools that there are bound to be vacancies somewhere for a new arrival who takes the trouble to present a professional image. As well as dressing smartly for an interview, try to project a relaxed and easy-going image.

There are of course far fewer opportunities outside Bangkok, though language schools and institutes of higher education around the country do hire *farangs*. For a job in a university you will probably have to show a degree or teaching certificate, neither of which will be scrutinized very carefully. The best places are Chiang Mai, the popular tourist destination in the north (where there will be a certain amount of competition from other travellers) and in the booming industrial city of Hat Yai in the south (where there will be none). In Chiang Mai the schools to try (as recommended by Steven Hendry) are INLC, the YMCA (as in Bangkok) and the Conversation Club opposite the Sri Tokyo Hotel. Chiang Mai University also hires native speakers with a BA to work for a semester (June to the end of September or October to late February). They guarantee a minimum of about 10 hours a week and pay B100 per hour.

If you find a town which suits and you decide to stay for a while, ask the family who runs your guest house about the local teaching opportunities. As an example, the Volunteer English School in the town of Sukhothai (the old Thai capital half way between Bangkok and Chiang Mai) recruits teachers through guest houses to teach evening classes at the local high school.

Freelance

Working as a self-employed private tutor is more lucrative but hard to set up until you have been settled in one place for a while and found out how to tap into the local elite community. Steven Hendry, a long-time travelling Scot who emerged from a Thai monastery in mid-1990 after a 2-year stint as a Buddhist monk, describes the steps to take to become a teacher:

> Be in town for at least a few months and get access to a telephone. Make up a little advertisement (half Thai, half English), get it produced properly and plaster it all over town as quickly as possible in universities, colleges, coffee shops, etc. It is definitely possible to get enough work in Chiang Mai and Bangkok to support yourself. I am teaching at present in Chiang Mai one hour per day at B130 (£3) which covers my day's expenses.

Placing an advert for private pupils in the *Nation*, the *Bangkok Post* or the US Consulate's monthly newsletter, *About Chiang Mai*, could also attract potential language-learners.

"The following persons will not be allowed entry: hippies, anyone wearing a headband, waistcoat or silk shorts, anyone barechested or not wearing undergarments."

REGULATIONS

All but the serious long-stay teachers in Thailand work on a tourist visa. Officially a work permit is required, but the authorities seem willing to turn a blind eye to transgressors, taking the view that, whatever the legalities, those who advance the cause of English are doing the nation a favour. In such a climate, governments might be expected to make work permits relatively available, but this is not the case in Thailand. Universities and established language schools may be willing to apply on your behalf provided you undertake to stay for at least two years and can provide evidence that you are highly qualified. According to the Berlitz School in Bangkok, it is necessary to pass a grade VI exam in the Thai language before filing an application with the Labour Department is permitted, which may account for the relative scarcity of work permits.

Tourist visas should be applied for in your home country and are valid for 60 days. Two one-month extensions are usually allowed though you may have to prove your solvency. Many teachers and travellers choose to nip over the Malaysian border to Penang where a new tourist visa can quickly and easily be obtained from the Thai Consulate. You might consider applying for a non-immigrant visa which is valid for 90 days.

As throughout Asia, it is a good idea to look neat and respectable when entering Thailand, especially if you intend to make a habit of it. Those entering from Malaysia should keep an eye open for the sign which reads, "The following persons will not be allowed entry: hippies, anyone wearing a headband, a waistcoat or silk shorts, anyone barechested, or anyone not wearing undergarments." In fact Thai border formalities are usually friendly and relaxed.

Anyone who stays in Thailand for more than 90 days in any one calendar year is supposed to obtain a tax clearance certificate from the Immigration Office (Soi Suanplu, Sathon Tai Road, Bangkok) before leaving the country. If you have stayed in Thailand more than six months it will be assumed that you are liable for some tax, though how this is assessed is hard to gauge.

CONDITIONS OF WORK

In a country where teaching jobs are so easy to come by, there has to be a catch. In Thailand, the wages for *farang* teachers are uniformly low. The basic hourly rate in Bangkok is 130 baht with a few schools paying less, though some promise considerably more, up to B350 (£7). If home visits are required — and hence a lot of time spent travelling — the rate should be higher than B130. Rates outside Bangkok are less, for example B80 (£1.50-£2) is fairly standard in Chiang Mai. (As a point of comparison, Thai teachers with a university degree earn B3,500 per month.) The handful of schools which pay wages at the top end of the spectrum have long waiting lists of hopeful teachers.

Some schools may offer advice but few provide or subsidize accommodation, so many teachers become long-term residents in budget hostels. If you stick at teaching, you may be able to find a suitable flat, though Bangkok rents have soared in the past two years. The English Language Officer at the British Council estimates that a gross salary of B20,000 (£465) per month will be required by an expatriate to live comfortably without the support that Thais have from family which is far more than most schools pay their full-time teachers. Again there is a large discrepancy between the expectations of the career teacher and those of a teacher traveller.

Before accepting a job, find out what teaching materials are in use, since some re hopeless, and will make life difficult. In class a show of anger will soon se the students' respect since the Thais go to great lengths to avoid showing nger.

EISURE TIME

It has to be said that Bangkok may be an exciting and lively city but it is not eautiful. It has very few parks, bad traffic congestion and polluted air. There also a great deal of what some might consider moral pollution, and there is certain element of the teaching fraternity in Bangkok who are there primarily r the easy availability of sex in the notorious Patpong district (despite the fact at there is a veritable AIDS crisis in Thailand). Although there are plenty of ight clubs and restaurants in Bangkok, there is a dearth of dance and film, and so of sports clubs.

Fortunately for teachers earning a low wage, the more innocent pleasures of hailand come cheap. Perhaps its greatest asset is completely free: its smiling, ourteous and warm-hearted people who are always willing to befriend *farangs*. iving expenses are not high. Tasty food such as grilled bananas and roast chicken egs can be bought from street stalls for as little as B10 and more substantial nd exciting meals exploiting the marvellous fresh fish and fruit cost no more nan B50. With a guest house room also costing about B50, there is no reason vhy even part-time teachers should not be able to afford to travel round the ountry, visiting jungle attractions like Kanchanaburi (where the Bridge over 1 River Kwai is located) and the islands like Koh Samui and Koh Phangan where ife is slow and the beaches are wonderful. Bangkok is also an important hub or travellers and cheap tickets are available to India, etc.

Richard Davies met a teacher-traveller whose experiences filled him with envy:

I met a Scottish guy teaching in Thailand. He got work with no problems and although the wages were drastically low, his lifestyle was paradise. A palm beach hut, children bringing him presents. His words were, "The best days of my life".

LIST OF SCHOOLS

AMERICAN UNIVERSITY LANGUAGE CENTER
179 Rajadamri Road, Bangkok 10500. Tel: (2) 252 8170.
Also branch in Chiang Mai, although vacancies here are rare.
Number of teachers: 90.
Preference of nationality: US, UK, Australia, South Africa, New Zealand; American accent preferred.
Qualifications: BA in language, social science or the humanities.
Conditions of employment: standard teaching stint is 6 weeks. 4-5 hours per day between 7am-9pm. Pupils aged 16 and above.
Salary: US$6-8 per hour.
Facilities/Support: participation in pre-service training session (20 hours) is required before teaching hours are assigned.
Recruitment: off the street.

BERLITZ
3 N. Satorn Road, Bangkok 10500. Tel: (2) 235 3846/235 3853. Fax: 238 5358.

Number of teachers: 15-20.
Preference of nationality: US.
Qualifications: BA or educated native speaker.
Conditions of employment: hours between 7am-9.15pm. No minimum period of work specified. Pupils aged from 11 years. Private tutoring on the side absolutely forbidden.
Facilities/Support: training provided (Berlitz method).
Recruitment: local adverts and local interviews, plus word of mouth.

ECC (THAILAND)
430/19-20 Chula 64, Siam Square, Bangkok 10330. Tel: 255 1856/7/8/9. Fax: 254 2243.
Number of teachers: 120 (normally have at least 2 vacancies each month).
Preference of nationality: none (but advertise in UK).
Qualifications: RSA Cert. plus 6 months experience.
Conditions of employment: contract length 6 months-1 year. Teaching hours 10am-12pm; 2-4pm; 5.30-7pm; 7-8pm. Pupils aged 9-30.
Salary: from B8,000 per month.
Facilities/Support: assistance given with finding accommodation. Bi-monthly workshops held. Plan to begin teaching RSA Cert. course this year.
Recruitment: adverts in *Guardian* and *TES*. Interviews not essential.

ELITE LANGUAGE SCHOOL
2nd Floor, Kongboonma Building, 699 Silom Rd., 10500 Bangkok. Tel: (2) 233 6620/1. Fax: 237 1997.
Number of teachers: 15.
Preference of nationality: 15.
Qualifications: BA, RSA Cert. (or equivalent), 2 years experience.
Conditions of employment: 1 year contracts. 25 h.p.w. Mostly evening work. School is open 7 days a week. Pupils aged 16+.
Salary: B15-25,000 per month.
Facilities/Support: assistance given finding accommodation. Monthly seminars held.
Recruitment: locally and through adverts in *Guardian*. Interviews not always necessary but can be held in UK.

ELS INTERNATIONAL (THAILAND)
419/3 Rajavithee Road, Phayathai, Opposite Children's Hospital, Bangkok 10400. Tel: (2) 245 8953/246 0426.
Number of teachers: 15.
Preference of nationality: none.
Qualifications: BA plus 1 year's experience.
Conditions of employment: 1 year contracts. Hours of teaching 8.30am-5pm. Pupils aged 20-40.
Salary: from B15,000 per month.
Facilities/Support: some training provided.
Recruitment: local adverts. Local interviews essential.

THE ENGLISH LANGUAGE SCHOOL
26/3, 26/9 Chomphol Lane, Lardprao Lane 15, Bangkok 10900. Tel: (2) 511 0439/511 3549.

Number of teachers: 8.
Preference of nationality: UK.
Qualifications: BA in relevant field or teaching qualification. TEFL qualification preferred and 1 year's experience. Should be active and adaptable with clear diction.
Conditions of employment: minimum period of work 6 months. Evening and weekend work essential. Pupils aged 10-70.
Salary: B150-200 per hour.
Facilities/Support: assistance given with accommodation. Training provided.
Recruitment: through local adverts. Local interviews essential.

INLINGUA SCHOOL OF LANGUAGES
7th Floor, Central Chidlom Tower, 22 Ploenchit Road, Pathumwan, Bangkok 10330. Tel: (2) 254 7028/29/30. Fax: 254 7098. 10 branches in Bangkok (related to ECC).
Qualifications: RSA Cert./Dip. plus 1 year's experience. Business experience helpful, since emphasis is on business English.
Conditions of employment: 1 year contracts. 25 h.p.w. Pupils of all ages. School also teaches French, German, etc.
Salary: average B12,000-20,000 per month.
Facilities/Support: assistance given with accommodation. Bi-monthly workshops held for teachers.
Recruitment: word of mouth.

LCC LANGUAGE INSTITUTE
8/64-67 Ratchadapisek-Lardprao Road, Bangkhaen, Bangkok 10900.
Number of teachers: 10.
Preference of nationality: UK, US, Canada, New Zealand, Australia.
Qualifications: BA, TEFL Cert. and experience.
Conditions of employment: preferred minimum length of stay 6 months. Hours of work between 9am-9pm. Pupils aged from 5 years. School also teaches French, German, etc.
Salary: B110-150 per hour.
Facilities/Support: help with accommodation. Wide range of course materials plus audio and video equipment. Some training provided.
Recruitment: local adverts and notices in Bangkok guest houses. Local interviews essential.

TCD COMPANY
c/o John Moriarty, 28 Suhkumvit Soi 24, Bangkok 10110. Tel: (2) 258 7036.
Number of teachers: 30.
Preference of nationality: UK, US.
Qualifications: TEFL/TESL training preferred, plus as much experience as possible. Preferably aged less than 38.
Conditions of employment: no minimum length of stay. Hours of work between 3.30-8pm. Pupils aged 6-60.
Salary: B200-350 per hour.
Facilities/Support: school provides list of cheap housing. Training given.
Recruitment: local adverts and word of mouth. Local interviews essential.

LATIN AMERICA

Spanning 75 degrees of latitude, the mammoth continent of South America together with the Caribbean islands and the eight countries of Central America, offer a surprising range of teaching opportunities. All but Brazil have a majority of Spanish speakers and, as in Spain itself, there is a great demand for English teaching, from dusty Mexican towns near the American border to Punta Arenas at the southern extremity of the continent, south of the Falkland Islands.

The countries of most interest to the travelling teacher are Portuguese-speaking Brazil, plus Chile, Colombia, Peru and Mexico. Certain patterns emerged during the research for this book, though sweeping generalizations are of limited value and will not apply to all countries and all situations. Inflation is so rampant that salaries and fees have to be adjusted at least monthly. New currencies have had to be introduced in Brazil and Bolivia — the latter knocked six noughts off its peso to create the Boliviano — while Peru now struggles with a currency worth 50,000 to the pound. This is symptomatic of economies in turmoil and quite often political crisis as well, all of which filter down to the situation for teachers.

Nevertheless the teaching of English as a foreign language flourishes amidst political and economic uncertainty, and demand increases in the various kinds of institution engaged in promoting English. Among the most important of these are Bi-National Centers, the American equivalent of the British Council. There are scores of these cultural centres in Latin America, including over 60 in Brazil and about 15 apiece in Argentina and Mexico. A complete list (under the rather worrying heading "American Republics" instead of "Latin America") is available from Room 304, US Information Agency, Washington, DC 20547. They are all engaged in the teaching of English, some on a very large scale; for example the *Haitian-American Institute* in Port-au-Prince employs 25 native teachers to cope with an average enrollment of 2,200 adult pupils. Although some funding comes from the US, these are all independent operations with their own individual teacher requirements. While some want a commitment to stay for two years, others are happy to take someone on for eight weeks. While some require only a good command of English (whatever the accent), others want teachers with an American BA in TEFL.

Britain also has cultural representatives in Latin America, especially in Brazil where there are about 30 *Sociedades Brasileiras de Cultura Inglesa* all teaching English. These national institutes represent the elite end of the market and normally require their teachers to have some specialized TEFL training and experience. Only a few recruit abroad so it is worth making local enquiries on arrival.

Several South American nations have a number of British-style bilingual schools. Although this book is not centrally concerned with English-medium schools, which are normally looking for teachers with a PGCE or full teacher accreditation, international schools in South America are mainly for local nationals (rather than expatriates) who want a bilingual Spanish-English education and have a very strong emphasis on English language teaching. Despite the prestige of these schools, some are willing to consider native speakers, with no formal TEFL training.

Finally there are private and commercial language institutes from International House (in Brazil and Argentina) through Berlitz (which is strongly represented in Latin America) to the cowboy operations where standards and wages will be extremely low. David Hewitt, a computer programmer from Yorkshire with no TEFL training or experience, was surprised not only to walk into a teaching job in Brazil but also to find himself giving lessons to the director of the school.

In whatever kind of school you teach, or if you just give occasional private lessons to contacts, you will probably find the local people extremely friendly and eager to help. The ethnic diversity and Latin warmth encountered by foreign teachers and travellers throughout the continent usually more than compensate for low wages and (in the big cities) a high crime rate.

Prospects for Teachers

With such a span of teaching establishments, there is a job somewhere for almost any native speaker, but especially North American ones. In a land where baseball is a passion and US television enormously popular, American (and also Canadian) job-seekers have a distinct advantage. The whole continent is culturally and economically oriented towards the States and there is a decided preference for the American accent and for American teaching materials and course books. Even in countries which have not traditionally shared this preference, such as Argentina, schools are busy marketing their courses in "American English for executives". In fact business English is gaining ground throughout the region, particularly in Chile, Venezuela, Colombia and Brazil, and anyone with a business background will have an edge over the competition.

The academic year begins in late February or early March and lasts until December. January and February are very slack months for language schools and in fact their doors may not be open then to receive job-seekers. But many institutes run 6 to 8 week courses year round and will be eager for the services of a native speaker whatever the time of year.

FIXING UP A JOB

A number of language schools welcome speculative enquiries from EFL teachers, either in advance (in which case you might be able to have a telephone interview and negotiate an official contract) or after arrival. What the principal of a girls' school in Lima wrote to us is echoed by many other institutes. "Anyone interested in a job is welcome to write to me at any time. If they happen to be in Lima they are equally welcome to come into school."

In Advance

Very few Latin American language schools advertise in the UK press. Even the most prestigious schools complain of the difficulties they encounter recruiting teachers abroad, mainly due to the low salaries they can offer and the very bureaucratic procedures for obtaining a work permit. As usual, you might succeed in persuading the British Council in the country which interests you to send a list of English language schools. (The most hopeful ones are Rio, Santiago, Lima and Caracas.) The British Council in London sells a *Survey of English Language Teaching in Colombia* (@ £20) which contains 59 addresses of language schools. South American Consulates in London and Washington are unlikely to be of very much assistance to the casual enquirer, though the Cultural Attaché might offer some advice to serious candidates.

The Latin American Union of Registered English Language Schools

(LAURELS) is relatively new and therefore quite small at present. So far it has just 12 members, only one of which is outside Brazil. But it is hoped that more schools will join from other countries in the coming years. For a list of member schools, write to LAURELS c/o the *Liberty English Centre* or *IBI*.

Recruitment organizations which might be of assistance to qualified TEFL teachers are *International House, Berlitz, inlingua* and the *Bell Educational Trust;* the latter sometimes recruits on behalf of *Culturas Inglesas* in Brazil. Certified teachers interested in EFL posts might like to contact Gabbitas, Truman & Thring, who send teachers to schools in South America on two or three year contracts; see for example the entry for *Craighouse* in Santiago, *Markham Cottage* and *San Silvester College* in Lima. School leavers should contact the *Project Trust* who have links with schools in Brazil as well as a challenging educational project with fishermen in the Honduran Bay Islands, and *GAP Activity Projects* who make placements in Mexico.

PGCE-holders who are committed Christians will be interested to hear that SAMS, the South American Missionary Society (Allen Gardiner House, Penbury Road, Tunbridge Wells, Kent TN2 3QU) recruits teachers of English for schools in South America with an Anglican foundation including the *British School* in Puntas Arenas, plus schools in Asuncion, Sanitago, Vina del Mar and Lima.

Americans should contact the AFS International Teachers Programs (313 East 43rd Street, New York, NY 10017) for information about its ESL programme in Argentina, Chile, Peru and Costa Rica.

The *TESOL Placement Bulletin* carries occasional notices of vacancies in South American schools. A few schools, including some of the biggest Bi-National Centers, attend TESOL Conventions (see page 63).

On the Spot

The concept of "job vacancy" is very fluid in many Latin American language institutes and, provided you are willing to work for local teaching wages, you should be able to create your own job almost anywhere. A number of the language schools which corresponded with us indicated that they would be willing to hire as many native speakers as they could get.

As throughout the world, local applicants often break into the world of language teaching gradually by teaching a few classes a week. Non-contractual work is almost always offered on an unofficial part-time basis. So if you are trying to earn a living you will have to patch together enough hours from various sources. Finding the work is simply a matter of asking around and knocking on enough doors. Try to charm the receptionist, librarian or English language officer at the British Council, Bi-National Center or any other institute which might have relevant contacts or a useful notice board. Check adverts in the English language press such as the *Mexico City News* or the *Buenos Aires Herald*. English language bookshops are another possible source of teaching leads, for example the English Book Centre in Guayaquil, Ecuador or Barreiro y Ramos in Montevideo, Uruguay.

There is more competition as well as more opportunities in the major cities, so if you are having difficulties rounding up work, you could try smaller places, especially if they are destinations for English-speaking tourists.

The crucial factor in becoming accepted as an English teacher at a locally-run language school may not be your qualifications or your accent as much as your appearance. You must look as neat and well-dressed as teachers are expected to look. Improving your personal appearance may be a problem if you have hitched down from the States with few possessions to your name but, if necessary, sell your camera and buy a jacket and tie or presentable dress, and while you're at it, have a bath, a haircut and a shave. Ask in expatriate bars and restaurants, check out any building claiming to be an "English School" however dubious-looking, and in larger cities try deciphering the telephone directory for schools or agencies which might be able to use your services.

Freelance Teaching

In most Latin American cities, there is a thriving market in private English lessons, which usually pay half as much again as working for an institute. It is not uncommon for teachers to consider the language school which hires them as a stepping stone to setting up as a private tutor. After they have familiarized themselves with some teaching materials and made enough contacts among local language learners, they strike out on their own, though this is far from easy unless you can get by in the local language and also have a telephone. Clients can be found by advertising in the quality press, or by placing notices on strategic notice boards.

REGULATIONS

Of course requirements vary from country to country but the prospects are dreary for teachers who insist on doing everything by the book. It is standard for work visas to be available only to fully qualified and experienced teachers on long-term contracts. Often you will have to present an array of documents, from university certificates and transcripts to FBI clearance, which have been authenticated by your Consulate abroad or by the Consulate of the host country. Although many schools will not offer a contract before interview and then will make it contingent on a work permit, the procedures must be started in the teacher's country of origin, which makes the whole business very difficult. All of this can take as long as six months and involve a great deal of hassle, not least for the employer.

The upshot is that a high percentage of teachers work unofficially throughout Latin America. It is hardly an issue in some countries, for example virtually no one gets a work permit in Costa Rica, not even the long-resident directors of language schools and no one seems to worry about it. Teaching on a tourist visa is a widespread practice in Mexico and Peru. Chile is one country in which it is often possible to turn a tourist visa into a work visa (see below). Meanwhile Brazil has become even stricter in its recent reforms and now all exchanges of money are supposed to be accompanied by receipts, which is likely to make life more difficult for casual teachers. There are ways round the regulations, for example to work on a cultural exchange visa (e.g. in Brazil) or a student visa (e.g. in Venezuela). Some prestigious organizations like International House, the British Council or Bell Educational Trust often smooth the way for their employees.

CONDITIONS OF WORK

The problem of low wages has already been emphasized, and these are quite likely to drop even further during the course of your employment since even the most assiduous school cannot adjust salaries fast enough to keep pace with inflation (running at 300% in Brazil at last report). An hourly wage of 1,000 pesos might be worth $2 one month and 75¢ the next. It is therefore essential to negotiate a rate in American dollars, the "parallel currency" throughout Latin America. This will be standardly US$2-$3 an hour. Insist on payment in local currency converted at the rate in force on that week's pay day. Actually getting paid in American dollars would be best of all, but this is almost always impossible, including at Bi-National Centers. Assuming you are able to save any of your earnings, you will be unable to convert it into a hard currency except on the black market.

Some schools offer perks such as 14-month salaries or return flights to teachers who stay for a year. A recent advert in the *TESOL Placement Bulletin* for an English Institute in Paraguay describes a typical situation: "Possible repayment of air fare through an accruing account, payable upon one year of service". Respectable schools will want you to stay for at least 6 months and preferably a year. A contract is often worth having, though if the employer seems over-eager for you to sign on the dotted line, be sure that there are no unacceptable binding clauses which might cause subsequent problems.

Teachers without an RSA Certificate are unlikely to encounter much snobbish disapproval, partly because this qualification is not part of the American TESL scene. Many institutes offer their own compulsory pre-job training (to be taken at the teacher's own expense) which provides a useful orientation for new arrivals.

One of the seldom-mentioned perks of teaching in Latin America is the liveliness and enthusiasm of the pupils. Brazilian students have been described as the "world's most communicative students". You may also be dazzled by the level of knowledge of Western pop culture, and should be prepared to have your ignorance shown up.

LEISURE TIME

Whether you are a serious student of Spanish or a frivolous seeker after the excitement generated by Latin carnivals, South America is a wonderful place to live in and travel. Women teachers may find the *machismo* a little hard to take, but will soon learn how to put it in its place. If you want to travel around, the *South American Handbook* definitely justifies the initial outlay of £20.

BRAZIL

The market for English teaching is not confined to the major cities of Sao Paulo and Rio. There are about 30 SBCIs (*Sociedades Brasileiras de Cultura Inglesa*) and 63 Bi-National Centers scattered all over the fifth largest country in the world. Schools in smaller places often notify cooperating institutes in the big cities of any job vacancies for native speakers. But speculative visits to towns of any size would probably be successful eventually.

The distinguishing feature of Brazilian EFL is the high proportion of well qualified Brazilian English teachers. Recruiting teachers from overseas is seen to be unjustifiably costly and is resented by the local teaching establishment. Even the most prestigious schools (e.g. the 11 members of LAURELS) do not consider it a priority to hire native speakers, except perhaps for very senior posts. For example the *Cultura Inglesa* in Recife advertised highly paid summer positions for teacher-trainers in a May issue of the *Guardian*. Brazilian law states that no more than a third of staff in any firm can be foreign. Work permits are available only to university graduates with three years proven experience.

Outside the prestigious *Culturas Inglesas*, Bi-National Centres and the 3 Britannia schools (affiliated to International House), native speakers can often walk into temporary jobs, which offer low wages and little security. There is also plenty of scope for private tuition at a rate of about $3 an hour (which is a high wage when compared to what an average Brazilian earns).

CHILE

Of course most of the opportunities are in the capital Santiago, though there are some relevant institutes in the Valparaiso-Vina del Mar area. The *Instituto Chileno Britanico* hires only highly qualified teachers but has a good library of teaching materials which can be borrowed after the modest membership fee is paid.

Edwin Hunt submitted a detailed report of the English teaching scene in Santiago based on the year he spent there as a teacher, including a brief assessment of selected schools (reproduced below), which is highly subjective and to be treated with some scepticism. According to Edwin, the commercial institutes in Santiago vary greatly in size, reliability in their treatment of employees and teaching methods. Some will not give you very much work — just a few hours each week — so you would have to obtain classes from several different sources. Others can be very demanding, particularly with regard to working during the peak hours of early morning and evening. Some of the smallest do not teach on their own premises at all, as they send their teachers out to do classes in the offices and homes of their client-students. The larger institutes mainly teach in their own classrooms, but many institutes do a mixture of off-site and on-site teaching.

Teaching at this level — the short-term, mainly casual work done by foreign visitors to Chile — is not well paid. Non-contractual work with the Institutes is usually paid by the hour, and they rarely pay much more than 1,000 pesos per hour. With your own private clients, you may be able to charge slightly more than 1,000 pesos; some well established private tutors charge as much as 3,000 pesos.

List of Selected Schools

Concord Chile Inc., Nueva York 57, Of. 501, Central Santiago. Tel: 724363. A small "agency" institute which teaches only by sending teachers to the clients. It is essentially a "one man and his accountant" operation run from a small office. Frequently takes on native-speaker teachers. Highly recommended.

Fischer English Institute, Cirujano Guzman 49, Providencia, Santiago. Tel: 490765. Teaches both on the premises and out at the clients' places. Recommended.

Lang International Ltd., Bucarest 046, Dp. E, Providencia, Santiago. Tel: 232 5955. Worth contacting.

Master, Orrego Luco 11, Piso 2, Providencia, Santiago. Tel: 231 8602/231 0366. Only hires women (or so they say).

Sheila May's, Napoleon 3070, Las Condes, Santiago. Tel: 231 1595. A small institute run by a helpful woman director. Recommended.

British English Centre, Dr. Manual Barros Borgono 79, Providencia, Santiago. Tel: 496165. Must be fluent in Spanish to teach here. Not recommended.

ELADI (Escuela Latinoamericana de Idiomas), M. Luisa Santander 0440,

Providencia, Santiago. Tel: 41241. Also: Jose Miguel Infante 927, Providencia. May be worth a try, though this large institute concentrates on the technology of language learning with a heavy use of videos and language labs.

Eurotron, Adelaida la Fetra 2375, Providencia. Tel: 231 9212/232 4222. Despite a rather posh atmosphere, friendly and worth a try.

John Kennedy Lenguage Institute (their spelling), Avenida Ejercito 20, Central Santiago. Tel: 696 1851. Not recommended.

Tronwell, Alcantara 82, Las Condes, Santiago. Tel: 246 1040. Director's office and Personnel department are at Regidor 66, Las Condes (tel: 232 5607). A fairly large establishment with their own controversial teaching methods, they could be worth trying.

Berlitz, Padre Mariano 305, Providencia, Santiago. Tel: 461681. Contact Sr. Cristian Lagarini in the first instance. Berlitz has a substantial establishment in Santiago. You may very well get at least an interview here, but be aware that the teaching is very strictly controlled by the management.

Santiago Language Center, Irene Morales 11 / Coronel Bueras 128, Central Santiago. Tel: 332599/398703.

Ichen S.A.E., Huerfanos 757, Of. 410-415, Central Santiago. Tel: 33 2921.

Sam Marshall, Avenida Los Leones 1095, Providencia, Santiago. Tel: 231 0652.

The majority of the larger Institutes — and some of the smaller ones — are mainly looking for a commitment to work for them for several months, so it won't be easy if you are only going to be in Santiago for a few weeks. Another problem concerns work permits and contracts. If you want to do more than just a few hours of casual teaching each week for more than a few weeks, then many Institutes will insist that you obtain an official work permit from the *Extranjeria.* To get a list of the documents you need to collect in addition to a contract of employment, go to the State *Intendencia,* which includes an *Extranjeria* section, on Moneda in the city centre just west of Plaza de la Constitucion. Then go to the main *Extranjeria* office which is at Santa Rosa 108. (If you are just staying in Chile a short time, you may not want to get involved in all this.)

Advertising for Private Clients

If you do not make a lot of personal contacts and use the grapevine, then the only way to obtain private clients is to advertise. The best results are obtained by putting a small ad in a magazine called *Ya,* which is the women's supplement in the Tuesday edition of *El Mercurio,* the leading quality newspaper. it will be at least two weeks before it appears, but then there should be a good number of enquiries. Other newspapers such as *La Epoca* and *La Tercera* have their classified ads sections, although they tend to be a little more expensive than *Ya.* There is a magazine called *El Rasto* consisting of nothing but advertisements into which you can place a small ad absolutely free of charge, and you can place it with just a phone call, although the results will not be spectacular. If you need to be written to rather than telephoned it might be useful to take out a Post Box number with the Chilean Correo, particularly if you are going to be changing your own lodgings fairly frequently.

A very useful option is to find a supermarket which has a noticeboard for small advertisements in their entrance halls. In particular the "Almac" chain of stores has such noticeboards. The best one is in Providencia on Avenida P. de Valdivia near the corner of Bustos. If you can translate between English and Spanish, it will be worth advertising yourself as a translator as well.

This sort of insider knowledge is invaluable for anyone considering going abroad on spec. One further avenue which Edwin's report omits is the possibility of teaching in English-medium *colegios* (of which five are included in the Directory), where a long-term commitment will be necessary and a reasonable salary paid (perhaps about half a teacher's salary in the UK).

Chile is a more attractive long-term destination now that democracy has been restored. The country has some of the most varied and spectacular scenery in the world — with glaciers at sea level, deserts where no rain has been recorded, active volcanoes and the highest mountains outside the Himalayas — and interesting cultural contrasts which encompass Mapuche Indians, high tech and a 1960s lifestyle. One of the drawbacks of life in Santiago is the smog.

COLOMBIA

If teaching institutes in Brazil and Chile have trouble attracting qualified foreign teachers, their Colombian counterparts have an even harder time, since most people's first association with Colombia is one of crime and violence. In fact foreign teachers are extremely unlikely to become involved in any drug-inspired tensions but are guaranteed to be welcomed by the locals. Memories will be of a local carnival rather than of a neighbourhood shoot-out.

Colombia is even more strongly oriented towards the US than elsewhere in South America, though there is a British Council DTO in Bogota, catering mainly for the executive market. But there are plenty of local language schools where untrained native speakers can find work, provided they are willing to accept low wages of about 1,000 pesos an hour (under £1/$2).

Only well qualified teachers are eligible to apply for a work permit. The Ministry of Education must approve the academic credentials, preferably an MA, and then will take two or three months to process the work visa.

PERU

Lima is one of the most lively EFL centres on the continent, as well as being one of the most stressful and dangerous in which to live. But many temporary visitors to Peru end up doing some English teaching once they have established a base in the capital, usually earning about $2 an hour. Although Dick Bird's experiences in Peru are not very recent, the situation hasn't changed significantly:

> *Lima probably has more language schools than Brighton. Teaching English as a foreign language is a growth industry and no English speaker has the right to feel unwanted in Lima. When we applied at an English institute (reluctantly recommended by the British Consulate) we were not asked to show any qualifications but we did have to attend an unpaid introductory course.*

Many schools are located in the well-to-do port area of Miraflores, and a door-to-door search for work might succeed.

A list of bilingual and English medium schools is available from the British Council in Lima. (The Cultural Office of the Peruvian Embassy in London can send a shorter list of 20 schools which function in English.) Not all are looking for certified teachers, so it is worth approaching them. The hours are more civilized than in a language institute, i.e. 8am-3pm rather than 8.30-10am and 5.30-9pm) and wages are higher. Certified teachers can earn British wages plus a 10% expatriate allowance. One of the pillars of the EFL establishment is *Newton College* in Miraflores which has an English department of 15, with about 70

British nationals on staff, half of whom are recruited abroad. They admit that among locally recruited staff, a qualification is not essential. Anyone who does decide to become qualified can do the RSA Certificate course on the premises.

Peruvian work visas are very rare and most people teach on a tourist visa, unless they have a long term contract. If this is the case, the relevant qualifications need to be notarized in the home country, checked by the teacher's Consulate and signed by the Peruvian Consulate.

ARGENTINA

Like Panama, Argentina has always had a substantial English-speaking population and so teaching jobs for unqualified foreigners are relatively scarce, especially if you don't have an American accent. Buenos Aires is a sophisticated city with a high standard of education. As mentioned earlier, the *Buenos Aires Herald* regularly carries a few job adverts for English teachers. There is also a useful notice board in the bookshop on Calle Florida (the main shopping street).

In addition to the Anglo-Argentinian cultural centres and Bi-National Centers throughout the country, there are two International House schools, one in Buenos Aires, the other in San Isidro 20kms north of the capital.

VENEZUELA

Oil money has resulted in a thriving market for English tuition and there are several reputable institutes in Caracas in addition to the *British Council* DTO and the *Centro Venezolano-Americano*. Proximity to the US means a strong preference for American accents and teaching materials.

MEXICO

As one language school wrote to us: "At present we do not employ foreign teachers due to the crisis in our economy." Yet plenty of opportunities remain. For example the 15 Bi-National Centers employ hundreds of native speakers mostly on a local basis, as do various British oriented schools scattered around the country. Without a TEFL background or at least a university education you are unlikely to break into these more upmarket institutes, but there are plenty of other kinds of school.

Stuart Britton is a world traveller who spent a couple of years in Mexico living on his teaching, often in a hand-to-mouth fashion. His initial job hunt took place in Ensenada, a tourist town in Baja California, as he describes in detail:

What a strange sensation it was to be in Mexico after the States, but the people were so warm and friendly and helpful as soon as I crossed the border — I could talk and relax — I felt more at home, although there I was in a land so far and so strange. I felt isolated yet I also felt that with these warm people around me, I couldn't starve or be "eaten up".

As far as work, I found a school from a fisherman who had befriended me at the bus station who knew someone who knew someone etc. etc. and then I finally found a commercial institute, a sort of training school for adults where they teach typing, tourism, English, etc.; there are many of these institutes in Mexico. Mostly the pay is very poor and conditions are basic.

The next week I went to the University Extension in Ensenada which is a snobby government-run establishment which hires qualified and university educated teachers *so I didn't have any luck there. But luckily I found purely by my careful observation of the reception area, an advertisement for a teacher at a school for bilingual secretaries run by nuns. I was accepted with hardly any questions asked about my qualifications or experience. They really are very unofficial in Mexico. The pay, however, was dreadful, only the equivalent of £9 a week — just over $1 an hour! It was just enough to pay for my accommodation. I had to find private classes also which I managed to do through more contacts of my fisherman friend.*

So, after about 18 months of teaching, finding other schools from contacts, giving a few hours a week per school, I decided to leave Ensenada. After only a day or two in Hermosillo, a desert town on the mainland, I phoned a well known American motor company. The pay was much better, the conditions were superb and the town was altogether much better. I also had no trouble finding classes in other schools and companies, including two banks and a plastics company, which made my income considerably higher than in Ensenada. I was coming up to $100 a week at times; again the problem was not having enough hours in one place to keep me going financially. I was constantly moving around for my students in those dreadful Mexican buses which you can hardly fit in at times and have to hang on for dear life. And the heat was tremendous.

Although the Mexican authorities take a fairly easy-going attitude towards the rules, you will have to be sure to renew your tourist visa every 90 days, either at a local government office or by crossing the nearest border and getting a new stamp on your return.

If you are looking for work in Mexico City, check adverts in the English language *Mexico City News*. Rupert Baker answered an advert and was invited to attend a disconcertingly informal interview at a restaurant (to which he still wore his tie). He ended up working for six months, starting on a peso equivalent of $2 an hour, rising to $3.50. Wages are normally much lower in Guadalajara and resorts such as Puerto Vallarta, Acapulco and Mazatlan where locals need to master English before they can be employed in the booming tourist industry. Private lessons are in great demand, and may be given informally in exchange for board and lodging.

LIST OF SCHOOLS
Brazil

BRITANNIA
Av. Borges de Medeiros, 67, Leblon, Jardim de Alah, 22430 Rio de Janeiro, RJ, Brazil. Tel: (21) 511 0143.
Number of teachers: 22.
Preference of nationality: UK, US, Canada.
Qualifications: RSA Cert. (Grade 'B') essential, BA (English, Modern Languages etc.) and, preferably, 3 years experience.
Conditions of employment: 1-2 year renewable contracts. 25-30 h.p.w. Pupils range in age from 16-45.
Salary: varies according to teacher's scale.
Facilities: subsidized assistance with accommodation provided. Training given.
Recruitment: through IH, London. Interviews held in both UK and US.

CAMBRIDGE SOCIEDADE BRASILEIRA DE CULTURA INGLESA
Rua Piaui, 1234, Cep 86010, Londrina, Paraná, Brazil. Tel: (432) 24 2901/24 1096.
Number of teachers: 2.

Preference of nationality: UK.
Qualifications: at least RSA Cert. and 3 years experience.
Conditions of employment: 1 year contracts. Hours of work 2-6pm and 7.15-9.15pm. Pupils range in age from children to adults.
Salary: unspecified hourly rate.
Facilities/Support: assistance with accommodation. Training provided.
Recruitment: interviews not essential.

CENTRO CULTURAL BRASIL — ESTADOS UNIDOS
Centro Rua 14, No 61, 74000 Goiânia, GO, Brazil. Tel: (62) 223 0315/224 4908.
Number of teachers: 4.
Preference of nationality: none.
Qualifications: previous experience essential, and TEFL qualification.
Conditions of employment: no standard length of contract. Hours of work 1-6pm. Age range of pupils from children to adults.
Salary: high compared with local rates.
Facilities/Support: no assistance with accommodation. Training provided.
Recruitment: interview essential.

CENTRO CULTURAL BRASIL — ESTADOS UNIDOS
Praça Duque de Caxias, 115, 13300 Itu, SP, Brazil. Tel: (21) 482 0267.
Number of teachers: none at present.
Preference of nationality: none.
Qualifications: high standard of English and previous teaching experience.
Conditions of employment: 3 month contracts. 16 h.p.w. Pupils mostly aged 14-24.
Salary: US$5.85-8.75 per hour.
Facilities/Support: no assistance with accommodation. Training provided.
Recruitment: interviews essential and mostly held in US.

CULTURA INGLESA
Rua Marechal Floriano Peixoto 433, Centro, Blumena 89100, SC, Brazil. Tel: (473) 227583.
Number of teachers: 3.
Preference of nationality: none.
Qualifications: minimum RSA Cert. and 2 years experience.
Salary: US$800-1,000 per month.
Facilities/Support: assistance with accommodation. Training provided.
Recruitment: through TEFL magazines. Interviews essential and were held in UK last year.

CULTURA INGLESA
Rua 12 de Outubro, 227, 7800 Cuiabá, MT, Brazil. Tel: (65) 624 2079.
Number of teachers: 1.
Preference of nationality: none.
Qualifications: at least 1 year's experience; preferably, RSA Cert.
Conditions of employment: 1-2 year contracts. Hours of work 8-11am and 4.30-9.30pm. 20-25 h.p.w. Pupils range in age from 8-60.
Salary: US$7 per hour, tax free.
Facilities/Support: assistance with accommodation. Training provided.
Recruitment: through direct application with c.v. Interviews over phone.

CULTURA INGLESA
Rua Jeronimo Coelho, 233, 89200 Joinville, SC, Brazil. Tel: (474) 22 7603.
Number of teachers: 3.
Preference of nationality: none.
Qualifications: RSA Cert.
Conditions of employment: negotiable contracts. Hours of work 7-10am and 2-9.45pm. 30 h.p.w. Pupils range in age from 7-50.
Salary: US$400-500 per month.
Facilities: assistance with accommodation sometimes given. Training provided.
Recruitment: through local adverts. Interviews not essential, sometimes held in UK.

CULTURA INGLESA
Av. Jõao Pinheiro 808, Uberlandia, 38400 Minas Gerais, MG, Brazil. Tel: (34) 234 8446.
Number of teachers: 1.
Preference of nationality: UK.
Qualifications: MA with at least 1 year's experience.
Conditions of employment: 1 year contracts minimum. 30-40 h.p.w. Pupils range in age from teenage to adults.
Salary: at local rates plus overseas subsidy in some cases.
Facilities/Support: assistance with accommodation. Training provided.
Recruitment: through the Sao Paulo branch of Cultura Inglesa.

CULTURA INGLESA
Rua Mamanguape, 411, Boa Viagem, Recife, PE, Brazil. Tel: (81) 326 1908.
Number of teachers: 10.
Preference of nationality: UK.
Qualifications: RSA Cert.
Conditions of employment: 1 year contracts. Hours of work 2-7pm. 25 h.p.w. Age range of pupils from kindergarten to OAP's.
Salary: £450 per month. £800 per month for teacher trainers with RSA Dip., for 3-6 month contracts.
Facilities/Support: accommodation in 2-room flat shared with another teacher plus cost of return air fare from UK and health insurance provided. Training given.
Recruitment: through local and UK adverts. Interviews carried out in UK.

CULTURA INGLESA
Rua Plinio, Moscozo, 357, Jardim Apipema, 40155 Salvador, Bahia, Brazil. Tel: (71) 247 9771.
Number of teachers: 4.
Preference of nationality: UK, Australia, etc.
Qualifications: RSA Cert. or equivalent, some experience required.
Conditions of employment: 1 year contracts. 25 h.p.w. Pupils range from age 7.
Salary: 21,000 cruzeiros per month (March 1990).
Facilities/Support: no assistance with accommodation provided. No training.
Recruitment: through Project Trust (see page 61).

CULTURA INGLESA
Rua Deputado Lacerda Franco, 333, Pinheiros, 05418 Sao Paulo, SP, Brazil. Tel: (11) 814 0100.
Number of teachers: 30.
Qualifications: BA essential, RSA Cert. and 2-3 years experience preferred.
Conditions of employment: 2 year contracts. 30 h.p.w. Pupils range in age from 8-60.
Salary: at local rates plus overseas subsidy in some cases.
Facilities/Support: assistance with accommodation. Training provided.
Recruitment: locally or through Bell Schools, UK.

IBI — INDEPENDENT BRITISH INSTITUTE
SEPS, Entrequadra 710/910 Bloco A, 70360 Brasilia, DF, Brazil.
Number of teachers: 12-15.
Preference of nationality: UK.
Qualifications: RSA Cert. (Grade 'A' or 'B'), BA, and preferably, 1-2 years experience.
Conditions of employment: 2 year contracts. 22-24 h.p.w. Pupils range in age from 8-80.
Salary: varies according to experience.
Facilities/Support: assistance with accommodation. Training provided.
Recruitment: through contract with former UK teachers. Interviews essential and held in UK and US.

LIBERTY ENGLISH CENTRE
Rua Amintas de Barros, N°1059, Curitiba, PR, Brazil. Tel: (41) 263 3586.
Number of teachers: 2.
Preference of nationality: UK.
Qualifications: RSA Cert., RSA Dip., PGCE.
Conditions of employment: 6 months-2 year contracts. 30 h.p.w. Pupils aged from 8.
Salary: US$1,000 per month.
Facilities/Support: assistance with accommodation if possible. Training provided.
Recruitment: interviews are essential.

NEW FRONTIER — CENTRO DE LINGUA INGLESA
Rua 86, No. 07, Setor Sul, 74310 Goiânia, GO, Brazil. Tel: (62) 241 4516.
Number of teachers: 4.
Preference of nationality: none.
Qualifications: RSA Cert. or RSA Dip./MA, and preferably 2 years experience.
Conditions of employment: 1 year contracts minimum. 26-34 h.p.w. Pupils range from age 7.
Salary: approximately £100 per week.
Facilities/Support: no assistance with accommodation. Training provided.
Recruitment: through direct application. Local interviews.

Chile

THE BRITISH SCHOOL
Casilla 379, Punta Arenas, Chile. Tel: (61) 223381.
Number of teachers: .5
Qualifications: RSA Cert.
Conditions of employment: 3/4 year contracts. Hours of work 8-1.40pm plus 2 afternoons per week. Pupils from age 4.
Salary: according to scale fixed by Anglican Church of Chile.
Facilities/Support: assistance with accommodation. Occasional training provided.
Recruitment: through the South American Missionary Society. Interviews essential and are held in UK, US, Canada and Australia.

CHILEAN-BRITISH INSTITUTE CONCEPCION
San Martin 535, Casilla 2607, Concepcion, Chile. Tel: (41) 221044.
Number of teachers: 1.
Preference of nationality: none.
Qualifications: must be qualified teacher of EFL/linguist.
Conditions of employment: 1 year renewable contracts. Mainly evening work. Pupils range in age from 7-45.
Salary: approximately £2.50 per hour in local currency.
Facilities/Support: no assistance with accommodation. Training provided.
Recruitment: through direct application with c.v. and interview; the latter is not essential for temporary employment.

CHILEAN CANADIAN LANGUAGE CENTER
Rafael Cañas 16-B, Providencia, Santiago, Chile. Tel: (2) 42095/225 3082.
Number of teachers: 5.
Preference of nationality: none.
Qualifications: TEFL/TESL or other teaching qualification.
Conditions of employment: 6 hours per day. Pupils of all ages.
Salary: US$5 per hour.
Facilities/Support: no assistance with accommodation. Training given.
Recruitment: through direct application. Local interviews only.

COLEGIO CHARLES DARWIN
Manantiales 0314, Punta Arenas, Chile. Tel: (61) 212671.
Number of teachers: 1-2.
Preference of nationality: UK.
Qualifications: experience with young children.
Conditions of employment: 1 year contracts. 30 h.p.w. Pupils range in age from 4-14.
Salary: US$300 per month.
Facilities/Support: assistance with accommodation. No training provided.
Recruitment: through the British Council. Interviews are not essential.

CRAIGHOUSE
Casilla 20007, Correo 20, Santiago, Chile. Tel: (2) 24 24 011.
Number of teachers: 7-10.

Preference of nationality: UK.
Qualifications: BA and education qualification (e.g. PGCE).
Conditions of employment: 2-3 year contracts. Hours of work 8am-4.30pm. Pupils range in age from 4-19.
Salary: unspecified.
Facilities/Support: rent allowance provided. Some training provided.
Recruitment: through adverts in *TES* and direct application with c.v. Interviews essential and take place in UK.

EUROTRON
Adelaida La Fetra 2375, Providencia, Santiago, Chile. Tel: (2) 231 9212/233 0008.
Number of teachers: 10.
Preference of nationality: none.
Qualifications: must be native speakers willing to teach.
Conditions of employment: 2 month contracts or more. 5-8 hours work per day. Pupils range in age from 15 upwards.
Salary: US$300-500 per month (September 1990).
Facilities/Support: no assistance with accommodation. Training provided.
Recruitment: through direct application. Local interviews.

INSTITUTO CHILENO BRITANICO DE CULTURA
Santa Lucia 124, Casilla 3900, Santiago, Chile. Tel: (2) 382156.
Number of teachers: 5.
Preference of nationality: none.
Qualifications: TEFL qualification or PGCE or equivalent and minimum 5 years experience.
Conditions of employment: minimum 1 year contracts. Hours of work 8.30am-8pm. Pupils range in age from 8 upwards.
Salary: £1-£5 per hour part- time. £300 per month full-time.
Facilities/Support: no assistance with accommodation. Training provided.
Recruitment: through local Chilean graduates. Local interviews essential.

INSTITUTO CHILENO-NORTEAMERICANO DE CULTURA
Moneda 1467, Santiago, Chile. Tel: (2) 696 3215. Fax: 698 1175.
Number of teachers: 15-20.
Preference of nationality: US, Canada.
Qualifications: MA in TESOL and 5 years experience in TEFL/TESL.
Conditions of employment: 1 year contracts. 30 h.p.w. Peak hours of work early morning and early evening.
Salary: US$400 per month.
Facilities/Support: assistance with accommodation. Training provided.
Recruitment: through adverts in *TESOL Placement Bulletin*. Interviews not essential although sometimes held in US.

THE INTERNATIONAL SCHOOL OF NIDO DE AGUILAS
Casilla 16211, Correo 9, Santiago, Chile. Tel: (2) 471007.
Number of teachers: 8.
Preference of nationality: none.
Qualifications: teaching degree, 2 years minimum experience and, preferably, MA.

Conditions of employment: 2 year renewable contracts.
Salary: US$15,000-21,000 per year.
Facilities/Support: assistance with accommodation. Training provided.
Recruitment: through recruitment fairs in UK and US. Interviews take place mainly in US.

SANTIAGO COLLEGE
Los Leones 584, Casilla 130-D, Santiago, Chile. Tel: (2) 232 1813.
Number of teachers: 6.
Preference of nationality: none.
Qualifications: BA/MA/certified teacher.
Conditions of employment: 1 year contracts. Hours of work between 8am-4pm. Pupils range in age from 4-18.
Salary: unspecified.
Facilities/Support: assistance given with finding accommodation. Training provided.
Recruitment: through local adverts. Local interviews essential.

Colombia

CENTRO COLOMBO AMERICANO (ARMENIA QUINDIO)
Carrera 14, 8 62, Bogotá, Colombia. Tel: (1) 463588.
Number of teachers: 1.
Preference of nationality: US, UK.
Qualifications: TESL graduates/senior students.
Conditions of employment: 6 month minimum contracts; 1 year preferred. Hours of work 7-9am, 4-6pm, 6.30-8.30pm. Pupils range in age from 20-35.
Salary: 1,000 pesos per hour.
Facilities/Support: assistance with accommodation. Training provided.
Recruitment: through the Michigan test (MTELP). Also through direct application with c.v.

CENTRO COLOMBO AMERICANO (BARRANQUILLA)
Carrera 43, 51-95, Barranquilla, Colombia. Tel: (58) 318084.
Number of teachers: up to 15.
Preference of nationality: none.
Qualifications: BA (English or Education) or TEFL/TESL/teaching qualification.
Conditions of employment: 1 year renewable contracts. Hours of work between 7am-8.30pm. Pupils range in age from 5-58 but mostly 18-25.
Salary: 1,600 pesos per hour plus 2 months pay and paid holidays after 1 year.
Facilities/Support: assistance given with finding accommodation. Training provided.
Recruitment: interviews not essential.

CENTRO COLOMBO AMERICANO (BUCARAMANGA)
Carrera 22, 37-74, Bucaramanga, Colombia. Tel: (7) 57816.
Number of teachers: 10.
Preference of nationality: none.
Qualifications: TEFL experience.

Conditions of employment: 2 year contracts. Hours of work 7-9am and 4-8pm. Pupils range in age from 12-35.
Salary: US$250 per month.
Facilities/Support: assistance with accommodation. Training provided.
Recruitment: interviews not essential.

CENTRO COLOMBO AMERICANO (CALI)
Calle 13 Norte, 8-45, 4525 Cali, AA, Colombia. Tel: (23) 685960. Fax: (23) 684695.
Number of teachers: 10-20.
Preference of nationality: US, Canada, etc.
Qualifications: at least a BA in an English teaching related field and a minimum 6 months teaching experience.
Conditions of employment: 1 year renewable contracts. 30 h.p.w. including evening work. Pupils range in age from 6-60.
Salary: average 115,000 pesos per month (1990), 150,000 pesos per month (1991).
Facilities/Support: assistance given with finding accommodation. Training provided.
Recruitment: through advertising in newsletters and at conventions. Interviews at least by phone essential; some interviews held in US.

CENTRO COLOMBO AMERICANO (MEDELLIN)
El Palo, No. 52-24, Medellin, Colombia. Tel: (4) 251 4416.
Number of teachers: 2+.
Preference of nationality: US, Canada, (if hired locally then no preference).
Qualifications: MA (Modern Languages, Education, English Literature).
Conditions of employment: 1 year contracts. Evening work compulsory. Pupils range in age from 15-40.
Salary: 100,000 pesos per month for an MA working 6 hours per day.
Facilities/Support: assistance with accommodation when necessary. Training provided.
Recruitment: through adverts in *TESOL Placement Bulletin* and direct application. Interviews sometimes carried out over the phone; otherwise selection made through references, etc.

CENTRO DE IDIOMAS
Universidad La Gran, K5, 13-13, Bogotá, Colombia. Tel: (1) 286 8200 ext 225/231.
Number of teachers: 1.
Preference of nationality: none.
Qualifications: BA and 1 year's experience minimum.
Conditions of employment: 950 pesos per hour plus social security for day work and 1,100 pesos per hour plus social security for evening work.
Facilities/Support: no assistance with accommodation. Training provided if necessary.
Recruitment: through direct application. Interviews essential.

CENTRO DE INGLES LINCOLN
Calle 50, No. 7-23, Bogotá, Colombia. Tel: (1) 288 0360.
Number of teachers: 2.
Preference of nationality: none.

Qualifications: RSA Cert. minimum, experience preferable.
Conditions of employment: 10 month contracts from 1st February-30th November but shorter contracts would be considered. 6 hours work per day between 7am-9pm. Pupils aged from 16.
Salary: 800-1,500 pesos per hour, 14 month salaries plus holidays.
Facilities/Support: assistance given with finding accommodation. Training provided.
Recruitment: through newspaper adverts. Interviews carried out over phone.

OXFORD CENTRE
Carrera 17, 58A-37, AA 102420 Unicentro, Bogotá, Colombia. Tel: (1) 249 9573/212 2528.
Number of teachers: variable.
Preference of nationality: UK.
Qualifications: ability to maintain good student/teacher relations.
Conditions of employment: 1 year contracts. 6 hours work per day. Pupils from age 7.
Salary: US$300 per month.
Facilities/Support: accommodation provided with host families. Training provided.
Recruitment: through advertising. Local interviews essential.

THELMA TYZON INSTITUTE OF ENGLISH
Carrera 59, No. 74-73, Barranquilla, Colombia. Tel: (58) 355867/ 323420.
Number of teachers: 10.
Preference of nationality: none.
Qualifications: specialized TESL training.
Conditions of employment: 1 year contracts. Hours of work 8am-12pm and 3-7pm. Pupils aged from 12.
Salary: 1,000 pesos per hour.
Facilities/Support: assistance with accommodation. Training provided.
Recruitment: through newspaper adverts and personal contacts. Interviews normal but not essential.

Dominican Republic

INSTITUTO CULTURAL DOMINICO-AMERICANO
Av. Abraham Lincoln 414, Santo Domingo, Dominican Republic. Tel: 533 4191.
Number of teachers: unlimited.
Preference of nationality: none.
Qualifications: preferably BA or equivalent in EFL or education and a good command of the English language.
Conditions of employment: 8 week renewable contracts. Hours of work between 8am-9pm weekdays and 8.30am-12.30pm Saturdays. Pupils range in age from 4-65+.
Salary: varies according to experience.
Facilities/Support: normally no assistance with accommodation. Training provided.

Recruitment: through direct application or through local adverts. Local interviews essential.

Haiti

HAITIAN—AMERICAN INSTITUTE
Angle Rue Capois et Rue St. Cyr, Port-au-Prince, Haiti. Tel: (1) 2 3715/3 4608.
Number of teachers: 25.
Preference of nationality: none.
Qualifications: BA and experience teaching EFL essential, commitment to Haitian people and experience living overseas also needed.
Conditions of employment: ethical commitment to stay for a minimum of 2 years. Hours of work 2-8 hours per day between 6.30am-8pm. Pupils from age 16.
Salary: US$6.50 per hour plus US$10 per hour after 20 years service.
Facilities/Support: informal assistance given to locate housing. Training provided.
Recruitment: through direct application. Local interviews preferred but employment possible through correspondence.

Mexico

COLEGIO INTERNACIONAL DE CUERHAVACA, SC
Apartado Postal 1334, Cuernavaca, Mexico. Tel. & Fax: (73) 13 29 05.
Number of teachers: 15.
Preference of nationality: none, fluency in English only criterion.
Qualifications: dedication, possibly some experience or training.
Conditions of employment: 2 year contracts. Hours of work 7.30am-3pm. Pupils range in age from 3-12.
Salary: varies according to experience.
Facilities/Support: accommodation arranged. Training provided.
Recruitment: through universities. Interviews held either over the phone or in California.

INSTITUTO MEXICANO NORTEAMERICANO DE RELACIONES CULTURALES DE CHIHUAHUA
Vicente Guerrero 616, Chihuahua, Mexico. Tel: (14) 12 61 65.
Number of teachers: 6-8.
Preference of nationality: none.
Conditions of employment: minimum 7 week extendable contracts. Part-time work 8-10am or 4-9pm. Pupils range in age from 5-60's.
Salary: approximately US$3 per hour.
Facilities/Support: assistance given finding accommodation. Training provided.
Recruitment: through direct applications. Local interviews essential in most cases.

INSTITUTO CULTURAL MEXICANO NORTEAMERICANO DE JALISCO
Enrique Diaz de Leon 300, Sector Juarez, CP 44170, Guadalajara, Jalisco, Mexico. Tel: (36) 25 41 01.
Number of teachers: 20-25.
Preference of nationality: none, but American English taught here.

Conditions of employment: minimum 6 month contracts. Minimum 5 hours per day. Pupils range in age from 4 upwards.
Salary: US$2-3 per hour plus benefits (25% extra).
Facilities/Support: assistance given finding accommodation. Training provided.
Recruitment: through direct application. Local interviews essential.

INSTITUTO MEXICANO NORTEAMERICANO DE RELACIONES CULTURALES, AC
Hamburgo 115, Colonia Juarez, 06600, DF, Mexico. Tel: (169) 53357.
Number of teachers: 30.
Preference of nationality: US, Canada.
Qualifications: minimum BA in EFL or related subjects.
Conditions of employment: minimum 1 year contracts. Hours of work 7-9am and 4-8pm. Pupils range in age from 15, average age 22.
Salary: US$13,000 per year.
Facilities/Support: no assistance with accommodation. Training provided.
Recruitment: through newspaper adverts and conventions. Interviews essential and sometimes held in US.

INSTITUTO MEXICANO NORTEAMERICANO DE RELACIONES CULTURALES DE TORREON, AC
Rodriguez 351 sur, Edificio Marcos 4° piso, Torreón, Coah, Mexico. Tel: (17) 12 20 96.
Number of teachers: 2.
Preference of nationality: none.
Conditions of employment: minimum 6 month contracts. Hours of work 8am-9.30pm weekdays with 3 hours per day for material development. Pupils range in age from 7-77.
Salary: 6,600 pesos per hour (April 1990).
Facilities/Support: board and lodging offered in exchange for teaching hours to avoid work permit problems. Training provided.

Nicaragua

UNIVERSITY OF NICARAGUA-UNAN
c/o Oxford Leon Association, Town Hall, St. Aldates, Oxford. Tel: (0865) 252581.
Number of teachers: 2-3.
Preference of nationality: UK (preferably from Oxford).
Qualifications: fluent Spanish and RSA Cert., experience preferred. Should be sympathetic to the Nicaraguan revolution and FSLN.
Conditions of employment: 1 year renewable contracts. 16-20 contact h.p.w. Pupils include university students and academic staff. Classes mostly for reading skills in technical English. Also should be able to give in-house training to Nicaraguan teachers, and handle twin town work with Oxford.
Salary: a nominal amount from the university; essentially teachers are volunteers and are expected to support themselves.
Facilities/Support: a house in Leon.
Recruitment: through adverts in local newspapers *New Statesman* and *EFL Gazette.* Interviews essential and held in Oxford.

Paraguay

PARAGUAY-AMERICAN CULTURAL CENTRE
Av. España 352, Asuncion, Paraguay. Tel: (21) 24 831/24/772.
Number of teachers: unlimited.
Preference of nationality: US.
Qualifications: EFL/ESL training and experience of living outside US.
Conditions of employment: 6 month or 1 year contracts. Hours of work between 7am-9pm. Pupils range in age from 7-40.
Salary: approximately US$4 an hour.
Facilities/Support: no assistance with accommodation. Training provided.
Recruitment: through adverts. Interview essential.

Peru

COLEGIO MARKHAM (Boys only)
Apartado 18-1048, Miraflores, Lima, Peru. Tel: (14) 460039.
COLEGIO SAN SILVESTRE (Girls only)
Apartado 18-0392, Miraflores, Lima, Peru. Tel: (14) 456740.
Number of teachers: 35 (Colegio Markham), 15 (Colegio San Silvestre).
Preference of nationality: UK.
Qualifications: BA and/or teaching qualification for Colegio Markham; classroom teaching qualification essential for Colegio San Silvestre. TEFL/TESL qualification useful.
Conditions of employment: 3 year renewable contracts. Hours of work 8am-3.15pm weekdays. 36 weeks per year. Pupils are aged 5-17.
Salary: Baker Scale plus 10% expatriate allowance.
Facilities/Support: no assistance with accommodation. Fares paid and medical insurance covered. Training provided.
Recruitment: through Gabbitas, Truman & Thring. Interviews held in London.

ELS PERU
Horacio Cachay Diaz 101, La Victoria, Lima 13, Peru. Tel: (14) 713780.
Number of teachers: none at present.
Preference of nationality: US, Canada.
Qualifications: at least 1 year's TEFL experience abroad.
Conditions of employment: 1 month renewable contracts. Hours of work 4-10pm, sometimes morning work also. Pupils range in age from 16.
Salary: average US$2 per hour.
Facilities/Support: assistance given finding accommodation. Training provided.
Recruitment: adverts in newspapers. Local interviews essential.

HIRAM BINGHAM SCHOOL FOR GIRLS
Paseo de la Costellano 919, Surco, Lima, Peru. Tel: (14) 481222.
Number of teachers: 1.
Preference of nationality: none.
Qualifications: TEFL qualification and a minimum of 1 year's experience preferred.
Conditions of employment: 1 year renewable contracts. Hours of work 8am-1.20pm. Pupils range in age from 5-17.

Salary: varies according to experience.
Facilities/Support: advice offered on accommodation. Some training available in Lima but not at the school itself.
Recruitment: carried out locally. Local interviews essential.

INTERACTION IN ENGLISH
Manco Capac 649, Miraflores, Lima 18, Peru. Tel: (14) 462503.
Number of teachers: 2.
Preference of nationality: UK, US.
Qualifications: RSA Cert., BA and experience.
Conditions of employment: minimum 3 month contracts. Hours of work early morning and early evening. Pupils range in age from 7-35.
Salary: approximately US$2 per hour.
Facilities/Support: no assistance with accommodation. Training provided.
Recruitment: through adverts in newspapers. Local interviews essential.

LEON PINELO SCHOOL
Los Manzanos 610, Lima 27, Peru. Tel: (14) 401730.
Number of teachers: none to date.
Preference of nationality: UK, US, Canada.
Qualifications: teaching qualifications or TEFL/TESL experience.
Conditions of employment: 1 academic year contracts (March-December). Hours of work 8am-3.30pm weekdays. Pupils range in age from 7-16.
Salary: varies according to experience.
Facilities/Support: no assistance with accommodation. Training provided.
Recruitment: local adverts via UK/US institutions and through personal recommendation. Interview essential.

NEWTON COLLEGE
Av. Ricardo Elias Aparicio s/n, Las Lagunas de la Molina. Apartado 5197, Miraflores, Lima, Peru. Tel: (14) 363211/790440.
Number of teachers: 15.
Preference of nationality: UK.
Qualifications: RSA Cert. or equivalent required for foreign contracts. Teaching qualifications not essential for local contracts.
Conditions of employment: 3 year foreign contracts. Indefinite length of employment for local contracts. Hours of work 8am-3pm. Pupils range in age from 5-18.
Salary: Baker Scale plus 10% expatriate allowance.
Facilities/Support: assistance in locating accommodation given. Training provided — school offers RSA Cert./Dip. courses for its teachers.
Recruitment: through adverts in *TES*. Direct application welcomed. Interviews are essential and are held in London for foreign contracts and Lima for local ones.

UNIVERSIDAD FEMENINA DEL SAGRADO CORAZÓN — UNIFE
Los Frutales s/n, Lima 12, Peru.
Number of teachers: 1.
Preference of nationality: none.
Qualifications: TEFL qualications and experience.
Conditions of employment: contracts are negotiable and are signed each semester.

Salary: varies according to experience.
Facilities/Support: no assistance with accommodation. Training provided when possible.
Recruitment: through personal recommendation. Interviews not essential.

WILLIAM SHAKESPEARE INSTITUTE OF ENGLISH
Dos de Mayo 1105, San Isidro, Lima, Peru. Tel: (14) 221313. Fax: (14) 712450.
Number of teachers: 6-12.
Preference of nationality: none, but must be native English speakers.
Qualifications: TEFL qualifications or teaching experience in South America. Senior posts demand 5 years experience.
Conditions of employment: 6 month-2 year contracts. $6\frac{1}{2}$ contact hours in an 8 hour day. Pupils range in age from 4-64.
Salary: varies according to experience.
Facilities/Support: excellent accommodation provided as part of contract package. Return air fares paid for 2 year contracts only. Training provided.
Recruitment: through IH and the Bell Trust; adverts in UK newspapers for senior posts. Interviews not essential but can be arranged in UK. Applications should include a recent photograph.

Venezuela

BRITISH COUNCIL CARACAS
Torre La Novia, piso 6, Paseo Enrique Eraso, Las Mercedes, Sector San Román, Apartado 65131, Caracas 1065, Venezuela. Tel: (2) 91 52 22. Fax: (2) 915943.
Number of teachers: 15.
Preference of nationality: UK.
Qualifications: RSA Cert. plus 2 years experience.
Conditions of employment: 1 year full-time contracts and some hourly paid part-timers. 25 contact h.p.w. Pupils range in age from 13 upwards.
Salary: between 18-24,000 bolivares per month (14 month year for full-time workers) and approximately 231-362 bolivares per hour for part-timers.
Facilities/Support: informal advice given on accommodation. Occasional training and an annual RSA Certificate course provided.
Recruitment: local and through British Council in London.

CENTRO VENEZOLANO AMERICANO
Av. José Marti, Edf, CVA, Urbanizacion Las Mercedes, Apartado 61715 del Este, Caracas 1060-A, Venezuela. Tel: (2) 751 5511.
Number of teachers: unlimited, 5 out of 110 at present.
Preference of nationality: US, Canada, UK, Venezuela.
Qualifications: BA or teachers with EFL/ESL experience. A written and oral test is given to all applicants.
Conditions of employment: indefinite period of employment. 2-8 hours work per day. Pupils aged 15-50.
Salary: US$222 per month plus benefits for full-time work.
Facilities/Support: no assistance with accommodation. Training provided.
Recruitment: interviews held locally but are not essential.

PART III

Appendices

Currency Conversion Chart
Embassies/Consulates in London and Washington
British Council Offices around the World

Appendix 1

Currency Conversion Chart

COUNTRY	£1 =	US$1 =
Argentina	10,650 Austral	5,465 Austral
Austria	20.7 Schilling	10.6 Schilling
Belgium	60.7 Franc	31 Franc
Bolivia	6.4 Boliviano	3.3 Boliviano
Brazil	191.5 Cruzado	98 Cruzado
Brunei	3.3 Brunei Dollar	1.7 Brunei Dollar
Bulgaria	5.4 Lev	2.75 Lev
Chile	607 Peso	311.5 Peso
China	9.3 Renminbi Yuan	4.8 Renminbi Yuan
Colombia	1,050 Peso	540 Peso
Cyprus	0.84 Cypriot Pound	0.43 Cypriot Pound
Czechoslovakia	63.2 Crown	32.4 Crown
Denmark	11.2 Kroner	5.8 Kroner
Egypt	5.5 Egyptian Pound	2.8 Egyptian Pound
Finland	7 Markka	3.6 Markka
France	9.9 Franc	5.1 Franc
Germany	3 DM	1.5 DM
Greece	296 Drachma	152 Drachma
Hong Kong	15.2 HK Dollar	7.8 HK Dollar
Hungary	119.5 Forint	61.3 Forint
Indonesia	3,627 Rupiah	1,871 Rupiah
Italy	2,212 Lire	1,135 Lire
Japan	242 Yen	126 Yen
Jordan	1,26 Dinar	0.65 Dinar
Kenya	45 Shilling	23 Shilling
Korea (South)	1,400 Won	718 Won
Malawi	5 Kwacha	2.56 Kwacha
Malaysia	5.3 Ringgit	2.7 Ringgit
Malta	0.58 Maltese Pound	0.3 Maltese Pound
Mexico	5,680 Peso	2,922 Peso
Morocco	15.8 Dirham	8.1 Dirham
Nepal	57.3 Rupee	29.4 Rupee
Netherlands	3.3 Guilder	1.7 Guilder
Norway	11.5 Krone	5.9 Krone
Pakistan	43 Rupee	22 Rupee
Poland	18,500 Zloty	9,500 Zloty
Portugal	260 Escudo	133 Escudo
South Arabia	7.3 Riyal	3.7 Riyal
Singapore	3.3 Singapore Dollar	1.7 Singapore Dollar
Spain	185 Peseta	95 Peseta
Sweden	10.9 Krona	5.6 Krona
Switzerland	2.5 Franc	1.3 Franc
Taiwan	53.3 Taiwan Dollar	27.3 Taiwan Dollar
Thailand	49 Baht	25 Baht
Turkey	5,343 Lira	2,750 Lira
USSR	1.1 Rouble	0.57 Rouble
Venezuela	95 Bolivar	48.7 Bolivar
Zimbabwe	5 Zimbabwe Dollar	2.5 Zimbabwe Dollar

Appendix 2

Embassies/Consulates
in London and Washington

AUSTRIA: 18 Belgrave Mews West, London SW1X 8HU. Tel: 071-235 3731.
  2343 Massachusetts Ave. NW, Washington DC 20008. Tel: (202) 797-3000.
BELGIUM; 103 Eaton Square, London SW1W 9AB. Tel: 071-235 5422.
  3330 Garfield Street NW, Washington DC 20008. Tel: (202) 333-6900.
BRAZIL: 6 St. Alban's Street, London SW1Y 4SG. Tel: 071-930 9055.
  3006 Massachusetts Ave. NW, Washington DC 20008. Tel: (202) 797-0100.
CHILE: 12 Devonshire Street, London W1N 2DS. Tel: 071-580 6392.
  1732 Massachusetts Ave. NW, Washington DC 20036. Tel: (202) 785-1746.
CHINA: 31 Portland Place, London W1N 3AG. Tel: 071-636 1835.
  2300 Connecticut Ave. NW, Washington DC 20008. Tel: (202) 328-2500.
COLOMBIA: Suite 10, 140 Park Lane, London W1Y 3DF. Tel: 071-493 4565.
  2118 Leroy Place, NW, Washington DC 20008. Tel: (202) 387-5828.
CZECHOSLOVAKIA: 28 Kensington Palace Gardens, London W8 4QY. Tel: 071-3966.
  3900 Linnean Ave. NW, Washington DC 20008. Tel: (202) 363-6315.
EGYPT: 19 Kensington Palace Gardens, London W8 4QL. Tel: 071-229 8818/9.
  2310 Decatur Place, NW, Washington DC 20008. Tel: (202) 232-5400.
FINLAND: 38 Chesham Place, London SW1X 8HW. Tel: 071-235 9531.
  3216 New Mexico Ave. NW, Washington DC 20016. Tel: (202) 363-2430.
FRANCE: 6A Cromwell Place, London SW7 2EW. Tel: 071-823 9555.
  4101 Reservoir Road NW, Washington DC 20007. Tel: (202) 328-2600.
GERMANY: 23-34 Belgrave Square, London SW1X 8PZ. Tel: 071-235 5033.
  4645 Reservoir Road NW, Washington DC 20007. Tel: (202) 232-3134/4645.
GREECE: 1A Holland Park, London W11 3TP. Tel: 071-727 8040.
  2211 Massachusetts Ave. NW, Washington DC 20008. Tel: (202) 667-3168.
HONG KONG: 6 Grafton Street, London W1X 3LB. Tel: 071-499 9821.
HUNGARY: 35b Eaton Place, London SW1X 8BY. Tel: 071-235 2664/4462.
  3910 Shoemaker Street NW, Washington DC 20008. Tel: (202) 862-6730.
INDONESIA: 38 Grosvenor Square, London W1X 9AD. Tel: 071-499 7661.
  2020 Massachusetts Ave. NW, Washington DC 20036. Tel: (202) 293-1745.
ITALY: 38 Eaton Place, London SW1X 8AN. Tel: 071-235 9371.
  1601 Fuller Street, NW, Washington DC 20009. Tel: (202) 328-5500.
JAPAN: 43/45 Grosvenor Street, London W1X 0BA. Tel: 071-493 6030.
  2520 Massachusetts Ave. NW, Washington DC 20008. Tel: (202) 234-2266.
SOUTH KOREA: 4 Palace Gate, London W8 5NF. Tel: 071-581 0247.
  2370 Massachusetts Ave. NW, Washington DC 20008. Tel: (202) 483-7383.
MEXICO: 8 Halkin Street, London SW1X 7DW. Tel: 071-235 6393/6.
  2829 16th Street, NW, Washington DC 20036. Tel: (202) 234-6000.
MOROCCO: Diamond House, 97-99 Praed Street, London W2. Tel: 071-581 5001.
  1601 21st Street, NW, Washington DC 20009. Tel: (202) 462-7979.
NETHERLANDS: 38 Hyde Park Gate, London SW7 5DP. Tel: 071-584 5040.
  4200 Linnean Ave. NW, Washington DC 20008. Tel: (202) 244-5300.
PERU: 52 Sloane Street, London SW1X 9SP. Tel: 071-235 6867.
  1700 Massachusetts Ave. NW, Washington DC 20036. Tel: (202) 833-9860.
POLAND: 19 Weymouth Street, London W1N 5AG. Tel: 071-580 0476.
  2640 16th Street, NW, Washington DC 20009. Tel: (202) 234-3800.

PORTUGAL: 3rd Floor, Silver City House, 62 Brompton Road, London SW3 1DJ. Tel: 071-581 8722/4.

2125 Kalorama Road NW, Washington DC 20008. Tel: (202) 256-1643.

SAUDI ARABIA: 30 Belgrave Square, London SW1X 8QB. Tel: 071-235 0303.

1520 18th Street NW, Washington DC20036. Tel: (202) 483-2100.

SPAIN: 10 Draycott Place, London SW3 2SB. Tel: 071-581 5921.

2600 Virginia Ave. NW, Suite 214, Washington DC 20037. Tel: (202) 265-0190.

SWITZERLAND; 16/18 Montagu Place, London W1H 2BQ. Tel: 071-723 0701.

2900 Cathedral Ave. NW, Washington DC 20008. Tel: (202) 462-1811.

TAIWAN: Free Chinese Centre, 4th Floor, Dorland House, 14-16 Regent St., London SW1Y 4PH. Tel: 071-930 5767.

Coordination Council for North American Affairs, 4201 Wisconsin Ave. NW, Washington DC 20016.

THAILAND; 29/30 Queen's Gate, London SW7 1QF. Tel: 071-589 0173/584 5421.

2300 Kalorama Road, NW, Washington DC 20008. Tel: (202) 667-1446.

TURKEY: Rutland Lodge, Rutland Gardens, Knightsbridge, London SW7 1BW. Tel: 071-589 0360.

1606 23rd Street, NW, Washington DC 20008. Tel: (202) 667-6400.

Appendix 3

British Council Offices

AUSTRIA: Schenkenstrasse 4, 1010 Vienna. Tel: 533 26 16/7/8.
BELGIUM/LUXEMBOURG; Rue Joseph II 30, 1040 Brussels. Tel: 219 3600.
BRAZIL: (Caixa Postal 6104), 70740 Brasilia DF. Tel: 272 3060.
   Av. Domingos Ferreira 4150, Boa Viagem (Caixa Postal 870), 51021-Recife PE. Tel: 326 6640.
   Rua Elmano Cardin 10, Urca (Caixa Postal 2237), 22291 Rio de Janeiro RJ. Tel: 295 7782.
   Rua Maranhao 416, Higienopolis (Caixa Postal 1604), 02140 Sao Paulo SP. Tel: 826 4455.
BRUNEI: Room 45, Fifth Floor, Hong Kong Bank Chambers, Jalan Pemancha (PO Box 3049), Bandar Seri Begawan 1930, Negara Brunei Darussalam. Tel: 27531.
BULGARIA: Boulevard Marshal Tolbukhin 65-67, Sofia. Tel: 885361/2.
CHILE: Eliodoro Yanex 832, Casilla 15-T Tajamar, Santiago. Tel: 223 4622.
CHINA: c/o British Embassy, 11 Guang Hua Lu, Jian Guo Men Wai, Beijing. Tel: 532 1961/5.
COLOMBIA: Calle 87, 12-79 (Apartado Aéreo 089231), Bogota DE. Tel: 236 3936.*
CYPRUS: 3 Museum St. (PO Box 5654), Nicosia. Tel: 442152.
CZECHOSLOVAKIA: c/o British Embassy, Jungmannova 30, 11000 Prague 1. Tel: 22 45 01.
DENMARK: Møntergade 1, 1116 Copenhagen K. Tel: 33 11 20 44.
EAST JERUSALEM: 31 Nablus Road (PO Box 136), Jerusalem. Tel: 282545.
EGYPT: 192 Sharia el Nil, Agouza, Cairo. Tel: 345 3281-4.*
   9 Batalsha Street, Bab Shark, Alexandria. Tel: 482 0199.*
FINLAND: Erottajankatu 7B, 00130 Helsinki 13. Tel: 640505.
FRANCE: 9 rue de Constantine, 75007 Paris. Tel: 45 55 95 95.
GERMANY: Hardenbergstrasse 20, 1000 Berlin 12. Tel: 31 10 99.
   Hahnenstrasse 6, 5000 Cologne 1. Tel: 20 64 40.
   Rothenbaumchaussee 34, 2000 Hamburg 13. Tel: 44 60 57/8.
   Bruderstrasse 7/111, 8000 Munich 22. Tel: 22 33 26.*
GREECE: Plateia Philikis, Etairias 17, Kolonaki Square, PO Box 3488, 10210 Athens. Tel: 363 3211.*
   Ethnikis Armynis 9, PO Box 50007, 54013 Thessaloniki. Tel: 235 236*.
HONG KONG: Easey Commercial Building, 255 Hennessy Road, Wanchai, Hong Kong. Tel: 831 5138.*
HUNGARY: Harmincad Utca 6, Budapest V. Tel: 182 888.
INDONESIA: S Widojo Centre, Jalan Jenderal Sudirman 71, Jakarta 12190. Tel: 587411/2/3.*
ITALY: Palazzo del Drago, Via Quattro Fontane 20, 00184 Rome. Tel: 475 6641.
   Via Manzoni 38, 20121 Milan. Tel: 782018.*
   Palazzo d'Avalos, Via dei Mille 48, 80121 Naples. Tel: 414876.*
JAPAN: 2-Kagurazaka 1-chome, Shinjuku-ku, Tokyo 162. Tel: 235 8031.*
   77 Kitashirakawa, Nishi-Machi, Sakyo-ku, Kyoto 606. Tel: 791 7151/2.*
JORDAN: Rainbow Street (off First Circle), Jabal Amman (PO Box 634, Amman). Tel: 63147/8.*
KENYA: ICEA Building, Kenyatta Ave. (PO Box 40751), Nairobi. Tel: 334855/6/7.
KOREA: Rm 401, Anglican Church Annex, 3/7 Chung Dong, Choong-ku, Seoul. Tel: 737 7157.*
MALAYSIA: Jalan Bukit Aman (PO Box 10539), 50916 Kuala Lumpur. Tel: 298 7555.*
MALTA: 89 Archbishop Street, Valetta.
MEXICO: Maestro Antonio Caso 127, Col San Rafael (Apdo. Postal 30-588), Mexico City 06470 DF. Tel: 566 6144.
MOROCCO: 22 Av. Moulay Youssef (BP 427), Rabat. Tel: 60836.*
NEPAL: Kantipath (PO Box 640), Kathmandu. Tel: 221305.

NETHERLANDS; Keizersgracht 343, 1016 EH Amsterdam. Tel: 22 36 44.
NORWAY: Fridtjof Nansens Plass 5, 0160 Oslo 1. Tel: 42 68 48.
PERU: Calle Alberto Lynch 110, San Isidro, Lima 14. Tel: 70 43 50.
POLAND: Al Jerozolimskie 59, 00-697 Warsaw. Tel: 287401/3.
PORTUGAL: Rua Sao Marçal, 1294 Lisbon. Tel: 347 6141.*
   Casa de Inglatera, Rua do Tomar 4, 3000 Coimbra. Tel: 39 23549.*
   Rua de Breyner 155, 4000 Oporto. Tel: 317321.*
SAUDI ARABIA: Dabab Street (off Al Washem Street) (PO Box 2701), Mura'aba, Riyadh
   11461. Tel: 402 1650.*
   Falasteen Street, Bani Malek District (PO Box 3424), Jeddah 21471. Tel: 672 3336.*
SINGAPORE: 30 Napier Road, Singapore 1025. Tel: 437 1111.*
SPAIN: Calle Almagro 5, 28010 Madrid. Tel: 419 1250.*
   Calle Amigo 83, 08021 Barcelona. Tel: 209 364.*
   British Institute, Residencia Universitaria, Esteban Terradas, Plaza de la Casilla 3, 48012
   Bilbao. Tel: 444 6666.*
   c/o British Consulate, Plaza Nueva 8 DPDO, 41001 Seville. Tel: 228873.
   General San Martin 7, 46004 Valencia. Tel: 351 8818*.
   Instituto de Ensenanza, Edificio Mecenas, Poligono Universitario, Fluente Nueva, 18003
   Granada. Tel: 201905.*
   British Institute, Goethe 1, 07011 Palma de Mallorca. Tel: 454855.*
   British Institute, Bravo Murillo 25, 35003 Las Palmas de Gran Canaria. Tel: 368300.*
SRI LANKA: 49 Alfred House Gardens, Colombo 3. Tel: 581171/2.*
SWEDEN: Skarpogatan 6, 11527 Stockholm. Tel: 667 0140.
THAILAND: c/o British Embassy, 428 Rama 1 Road, Siam Square 301 2, Pathumuran,
   Bangkok 10330. Tel: 252 6136-8.*
   198 Bumrungraj Road, Chiang Mai 5000. Tel: 242 103.*
TURKEY: Kirlangic Sokak 9, Gazi Osman Pasa, Ankara 06700. Tel: 1228 3165-9.
   Ors Turistik Is Merkezi, Istiklal Caddesi 251/253, Kat 2,3,5, Beyoglu 80060, Istanbul.
   Tel: 152 7474/8.
USSR: c/o British Embassy, Naberezhnaya Morisa, Toreza 14, Moscow 109072. Tel: 233
   4507.
VENEZUELA: Torre La Noria, Piso 6, Paseo Enrique Eraso, Sector San Roman, Las
   Mercedes (Aptdo, 1246), Caracas 1010A. Tel: 915222.*
ZIMBABWE: 23 Stanley Ave. (PO Box 664), Harare. Tel: 790 627-9.

Offices marked with an asterisk have their own English language teaching centres (DTOs).